The Christ and the Faiths

Also by Kenneth Cragg

The Call of the Minaret
  (O.U.P., 1956; new revised edition, Collins, 1986)

This Year in Jerusalem
  (Darton, Longman & Todd, 1982)

Paul and Peter: Meeting in Jerusalem
  (Bible Reading Fellowship, 1981)

Muhammad and the Christian
  (Darton, Longman & Todd, 1984)

Jesus and the Muslim
  (George Allen & Unwin, 1985)

The Pen and the Faith: Eight Modern Muslim Writers and the Qur'an
  (George Allen & Unwin, 1985)

The Christ and the Faiths

Theology in Cross-Reference

Kenneth Cragg

First published in Great Britain 1986
SPCK
Holy Trinity Church
Marylebone Road
London NW1 4DU

ACKNOWLEDGEMENT

The extract from 'Canto XLV' by Ezra Pound is reprinted by
permission of Faber and Faber Ltd from *The Cantos of Ezra Pound*.

British Library Cataloguing in Publication Data

Cragg, Kenneth
    The Christ and the faiths: theology in
    cross-reference.
    1. Theology   2. Christianity and other
    religions
    I. Title
    230   BR118

    ISBN 0-281-04240-3

Printed in Great Britain at
The Bath Press, Avon

For

Albert and Emily

Amor in Initio
Ab Initio Gratia

Contents

Foreword

by the Archbishop of Canterbury

Kenneth Cragg has lived for many years in the midst of other faiths, especially Islam. In recent years he has written a number of books on the Christian presence in the various 'households of faith'. *The Christ and the Faiths* is the culmination of these reflections. In it the author does not ignore the strong claims to finality which each religion maintains. His purpose is to ask how each religion might see the particular Christian claim contributing to its own understanding.

Dr Cragg invites Christians to abandon the narrowly parochial and return to a sense derived from the original Greek *paroikia*: 'theology has somehow to reverse what has happened to *paroikia* and pass from the sedentary to the active, from congenial familiarity to strenuous encounter with the uncongenial scene'.

The author makes no appeal for syncretism or for ignoring the depth of difference which millennia of quest and test have opened up between the different religions. Nor does he diminish what God in Christ offers to all people. What he claims is that the gospel can only *be* gospel when it is involved in the process of life and faith through which each religion brings forth from its own treasure those things both new and old which are its truth for today.

It is a profound and patient task to which Dr Cragg invites us – and by 'us' he means not only Christians, but those whose faith and perception have been nurtured in different soils. It is a task I welcome and commend. If the invitation is refused, the dangers of division and isolation will be multiplied, and the seed of God's word will fall indeed on stony ground.

March 1986   ROBERT CANTUAR:

Preface

What are the 'frontiers of theology'? A Cambridge Inaugural Lecture in Divinity with that title in 1981 saw them in the adjacent disciplines of history and philosophy. Theology was taken to be the story of Christian convictions, the understanding of their developing character in the thought and institutions of the Christian Society. Theology meant investigating the religious language habitual to that tradition. There must certainly be constant reference to religious experience but it seemed that its borders were within its own perimeter. The frontiers of theology were not seen to lie within the sphere of the Hindu, the Muslim, or the Buddhist.

The assumptions are familiar enough. Theology must be in control of its own data. Like sovereignty its range is confined to its territorial waters. For many it would cease to be theology, as an academic discipline, if it ventured into open seas. But can it truly be authentic if it hugs familiar shores? If it is indeed about God, is there anything it can appropriately exclude from its liability, on condition, of course, that its inclusiveness is in God's name? Will it really be in good faith if it counts anything alien to its sympathy, in tension with its convictions as such sympathy may be?

There would seem to be today a growing recognition that Christian theology must justify its being 'Christian' by undertaking a theology of religion at large and incorporating this into its traditional responsibility for its own distinctiveness. It is these – Christian theology in harness with a theology of religion and tethered around the theme of the Christ – that this book aims to take in hand. Hence the *bona fide* and the *bona fiducia* of the opening and the closing chapters. For good faith in relationship cannot well be had without content and substance, credally confessed and communally sustained through time and change. Such possessing is *fiducia*, but always on behalf of *fides*, the mutuality of faith and faithfulness.

Both, we must now acknowledge, belong in the plural world. It is not that, with the Persian poet, Sa'di of Shiraz, 'we should agree with everyone about their religion'. That would be a counsel of indifference, or cynicism, or even of despair. To a degree, it might also be a counsel of peace and charity. For religions display a long and tragic capacity for intolerance and pride. Contradiction has often been their stock in trade. Both dogma – and its repudiation – have a way of descending to anathema. Any claim to interpret and transact things ultimate cannot easily reconcile to the idea of being optional. 'To be or not to be' absolute – 'ay, there's the rub'.

Yet, in practical terms, to concede that all are options is what we must allow. In that sense, Saʿdi was right. 'About everyone's religion' we have 'to agree' the fact that they have it. Faiths do share the human world and occupy the contemporary stage. Meaning and mortality are common to them. 'Ours' and 'theirs' is the way the situation is about faiths. The interior convictions of each are in the external presence of all. They can be said to be options available. To be sure, there is no optionality for vast masses of mankind. Geography, history and culture make adherence wholly static. Given poverty and illiteracy and much else, the next meal is more significant than another faith. But theology means, or ought to mean, just that presence of mind for which the content, and therefore the credential, of faith has become a live issue and so, in turn, a conscious alertness of belief. The more intelligent and faith-caring that alertness becomes, the less we can 'agree with everyone', but the more we must heed the fact of their believing as they do.

This brings us, in another idiom, to the question of prepositions – those intriguing beguilers of meaning. What we have been saying adds up to the distinction between 'truth *for*' and 'truth *of*'. The fact is that faith-X is taken as truth *for* (because 'by') X-faithful. It is what *they* hold true. Whatever the faith may be, in the plural world there is the truth as credence within the discipleships it merits and sustains.

But what should we say about the truth *of* it? Some would say that no issue between *for* and *of* can well be undertaken. For them, at least where religion is concerned, no 'truth' exists other than a taking to be true. There are, it is said, no final criteria that could justify conclusion inasmuch as all criteria have only actual credence for their assumed authority. All that might resolve the issue has to be seen as caught within it.

Here, surely, if there ever was one, is a theme for theology. Current pluralism will not let it rest, as for too long it has been rested, in the instincts of all faiths to secure themselves either by ignoring it or leaving it in the silence of their own assurance. It can no longer be – if it ever was – good faith to do so, least of all for a Christian liability to and for the world.

One difficulty of truth-claims and truth-credentials lies in the fact that faiths know themselves from within and all others from without. Those who can inhabit two faiths are few. So their inwardness is not outwardly known and the external reckonings may well not comprehend. The first task is somehow to surmount this mutual miscarriage. Hence the attempt, in the four sections of this book, to see the several points of crux in Christianity from within the prescripts of four other faiths, and in each case to interpret the one into the concern of the other. In this way it may be hoped to bring two inwardnesses into relevance or, if this be too aspiring, to reduce the externality of either to the other so that, in some measure, they may meet for what they are rather than as they have seemed. Such an enterprise warrants the hope that the issues present in moving from a pluralist situation of 'truths-for' towards a conviction and confession as to that 'truth-of' which is 'in Christ' can be resolved. The warrant of hope is only in the going – the going which *The Christ and the Faiths*, with all its limitations, aims to make. Its sequence is through certain central themes of four world-faiths that are deeply mediatorial of themes crucial to Christianity. The chapter headings indicate how these move through transcendent lordship, sovereignty and revelation, to messianic intention and history, Christology and Christologies, and thus to the self as desire and as undesiring. These are all waymarks through territories Islamic, Judaic, Hindu and Buddhist where Christians have now to find their dimensions of theological discourse and duty.

That they are dimensions far exceeding any single competence must be apparent to all. Many risks attend a Christian theologian who sets the task squarely within the mental and spiritual habitation of another faith. Mere physical location cannot ensure that the risks are taken, still less overcome. The chapters here, especially 2 to 7, take their shape from four and a half decades of intermittent residence, in both pastoral and academic ministry, in the Middle East. Beirut, Jerusalem, Cairo and many other locales in more transient experience from Morocco to Oman, Sierra Leone to Kabul, have aroused the thoughts which inform these chapters. No one can live sensitively within the deep trauma of contemporary Zionism and its bitter entail of tragedy and not struggle desperately with their meaning within Judaism and for Islam.

Tenure as Warden in Canterbury of the (then) Central College of the Anglican Communion, sojourns in India, and a five-year Readership in Religious Studies at the University of Sussex, required – and I hope educated – a wider liability. The Chavasse Lectures at Wycliffe Hall, Oxford, in 1983, and the Daniel Sprigg Lectures at Virginia Theological Seminary in 1985, gave occasion to develop and shape some of the book's contents, though in slighter form and more tentative character. I confess my deep indebtedness to the stimulus, the lively privilege, of all these circumstances of mind. The Central College venture at Canterbury housed a splendid vision but was allowed too brief a lease of life to fulfil its calling. But its joy and inspiration are latent here and make still more warm my gratitude to His Grace the Archbishop for his willingness, in a Foreword, to underwrite the central urgency of the theme.

Can it be that for too long our theology in its preoccupations has been too readily domesticated, suggesting a situation of neglect of the religions akin to that of the modern poet who wrote concerning a famous poet-predecessor:

> Whether or not we read him, we can feel
> From time to time the vigour of his name
> Against us like a finger for the shame
> And emptiness of what our souls reveal
> In books that are as altars where we kneel
> To consecrate the flicker, not the flame.

To respond to the vigour of the faiths merely with another book, though one where we kneel, does not suffice. But there are times when the flicker can be prelude to the flame, the flame which, in Charles Wesley's plea, will 'trembling to its source return' – to the Christ within, beyond and on behalf of, all the faiths.

Oxford, 1986   KENNETH CRAGG

The Christ and the Faiths

1

Bona Fide Christiana

I

Yesterday I was at work teaching Christ to lift his cross . . . I inspected his feet to see that they should be worthy of the nails. I see to it that he is dumb and stands to attention before his accusers. With a piece of silver I buy him everyday, and with maps I make him familiar with the topography of Golgotha.[1]

Who and where is the writer and what 'Christ' can he mean? A poet of the First World War and a passionate lyricist against all wars, he writes of Flanders in 1918. Wilfred Owen's 'Christ' is the common soldier whom he and other officers drill and groom for battle. Gethsemane is in the trenches and 'Christ' the point of the pathos in the enormous tragedy, the sufferer on whom entails the burden of wrongs – vast, anonymous, imponderable – that belong elsewhere in the pride and malice of the world.

Owen situates the horror of his days, the angry oblation of the youth of his generation, within the drama of Good Friday. His pity was as generous as his passion was intense. It would be fair to reverse his imagery and use it on himself. For, though commanding others, he knew himself a conscious victim. Generously seeing those in his charge as bearing in their own persons the evil enmities of nations and himself a marshal of their anguish, he was reading also for himself the maps of Golgotha. There was a self-oblation in his duty and his poetry. Ardently repudiating the institutional crime of war he nevertheless chose to identify with its human tribulation. Those who recognize where 'Christ' is are the more likely to be there too.

But what do the victims of war, dumbly drilled or superbly articulate, have to do with Jesus and Gethsemane? The only swords there, a mere two, if wildly drawn, were promptly sheathed. The question: 'Whom do men say that I am?' has many incongruous answers. But, as with Wilfred Owen, answers are eloquently made and fervently meant. The events of the Gospels' climax in Jerusalem have gathered to themselves a wealth of invocations of their pattern, situations to be interpreted by their light. The Christ, they seem to say, can only be one in this strange capacity to be many.

The religions of the world, it seems, are no check to this wide and far diffusion of the Christ image. On the contrary, for all their tenacious differentiation of themselves from 'Christianity', they readily accommodate the Christ to their own equations, on their own terms. Whether the Christ-victim or the Christ-saviour, he can be freely identified with the aspirations of other faiths and brought within their constraints, or even aligned with the legendary figures of mythology. Poets and philosophers, if not theologians, suggest where his manifold image may be recognized. Thus, for example, John Keats. The Christ of Christians is one with Oromanes and Vishnu, in diverse 'palpable and personal schemes of redemption'.[2] In his familiar tale of 'the great Pan', Francis Rabelais understands 'this Great Shepherd' in whom all have their being to be 'that Great saviour of the faithful who was shamefully put to death at Jerusalem'.[3] Examples are many. The four major faiths with which we are concerned in these chapters each have their characteristic – if also inwardly debated – versions of the Christ. In disallowing the Christian verdict – itself also vigorously interrogated – they substitute their own reckoning and bring 'the Christ' within their own constraints. Authors may write of 'the unknown Christ', or 'the anonymous Christ' of other faiths.[4] But the paradox, rather, is not that he is unknown or anonymous. It is that they know him by their own naming. 'The Christ and the Faiths', therefore, as a title and theme, has to do not only with a presentation, but with a prepossession. It has to do with a theological vision the Christian knows to be distinctive. But the trust of it has to be discharged in a context of assumptions already thought to be in hand.

It follows that to be *bona fide Christiana* in this situation means a dual task. It requires Christians to bring to all prepossessions about Jesus and the imagery by which he is interpreted everywhere the understanding of his Christhood by which Christianity exists. The two duties inform and serve each other and could be likened to the art of translation. Attitudes and instincts already present, as determined by the mind of other faiths, are the setting into which the Christ of the New Testament must be expressed. As in literature, so in theology: meanings are transacted only as languages are translated. This is the sense of 'cross-reference' which we have here in mind. The aim is to take the Christ whom the New Testament had in view in that most characteristic of its cherished usages, 'our Lord Jesus Christ', into those thoughts or inklings of him in the comprehension of other religions. In this way Jesus as the Christ can be studied both as the crux of Christian theology and also as the touchstone of all faiths insofar as these shape their image of him by the data of their own experience and their verdict on the human scene. The proposal is to locate around the Christ-theme the fulfilment of a Christian obligation in the conscious coexistence of religions today and to do so in the conviction that the Christ-theme is where the obligation crucially belongs and can most comprehensibly be undertaken.

II

There is nothing new about such coexistence. Faiths have been interpenetrating and interacting through all their histories, often with a strange non-cognizance of their mutual debts. What is new in the present is the degree of their involvement with each other. Global exchanges, mobility, migration, international politics, technology and problems of world ecology and world economy, demand that they converse and that they repudiate assumptions of self-sufficiency. To be duly contemporary is to be mutually related. We are no longer physically self-enclosed: it is urgent that we should be realistically open, each to all, in custodial doctrine and tradition.

This means that all faiths are required to respond, in some measure, to the same questions. Their responses, therefore, to the world around them can no longer remain, as they have long been, private or domestic to themselves. For all their ancient interplay, the major faiths have frequently privatized their diagnoses and their remedies, conducting their societies only by in-discussion with themselves. The sanctions of culture, issues of authority, a congenial idiom, have all contributed to this posture of inclusive self-reference. They have a firm preference for their own criteria, a will to suppose that their only loyal future is their past. Classic Christian theology has, for the most part, been a strictly domestic affair, pursued in respect of its own major concerns, by reference to its own canons and the interests its own cultures dictated. It has only feebly responded to the intellectual and spiritual bearings given to it, for example, out of Asia. Today its cast of mind can no longer properly be only patristic, or Thomist, or reformed, or neo-orthodox. Some would even say that, in a certain sense (to be pondered in Chapter 14) it can, for the same reasons, no longer be *only* biblical. Thus the major obligation of any and every faith today must be its relation to others, with all the questions this entails as to authority, language, vocabulary and tradition. 'It is likely', Michael Ramsey wrote in 1975, 'that Christian theology will in the future be tested less by in-discussions of people of Christian allegiance than by the questions received from those outside the Christian tradition.'[5]

Different faiths are differently equipped, both by content and temperament, to undertake lively cross-reference outside themselves. To many within them the obligation is disconcerting, or may be perceived as a threat. Each faith, and within them – in a sense to be argued (also in Chapter 14) – each personal believer, must venture their own task. There is no desire in anything that follows here to do it for them, but only to undertake *a* Christian discharge, a *bona fide Christiana*, in the cognizance of religious diversity.

But though the response must be inward, by inward lights and initiatives, there is much that is common in the pressures from within which it must come. The psyche is as important as the mind. The growing sense that faiths are multiple can spell insecurity of soul as well as bewilderment of thought. The timid or the assertive will see the very fact of other belief-systems alternative to their own as disturbing. For it suggests a certain optionality, once it is realized how far an accident of birth may have determined the convictions in one's sincerity.[6] Let us hasten to add that for vast numbers this optionality is never present in practice. There are relatively few who can take private initiatives of changed belief. Illiteracy, cultural determinism, poverty, and much else, preclude them. Nevertheless, once the idea interposes itself that circumstance has entered far into allegiance, that faith may be fortuitous, what of their finality? Will they still seem absolute? Living with pluralism implies the paradox that tenacity of adherence proves only the intensity of conditioning.[7]

If Christian relation to other faiths in these situations is to be *bona fide* it must take sensitive note of the mood as well as the matter of their reactions. 'Shanti! Shanti! Console, console, my people', cries an Indian writer, 'the whole of India is standing round the death-bed of God.'[8] Secularity has its obtrusive and ambiguous pressures everywhere, bringing liberation for some from the tyranny of oppressive beliefs or apathetic traditions, but inducing fear and bewilderment in others by its erosion of spiritual loyalties. A Muslim observer comments on the spread of secular attitudes in a delightful metaphor. They are, he says,

> . . . like the badu in the proverb who, on a cold night, let his camel put his neck in the tent. The result was that after a while the camel had the tent to himself and the poor badu spent the night out under the open sky.[9]

Determined to resist dislodgement when faced by factors that threaten to render them marginal or obsolete, many in the faiths resort like Saul of Tarsus to vehement assertion. They adopt a siege mentality. Out of fear for the loss of identity, they bolster authority and call up the forces of political nationalism, anticolonialism, and rejectionism. They sustain their emotional security by their religious fidelities and then repudiate as compromising the very tasks of thought and spirit vital to any wise or sure relation to their future.

We do not here take up the politics of inter-religion. Our themes are theological. But, as such, they must be realist about the passions within which they move. 'My way of getting even', wrote a recent Jewish correspondent, 'is by practising my religion with fervour and enthusiasm.'[10] It is that kind of world in which faith-commendation has to make its way. To reckon duly with a passion may be as urgent as to wrestle squarely with a doctrine. Cross-reference in theology is no placid consulting of the columns of a dictionary: it is a patient and perceptive ministry in human crisis.

III

Whether intimidated or defiant in face of modern pressures all the faiths have built-in resources of assurance. In respect of pluralism these are a large part of the problem. For they are for the most part self-warranting and not readily open to criteria outside themselves. In one form or another their authority is their finality. They tend to be self-secured by the twin concepts of their once-for-all-ness and the notion of 'development' by which they are insured against the time-experience which might otherwise be thought to chasten or to challenge them. Thus, for example, A. H. Rabinowits writes:

> God showed Moses in advance all the subtle details of the Biblical law and its scribal interpretations and thus 'the words' (cf. Deut. 9.10, i.e. God's to Moses) embody Holy Writ, Mishnah, Tosephoth, Haggadoth and all that a conscientious student may develop from them in the future.[11]

'Conscientious', here, is the safeguarding word. But the idea that all within a faith's history is somehow by its own sufficient warrant is precisely the citadel of immunity which cross-reference must try to penetrate. The Judaic sense just quoted has a parallel in John Henry Newman's theory of 'the development of Christian doctrine.'[12] The resulting entrenchment of authority tends to pre-empt the thoughts arising from inter-faith relationship which might give it pause.

Doctrines of revelation give the same posture, but diversely with the variety of revelations. Thus, for example, John Calvin asserts in his *Institutes of the Christian Religion*:

> Any opinion of the heavenly mysteries which has been formed by men themselves . . . is the mother of error . . . It is no inconsiderable sin to worship God by guesswork (*fortuito*).[13]

The Qur'ān has its own *fortuito* idea in the term *zann*, meaning 'supposition' or 'surmise' which it uses repeatedly in its reproach of those who merely 'suppose' about God and his Scripture. But, of course, the Islamic revelation does not tally with John Calvin's. They have differing positions about 'guesswork'. Their anathemas, therefore, go in different directions and start from differing premises.

Ibn Khaldūn, the great Muslim historiographer, brought remarkable acumen to his analysis of society, but his theological position was thoroughly self-enclosed. 'The Qur'ān', he wrote:

> is the greatest, noblest and clearest miracle . . . It is its own proof. It is the clearest proof that can be because it unites in itself both the proof and what is to be proved . . . a miracle which is identical with the revelation.

'The proof of what is to be proved' would be many a Christian's confidence in the Bible or a Hindu's in *Sruti* writings. How may genuine cross-reference escape from these self-enclosures? What persuades Ibn Khaldūn does not persuade the Jew or the Christian or the Buddhist. Indeed, it is not even accessible to them. For it resides in that *i'jāz* or matchless Arabic eloquence of the Qur'ān which none but the born-Arab can appreciate. Ibn Khaldūn goes on:

> The Qur'ān is alone among divine books in that our Prophet received it recited to him (*matlū*) in the words and phrases in which it appears. In this respect it differs from the Torah, the Gospel, and other heavenly books. The prophets received them in the form of ideas during the state of revelation. After their return to a human state, they expressed their ideas in their own ordinary words. Therefore these books do not have 'inimitability'.[14]

Muslims find this contrast in the shape of 'inspiration' altogether convincing. It spells a total guarantee of status and content. But to other minds a purely linguistic miracle quite fails to convince, since it cannot even register and has to be taken on trust by those outside the privilege of Arabic. And, further, there can be grounds for feeling that this syllabic idea of verbally recited revelation has less claim to credence than that in which the human spirit wrestles, and masters language in being mastered by truth.[15] The immediate point, however, is not debate about that issue, but simply the disparity in the very canons by which decision may be reached. We are all liable to be appealing to warrants which are themselves on trial.

Ibn Khaldūn had many Christian parallels of the proof and the proven. The Eastern Christian theologian, Vladimir Lossky, writes:

> Itself the source of all revelation as of all being, the Holy Trinity presents itself to our religious consciousness as a fact, the evidence of which can be grounded only upon itself.[16]

'Our' is the crucial word here. Being 'grounded only upon itself', as affirmed of a doctrine, disallows to coexistent faiths any appeal to common thoughts which might mediate between convictions, whether about God or about a Scripture.

In this regard, the retreat or the advance – whichever it be – into mysticism is neither a mental nor a spiritual solution. We may all concur in the view of Hilary of Poitiers about the unwillingness [of theology] to be compelled into exposing to the uncertainty of human language the mysteries which should be contained only in the adoration of our souls.[17]

It is, however, the adoration of our souls which somehow we must aspire to share. Unless it is inherently incommunicable we are surely duty-bound to give it voice and so to return to communicable thought. When we will ourselves to do so we confront this formidable situation of self-warranting otherness reciprocal to our own. Theology's first task, therefore, is to interrogate this diversity of self-legitimation, its own and that of others, and seek what might establish between us the sort of *bona fide* relationship which does not exempt its own credentials from engagement with the other. Otherwise, the closed-shop nature of what, in most religions, purports to be of universal relevance, will persist and harden. In practice we concede the givenness, the there-ness, of other faiths in the world scene and their immense liabilities for society and the future. How then do we do so theologically?

That question will not, here, be sidetracked into speculation about 'providence' in their existence. It is not, here, a theology of the presence of religious diversity which we pursue, but a theology of a present 'good faith' with each other. How divine sovereignty relates to multiple religious forms and not to one all-comprehending system of faith and a unanimity of worship is a theme in which we could easily be lost in idle conjecture and be caught in bewildered indecision. Meeting is more urgent than surmise. Pluralism does not primarily require of our theology hypotheses about its being so. It awaits a Christian fidelity of mind and will in the relationships it entails and offers.

IV

A Christian fidelity. The decisions any faith makes about its neighbours in the world must be its own. Each has to be its own assessor. Only out of inward criteria can relationship emerge. By the very nature of the situation just reviewed, those criteria are a large part of the issue. The onus on internationalism is, precisely, nations. The burden of inter-faith is, precisely, faiths.

Defined and motivated by its own *bona fide*, and out of its own *fiducia* – the term to be taken up in the concluding chapter

– a Christian theology has first to listen to the questions explicit
for it in other religions. It has then to undertake them in the
common denominator of human experience as the place from
whence they all emerge and to which answers must return.
Shared humanity, interpret it how we may, best conduces to
realism in our response. It is the best hope of relevance translated and received.

It will be evident in each of the four main sections of our
study how readily and pointedly transitions of meaning arise.
There is what might be called a Christian resonance in so much
of the inter-thought of which a cross-reference theology
becomes aware. It is not that a Christian has to silence the
other, as some in controversy have long assumed, but rather
to transpose what he hears into another key. A purely literary
example may clarify the point. For inter-language translation
affords many parallels for inter-theology. Boris Pasternak, the
Russian poet and novelist, spent long years under Soviet duress, in which he sustained himself by working as a translator.
It was a meagre livelihood but it had other usefulness. When
direct writing and publishing were not possible, translation
might drop hints, imply meaning, and transpose comprehension from one context to another. It could communicate by
inference, its fields deliberately chosen for their implicit 'explicitness'. Inter-theology has to learn to do likewise, not – as
in Boris Pasternak's situation – because of political duress
(unless this exists), but in coping with dogmatic entrenchments
we have earlier noted. What there may be no mind to receive
there may be a necessity to recognize. Where statements would
be precluded, inferences cannot be. Points may be seen inside
the barrier which otherwise would shut them out. Meanings
may thus elude their own exposure to veto.

Consider Pasternak's Russian version of lines from Shakespeare's *Hamlet*. The original runs:

> For who would bear the whips and scorns of time,
> The oppressor's wrong, the proud man's contumely,
> The pangs of dispriz'd love, the law's delay,
> The insolence of office, and the spurns
> That patient merit of the unworthy takes . . .?

Pasternak's Russian, back into English, ran:

> Who, otherwise, would tolerate the spurious grandeur

Of rulers, the ignorant rudeness of potentates,
The universal hypocrisy, the impossibility
Of pouring out one's heart, unhappy love,
And the belittling of merit by non-entities . . .?[18]

The relevance of Hamlet's words in Stalin's world is unmistakable. But it happens by a resonance, a cross-reference. What is there in the source takes on and takes up the pith of what it seeks out. Pasternak was in love with Shakespeare and chose his pieces with the double motivation of their meaning and their aptness as determined by their destination. So it must be with theology in trust in every human situation. This is the way of the Incarnation.

Let us have the parallel rightly. The example of inference for things Stalinist *via* things Shakespearean could only be wholly accusatory. It is far from so with us. Resonance may be positive and warm, as when the Gospel's: 'You are not your own' speaks into the Buddhist version of the same discovery. It can be so when we translate the reverberation of the way of Jesus' cross into the central question of the pre-Hijrah Muhammad. The *Sīrah*, or life-course, of the latter at that point is squarely within the burning issue of pre-Gethsemane, namely how a truth, and its bearer, believed to be God's, appropriately respond to the obduracy of the hostile world. The political decision, by which Islam lives and to which the Prophet came, carries within itself the counter-relevance of the other decision by which Jesus defined and achieved Messiahship. Christian theology is, therefore, not on alien ground in the territory of Muhammad's Mecca: it occupies it in the contrasted idiom of Jesus. Christians involved in multi-faith schools, for example, need have no compunction about objective, perceptive study of Muhammad's mission. In the study of Islam they are squarely within the dimensions of the gospel. They are involved in an act of translation by which an issue, basic to all truth and 'establishment', is read when translated from the language of power into the language of grace.

Such resonances have always been assumed – if in other forms – in the typology by which the New Testament inherits from Hebrew Scriptures. One can translate the Joseph saga into the key of gospel salvation. Supremely, of course, the ancient theme of election to vocation translates into the continuous, yet vitally contrasted, self-understanding of the

Church. What in the one is inherently private to the ethnic identity of those not-Gentile, in the other is accessible and ful-fillable by 'whoso-ever will'. As between languages, so in theology: meanings are transitive. They go across, and what they bring has to find its bearing, or its bearer, in the terms and constraints which avail. These, as also in language, may be re-minted, elasticized, enlarged, precisioned, in the process. But unless what the other has is recruited, engaged, excited, no resonance will be heard. And our love is with our translation, and not only our perception of relevance. If we mean to live in this world, it has to be said that cross-reference theology is the only one there is.

V

In the four main sections of this book, each with three chapters, a Christian care for meanings and bearings in this sense is studied in respect of four major faith-systems. Other directions of Christian obligation are not attempted and within the four major faiths only severely selective themes. The selections, however, are central. The effort, though sadly limited in its range, may serve to illustrate what cross-reference involves. There is a deliberate sequence in the four movements of thought, each ending on the threshold of the next.

We begin with Islam and the theme of God. The characteristic Islamic reading of divine transcendence is seen to be in partial harmony, yet radical contention, with the Christian reading. In the view of the Muslim, with his compelling Allāh-consciousness, the Christian's worship and theology fall short of radical transcendence. There is, for the Muslim, in 'God in Christ' a compromise of divine exaltedness and in Incarnation a forfeiture of due sovereignty. It is thought that the imperative of the divine will is somehow diminished by what Christianity affirms as divine condescension manward. The Christian's sense of 'the knowledge and love of God' is read as unwarranted trespass on the doing of his will, with which alone revelation is concerned.

This inclusive question of transcendence between two theologies deeply involves the theme of Jesus, his status and significance. Christian theology embraces, indeed requires, Christology: Islamic theology forbids it. Islam, therefore,

encloses Jesus strictly within the dimension of prophethood
– the exclusive category, as the *Shahādah* tells, in the Creator's
relation to his human world and the acme of his mercy to it.
For Muslims, Jesus must be comprehended within this rubric.
The other, theologically ampler, significance he carries for
Christians must be rigorously disallowed.

Further, the Islamic sense of divine sovereignty, relating to
humanity only through messengers, demands their manifest
success. Hence the necessary alliance of the Islamic-religious
with the Islamic-political. Prophetic revelation – at least the
final one – must become operative and victorious through a
state regime, divinely sanctioned and divinely established. Man
has to be under enforcible command and prohibition, not
merely in respect of crimes and evils society must suppress
but also in respect of religious attitudes and actions *in toto*.
So insists the great jurisprudent, Al-Shāfiʿi, commenting on
Surah 75.36, which asks: 'Does man reckon that he will be left
to roam at random?'[19]

The entire assurance here about the political and legal aegis
feasibly controlling all things spiritual proceeds upon an Islamic
view of human nature which other criteria must regard as sanguine. It ignores the dark areas of human tragedy, of perversity
not amenable to political correction or not even cognizable in
legal terms. The history of prophetic vocation alone would bear
tragic witness to the intractable character of human wrong and
reaches of our need and despair which go far beyond what
exhortation can retrieve or power correct.

In all these ways there are things seriously at issue between
Islamic and Christian theologies within their common faith in
transcendence and sovereignty. Chapters 2 and 4 take up this
study, while Chapter 3 explores the fascinating inter-field
which exists between prophethood and Incarnation. Only in
a careful attention to the Muslim partnership with us *and* the
Muslim consensus against us can a Christian theologian clarify
and pursue the one and interpret into the other.

VI

Much that is at stake between Islamic and Christian theology
around divine transcendence, prophethood and tragedy, reflects the absence of Christology in the one case and its

centrality in the other. To pass – albeit on behalf of theology
– into the theme of the Christ is to take up issues Judaic and
biblical. There is thus a clear sequence from Chapters 2, 3 and
4, into Chapters 5, 6 and 7. The messianic hope, in its Jewish
context, is emphatically a confidence in the sovereignty of God,
his fidelity and power. Jew and Christian are one in their belief
in the messianic dimension (if we may so speak) within a theology of creation, covenant and history. They differ in whether
and where that hope is realized and fulfilled. Jesus as the Christ
is the key to Christianity, because Messiahship is the key to
Jesus. That messianic realization is the genesis of the Church.
In ongoing dissuasion from this Christian messianic actuality,
acknowledged in Jesus and incorporate in the Church, Judaism
puts our Christology under insistent interrogation. Its own rich
continuity has to receive a positive Christian reckoning within
a firm conviction of the new openness of peoplehood for God.
Chapter 6 takes up that large concern.

But new peoplehood derives from messianic event, from
Christhood according to Jesus. In the broad Judaic view, this
Christhood can only be read as Christian romanticism. The
world is manifestly unredeemed. It must be fictitious to cluster
all hope and faith around a single cross, a *Salvator mundi* in
such guise. All the evidence – not least that of Jewish agony
in history – cries out against its credibility as a bearing of 'the
sin of the world'. Jewish identity witnesses to the conviction
that there is no realized Messiahship – at least not yet, perhaps
never. Did not our own Paul write, though in another connection: 'That which is seen is not hope'? (Romans 8.24). The Jewish case gladly borrows his words. To have the Messiah, to
identify him, is no longer to await him. It is to antedate deliverance with evil still postdating him. Easter is at best premature,
at worst illusory.

Our faith in the real, actual and historical redemption at the
cross has much listening here. If we can bring it, it will deeply
inform as well as inspire the response. This must be firmly
linked with the other emotive area of Judeo-Christian relation
which concerns community in Messiah. If it be Messiah Jesus
then that community lives beyond all discrimination of Gentile
from Jew. It knows no *goyīm*. Conversely, it was, and is, the
Judaic unreadiness for Messiahship according to Jesus crucified
which underlies the Jewish disallowance of any Jew-Gentile
integration, any church-concept transcending categories ethnic

and territorial. Such a concept, like its source in Messiahship, must be regarded as romantic. Its universal reach is either imaginary or hypocritical. Jewry maintains a steady disclaimer of any 'chosen peoplehood' not its own, any admissibility to it of 'all believers'. Indeed, that phrase of the Creed may simply be the Christian version of a necessary 'circumcision'. Particularity remains crucial to divine purposes and Israel alone and for ever has it. The necessary perpetuity of the Gentile condition is for Gentiles' sake.

Christian theology in these realms of 'cross' and 'Church' has much to gain from moving out of its traditional in-discussion, soteriology and ecclesiology, and into the Judaic mind about them. Jewish exceptionality under God and this strong non-Messianism, at least in Christian terms, proceeding together as they do, make exacting demands on mind and heart as we live in mutuality. The several dispositions which obtain in this highly charged context are studied in Chapters 5, 6 and 7. The whole *raison d'être* of the New Testament is at issue. So also is the question whether there should ever have been two Testaments bound up so confidently in a single Bible. Has the confession of a world's Messiah and his open community been too unilateral in its sense of antecedents? What does its universality really mean for the role within it of those non-Hebraic cultures, and *their* histories, which it claims to embrace? Few matters of cross-reference can be more radical than these. They have, moreover, to be undertaken in the tensions born of contemporary Zionism, the anguish and entail of the Holocaust, and the painful ambiguities of the State of Israel.

VII

Non-Hebraic cultures and, we had better add, non-Mediterranean cultures, what of them? This is the query instinctive to Hinduism. It interrogates us about singularity. Why just *one* Christ, our Christ? The Christian sense of divine solicitude about man to the length of the cross vexes the Muslim in jealousy for *Allāhu akbar*. Christian Christology in that tragic dimension vexes the Jew in its identification of what can only properly be 'not so' and 'not yet'. What India wants to challenge is monopoly. Why not plural Christologies where saviourhood is fulfilled in welcome diversity? Semitic faiths are by instinct unilateral and intolerant, whether about 'God and his people', or 'God in Christ', or 'God and his apostle'. Why take the name of any god in vain?[20] May we not think of an inclusive variety of 'Christic' identities, in sundry times, persons, cultures and symbols?

India's is the ethos with which to associate this cast of mind. Hinduism has long impressed with its capacity to relish a neutralizing of all contradiction, to contain incompatibles, to tolerate anything except intolerance. Understanding Hinduism might be likened to embracing a cloud. It escapes you as you will to grasp it. It will not be tied down. It is capable both of zeal and apathy, of subtle sophistication and indolent vulgarity. The emergence of Buddhism from its Hindu context may be seen as a bid to organize and discipline its fertile vagaries and lofty aspirations. Its genius confronts the fundamentals of Christianity with multiple and disconcerting questions. Christian cross-reference to India brings all Judea, Greece and Rome, within the gospel, to a lively trial of contrast.

Furthermore, Hinduism calls in question the basic confidence of Christianity that it is called to be open to the world. The Christian gospel is conversionist through and through. The singular Christ requires the soul-seeking Church. This ardent hospitality, as baptism seals it, is inappropriate, say Hindus, outside the family circle of Christian nurture. The pluralism of faiths ought to mean the static pluralism of communities, and the latter should command mutual respect and preservation. To welcome new allegiance is improper: to seek it is deplorable. Religious truths being what they are, there is no point in changing or transferring them. Such was the insistent view of Mahatma Gandhi. There were, doubtless, elements of political nationalism at work in his view, but these only sustained a passion religiously held.

It might be argued – even on Hindu premises – that sacred pluralism indicated a complete indifference about changed adherence or conversions responding to diversity. But such logic apart, Hinduism has long and often proved capable of resenting ex-Hindus. Either way, a no-conversion stance faces Christian faith with a sharp challenge. The will to recruit confronts the cultural determinism of the karmic law. There is neither point nor reason in the evangelism which would undo it. Undoing, anyway, is a forlorn quest. Chapters 8, 9 and 10 attempt a response to these and related aspects of the feel of India.

VIII

What of Buddhism? Here, in large measure, and despite some interpretations to the contrary,[21] we leave theism behind. The focus has to be the self and the double meaning, physiological and moral, of 'egotism'. Is our undeniable egocentric situation in the life of the body and the person a delusion, a snare, a setting in which 'unselfishness' is inherently impossible? Or is it the ground and setting of a crisis about selfhood, in which there is, indeed, a self to abnegate and let die but only on behalf of a self legitimated by unselfishness? The second is, of course, the Christian view, grounded in the meaning of creation and Incarnation, and met by divine resources of grace for a right resolution of its crisis. Our concern with Buddhism, therefore, lies in the vital distinction between selfhood and selfishness, between a physical, personal egocentric situation (where we all are) and what we make of it in moral egoism.

What is at stake in this distinction can well be comprehended in the ambiguities of the word 'desire', itself a central term in almost every faith. 'One thing have I desired of the Lord', sang the psalmist (Ps. 27.4). 'With desire have I desired', was the word of Jesus in the culmination of his ministry (Luke 22.15). He himself as 'the joy of man's desiring' has been the theme of music and devotion. *Ibtighāʾ waj Allāh*, 'desiring the face of God', is the Qurʾān's prescript in moral issues as well as in soul-devotion.[22]

In making 'desire' central, Buddhism has its own 'way' concerning it. How should we take the seeming negativity of that 'way', utterly contrasted as it is with the 'negative capability' of which John Keats wrote so tellingly? Plainly the Buddhist abnegation of 'desire' has a certain kinship with Christian baptism and the 'No' we must say to self. There *is* point in the menace we can be to ourselves. There is a self to mortify, as Paul had it in Romans (Rom. 8.13; cf. Col. 3.3), to 'let die', as the *Dhamma* has it. But what 'self' is it?

Here the most positive and radical Christian reference into Buddhism belongs. We need not press crudely the loaded question about what it is that enters *Nirvāna*. 'Nothingness' is not extinction, if there really was nothing to become extinct. All faiths in any event have their paradoxes. The Christian has a vital one in the Incarnation. A wise inter-theology will know that all faiths can be controversially embarrassed if we are crude enough to misconstrue them. The puzzle of the self deserves better of our perception than easy argument. Yet we must insist that it is not to be evaded by retreat into mystery or prevarication. Whatever its thesis about samsaric flux, Buddhism is caught, as we all are, in urgent and concrete circumstances where selfhood is beset. There are, for example, tensions in Sri Lanka, about politics, racialism and society, about the *Sangha* and the world. History requires to be interpreted and handled. Will a detached neutrality ever be more than either a retreat or a treachery? Disinterested involvement must seem either a contradiction or an illusion. Maybe the sheer 'desire' to be unselfed will be yet another, perhaps deluded, form of self-pre-occupation?

For the Christian it is clearly all familiar territory, yet profoundly dissimilar. The cross-references are fascinating to note and exacting to explore. They have to do with personhood, time, flux, mortality and meaning. There is no more bracing field for Christian theology in the trust of Christ and grace, of creaturehood and fulfilment, than the neighbourhood of the Buddha and his Four Noble Truths, as Chapters 11, 12, and 13 discover.

IX

With what, then, in sum, do these four faiths confront us in venturing out of our familiar in-discussions into a theology eager for their stimulus and minded for their points of substance? We must reconsider what can be thought of God if we are not to be found in compromise of divine transcendence. We must dissociate God's prerogatives from human interrogatives and draw no clues as to divine power from our human wistfulness for grace. In this context, we must restrict what is revelatory to the prophetic and, so doing, re-semiticize a Jesus whom our Fathers reinterpreted, without warrant, for Greece and Rome. We must de-romanticize our understanding of salvation. We must renounce our conviction of a human community authentically gathered around the cross, for the more realist, the primary, nexus of nation, tribe, territory and blood. We must be content to be *ethnē, Gentiles,* and concede that there is no viable, spiritual *e pluribus unum,* such as the

apostolic Church believed itself to be. That most ambitious of
all visions, in the New Testament, about 'no more strangers',
but rather 'fellow citizens . . . the household of God' (Eph. 2.19)
must be seen as insubstantial. All this they say to us.

Christology, furthermore, must be de-monopolized to admit
of numerous saviourhoods, multiplying or diversifying the
paradigm (as we esteem it) of the cross on Calvary. The
endlessly varied psyches of mankind, their myth-making fertility, their primordial image-ing must be allowed free rein. The
distinctiveness of the Christian gospel and the resultant will
to a missionary inclusiveness of human range must be aban-
doned. We must surrender the will to recruit the world. At
best, pluralism suggests to us, there can only be a sort of common market of 'salvations', each by its own lights and means.
We have too readily said that around the cross of Jesus all
the ground is level and that 'whosoever will may come'. Asia
caps these warnings by assuring us that our Christian sense
of personality conspires, in fact, to its own deception by affirming its loved and cherished creaturehood, a loved and redeemed
identity, heir to eternal life.

These, in brief, are the terms of our summons to a theology
which seeks no immunity or relief but wills to relate *bona fide*
to the cross-examination of the world it claims for its parish.
That word 'parish', in an odd way, has in its fortunes the very
nub of our theme. Its current sense is of things severely local
and, for that reason, familiar, enclosed, unadventurous, just
'parochial', whereas *paroikia* in its Greek sense (cf. 1 Pet. 1.17)
was precisely where men were not at home but were on
the road, open-ended and moving on. Theology has somehow
to reverse what has happened to *paroikia* and pass from the
sedentary to the active, from congenial familiarity to
strenuous encounter with the uncongenial scene. Whatever we
have to do (according to our mentors) with re-semiticizing,
de-romanticizing, disillusioning, and the rest, will mean some
de-parochializing of our instincts and our concerns. Any
response here can only be summary and selective. But a final
chapter will need to look back over the experience and relate
it to the heritage of faith, the *fiducia*, in which we live as
Christians and by which alone we are identified. There is
neither point nor loyalty in encounter with pluralism if 'the
salt has lost its savour'. The summons is not met if we forfeit
what is heeding it.

How, then, does 'the faith once delivered', as Jude 3 has it, not merely ensure, but fulfil, itself in the duty of cross-reference? We hold to 'God in Christ' as theology's credential, the disclosure in grace of the God of creation and history. We hold to Jesus as this Christ, the active, trustworthy referent for God because in Jesus as the Christ we find God, self-given to humanity. We hold to the mandate of the Christian to be, through grace and holiness, the referent for Christ. We hold the people of that reference to be the custodian community through whose life and ministry of word and sacrament this 'knowledge and love of God' avails for all mankind. We hold that this community of faith comprehends all human diversity of tribe and culture and excludes none. Our faith, it could be said, is in fact a harmony of referents – of God to Christ, of Christ to God, of Jesus to Christ, of the Church to God in Christ Jesus, and of all these to the heart of the person. Cross-reference theology, we might further say, is none other than the conscious, loving, tireless, hopeful trust of these referents together and the patient interpretation of the theme of their consistency.

X

There are three clear obligations, in the closing chapter, for any theology intending to be both loyal and relational. One must concern the sustaining of the central and distinctive identity of Christianity – as just now defined – in respect of the wealth of sometimes bewildering debate over any definition. As we must see in dealing later with the mind of India, and its complaint about singular theology, Christianity has great range of diversity within itself. Interpreters with the ambition to relate it to other faiths must acknowledge inward issues which divide Christians. These go some way to illuminating cross-reference into the other religions, where questions of quietism, gnosticism, mysticism, the exoteric and the esoteric, and hermeneutical controversies, also arise. Questions turning on Jesus and history, New Testament exegesis, theology and culture, pressures of secular origin, the demands of liberation, bring sharp and serious tensions into Christian self-understanding, as do also vexed matters of church authority, and even church authenticity. There can be no neglecting, and certainly no concealing, these factors. No Christian engagement with other faiths has a mandate to be 'plenipotentiary'. Cross-reference has rigorous duties with its own *credenda* and must be prepared for their presence in all exterior ventures and relationships. There is, indeed, no major faith whose commendation may not justly suffer the retort: 'But that is not what . . . proper really says!' Or: 'What we hear *you* saying does not coincide with how others among you characterize your religion!'

This situation is not one for despair. Lively, intelligent Christians are not likely to think they lack a positive, glad and communicable identity, a faith they hold and by which they are held, capable indeed of breadth and freedom, but nevertheless defined by an integrity both of doctrine and of worship.[23]

The second obligation stems from the first. It wrestles with the fact that apostolic cross-reference within the New Testament had to do only with Greece and Rome outside the original Hebraic matrix. That apostolic cross-reference, furthermore, is sealed and documented in the Canon, which thus excludes from scriptural status and (thus far) from liturgical usage any present cross-reference, indeed any subsequent to the New Testament writers. This is clearly a radical problem in and for a faith which purports to embrace all mankind and to be the 'desire' of all cultures, a faith whose theology of conversion must assume that all men's antecedents – and not simply those of the Jewish order – have authentic place within its heritage, its liturgy and its expression.

The New Testament writers, within the Canon, were totally oblivious of Asia. The Islamic shape of mind about divine omnipotence was then still six centuries away. The Buddha was never within the ken of Peter or of Paul. Mercifully, the New Testament precedents are ours. We have *their* cross-reference into Greek vocabulary as well as Hebraic clues to sacrifice and suffering. But any present emulation of these patterns, in the still more exacting fields which they ignored, is wholly in our hands. The Fourth Gospel may suggest ideas to Christian thinking in India. But it will not write them into Scripture. Romans makes fascinating reading in the Buddhist scene. But the Canon is closed. We can only be scriptural in our world cross-reference by our own resources and our own responsibility in the Holy Spirit.

Here we are in deep waters. The Canon will not be reopened but are we well served by its closedness? Maybe the assumption

which bound the whole Bible into one, supposedly harmo-
nious, supposedly sufficient, volume, was premature. Its 'suffi-
ciency' – in the Anglican term – must lie, not in a world-
awareness it does not possess, but in a living loyalty by which,
somehow, we make good its geographical inadequacy. In that
sense, today's Church has to be more widely, more ambitiously
apostolic than the first apostles – unless we are to suppose
that all the world is still around the Mediterranean.

It is from these thoughts that we reach our third obligation.
It has to do with the role of the personal Christian and the
role of the whole Church. It is people, not structures, that meet.
What should we think about the collective guardianship and
the individual initiatives? How free can the person be? What
are the limits to those reservations of interpretation which even
the most authoritarian church-structures must partially allow?
Is there legitimate disparity between what is required in a creed
and what obtains in a *credo*?[24]

It would be idle to think of cross-reference theology as a
sort of 'negotiation'. That word in its current meaning belongs
with diplomacy and trade, not with the things of the Spirit.
Yet in its Latin derivation it can be very close to a theology
with the will to love: *Neg-otium* – saying No! to sloth, to torpor,
to ease, to repose.

NOTES

1 Wilfred Owen, *Collected Letters*, ed. Harold Owen and John Bell (London
   1967), p. 562. Letter to Osbert Sitwell, No. 634. The same theme recurs
   in the imagery of Wilfred Owen's war poetry.

2 *Letters of John Keats: 1814–1821*, ed. H. E. Rollins, 2 vols. (Cambridge,
   Mass.), 1958, vol. 2, No. 159, Letter of 21 April, 1819, to George Keats,
   p. 103. Oromanes belongs in an oriental fairy tale current in Keats's time,
   i.e. *A History of the Merchant Abudah, or: The Talisman of Oromanes*. See
   Charles Morell: *The Tales of the Genii*, 2 vols, London 1764.

3 Quoted from T. R. Henn, ed., *Passages for Divine Reading* (London 1967),
   p. 121 modernized from Francis Rabelais, *Works*, Book iv, Chap. 28, trans.
   of 1653 by Thomas Urquhart, Navarre Society edn.

4 See Chapter 8, notes 10 and 12; and Chapter 10, note 2.

5 In *Religious Studies*, Cambridge, vol. 11, No. 2 (1975), pp. 193–200. Among
   sociologists also is this sense that too limited judgements have been made.
   Thus, for example, Peter Berger, *The Heretical Imperative*, London 1980.
   He sees his work in the sixties as sadly lacking in range and advises anyone
   seeking an understanding of Christianity today to widen their ecumenicity.

He means by this term not merely inter-Christian relations, but the world relations of all religions.

6   Islam has traditionally taught that it is parents who 'make' children Christians, or Hindus or Buddhists etc., by upbringings which preclude the natural Islamic bent within all human life as it obtains at birth. It is open of course to all faiths to opine that mankind is 'naturally' themselves. The point here, however, is the degree to which a sense of having been born (and raised) as such-and-such brings a fortuitous quality into a received 'finality'.

7   Conditioning sometimes survives even abandonment of commitment. Thus, for example, James Joyce observes in: *Portrait of the Artist as a Young Man* (London 1930), p. 240: 'It is a curious thing how your mind is saturated with the religion in which you say you disbelieve.'

8   J. H. Anand, 'Tradition and Modernity in Recent Hindi Literature', in C. D. Jathanna, ed., *Dialogue in Community* (Mangalore 1982), p. 75.

9   Mushir al-Haqq, *Islam in Secular India* (Simla 1962), p. 21.

10 R. R. Brenner, *Faith and Doubt of Holocaust Victims* (New York 1980), p. 59. This work was based on extensive questionnaires to survivors concerning their attitudes to Judaism. Some felt a blank necessity to repudiate all sense of a 'God of Israel'. Others embraced and practised their religion with ardent zeal as a way of 'spitting on the Nazis' graves'.

11 A. H. Rabinowits, in *The Values of Judaism* (Tel Aviv 1953), p. 47.

12 John Henry Newman, *Essay on the Development of Christian Doctrine*, London 1845.

13 John Calvin, Libr. 1, Cap. v.

14 *The Muqaddimah of Ibn Khaldun*, trans. by Franz Rosenthal (New York 1958), vol. i, pp. 192–3.

15 See further in Chapter 3 below and my *Muhammad and the Christian* (London 1984), Chapter 6, 'The Prophetic Experience'.

16 Vladimir Lossky, *The Mystical Theology of the Eastern Church* (London 1957), p. 65. His reference, of course, is not to 'the divine essence', of which in his tradition, 'there is no place for a theology', but to the *doctrine* of the Holy Trinity.

17 *Patrologia Graeca*, 36, 141B.

18 Ronald Hingley, *Pasternak, a Biography* (London 1983), p. 168. The lines are 70–4 of *Hamlet*, Act 3, sc. 1.

19 See M. Khadduri, *Islamic Jurisprudence*, being a trans. of Al-Shāfiʻi: *Risālah*. The verse might be translated: 'Does man think that he is left on the loose?' The revelation of the Qurʾān is understood as the religious authority in and through all law, civil, criminal, constitutional, and moral. A transcendental order behind the duty of law-abidingness is common to the Semitic faiths. What is distinctive about Islam is explicit and inclusive state aegis as sanction and instrument. Personal autonomy is taken wholly into Islamic constraints. See also Chap. 2, note 25.

20 Quoted from Herbert Birks, *Life of Thomas Valpy French*, 2 vols (London

1985), vol. 1, p. 58. French, first Bishop of Lahore, taught at Agra. He invited an essay from Hindu teenagers on their first choice among the Ten Commandments. One student chose the Third and began his essay with this query. French thought he was being provocative. But the reaction takes one to the heart of Hinduism. On the point of Semitic intolerance, one may note the cry of despair about contemporary Jerusalem from an India-lover of long sojourn there: 'This city needs a strong dose of Hinduism: they are all so sure that they alone are right!'

21 Notably Lynn De Silva. See Chap. 11, note 23.

22 See: 'Desiring the Face of God', in my *The Mind of the Qur'ān* (London 1973), pp. 163–81.

23 In a revealing passage in 2 Cor. 1.17–20, Paul responds to ill-will and charges of insincerity by affirming the fidelity of God enshrined in the gospel he preaches and then linking his own sincerity with that of the gospel. The two, he says, characterize each other. The ministry must partake of the authenticity of the faith it tells and serves. Equivocation is no part of the gospel nor, therefore, of its bearers. This is the double point of *Bona Fide Christiana*.

24 Cf. the hint in Robert Bridges, though noted in order to be denied, about Thomas Aquinas:

> Some . . . say that the saint himself held not the faith
> Which universal credit compelled him to assume
> If he would lead and teach the Church . . .

Robert Bridges: *Poetical Works* (Oxford 1953), 'The Testament of Beauty', p. 583, lines 480–2, Book 1.

God and Islam

2
Theologies of Magnificat

Prove to me only that the least
Command of God is God's indeed,
And what injunction shall I need
To pay obedience?[1]

Islam lives by the assurance that the need of 'proving' has ended
with itself. 'Command of God' obtains, and so must the human
obedience. Religion, in Islam, is centred in divine imperative
– the imperative to which being *muslim* responds in the witness
of faith, the duties of *Dīn*, the society of the *Sharī'ah*, and the
solidarity of the *Ummah* of the Prophet. All these are grounded
in that total sense of the divine authority steadily and intensely
confessed in the *Allāhu akbar* of Islamic life and liturgy. No
reference into Islam from outside it can properly begin except
from this inclusive, incorporating sense of divine command
and human surrender. The outsider must come to terms with
what may well be considered the most comprehensive God-
consciousness, credally, ritually and politically institutionalized, that history knows.

But, distinctive and, therefore, sharply self-oriented as Islam
is, in its version of God and man and the world, its theism
in the imperative mood has vital kinship with both Jew and
Christian. The more confident and, in some ways, the more
immune from need of others its autonomy appears, the more
urgent the recognition – theirs and ours – of how much it shares.
It could not be otherwise with an intelligent theism. For one
can hardly be sanely monopolistic about God. It is these affini-
ties this chapter is set to understand as central to any cross-
reference in questions posed and thoughts transacted.

They are well formulated as theologies of *Magnificat*, using
the Latin verb which has come to be so closely linked with
the Song of Mary but which we find, for example, in the Vulgate of
Psalm 34.3: *Magnificate Dominum mecum*, or *Magnificetur Dominus*
in Psalm 40.16 and elsewhere. Such joyous and perpetual celebration of the greatness of God (in that sense 'making' him great)

belongs squarely with the Qur'ān of Islam, in its own idiom. *Kabbirhu takbīran*, says 17.111, using the familiar absolute accusative: 'make him greatly great'. The cry: *Allāhu akbar*, the liturgical form in which 17.111 is obeyed, is the *Takbīr*, the clue to all Islamic theology. That God is *Al-Mutakabbir* (59.23), 'the Self-aware great', is the transcendental counter-part of *Takbīr*. The believer bestows no greatness: he acknowledges how transcendent it is. That such acknowledgement should be requisite is a fascinating theological point to which we must return. For the moment it carries every believer, however lowly, into surrender to divine Lordship responding to what perhaps we may call the annunciation of existence, the awareness of a selfhood summoned into divine obligation.

We can perhaps best pursue this theme, from *Takbīr* into *Tauhīd*, or 'unity', by pausing to review the preoccupations of Muhammad's mission, or *Risālah*, resulting from the immediate setting in which it was fulfilled. For there is a real sense in which any faith is shaped and predisposed by the constraints of its locale, the concerns which weighed in its genesis.[2] When Sākyamuni – to give the Buddha his personal title – the wise man from the Sākya country in the foothills of the Himalayas, took his way out of the palace he encountered first a sick man, then an old, decrepit, man and finally a dead man. His concerns were decisively with impermanence, disease, transience and mortality. He did not, vocationally, confront a slave man, an exploited man, an alienated man, or an imprisoned man. It was these who were in the path of Moses when he renewed his roots in Jacob and opened himself to his people's oppression, and their slave mentality. It followed that exodus *via* leadership, under God, became the definitive event for Moses' people, and, with exodus, the abiding conviction as to covenant and 'God and His people'.

With Muhammad it was neither transience nor *dukkha*, neither expatriate enslavement nor ethnic migration. We need not presume more precise knowledge than a sound scholarship can warrant, about the pre-Islamic Meccan world and the Prophet's travels, to gauge the motive circumstances within the Quranic scene. The Scripture itself informs us: the paramount factors were an encounter with pluralism in deities and division among Arabs. It is likely that the two belonged together. Something like Elijah's issue with the *baalīm* in his Samaria breathes in Muhammad's repudiation of the polydaemonism of Arabia.

Shirk, or pseudo-worship, is the multiple 'Pharoah' of Quranic 'exodus'. Liberation from the idols is the central motif of the Prophet's story.

That liberation from *Shirk* was a precondition of a new order. Muhammad knew of months of truce and no doubt his merchandise profited from them. But why were they necessary? Why could they not become perpetual? Chronic tribalism, the tradition of blood revenge and, with it, the cultic esteem of *murūʾah*, or manly courage – courage for its own sake – these were the afflictions of Arab society, on their own soil, to which pre-Islamic poetry bears both proud and plaintive witness. It was these evils which Islam was either to banish or baptize into its unifying ethos and doctrine. We need not impugn what is so precious to Muslims, namely the direct divine source of the Qurʾān, to appreciate the circumstantial setting which determined – or perhaps we should say coincided with – its incidence. For belief in revelation means a readiness for its time and place. The outsider can certainly trace in some of the instincts of Islamic theology the attitudes of Meccan/Arab ways, whereby thought about God was readily aligned with assumptions about power and social will.[3]

To these we may return later. Meanwhile it is clear that Islam's sense of divine greatness, and of the duty to affirm it resolutely, have their historic context in the 'idolatry' against which its vocation was formed in the markets of Mecca and the conflicts of the tribes. That there were also, undoubtedly, influences deriving from the earlier Judaic and Christian monotheisms does not alter the basic quality of Muhammad's preaching as determined by the duty to counter and eliminate *shirk* and the deities it invoked. Only by such firm and final rejection could the sole Lordship of *Allāh* be enthroned in the hearts as it was in the heavens. The absence in Arabia, apart from the *Hanīf* movement,[4] of any native monotheistic tradition, meant that the Prophet's theme of divine unity had necessarily to be urgent and combative. The biblical prophets, by contrast, are seen by the Hebrew historians as resisting alien, Canaanite temptation into nature worships and idolatry, and doing so from within an already established Judaic conviction, if not of the inclusive unity of Yahweh, at least of his singularity as 'the God of Israel'. It is important to keep always in view the iconoclastic achievement of Muhammad where no such long, Mosaic-style, tradition existed.

II

This distinctive prophethood of divine unity, however, in the
Arabian context, had two consequences which have dominated
Muslim theological thought ever since. It tended to a concern
for unity as a theme of number, the singular in denial of the
plural. Further, it entailed a rigorous dissociation of God from
the human realm, a passion for divine exaltedness, which –
as we must see – strained the associative implications of the
Qur'ān's own clear and ardent confidence in divine creation,
human creaturehood and divine legislation.

'Say: " He is God, the One"' (Surah 112.1). The word *Allāh*
is incapable of being made plural, or of being in construct,
or 'possession', to any other noun. The generic noun *ilāhun*,
'a god', is used for the absolute negation in the *Shahādah*: *Lā
ilāha illā Allāh*, 'There is no god save *Allāh*.' This sole Lordship
of *Allāh* as the core of Muhammad's witness constitutes the
utter incomparability affirmed in the words: *Allāhu akbar*,
'greater is God' – a grammatical comparative not further elaborated by 'than . . .' since nothing is worthy of entering into comparison. *Takbīr* and *Tauhīd* together assert and celebrate this
entire transcendence. Yet this faith in the divine unity is not
adequately confessed merely in terms of 'number' alone, that
is, as something to be affirmed in rejection of 'deities' in the
plural, of idols many. It has to do also with the inner 'self-
consistency' characterizing the inclusive sovereignty of God.
For, as the eleventh-century Rabbi, Solomon Ibn Gabirol,
observed: 'Thou art One, but not as the one that is counted
or owned. For number . . . cannot reach Thee.'[5]

'Number' cannot qualify God, because the word *Allāh*, God,
Gott, Deus, Dieu, does not have to do with a genus or class
to which others could belong. It is in *not* being a generic word
that it is incapable of plural. When we say: 'God is One', the
sentence is not like: 'Carpentry is one (profession)'. For there
are many others in the genus 'profession'. The Islamic *Shahādah*
is not confessing: 'There is no god but God', in any sense analogous to saying: 'There is no star but Polaris, there is no constella-
tion but Orion.' For there are innumerable stars and endless
constellations. Sentences of this kind, purporting to be restrictive and nugatory, negate where the entities concerned are only
'ones' in instance because they are 'many' in fact. The unity
of God is not about counting in a (potential) sequence which

never got past one, as in 'an only child'. The Arabic word *Allāh* has just this force of non-generic singularity, which English intends to indicate by the capital letter.

There would be point in saying that 'There is no god but God' is a sentence comparable to one which says: 'There is no king but Caesar.' There are, in fact, many kings and rulers. But 'no king but Caesar' is a political statement: it is restrictive, not about existence but about 'right' or 'validity'. It is an assertion from loyalty, not from sheer fact. *Mon*archy, at least, in the same territory, must be exclusive.

If we put these two formulations together we reach something close to the witness of Muslims about God. For 'gods', (*ālihāt*), do 'exist' in the imagination or perverse allegiance of 'polytheists'. These are the pseudo-deities meant in the negation in the first part of the *Shahādah*, for which Arabic uses a different noun (*ilāh*) which is capable of plural (*ālihāt*). English can only indicate this with the same word with, or without, the capital initial letter ('god' and 'God'). Such 'gods many and lords many' *do* have an actual, albeit false, tenure in the faiths of men. Otherwise there would be no need for prophets to deny them. They are not real: they are figments of the pagan mind, the folly of the *mushrikīn*. Essentially there is no need to deny the non-existent, but practically there is every need, as in our 'political' example. The real authority of 'Caesar' requires the 'non-king-ing' of any other claimant ruler.

Theology, Jewish, Christian, Muslim, lives by this fact of divine unity and by devotion to it as also a task. It rejoices in the assurance that 'only God is God', yet has also to strive to make it so. What is blessedly and unassailably has to be *let be* so. This is the paradox of the divine unity. Its transcendental 'undoubtedness' is, however, continually called in question by a 'political' non-recognition which – in the sense of our analogy – has another 'king' (god) but God, which needs to be dethroned, so that men '*have* no other' God, as distinct from merely saying that there is none.

There is point in this 'political' language, not least with Islam, since there is a strong 'sovereign' element in its thought of God, a monarchical sense in its religious emphases, and, indeed, a final policization of its patterns of religious establishment. The Qurʾān does not hesitate to see Muslims and their opponents as *hizb-Allāh* and *hizb al-shaitān* (Surahs 5.56, 58.19), 'the partisans of God and of Satan'. Such was the price of its

very fervour 'in the way of God' in the setting shaped by the
chronic tribalism and pseudo-worships with which Muhammad was confronted in his mission. To the 'zealous' aspect
here we will return in Chapter 4 below.

Here the immediate point is to appreciate the significance
of the disallowing of the essentially one divine authority, the
wilful, albeit unreal, making plural of the worship that can
properly be only one. It means that, as well as truly being
One, God has to be let be One, and that this 'letting be' hinges
on man, on you and me. The divine unity is one which we
are capable of making pseudo-plural by disallowing a true worship and invoking, asserting, trusting, gods which have no
being outside our invoking, or asserting, or trusting. To give
the lie to them will require the reversing and forsaking of all
these acts and attitudes of ours by which they falsely 'exist'.
Hence the wide reach, conceptual, emotional and practical, of
the repudiation of *Shirk*. The situation of our falsehood
demands negation of our notions about 'gods'. More, it requires
the winning of our emotions and the cleansing of our imagination, until 'we have such gods no longer'. Islam has always
been inclusive, in this way, in its care for a whole theism, even
if its *Shahādah* has remained severely propositional. There is
no doubt that the sequence of a true *islām* moves from: 'There
is no god but God', to: 'Thou shalt have no other gods . . .'
to: 'Whom have I in heaven but thee?'

The mysterious fact that God, the One, the only, can nevertheless be the slighted, the denied, the ignored, the displaced,
the neglected, must be allowed its full import. Theology, in
a strange way, is really about 'letting Being be'. *Allāhu akbar*
is a fact but it is also a confession. It is the sort of fact that
can go unrecognized. Where confession is withheld, the 'absolute' has submitted to be relative to our 'consent'. This, so stated,
may be an unpalatable truth to Jews or Christians, and to Muslims instinctively most of all. Yet it is inseparable from our
living theism. It tells us much about the patience of God –
enough to give pause to the impatience of men about the divine
dishonour it entails. It tells us much, too, about the dignity
of our human-ness and about the crisis in creation.

We can illuminate the point at issue here, about the strange
forbearance of the heavenly sovereignty, from two very different perspectives. It would be supposed by most theism, certainly by Islam, that iconoclasm is its duty, denying and

eradicating pseudo-worships, and destroying the idols. The true believer must emulate Elijah, as he emulated the Quranic Abraham, and Muhammad emulated both. Not at all, Karl Marx would argue, and did in his writings. Once we have understood how man, in nature, is all there is, *both* theism *and* atheism become meaningless and no longer need to be denied. When positive human self-consciousness is attained (Marx's phrase), atheism, as a *necessary* denial, will go the same way as theology, into limbo. It is only necessary to deny God and gods as long as their illusoriness persists.[6] Could there, conceivably, be a more telling measure of how total 'the exclusion of God' (the Qurʾān's repeated phrase)[7] could supposedly be, so total that denial itself has become superfluous? God, gone without a trace, by a certain interpretation of the human!

Let us move for our second perspective from Karl Marx to John Milton, the seventeenth-century English poet and no mean theologian. He can help us understand how the sovereignty of God, which we are saying calls for recognition, is of such a sort as to await a recognition which is not imposed but loved and wanted by the submission bringing it. Otherwise, God himself is somehow misconstrued and his very sovereignty is misread as a compulsive monarchy. This is the significance of Milton's Satan in *Paradise Lost*. It is worth exploring briefly as a pointed, if also subtle, witness in our argument.

There was much, no doubt unconscious, Islam in John Milton, not only for his interest in Satan, also a vital figure in the Qurʾān,[8] but for his rugged Islamic sense of idols to be dethroned in the vindication of God's Name. Thus Samson, the great hero in *Samson Agonistes*, now captive and blinded in the idol temple, yields his cause to God.

> The strife
> With me hath end: all the contest now
> 'Twixt God and Dagon; Dagon hath presumed,
> Me overthrown, to enter lists with God,
> His deity comparing and preferring
> Before the God of Abraham. He, be sure,
> Will not connive or linger, thus provoked,
> But will arise and His great Name assert:
> Dagon must stoop.

Samson's old father, and Milton's commentator, Manoah, concurs:

            God
Nothing more certain, will not long defer
To vindicate the glory of His Name
Against all competition, nor will long
Endure it, doubtful whether God be Lord
Or Dagon.[9]

Strongly Islamic sentiments!

But, in *Paradise Lost*, Satan somehow runs away with the
poet's theology, if not with his intentions. For Satan emerges
as a hero, assertive, defiant, and resolute. 'Better to reign in
hell than serve in heaven', he cries. God, reciprocally, is seen
as almost worsted by this defiance, Lord of a sovereignty which,
if still outwardly enthroned, is none the less successfully
denied, and thus essentially frustrated. The reason? It lies in
the unduly 'logical' and stringently monarchical role in which
God is cast, issuing commands and wielding a governance
which Satanic courage and pride can still reject and deny and
seem admirable in so doing. Logic and reason cannot fault the
situation. To be God is surely to rule: to be under God is to
be subject to divine imperative. Yet the imperative service
can be denied in a manner which seems to re-present that Lordship as a tyranny oddly mastered by what Satanically frustrates
it.

When we take the measure of this puzzle, a vital clue to
theology for all of us emerges, though one which some of us
are loth to concede. It is that the sovereignty of God is of a
nature to be realized in human life only when it is inwardly
loved and wanted. Its claim on us wills to be willed in return.
There has to be *islām*. We *may* defy if we will. To do so is
against the truth, the logic, the rule, behind all things, against
the law of God. But, paradox as it may be, these do not avail
to subdue us if we choose to be defiant, and if we so choose
God's being God is something *we* distort into an image of
oppression or frustration, inviolate and blessed as it essentially
remains.

To read this clue rightly – and it is written large in history
and in life – can bring us to an essential fact about *islām*, as
a term. It is that the divine imperative addresses freedom, a
freedom of ours which God has willed to be the context of
his own will. To submit to God is to will a conformity to his
will. In terms of the poetry of Muhammad Iqbal, who needs

to be read watchfully, our true fulfilment as finite selves consists in taking God's will freely into our own.[10]

> Even though you are single in essence,
> Yet You have created for Yourself a world of plurality.[11]

Within that plurality we in humanness are the sentient part with a volitional role. There is no denying the actual pluralism of all that is and no sanity in the attempt to reduce its manifoldness to some pseudo 'unity'. The very pluralism is the sphere of a genuine *Tauhīd*, in which divinely willed plurality is subdued to the divine order by the consecration of man in due creaturehood and 'dominion'. In that 'religion', as Surah 2.256 has it, 'there is no compulsion'. It is on this ground that we must deal together in 'theologies of *Magnificat*', acknowledging and measuring aright the annunciation of existence which we learn to heed by this awareness of how God wills to be God and how we are to confess it so. 'My soul ... my Lord ... magnify.'

III

The *Magnificat* of Mary, according to the Gospel, was firmly within the covenantal theme of Jewish chosen-ness. We sense that the inclusive 'generations' of which she sang were Jewish, while some of the allusions in the Song are drawn from celebration of the Maccabean heroes. Patriarchal contexts apart, the Qurʾān, by contrast returns back from ethnic covenants of peoplehood to the elemental covenant of nature and of husbandry, the covenant with 'the good earth'. Its theology is the theology of creation. The patriarchs it sees not as dynastic but didactic, not people–progenitors but breakers of idols and teachers of *Tauhid*. They are participants, not in an elective history but rather in the divine demand for a pure worship. As if to underline this contrast, Ishmael replaces Isaac in the different idiom of the building of the Kaʿbah, and the founding of Mecca.[12]

But there is a haunting identity of conviction in the phrase of Mary's Song: 'His mercy is on them that fear him.' *Rahmah* and *taqwā* are at the heart of the human annunciation in the Qurʾān. To discover these anew, with their impulse to the ruling Quranic themes of praise and gratitude, and the intimations present from God in the experience of human life, will bring us into shared theology and open the way into a vexed question between us, in Islam and Christianity, about whether and when the sacred becomes secular or the secular made sacred.

Rahmah and *taqwā* are among the most frequent roots in the Qur'ān's Arabic and they are clearly linked. The one is the noun denoting all that is comprised in the *Bismillah's* use of the divine Names: *Al-Rahmān al-Rahīm*, which, in its double usage of the R H M root, sees 'mercy' *of* the essence and also *in* the action of God; the other is the fundamental human posture of awe and wonder and reverence in respect of God as his *Rahmah* shows him to be. It is that 'fear of God' which preserves and hallows the believer, in soul and conduct, and so holds him within the prescriptive order of the moral law. This 'fear', as Fazlur Rahman is careful to point out, in describing *taqwā* as 'perhaps the most important single term in the Qur'ān',[13] is not a crude 'fear', like fear of a wolf, but a conscience which guards the self from wilfulness and self-wronging (*zulm al-nafs*). It may be seen as analogous, to a degree, with the Christian sense of the Greek noun *sōphrosunē*, the 'wisdom' that guards and saves the self from *superbia* and all that follows from inflated notions of oneself.[14]

But if *taqwā* is regulative and protective of a right behaviour it is everywhere reciprocal to divine *rahmah*. To be 'squarely anchored within the moral ... "limits of God"'[15] is to know and cherish the mercy which made them so. The alertness to the subtlety of evil which *taqwā* brings rides with the *dhikr*, or 'reminder' which God's mercy makes in the revelation of the Qur'ān and the provision for its recital. That divine judgement, acknowledged in *taqwā*, far transcends human reckonings of utility or convention. It is God's mercy which has it so. Without God's law our liberties might *seem* greater but our case would be abysmal. Were there no tether our straying were our doom. All this *taqwā* registers with gratefulness to the All-merciful, *al-Rahmān*. 'There is no haranguing him that they may take upon themselves.'[16]

For many in the centuries of Islam *taqwā*, and God's mercy as having no counsel but its own, have dominated all thought and anticipation of the future life. But in the present context, *rahmah*, disclosed in law and the fact of the Qur'ān, is present antecedently to *wahy*, or revelation, in the fact of nature and the earth and man as their trustee. It is here that a common theology of *Magnificat*, if all too seldom recognized for what it is, is most surely recognizable between Muslims and Christians. Mary, it might be protested, was not concerned with ecology and the Quranic Miriam sings no song, though there is a comparable aura of wonder and godly fear in her annunciation according to Surahs 3 and 19. Yet a deep, not to say urgent, theology of human life and the order of nature belongs with her significance. It will be well to make our way into an inclusive theology of praise responsive in, and to, creation by pondering where *Magnificat* will take us if we begin reverently with birth.

Islam and Christianity will never be at one about Jesus' nativity. For the latter it is within the larger wonder of the Incarnation. That mystery may be served and symbolized by a break in genealogy. For the Muslim the break occurs without the larger wonder, to signify a prophet's vocation. The two 'nativities' are, therefore, quite in contrast. In the one 'the Word is made flesh', in the other 'a word is born'. Either way, there is motherhood and there is birth. These, in every event are inclusive index to the human trust, the token and the instrument of the authority to be which God, in creation, has given and maintained to us. Procreation, on our part, is creation's investment in itself by contracting for our management and ordaining such management in generations. Wombs, we may say, are the pledge and method of the divine commitment to our kind and of our kind to the possession and celebration of the earth. They are normally fulfilled by the partnership of sex, but whatever may, or may not, be signified by an abeyance of that partnership, it is birth that happens and life which ensues. On this we are at one, 'involved in mankind'.

The Qur'ān is often found marvelling at the mystery of birth, all birth, and at the strange progress of the embryo into life. It is there in Surah 96.2, in the ʿalaq which rhymes with khalaq, the biology and the Lordship, and gives its title to the Surah. There are frequent passages which rehearse the cycle of the womb from the onset to the climax of fertility.[17] 'The love and tenderness' which God has appointed between partners in sexuality are 'among his signs' (Surah 30.21), a conviction immediately linked with 'the creation of the heavens and the earth'. This reverent celebration of the trust of birth and of the sexual will and power within it are, as it were, the lowliest of *magnificats* and, by implication, make all experience in child-coming (an experience which male and female may share) an annunciation. Existence, we may say, in its genesis as well as in its ensuing, is annunciatory and may be so known in every human instance. Our casualness, our grossness, our brutality, our blasphemy may well, at this point more than any other, betray the meaning of the trust and human lives are often inaugurated in such 'exclusion of God'. But the vocation remains, and the Mary of both the Gospel and the Qur'ān is a perpetual figure-of-truth as to the divine 'high regard of man' which birth perennially tells and, telling, invites us out of 'mercy' into *taqwā*.

A procreative creation, then, is the biblical/Quranic *mise-en-scène* of mankind. What we should learn from its cycle of inauguration is seen as the clue to its whole quality as a divinely given field of sense and faculty and worth, to be tenanted as a place, occupied as a span and achieved as a grace. Mary's motherhood, whatever its exceptionality for the sake of and by virtue of the Jesus she bore, has this wider significance for us all. It was of her body that she sang in *Magnificat*, for it was physically that being 'handmaiden' was fulfilled. Those who understand her vocation within the Incarnation have the greatest cause of all to learn the hallowedness of their own flesh, the 'where' and 'wherein' of God's self-disclosure. But all who are 'in the body' owe themselves to birth, to a birth which they should read as a sacrament of divine intention, the divinely meant initiation of themselves to 'this fair earth'. They have 'arrived' and even if, with Thomas Traherne, they do not inquire where they have 'not been' so long awaiting being, at least they may sing a praise of their own:

> A stranger here
> Strange things doth meet, strange glories see,
> Strange treasures lodged in this fair world appear,
> Strange all, and new to me.
> But that they should be mine, who nothing was,
> That strangest is of all, yet brought to pass.[18]

Such personhood, so read, is the sum of doxology, the meaning of the faith which theology formulates. The senses with which we are physically endowed and the powers of mind behind them make us 'lords of all created excellence'. Both senses and mind are purified by their proper employment under God. Their sphere is both science and art, the mastery and the mystery of things, the capacity to exploit and technologize and the quality to hallow and enjoy.

> The heavens were an oracle and spoke
> Divinity: the earth did undertake
> The office of a priest.[19]

but only because of human will to a 'noble subservience ' to God. Or, as Wordsworth had it:

> The human form
> To me became an index of delight,
> Of grace and honour, power and worthiness.[20]

The 'power' is what the sciences explore and harness, extending the bodily competences by the means that nature affords for their recruitment in the varied skills and processes of the sciences, both physical and applied. The 'worthiness', however, belongs *via* the body in the beauty and diversity of human experience, in the celebratory arts, and in the partnership of other experiencing selves within society, with its memory, its mutuality and its culture.

All these may be said to lie behind the Quranic theme of praise, its *al-hamdu li-Llāhi* to be sounded in response to our annunciation into life, initially and steadily. There may have been, in the story of Islamic philosophy, a proneness for the sort of 'occasionalism' which finds no intrinsic quality in things and events and phenomena but relates them all to an immediacy in God's action whereby leaves fall, snows melt, knives cut and shadows lengthen, by divine *fiat*, at once the cause and the effect. But this bypassing of natural order and organs and factors and forces, derivable as it may be from some exegesis of the Qur'ān, in no way denies us the reading which takes such order and its patterns as, in fact, the dependable fabric of a world discoverable and amenable to man.

In its different idiom, some biblical theology, not least in Germany, has depreciated the whole relevance of nature intrinsically, seeing it as somehow only the arena for 'redemption' – a redemption awaited as what alone creation significantly experiences of God. There may be biblical accents which arguably sustain this, partly because the Hebraic tradition has a strong bias against all things Canaanite and, therefore, against what might otherwise have been legitimate in fertility thankfulness and nature festivals. The poetry of the Psalms, as well as the imagery of Hosea, however, forbid us to think biblically of the universe as other than a celebration of divine majesty and power.

When they are wisely alert both Islamic and Christian theologies make for human doxology with the natural order as its ground and theme. All that has to be said about Quranic law and God as 'the Lord Chief Justice of the world', or about New Testament Incarnation hallowing 'the flesh' by its receiving of 'the Word', requires and presupposes the good earth, and time, and things, and history, as the context of these mercies and the awe, the *taqwā*, they kindle in us. However differently they proceed, they both mean that the human experience is everywhere sacramental. Such is the sense the Qur'ān conveys in almost every Surah, in its constant accent on the *āyāt*, the 'signs', discernible to the perceptive, if hidden from the casual, by which phenomena are understood. This Quranic emphasis effectively 'marries' the scientific and the 'spiritual', the mastery and the mystery of man in nature and nature with man. For the same signs which excite the skills and enable the technologies also excite the wonder and the gratitude which hallow occasions, inspire the arts and impel the soul to praise of God. The Qur'ān has a multiplex of 'signs', in earth and plough, fire and iron, cloud and rain, seed and harvest, sun and shade, sleep and wakefulness, shower and a greening land, palm and oasis, wind and sail. The familiarity of these is always strange, their recurrence endlessly surprising. The Adam in the husbandman, the artisan, the master, knows them all to derive from the *adama*, from the earth. His having their names is Quranically seen as the Lord's doing, the divine gift. Their naming under him is his authority over them. In pursuing their significance to him, for sustenance, for nurture and for culture, he finds his *khilāfah*, his 'dominion', and at once the temptation to self-sufficiency, to ingratitude, to divine 'exclusion' is with him, and with him as something to be deliberately overcome, refused by that exercise of will which is the theme of his creaturehood and the purpose of his annunciation.

It is this, in its positive claim, that underlies the heinousness of *shirk*, understood as worship withheld, diverted, repudiated. *Shirk* is the human denial of the divine relationship. It is the rejection of the sacramental quality of our human situation in the economy of the world and the exchanges of society as these obtain within our personhood. In its crudest form – with which parts of the Old Testament, and much of the Qur'ān, through circumstances of time and place, were most concerned – it means the misreading, the idolatrizing, of items of nature. These are then 'signs' to be noted, feared, propitiated, but not 'signs' pointing beyond themselves to give index of processes amenable to man and of mysteries within the single authority of God the ever merciful. When the signs are rightly read they spell the status of man, as executant and celebrant: they tell the nature of God as purposing man's creaturehood as an enterprise of response.

IV

These Christian/Muslim truths of God and man, of man in nature as custodian in sacraments of meaning waiting for his recognition and his will in soul and act, shared as they are, take us into a vexed area of contemporary theology concerning the sacred and the secular. The terms are much confused. If this sacramental, sign-quality of all our experience in the natural world under God is true – as for both our faiths it is – then clearly all things are the field of sacredness. There can be no secular in the sense of an area, or of entities, excluded from this human vocation to receive responsibly and to count a trust from God, or in which we do not repudiate *shirk*. It is in this sense that Muslims insist how, in Islam, there is no secular. It is an insistence with which the Christian agrees, a truth about the world as meant for God.

But, inasmuch as the vocation, thus accounted shared, is set, by God, within the will and option of mankind, the secular will happen where the sacramental meaning and the *āyāt* are ignored or belied. When it happens the world will remain meant for a hallowing which *we* will have disallowed. The Qur'ān is eloquent of this aspect of the human scene where 'most of them give no thanks' (Surahs 2.243; 10.60; 12.38; 27.73; 40.61), and where *kufr*, or rejection of God's rule, is frequently indicted. Those strictures in the Qur'ān refer to the pagans outside Islam. The question persists, however, whether they can be warranted within Muslim society.

There are those in contemporary Islam who believe so and state their indictment vigorously, even comparing the Muslims of whom they feel ashamed to the people of the pre-Islamic *Jāhiliyyah*.[21] The nostalgia for a lost 'golden age' which has never recurred in Muslim history since the first four Caliphs points to the same conclusion. Insofar as it is true a secularity obtains, not because things are ever outside God's rule but because they are only submissively within it by the human submission and this may be withheld.

The point at stake here may be focused if we return where we began to the divine imperative so central to the Qur³ān and to the sense of *Tauhīd*, or divine unity, which is best caught in the analogy: 'No king but Caesar'. The area of thought in that statement is 'political' and differs significantly in its 'feel' from a formula which says: 'There is no real but the Real'. The latter is philosophical and some Islamic metaphysics has understood the *Shahādah* that way. But the other form of analogy is more in line with the instinct of Islam because faith in *Tauhīd* demands the active dethroning of the false gods, the elimination of the false worships, what we called earlier the no-king-ing of all that is pseudo. The career and decisions of the Prophet, turning on the hinge of the *Hijrah*, plainly proceeded in 'political' terms in thought about the way God has his way, in the whole issue we are discussing as to man, in creation, under God.

It is hard to be sure which determined which, but clearly they inter-depend. The preached message and the religious summons of 'No god but God' was implemented or institutionalized in a form and a context which answered to the analogy: 'No king but Caesar'. The bringing of the human vocation to be under God was taken to be a political possibility, achieved in power. The Prophet became the ruler and *islām* as the human tributariness to God became Islam, the accomplished fact. Indeed, the verb *aslamnā* came to have a double meaning, in the sense of having two legitimate 'objects' to which it is 'transitive', namely surrender to God and submission to prophetic and caliphal rule. Surah 49.14 is a striking case in point.[22] There are those who consider that in the given circumstances of Quraishī Mecca and tribal Arabia, Muhammad had no other option.[23] All faiths have definitive origins and, in circumstances attending them, it is their own decisions which determine how their constraints are handled. This is true of Gethsemane also.

Has it not been Islam's instinct for the 'political' reading both of the analogy and the demand in 'no god but God' which explains its confidence that it has no need for the disturbing distinction between sacred and secular? If a 'regime', a *Sharī'ah*, an Islamic state, can institutionalize the Islam God wills, will not that be the 'fact' of the sacred and the 'non-fact' of the secular? So many would assume. Yet, what of *islām*, the inwardness of a divine submission? Will the external ever be the authentic? Can a divine sovereignty be politicized? Does not any modern state have to become, to a degree, 'secular', in the sense that it acknowledges credal diversity and allows the care for the sacred to be de-monopolized? Can divine law and one religion be identified? If it is recognized that the task of spirituality cannot be unilateral, will not the experience of the sincere Muslim, facing it by his lights, come to resemble that of his concerned Jewish and Christian neighbour? Further, if there is no unilateral monopoly in striving for a God-acknowledging world gratefully alert to his *āyāt*, will there be any unilateral escape from the pressures and temptations of secularization? There are those in contemporary Islam who call for a complete 'de-westernization' (their name for the secular) in all areas of education, so that an Islamic sociology, psychology, political science, as well as an Islamic physics, chemistry and technology, can emerge to preserve all Muslims, and the educated young especially, from secular contagion.[24] But is human experience geographically distinguishable in this way in modern terms? Are there any religious or cultural immunities to be had from current history?

This is not to say that irreligion is inevitable or that secularizing trends are irreversible. Indeed, as we must see in Chapter 4, vehement religious *re*-assertion is a characteristic of our time. But it is just this temper of credal, cultic and communal assertiveness in religion which is least able to register what the *āyāt* require of us or to read them aright. Moreover, there lies behind what our faiths see, and deplore, as secularization a claim to that human autonomy which, in proper discipline, is entirely within the dominion/*khilāfah* of man which we both confess to be divinely given. That sense of autonomy, of being given the reins, easily turns into the delusion that the reins have not been 'given' but simply taken. Technological man is tempted to feel that he is not 'referable' at all, unless it be to social or technical constraints, certainly not to any divine ones. Islam, as a faith in such emphatic referability of man in all things to God, a referability couched in strong imperative and absolutist proposition, is liable, more than any other faith, to collide head-on with the modern assumption of autonomy 'to the exclusion of God'. It will not help to a true spirituality to see it in defiance of techniques, or in reversal and arresting of history. It can only come in the consecration of all that cannot be disinvented but must be taken up into a comparably dynamic will to *taqwā* and an equally insistent recognition of *rahmah* in, not despite, all our occasions. When Surah 75.36 asks: 'Does man think that he is left on the loose?'[25] that is just what secular man, in his pretensions, thinks to be the case. Those who – to adopt the Qurʾān's phrase about *hizb-Allāh* – seek to be 'partisans for God' in today's world have a more taxing, more lively, more imaginative task than any previous generation, but only because mankind now is in the most ultimate (thus far) dimension of the ancient privilege to be and to achieve.

We have not understood the 'secular' if we think of it in a static way over against the 'sacred', nor appreciated the 'sacred' if we suppose it ensured by rule and decree in insulation from the 'secular'. All things are a potentiality for sacramental meaning, realizable within what, otherwise, is secular, denied in what, otherwise, were sacred. If we assume the 'sacred' too complacently or suppose it organized by establishment, we mistake its real task and its truly spiritual nature. We are then either sanguine about the secular or trivial about the sacred.[26]

V

What, then, of the all important rites and symbols which, in any faith, must focus sacramental meaning and, as it were, steadily enlist attention to the 'signs' the Creator has enshrined in the annunciation of existence in our creaturehood? In pagan, primal religions, phenomena themselves were taken as 'enchanted', the numerous points of deification plurally attributed. Theology in the monotheisms 'disenchants' nature in such terms, eliminates the deities in the confession of a single Lordship. But there must still be a point of transaction whereby *taqwā* and *rahmah* meet as the conscious and the real. In Islam this sacramental encounter of the soul of the faithful with the law of the All-merciful is in the pattern of *Salāt*, or ritual prayer, where the postures of the body, in line with the phrases of *Tasbīh*, or praise, both tell and take the meaning of *islām*, or surrender. The confession here of *Allāhu akbar* is fulfilled in the significance of rhythmic prostration and erectness, with the body as the agent in the celebration.

The human form may itself be taken as a reading of the human dignity. The erect posture takes in the horizons and commands the scene. Mobility is by two limbs, leaving two for the dexterity on which all skill and power to attain depend. The mind presides over this human 'engineering' through nerve, sense, faculty and will. So the mind, in the head, is brought in lowliness to the ground in the sequences of the *Salāt*, affirming the tributariness to God of all that man is and man attains. But this posture alternates with the return to erectness, just as the erectness acknowledges its privilege and mystery in the prostration.

VI

It will be wiser to study the Christian transaction with life's call to *Magnificat* in the context of Chapter 4. Occupied as we have been here with selfhood, with birth and the body, with the annunciation of existence, and with a sacramental theology of creation and humanity, we have said nothing of 'Holy is his Name'. Nor have we taken note of those other phrases of the Song of Mary, as a clue to our theologies, about the putting down of the mighty, the scattering of the proud, and the filling of the hungry. These have to do with what old writers called 'theodicy', with the action – and so the credibility – of God, the God of responsible creation, in the sequential world of history, the drama and tragedy of human time. These any authentic theology about divine *rahmah* must take up. Increasingly they compel us into eager and receptive cross-reference between us in our readings of God and man and things. *Magnificats*, as Mary's Song so plainly realized, must hold conviction in the real world, where, by creation and by procreation and, as faith sees it, by annunciation, we find ourselves.

This logic, from creation to theodicy, takes us into 'revelation', and what may be expected of it. Will its aim – shall we say its duty – be primarily to legislate and enjoin, to issue imperatives, to summon us to destiny? Or, as coming from the God we discern in our sacramental experience, is there more that 'revelation' might do, in fuller interpretation of our creaturehood and in divine concern about the crisis it entails within us and about us? These questions would seem to require some study of 'the capacities of revelation'.

NOTES

1 Robert Browning, *Poetical Works* (Oxford edn 1940), p. 410, stanza ii, 'Christmas Eve and Easter Day'.

2 See author's Note in Muhammad Kamil Husain, *City of Wrong* (Amsterdam 1959), pp. 223–5, for a suggestion about exodus, the cross and the Battle of Badr, as the decisive constraining factors in the self-awareness of the three faiths, Judaic, Christian and Muslim, respectively.

3 cf. M. M. Bravmann, *The Spiritual Background of Early Islam: Studies in Ancient Arab Concepts*, Leiden 1972. On his view of the evidence, divine prerogative resembles rulership patterns in tribal society. Injustice is within the power of him who has 'subjects': there is no subjects' complaint: favour has nothing to do with deserts.

4 The *Hanīfs* (*hunafā'*) were monotheists, heirs of an Abrahamic tradition, it would seem, whose stance would seem to have influenced Muhammad, though there remains much that is uncertain in detail concerning them.

5 *The Kingly Crown*, tr. by Bernard Lewis (London 1961), pp. 28–9. Ibn Gabirol (Avicebron) (1020–70) was a Spanish Jew who wrote in Arabic. He saw the unity of God as essentially inexpressible but saw, also, that God could, and must, 'be unified ... by those who declare His unity'. He also had a lively sense of an 'annunciation', writing 'Before I was Thou didst greet me with Thy mercy and breathe spirit into me ...', p. 55.

6 *Karl Marx, Early Writings*, ed. T. B. Bottomore (New York 1963), p. 251.

7 The phrase *min dūni-Llāhi*, lit. 'in without-ness of God', better: 'to the exclusion of God' is a state reiterated in the Qur'ān of any and all whose attitudes of trust, belief, habit or concern take no account of divine law or mercy or proceed in repudiation of them.

8 See Surah 2.30–7 where Satan defies God's appointment of man (Adam) as viceroy in the earth, refuses to prostrate to the creature and becomes the 'accuser' whose aim, in flouting God's will, is to confound Adam, bring him to evil and so discredit the divine design. It is for this reason that we must 'give the lie to the liar' and so vindicate God's wisdom in our creaturehood.

9 John Milton, *Samson Agonistes*, lines 460–8 and 473–8.

10 In Muhammad Iqbal, *Asrār-i-Khūdī* (Secrets of the Self), tr. R. A. Nicholson (London rev. edn 1940), pp. 44f. Iqbal does not see God as an absolute in whom all other selves are lost but in whom other selves have meaning. True Islam is to be obeying God so completely that one's will mirrors the divine will. See *Secrets*, introd. p. xvii, and Iqbal's *The Reconstruction of Religious Thought in Islam* (Lahore 1930), p. 71. He has to be read with care because of his elusive style and his poetic freedom.

11 *Asrār-i-Khūdī*, p. 89.

12 Ishmael has been studied and interpreted by several Christian Islamicists concerned for biblical criteria, as a symbol of 'Abrahamic' community between the two faiths and a possible ground for covenantal 'fulfilment' in the history of Islam. Others prefer to ground the whole inter Christian-

Muslim relationship on the surer basis of doctrinal affinity and spiritual meanings, rather than on the unsure significance of Old Testament personalities and traditions.

13 Fazlur Rahman, *Major Themes of the Qurʾān* (Minneapolis 1980), p. 28.

14 The Greek word occurs in 2 Tim. 1.7. The classical Greek meaning takes us to thought-habits which do not, by their immoderation, presumption or disproportion, jeopardize the self. 'The quality of a mind whose thoughts are safe' might be a rendering. Man can be his own worst enemy by pretension, 'over-arching ambition which falls on the other side' in ruin. *Sōphrosunē*, one might say, is protective discipline.

15 Fazlur Rahman, op. cit., p. 29.

16 Surah 78.37 – a verse which is an interesting example of how translation can vary oddly. Pickthall has: 'the Beneficent with whom none may converse', and Arberry: 'the All-merciful of whom they have no power to speak'. *La yamlikūna minhu khiṭāban* carries a denial of the right or power to assume any 'pleading' handle on God. 'Harangue' suggests this brashness. It would make folly of all prayer to translate it as if God could never be addressed. The meaning is not far from the poet Raleigh's lines about 'heaven's bribeless hall' – 'no shuffling (of the cards) there'.

17 Surahs 22.5 and 23.12–14, and also, more briefly, 16.4; 18.37; 36.77; 53.46; and 76.2, where the *nutfah*, or seminal emission, is joined directly with God's creating. Note also 80.17–19: 'Tragic humanity! how thanklessly unbelieving! From what did the Creator fashion him? From a drop of sperm he created him and set the measure of his being.'

18 Thomas Traherne, *Centuries, Poems and Thanksgivings*, 2 vols., ed. H. M. Margoliouth (Oxford 1958), 'The Preparative', vol. 2, p. 22, stanza 4.

19 ibid., vol. 2, p. 6, st. 7, 'The Salutation'.

20 William Wordsworth, *The Prelude*, Book 8, lines 279–81.

21 The opprobrium in the term *Jāhiliyyah* makes its application to contemporary Muslims the more remarkable. It equates them with the uncouth and perverse Quraish resisting the Prophet himself. See, for example: Muhammad Qutb: *Jāhiliyyah al-Qarn al-ʿAshrīn* (The Jāhiliyyah of the 20th Century), Cairo.

22 The passage in which certain bedouin came to Muhammad and said they had 'believed' (*amannā*). He halted them and told them that 'faith had not entered (their) hearts'. They were to say, rather: 'we have submitted (*aslamnā*).' The distinction between a political surrender and an authentic faith could not be clearer. *Aslamnā* is the 1st pers. pl. past tense of the verbal form which yields the verbal noun *islām*, i.e. 'we have become Muslims', whether by accession only or by faith also.

23 See Kenneth Cragg: *Muhammad and the Christian* (London 1984), Chap. 3. cf. also the contrasted thesis among Muslims about Jesus, namely that he was non-political merely for lack of occasion in the Roman Empire. See, e.g. Ziya Gokalp, *Turkish Nationalism and Western Civilization*, tr. N.

Berkes (London 1959): 'The first reason for the existence of a fundamental opposition between Christianity and Islam should be sought in the social conditions at the time of their rise. Christianity originated within a community that was under the domination of a powerful state and that had no hopes of political independence. Islam, on the other hand, flourished among a people free from external domination who had the capacity to establish an independent state' (p. 214). cf. also Muhsin Mahdi, however, in J. Kitagawa, *Modern Trends in World Religions* (La Salle 1959), pp. 1–27 who notes that the ideal form of a politicized Islam was that of the city state in Medina and that frequently in Islamic caliphal history the champions of Islamic law and theology were often at odds – to their personal cost – with political rulers whose power exercise was seen as inimical, or disloyal, to a true Islam.

24 See, e.g., Syed Muhammad al-Naquib al-ʿAtta, *Islam and Secularism* (Kuala Lumpur 1978), who calls for a total 'de-Westernization' of knowledge.

25 Surah 75.36 variously translated. Some take it that there is an analogy between wandering, untethered camels and mankind, or that man should not imagine himself other than mortal, or that his life is a vain thing. 'Left at random, or on the loose' would seem to take the force of the question. 'If we can we may' is often the assumption in scientific efficiency. It is this pretentious autonomy the Qurʾān is ironically calling in question. See also Chap. 1, note 19.

26 cf. the comment of Walter Hobhouse, *The Church and the World in Idea and History* (London 1910), p. 209: 'The system of the Medieval Papacy tended to secularise the church more than it spiritualised the world.'

3

Capacities in Revelation

I

The spiritual communion between God and Muhammad wrought a unity of purpose. Muhammad's will and purpose were completely subordinated to those of God and were, so to speak, fused with them. This spiritual fusion is metaphorically expressed in the Qur'ān as 'one cord serving two bows and even closer'.

Citing in unusual terms the classic passage in the Qur'ān about the Prophet's revelatory experience,[1] Muhammad Zafrullah Khan continues:

> The Prophet explained this experience very simply. He has said that if a servant of God submits himself wholly to the will of God and commits the whole direction of his life to it, he gradually achieves a condition in which God becomes the eyes with which he sees, the ears with which he hears, the hands with which he labours and the feet with which he walks. This comes as close to expressing the mystic spiritual reality as it is possible to do within the limits of human speech.[2]

Such is one view, a very idiosyncratic one, of the phenomenon of revelation in the Qur'ān. There are very different readings, metaphorical or otherwise, of Surah 53. But this one serves well to introduce the crucial issues that relate to the nature of revelation, and its expression in scriptures, *via* the interaction of divine initiative and human receptivity. They are issues which arise directly from all the previous chapter has examined in theology.

'Capacity' is a wise choice of word. But we must have it in the plural, and with its twin meanings. 'I am here', a man may say, 'in my capacity as . . .'; be he ambassador, salesman, canvasser or constable. The word signifies that *as which* he comes or acts. It also covers what such coming or action is competent to do. *Capax imperii*, for Tacitus, meant 'being equal to the task of empire'. People of capacity have, we might say colloquially, 'what it (i.e. the situation) takes'. *Capax* to Romans meant spacious and roomy. 'Capacity,' then, is both function and ability; it brings competence to an office and an office to competence.

What should we understand of the human capacity in revelation, in both senses of the word? The question has the advantage of avoiding, in the first instance, the familiar puzzles and prejudices of words like 'messenger', 'seer', 'apostle', 'son', or 'Son'. It invites us to face squarely what it takes to be revelatorily 'on behalf of God', and what 'having it' might mean. Answers will have to explore the manner of inspiration, the measure of relevance, the status of the role and the role of the status, and how – in the divine ordering and the human participating – the 'capacities' entailed in revelation are rightly received in the event and acknowledged in the sequel.

Everything that has to do with God in Islam is finally within the context of the prophethood of Muhammad. The two parts of the *Shahādah*, or confession of faith are not, credally, separable. 'There is no god but God: Muhammad is the *Rasūl* of God.' 'Obey God and obey the *Rasūl*' is the steady injunction of the Qur'ān.[3] Muhammad as the vehicle of the ultimate revelation marks the climax of God's directives to humanity through a long series of prophetic agency beginning with Adam. The crown and touchstone of them all is the final Qur'ān. That God is man-directing and world-ordaining is central to the whole nature of Islam which, as a term, is defined as a duly obedient human response to God's directing and ordaining. The conception and reception of revelation are, therefore, the decisive theme in theology. The whole 'feel' of faith about God is determined by the nature of the agency through which it is construed and educated, namely the apostolate of Muhammad.

Such interaction between what is believed of God and what is received through the Prophet is fundamental even when, as in Islam, it is strenuously non-incarnational.[4] Though revelation is everywhere in the Semitic faiths a *theological* event, a theological mystery, each of them has a distinctive interpretation of the form of the divine-human enterprise which, on any and every showing, revelation entails. The Quranic form, in the person and prophethood of Muhammad, differs from the Hebraic in being unilateral, not multiple, in its

incidence, and in being essentially verbal as a celestial communication – in Quranic terminology – by a 'downward' bestowal. Albeit situational – as revelation can never fail to be
– it is not participatory, as Job and the Psalms, or Amos and
Jeremiah.

Still less does it admit to be comprehended within New
Testament criteria as to how the divine and the human belong
within the event of revelation. The Qurʾān requires us to
understand its status as 'the Word of God' as meaning 'the
Word *from* God', of which we may in no way say, in the careful
Greek of John 1.1: 'and God was the Word'.[5] It is these disparities which we have to explore in this chapter and we must
do so not only as studies about revelation but – as they most
surely are – indices to theology. They belong diversely with
the theme of the divine greatness we have just shared. How
God may be understood to have revealed, in what measure,
to what intent, by what means, through what order of sending
or of giving, must surely define for us how God may be understood.

II

The familiar and, perhaps in some users, trite, distinction
between revelation of the divine will and revelation of the
divine nature – which, in sounder language must concern us
later – should not deter us from realizing the unifying factor
between Jew, Christian and Muslim in the conviction that we
stand under divine revelation. What urgently differs belongs
with what unites. Our common theology of creation commits
us to shared belief in the relevance of God to the world and
the relevance of the world to God. While the first relevance
may be so awesome as to make 'relevance' almost an irreverent
word, the second relevance is no less real. Somehow, *Allāhu
akbar* needs to be said and only humanity can say it with intelligent intent.[6] There would be no point in prophets if men were
automata, nor in messengers from him if God were tyrannical.
Divine authority, as we have seen in Chapter 2, is reciprocal
to human vocation. It is creaturehood which is the constituency
of prophethood and both are the sphere of divine purposes
entrusted to mankind. There is a sense, common to the Scriptures, biblical and Quranic, in which creation has engaged the

will of the Creator with the will of the creature. So much revelation, *per se* signifies, however diversely we receive its contents and recognize its forms. The capacity for revelation through prophets as instruments relates to the capacity for revelation in people as listeners. Both capacities, as vocation and obligation, belong within the created order understood as the realm of divine–human relationship, whether of will only or also of communion and fellowship. Creation and revelation alike bespeak a responsible transcendence and assume, because they address, a responsive humanity.

Taking this common point in the Muslim/Christian situation, in all its implications, it will be wise to proceed by considering the related themes of language, personality and final significance within the incidence of revelation. The first has to do with the ability of speech and Scripture, in the temporal, plural world, to convey and house eternal truth. The second concerns the role of prophet or messenger in the experience of words on God's behalf, the nature of what Islam calls *wahy*, and Christian thought 'inspiration', in the mediation of meaning from God to man. The third has to do with the manner in which the credentials of such personal, scripture-shaping capacity on behalf of God are finally tested, received and institutionalized in obedience. Such 'finalizing' into a received faith in, or about, such personality must hinge, in large measure, on the sequel to his impact, on the way in which the burden of the word becomes the issue of its pain and 'victory'. This, which the Qur'ān calls 'vindication', must mean that the divine is significantly staked in the prophetic, in that a will which is divine has spoken in search of submission. It, therefore, further means that how the prophet, for God, experiences his world and responds to what his role entails on him there, must be an index, arguably deeper than words themselves, to a knowledge of the Lord who sent him. It is here that Christian faith reads the cross as supremely revelatory and, for the same reason, finds the prophetic essentially deepening into the incarnational because the verbal has become the situational, or 'the Word the flesh'.

III

The Qur'ān firmly understands itself in strictly verbal terms and excludes any incarnational dimension as either proper or necessary to prophetic revelation. As Scripture it has been understood by Islam as the final revelation, given in a form that is clear and mandatory and, to that end, explicit, and entrusted to one language, a language to which it is necessarily bound by virtue of an inalienable unity of form and meaning. By these qualities it can be seen as 'fool-proof'. If slips of the tongue, on the part of the Prophet can be, and are, blessedly prevented, and scrupulously excluded by the piety of the reciter – as slips of the pen are by the care of the calligrapher – then the revelatory truth is secure and present to tongue and pen and mind.

This character of revelation requires rejection of the pre-supposition on which the New Testament and, in part, the Bible generally, proceed. There revelation is directional, to be sure, but leaves an active, sentient place in its incidence and reception. This it finds the more congruent with its summons to a free, voluntary, creaturely response. Clearly this response is not decreed and *ipso facto* ensured. If that were the case no prophethood would be necessary. Is it not arguable, then, that the manner, as well as the goal, of revelation should leave room for the responsive liabilities of the human factor and invite in its incidence as well as in its substance the active participation of mind and personality? Doing so, would not revelation be more consonant in its method with its intention, as something divinely proposed but humanly transacted? Can what is purely arbitrary either suit Godward or avail manward?

It is necessary, then, to ask whether the Qurʾān is either rightly received or truly conceived in the manner of arbitrary dictation from above which traditional Muslim theology has understood? A universal revelation, using *a* language in this way unilaterally, would need to employ a universal one. No such universal language exists. Any revelatory language must surely be susceptible of translation within a multilingual humanity. It needs to be viable and capable of obedience within all the exigencies of human grammars and cultures, in potential correlation to all the vagaries of society and history.

These, furthermore, include the time factor of incidence. Even if not situational in the sense of incarnational, all revelation is bound to have a particularity of place and point in time at which, somehow, all points and places are to find illumination.

The translation will always have to be from its 'there-and-then' to some other 'here-and-now' and this translation of time-context will add to the complexities of the purely literary one. For even the most strictly 'literal' language must proceed by metaphor and allusion and these are in the flux of the changing world. Some Islamic exegesis today is alive to these aspects of its task.[7] But it remains difficult of solution within the traditional prescripts about the nature of the Quranic text as 'an Arabic Scripture', in the literal sense revelation's final 'document'. The question persists whether receiving any Scripture as an authoritative book in a static way can ride with any lively understanding of the vitality of meaning within language.

Here, of course, belong all the current attitudes about language and 'fact', about verification and 'statement', tending to easy scepticism about any religious 'truth' – attitudes arising from the popular prestige of science and its exclusive claim to significant 'factuality'. We need not stay over these as they presuppose a positivism, denying meaning to metaphysics, poetry and theology alike, such as no intelligent Muslim or Christian could accept. But given our common faith in the feasibility of theological statement which is inseparable from our conviction about divine revelation, there remain, in loyalty to that very conviction, lively questions about what the 'meanings' really are. How should metaphors be understood? How is the reader to 'take' the ambiguity which language often implies and often at the most crucial points? Even plays on words are not unknown in the Qurʾān[8] and the intention of critical phrases may be at issue.[9]

The problem is familiar wherever there are Scriptures. The Jewish sage, Abraham Ibn Ezra (1089–1164) said: 'Our learned ones have said that no biblical verse ever departs from its literal meaning', adding: 'It is, therefore, proper to pray only in a literalist manner and not in a manner containing mystery or parable.'[10] But Rabbi Eliezer said: 'Everyone who interprets or translates literally a word from the Bible is a liar. Everyone who adds something to it, however, is a blasphemer.'[11] The margins of the Qurʾān herein resemble those of the Talmud. When Jalāl al-Dīn al-Suyūtī (1445–1505) wrote his famous compendium on Quranic exegesis he aptly entitled it: *Al-Itqān*, 'The Mastery'. But is it ever achieved?

The issues are peculiarly acute where, as in the Qurʾān, revelation to a prophet is understood as an auditory experience, that is, a revelation which is itself *in* language. In what is linguistically received, the text *is* the revelation. On a different view, revelation might be, not a content but a presence, or what Martin Buber called 'the unformed, undifferentiated, pre-linguistic "word" of immediate experience'.[12] Writing is, then, the subsequent reflective responsive task of the prophet himself or, more likely, of the disciple who is such as his 'hearer'. While, it would seem, the Qurʾān was written by disciples, not by Muhammad himself,[13] such writing was, so to speak, at the Prophet's 'dictation' of what he had himself 'heard' in celestial 'dictation' from above. In that Quranic situation the writing 'terms' are not derivative but definitive: the revelation and the terms are one. Where, as in Buber's argument, the expression in language is secondary to the immediacy of the presence, the role of language – and so of exegesis – is less critical, since the reader learns to go behind the words to the experience which was, essentially, the meaning in a way that they were not.

It might, no doubt, be possible to comprehend the Qurʾān also in something like the Buber sense, as, indeed, in the example with which this chapter opened. To do so, even in less explicit form than that of Muhammad Zafrullah Khan, could fit certain aspects of Muhammad's experience to which we must come below. It might also relieve some of the problems of language involved in the traditional view by which words and revelation are one. But it would open out in a bewildering way the esotericism which turns the verbal into the enigmatic and language into a cypher for all but the initiated.

For orthodox Islam the whole issue of revelation as Scripture, of Scripture as revelation, is gathered up into the theme of *tanzīl*, where – as with so many issues in theology, whether Islamic or other – it is contained rather than resolved. The Qurʾān, as *Umm al-Kitāb*, is immutably in heaven. When mediated *via* Muhammad into human awareness, speech and language, it is heard, received, recited and set down, as 'an Arabic Qurʾān'.[14] The vocabulary, the grammar, the meanings were those necessarily familiar, albeit inimitable, to the immediate context of the Meccans. When the Quraish heard the words *Allāh*, *akbar*, *khāliq*, or imperatives like *utīrū*, *ʿūdhū*, *ittaqū*,[15] they were already familiar to them, however amply the connotation was being enlarged. That heaven should use the Arabs' language was implicit in the very notion of intelligible *tanzīl*. Only in their own diction could they be informed. We have to say, within the meaning of *tanzīl*, that mediation itself through Muhammad's recipience and utterance bridged the eternal into the temporal so that, when revelation happened, existing language intelligibility proved to have been its vehicle. In the immediate context the problem of how a single language could convey 'a mercy to the worlds' (Surah-21.107) did not arise. The role and capacity of Arabic are simply taken as a fact of the revelatory situation and providential decree. Such faith does not absolve believers of the exegetical tasks that attend it, but it does exempt them from pursuing further the question how it could be so. The Qurʾān reciter has implicit confidence in the capacity of language, that is, Arabic language, for the role he believes it to fulfil in the economy of God and the prophethood of Muhammad.[16]

It is time to turn from the linguistic to the personal in the phenomenon of the Qurʾān, from questions latent in the words to themes about the messenger.

IV

It might be said that the divine economy which capacitates languages to be declarative of the divine will likewise capacitates the Prophet to be the sole and personal recipient of its Quranic form. Is there, then, no study or inquiry that need engage us? Very many Muslims would believe so. But, for any cross-reference between Quranic and Christian faiths, personality in revelation must emphatically be seen and explored as a theme central to theology. It is a clear upshot of all that has been already said about the capacity of language. Given a keen perception it can vitally educate our respective theologies.

Muslims in general have long held that Muhammad's role in the Qurʾān was essentially passive. His personality was purely a receptacle for a serial, auditory communication of a celestial Book, his receiving of which did not entail any conscious composition nor any deliberating mind or soul. *Wahy* – the technical term for such revelation-inspiration (in one) –

did not recruit his mental powers nor turn upon his personal will.

This Muslim conviction as to Prophet and Book is, of course, in the interest of religious certitude. On this view, the less the revelatory action is thought to be man's the more surely it can be held to be God's. The more humanly unaccountable, the more securely from God. Where the human factor is no more than a relay-er of divine messages the more dependably the divine will is heard. The Qur'ān has its authority, one might almost say, for Muslims at large as a cumulative 'communiqué' from God to mankind, delivered by Muhammad. 'Cumulative', as we must see, is an important word. The sequence occupied some twenty-three years of Muhammad's *Sīrah*, or life-story, and the revelation never came through any other.

This, faith's, esteem of the Qur'ān, dominant in Islam for fourteen centuries is, of course, sustained by the traditional belief in his complete illiteracy and, paradoxically, the Book's inimitable eloquence as Arabic. On both counts the Qur'ān demonstrates literary 'miracle', or *i'jāz*, the capacity, that is, to defy all imitation. This matchlessness was both the proof and the proven. Faith in it constituted a linguistic quality the guarantor of divine origin. The guarantee was held to be reinforced by the total *in*capacity of Muhammad, in and of himself as *ummī* (Surah 7.157–8). By that 'illiteracy' his very capacity for *wahy* lay in the absence of any ability of word or speech.

It is here that a reverent, mediating theology needs to pause and consider, beginning with the vital single passage just cited about Muhammad's being *al-rasūl al-nabī al-ummī*, 'the unlettered apostle-prophet'. Does it really mean that Muhammad was (if the phrase may be permitted) literally illiterate? His expertise in commerce and the management of caravans would certainly argue to the contrary. It is true that the Qur'ān refers to his not having hand-written the Book (Surah 29.48). But this may well mean, not that he could not write, but that he used scribes. In any event, it is not so much hand-writing that is at issue, but composing. And composing is an ambiguous word. On any count a true sense of *wahy* must certainly exclude the kind of conscious, self-reliant, deliberate authorship by which writers express themselves and produce their works. But need a genuine recognition of the revelatory origin of the Qur'ān necessarily exclude a participatory personality, subject

indeed to 'revelation' but with an active mental part in its coming into 'Scripture'? Need such a dimension in any way detract,
by its presence, from the reality of *waḥy* or the status and 'security' of the text?

In any event, it is probable that *al-ummī*, descriptive of
Muhammad, does not mean any actual illiteracy but rather
refers to membership in a people as yet without Scriptures.[17]
It is clear that Jews and Christians were 'people of the Book'
and that this quality, together with the phenomenon of past
prophethood as its condition and ground, was a crucial image
in the background of Muhammad's experience. By contrast,
Arabs were *not*, as yet, 'people of a Book': they were *ummiyyūn*,
'unlettered' in the sense of 'unscriptured'. Would not an Arabic
revelation and, as a means to it, an Arab prophethood, be
necessary to their rescue from that deprivation? This reading
of the Arab *ummiyyūn* and the *ummī* messenger of their own
kin and kind (an important feature of Muhammad's appeal)
accords well with the clear emphasis in the Qurʾān on its being
an Arabic book.[18]

If this reading is accepted it in no way detracts from the
Qurʾān's quality as given, not composed, but it does return
us squarely to study of Muhammad's role and here, in a strange
way, the Qurʾān can be our surest ally. For the traditional view
about pure passivity conflicts with so many of the Book's own
emphases and implications. There is no doubt that it was intelligible in its incidence on human audience. Should it not be
understood, then, as intelligible within the mind of the prophet-
auditor? If it were so, must not his faculties have been engaged,
indeed heightened and tensed, given the critical context into
which it had to be spoken? When Muhammad preached he
was not utilizing words not antecedently employed, nor confronting a setting not consciously experienced. Could those
facts allow of total passivity in the transactions of inspiration
by which he became aware, from beyond, of what the divine
address to the setting would be?

It was in relation to the setting and the situations that the
Qurʾān accumulated. It could not be sent down all at once.
It was necessarily 'at intervals' (17.106). It needed to engage
with reactions to its own impact as gathering controversy
shaped the Prophet's encounter with idolatry and its vested
interests in prestige and the economy. Such controversy is built
into the very texture of the text, with exchanges like: 'They

say . . .', 'Say thou . . .', prescribed, indeed, in *wahy*, yet also required by the actualities of its enterprise in the mundane world. Do we not, therefore, have to concede some conscious, spiritual participation by Muhammad in the reality of its incidence in the soul, given his evident participation in its incidence in the society? Will not this whole situation require faith to look again at the notion of passivity and the thesis that God's activity proceeds only by the human abeyance?

V

There is evidence not only from the Quranic situation itself but also from Muslim scholarship in the Scripture that the Book of Islam *is* thought of in other terms than those of traditional belief. Such evidence is of vital importance for any Christian mediation of New Testament norms about the person of Jesus and the genesis of Scripture. Implications of a conscious dimension in the view about Muhammad and his role – without in any way impugning *wahy* – are frequent in several quarters. Some arise from the time and translation factor already noted. For legists this is perhaps more obvious than for theologians. Thus, for example, the revered Shāh Wāliullāh, the eighteenth-century mentor of Indian Muslims, writes in general about prophethood that when a *sharīʿah*, or sacred law, is revealed it takes special note of the culture to which that prophet is sent and the prophet applies its universal principles, having in mind that culture. Whether he does so within, or outside, the Scripture text, it is clear that he is actively involved in its incidence and, even more, its concrete meaning. This makes, of course, for flexibility in the application of what is revealed but it also bears upon its very content, as discerned within the prophetic consciousness.[19]

Similarly, we find in the artistic or literary appraisal of the very *iʿjāz*, or incomparable eloquence of the Qurʾān as Arabic, a tendency on the part of those familiar with literature and its criticism to advert to Muhammad's genius or skill. This may be only half-consciously at odds with the traditional view of inspiration, but at least it betrays a strong temptation to think of Muhammad creatively within the Qurʾān. Thus, for example, the twentieth-century leader and martyr of the Muslim Brotherhood, Sayyid Quṭb, expresses his thrill as a literary critic, with the Arabic of the Scripture.[20] Or, conversely, we have sociologists or jurists attributing to Muhammad's acumen or discerning leadership patterns of law and behaviour, like the fast of *Ramadān* or the paying of *Zakāt*, which more properly belong solely with the *fiat*, or injunction, of revelation.[21]

Furthermore, when we come to the philosophers in the centuries after its origins when Islam took stock of the Greek philosophic tradition, the phenomenon of prophethood, and Muhammad's most of all, is freely associated with the universal wisdom. Far from being a mere recipient of an arbitrary *wahy* which neither requires nor seeks his consent and mind, he becomes almost like a divine deputy, the philosopher-king, the intellectual repository of the divine wisdom. For Ibn Sīnā, the prodigious eleventh-century polymath, Muhammad in his Quranic role emerges not simply as the lawgiver, philosopher-king in the Greek vein, but also as receiving the Scripture from celestial intelligences through the mediating active intellect. The sanctions of the Scripture in moral life are rationally related to the needs and situations of the society it addresses and concerns. The active intellect by which they are prophetically received is the intuitive endowment or imagination possessed by the prophet.[22]

These innovative ideas which became widely disseminated in philosophic circles were in no way conceded by the strict theologians. In his *Al-Irshād*, the redoubtable 'Imām of the Twin Shrines', Al-Juwaynī (died 1085), a Persian divine and heir of Al-Ash'arī (873–935), resisted them fiercely. His view was that there was no explaining *wahy*: from start to finish it was God's act. To be God's messenger is simply to reiterate God's sayings, to bear *al-balāgh*, the communication, in the plainest sense, to the auditors. Revelatory acts of God have no necessary relation to the knowledge any prophet possesses, nor to his sense of being one. No natural causes are to be identified in the phenomenon of *wahy* and nothing intrinsic to the human bearer. To Al-Juwaynī any 'Platonizing' of Muhammad or the Qur'ān was wholly reprehensible.[23]

Nevertheless, the instinct to doubt the minimal and in some form stress the maximal role for Muhammad in the experience of the Qur'ān has persisted and grown. It is at its most insistent among the mystics who, more than the lawyers, the littérateurs, or the philosophers and social thinkers, see Muhammad as living and speaking within a divine intimacy where mind and will are at once human and divine. Sufism in its mystical esteem of the Prophet, its cherishing of the light of Muhammad, its techniques of absorption, proceeds upon a near identity of God and his Word and engages with the Qur'ān in its own esoteric vein where surface meanings and, with them, a merely functional concept of Muhammad, are far transcended. There is no space to do them justice here.[24]

VI

But why, we must ask, does it matter what should be thought of the status and role of the Prophet in the Qur'ān? What is there that turns on the issue? Implications for the liveliness and responsibility of commentary are only part of the answer, important as they are. Exegesis, to be sure, will be more relevant and alert if it is free to argue from then to now and to 'read' Scripture as the sphere of intelligent, rather than merely static, obedience. But there is more. A dynamic sense of the Qur'ān *in situ* can help to move submission to its meanings away from simple legal conformity to a blue-print towards engagement with a total relevance. Indeed, the measure of relevance will be larger if we appreciate that we are not simply coming to a document which directs and legislates but to a dramatic focus of religious existence to which we must respond.

In this sense to study Muhammad, as it were, existentially, to reckon with his role in the Qur'ān intensively, is to realize a situation which can bring us, and perhaps Muslims with us, closer to what is the vital clue within the New Testament. The clue is the fact that the more existential, as distinct from mere message-bearing, we see prophethood to be, the more we discover that it takes on, and takes over, personality. It becomes biographical. This may still be far from what the New Testament, in gathered consensus, understands about Jesus, but it is surely an index to it. To develop this point will lead our argument about capacity in relevation into its final phase.

We begin throughout with the verbal. 'Jesus', too, says the Gospel, 'came preaching'. He, too, was 'a prophet, mighty . . . in word', 'the prophet of Nazareth in Galilee'. Certainly it is with speech for God that the Qur'ān begins – and, as many would say, ends. 'God and his Messenger', is how the *Shahādah* has it. But all such speaking on God's behalf merges, inevitably, into biography of the speaker. The word, however severely oral and verbal, distinct as message, from messenger, takes on a destiny mingling to a degree with that of the bearer. If there is hostility to it – as there normally is in this human world – that cannot be separated from hostility to him. Rejection of the one is *ipso facto* rejection of the other. The encounter of the embassy with the setting becomes an encounter with the ambassador. The Qur'ān, as we have seen, bears clear indication of this fact with its patterns of controversy and its 'occasions of revelation'. But, outside tradition, which in turn is outside the Qur'ān, Islam has not, with the exceptions we have noted, vested the revelation in the experience around the word but only in the word itself. The Prophet remains always the messenger.

With Jesus according to the New Testament it is emphatically otherwise. The preaching and the person are seen and heard as truly inseparable. But before we explore this as a vital point of cross-reference, it is wise to pursue further, within Quranic limits, the potential towards a New Testament situation. In the latter it is precisely the prophetic vocation of Jesus which engages his filial consciousness. The motive which sustains him in the gathering encounter with the setting and its hostility is the vocation which both expresses and requires what he calls his 'sonship' to 'the Father'. In the case of Muhammad there is no doubt that the struggle with Quraishī obduracy, which tests his mettle as prophet, also sifts his personality, demanding the persistence, the tenacity, the *sabr*, which he brings. These, in turn, necessarily become significant as part of the overall message. They are no more detachable from his impact on society around him, than they are separable from his identity as, by these proofs, veritably prophet. To that degree the message becomes the messenger. Its reception is the measure of his: his response to that reception not only serves it by endurance but to a degree assumes its character. Were he to default it would be disowned. Because he persists, it holds the field.

What marries message and messenger in these external ways, by circumstance of their twin story, also translates into inward experience. The sense of identity which the original and continuing commission bestows deepens in the going. What the Qur'ān calls the 'burden weighing down his back', the burden of the message, is also that which 'exalts his fame' (Surah 94.2–4). That 'fame' (lit. 'mention' or 'renown', *dhikr*), is an interior consciousness as well as an exterior repute. He may still be only a bearer but there is a significance in his bearing (in both senses of the word). It cannot be otherwise, in a context so fraught with tension and crisis. However emphatically it has to be said that Muhammad is 'only a *rasūl*', that message-carrying capacity is only fulfilled as it is enlarged into a personal significance.

The interior side of this experience is sweetly expressed, in a different idiom, in the words of Wisdom 7.27, where 'wisdom', as the active power of God, is described as 'entering into holy souls, making them friends of God and prophets'. Perhaps we are reversing the order which the writer in The Wisdom of Solomon preferred. It is the 'making', no mere 'sending', with which we are concerned – something which the prophets *are*, deeper than, prior to, what they *say*. What they are, they are by an intimacy with the counsel, if not with the society, of God, whereby they are 'friends'.

What such relationship, in fact and not merely by function, with God signifies can be most radically illustrated by reference to the biblical prophet, Jeremiah, with whom prophecy becomes deeply autobiographical. Jeremiah's prophetic vocation, more than usually tragic, provokes in him those so-called Confessions, in which he bitterly expostulates with God about his experience in an unrelenting mission amid an unrepentant people (Jer. 8.18—9.3; 12.1–5; 15.10–18; 20.7–9; 20.14–18). Why should these have been retained in the text and not expunged by a redactor, unless they had sharp relevance, despite (rather, in fact because of) their puzzling and daunting character? It is possible to see in them the very germs of the new covenant. For Jeremiah's only solace is to be assured that his fidelity, however solitary and lonely, is of abiding value to God though a whole nation be apostate. But however we read the Confessions, there is no doubt that here experience within prophethood has become more ultimately significant than the message verbally delivered. The verbal has become the personal. The prophethood has become the personality, in the sense that the final significance is carried by a figure in a setting, not essentially by a verbalism in a mouthpiece.

Though Jeremiah is undoubtedly the most signal example of this truth, it is evident elsewhere in the biblical tradition.

Hosea draws his prophetic vocation and much of his imagery from his own domestic sorrows and betrayal. Amos, challenging Samaria, the Northern kingdom in the eighth century BC in its luxury and oppression, is as much a prophet by his gaunt appearance, out of his Tekoan distance and into the gilded courts of power, as he is in the verbal message he brings. In many other biblical situations who and how the messenger is carries the meaning and the summons more eloquently than what he is merely commissioned to say.

Some biblical scholars, perhaps surprisingly, noting this phenomenon, have sought to withdraw the status of prophet from these figures of meaning-in-life. Thus Gerhard von Rad notes that in Jeremiah we pass from speaking a prophetic word to biographical interest and personhood. But, since this is not 'God-speech', not 'proclamation, but remonstrance with God', he adds: 'It is clear that Jeremiah with the actual words of his Confession has left his prophetic office ... his words do not proceed from above to below, but from below to above and what he bears witness to is primarily *not* a word of God but his inner doubts, his suffering and his despair ... Is it not true that in these confessions the prophetic office in a very real sense has come to an end?'[25]

This comment might be said to have a very Islamic ring, in that it assumes that prophethood can only ever be a verbal charge and not a personal burden. Jeremiah, contrary to von Rad's demur, is still 'a bridge for God's word', indeed even more so, because like the psalmists and the author of Job he lives and feels his encounter with the world on God's behalf and we take cognizance, revelatorily, of the ways of God from such encounter most authentically. His experience becomes itself a dialogue with God and 'revelation' – to him and to us – is on the further side of such anguish. As Davidson observes: 'Prophecy had already taught its truths: its last effort was to reveal itself in a life.'[26]

Such thoughts point eloquently towards the New Testament faith about Jesus, where 'the Word is made flesh' in a kindred but more ultimate sense. But before a brief attempt at a possible joint Muslim/Christian theology in this field, it is important to note how something of the same situation within personality belongs within the Qurʾān, *mutatis mutandis*.

VII

Refusal of Muhammad's message by the Quraish produced a new situation in the *Sīrah* of Muhammad. The original call is tempered by adversity. Rejection sharpens its content and heightens its intensity. There is a parallel progression between what has to be uttered and how it is received. The collection of Quranic utterances, however we understand the details, certainly belongs within the constraints of opposition. Herein there is a resemblance to biblical prophethood. In Amos 7.10–17 it seems that it is resistance, precisely, which leads to the writing down. In Isaiah 8.16f. the rejected words are 'bound up', held for the future, entrusted to a circle of disciples, reserved for the positive reception to which they must one day come. To those who say: 'Let us hear no more of the holy One of Israel' (Isaiah 30.11), it must be ensured, by setting it down in writing, that they shall hear more. Is it not comparably so with the Qurʾān?

There, too, are suffering and obduracy. The Prophet is warned that he may die before he sees what awaits his detractors (Surah 10.46). The crisis into which Muhammad's story moved through the thirteen years prior to the *Hijrah* is familiar enough, as well as the trauma of that emigration by which he sought his way out of oppression and into mastery. The contrasted militancy and success of that solution should not obscure from us the antecedent reality of testing and tribulation incurred as God's messenger because of God's message, as Islam sees and believes it to have been.

If, in spite of certain features of the Qurʾān which might deter us, we can keep an issue clear here it may serve to pave a way into an interpretation of what Christians mean by Jesus as 'the incarnate Word'. The possibility lies in the fact that this dimension of prophethood being 'on behalf of God', even in the most severely 'oral' sense, means that a certain parallel is seen to exist between enmity to the prophet and enmity to God. The obduracy in the people which greets the messenger relates to the Lord who sends him. The written Scripture which registers and takes issue with that obduracy is both God's word and the messenger's, by lordship in the one case and charge in the other. In the whole prophetic tradition we find that obduracy spelling pain and suffering for the messenger. It then

becomes fair to ask whether this extends to God, since it is
for God it is incurred.

In the biblical case of Jeremiah there is a clear sequence from
the prophet's sorrow to God's. What Jeremiah undergoes is
held to be a far, frail index to the sorrow of God. While the
prophet deplores a fruitless ministry, the Lord grieves over
the human rebellion (Jer. 12.5–11). In the story of the burning
of the scroll in Jeremiah 36 by the obdurate king, Yahweh himself is made to undergo, as it were, a fiery rejection. For his
Scripture is assigned to flames. In Isaiah 50.4–9, the spokesman
for God (he has 'the tongue of one taught') senses God 'standing
by' to share the confrontation with the scoffers.

It will be said that this sort of 'association' between the divine
and the human within prophetic tribulation is utterly unthink-
able in Islam. But before we hasten to exclude it, let us be
aware that, in doing so, we will endanger the whole reality
of that divine stake in mankind and thereby make incredible
the entire phenomenon of prophethood, the Quranic included.
To assume divine indifference here is to make fools of prophets
and of creation a fraud. Christian and Muslim alike are committed to the reality of both, under 'the Lord of the worlds'. There
can be no question about the divine involvement with the
human world. The only questions will be, How? and, How
far? What can we really believe about God because of prophethood in his Name?

VIII

How, and, how far, can we find God to be within, as well
as over, what eventuates in the encounter that is set between
the prophethood he sends and the creaturehood that is both
his and its field of summons and expectation? The answer,
when we reach it in Christian terms, is what Christian faith
and Scripture mean by Incarnation and the cross. If, so to speak,
prophets carry, as it were by proxy, an enmity to God within
the enmity to themselves, may they also be seen to be carrying,
also by proxy, a redemption of that enmity which, through
their story, can be recognized as God's? If, as we well may,
we think of prophets as God's activists in this world – using
a current term – what might be the divine activism reciprocal

to theirs? Is the need for it not implicit in the mandate by which
they came in his Name? Unless we are to disconnect them from
God in their coming, which is his sending, we can scarcely
disconnect him from them in the sequel.

The language of 'sending' about prophets is common to both
Bible and Qur'ān. 'Coming' and 'giving' are further, more intimate, terms in the New Testament. They deepen the measure
of what divine involvement might be. 'Sending' may imply
remoteness, a circumscribing of concern, a posture more of
requiring than of yearning, of sovereignty and not also of love.
But, whether 'sending', 'coming', or 'giving', the stake in the
human scene of 'God and his prophets' – whoever they be
– is plain.

How, then, is God *ghālibun ʿalā amrihi*, in the telling phrase
of Surah 12.21? How is God 'mastering what he has in hand'?[27]
In the immediate passage in 12.21, the meaning is about God's
providence in the sale of Joseph by his brothers and his prosperity in the household of his Egyptian owner. In the inclusive
theme for which we borrow it, of creation and the prophets
and God's grand design through 'revelation', what, can we
say, eventuates worthily of God? Clearly we cannot believe
in him and suppress the question. The prophets' 'vindication'
– to use another term – has, in a sense, to be God's also. Much
in the Qur'ān would witness that judgement is the answer.
Prophets – and God – are 'vindicated' in political success, in
eschatological fire, in the finalities of heaven and of hell. But
must we see these as the only worthy sequel to what was at
issue when the prophets were sent and suffered in the going?
Or is there no intervening way of divinely 'mastering the matter' that is between creature and Creator?

What is meant by Christian faith, within this common context
of a divinely liable world and a world-liable God, by the Incarnation and the cross, is a mastering of the matter by the love
that suffers and redeems. The prophetic service which we all
recognize in Jesus, deepens within his vocation and fidelity,
into a crisis of human enmity which, in deliberate readiness,
he undertakes to bear, and so bear away, in obedience to what,
messianically, he reads as God's way whereby what is wrong
with the world, as 'God's affair',[28] is truly overcome. The deliberate self-giving of Jesus is acknowledged, by faith, as the
actual meaning and fulfilment of his 'sonship', because it is
sustained throughout by awareness of his 'Father'. That

faith is formulated, in the sequel – where alone it could be reached – as the expression of the eternal mind, as the very 'activism' of God, the action which, responding to what, through prophetic experience, has taken inclusive issue with his sovereignty, both affirms and discloses where, and wherein, that sovereignty is. This is the Christian's meaning in saying that 'the Father sent the Son'. God is *ghālibun ʿalā amrihi*, Master by this mastery.

It is in this way that prophethood has passed into sonship and that 'revelation' duly concerning God's will has passed into 'revelation' blessedly denoting God's nature. That enlargement of its range and generosity fulfils all the implications of law and Torah, of summons and appeal, by an initiative of grace which both registers and transcends them. The antagonism which Jesus incurs, though continuous with all prophetic travail, can be seen as qualitatively inclusive of all that is wrong with the world. Such realization is part of the confession of the Incarnation, in the sense that here history is epitomized. By the same token the grace which bears that symbolically inclusive evil, has to be identified comprehensively with divine Lordship within the creation that undergoes it and the history it characterizes. It is by this warrant that the Christian must say: *Allāhu akbar*.

It falls to the next chapter to explore this warrant further.

NOTES

1   Surah 53.1–17 is a crucial passage concerning Muhammad's experience in recipience of the Qurʾān. Verse 9 here quoted is usually taken to refer to the distance to which the revealing figure approached Muhammad as he moved down from the far horizon, 'until he was a mere two bow-lengths away or even nearer'. Muhammad Zafrullah Khan takes the three words *fakāna qāba qausain* to refer, not to spatial distance of approach, but to the intimacy between the celestial and the human participants. *Qāb* is defined as the space between the extreme end of the bow and the point on it which the hand grasps or, alternatively, the space between the string and the hand-grasp when in use. Yet again the sense may be simply the length of two bows from end to end.

The reading followed by Dr Khan is hard to sustain, the more so in view of what follows: 'or nearer yet', which, along with the whole context seems to refer to spatial distance. Moreover, two bows with one cord seem a strange thought. Nevertheless, there is support elsewhere in Muslim interpretation, especially within Sufism, for the idea of such an intimacy between God and the Prophet, safeguarded, as here, by the word 'meta-phorically'.

2 Muhammad Zafrullah Khan, *Islam, its Meaning for Modern Man* (London 1962), p. 76.

3 e.g. Surahs 3.32 and 132; 4.59; 5.92; 8.1, 20 and 46; 24.54; 47.33; 58.13; all in the imperative verb. There are other passages in the indicative describing Muslims as those who 'obey God and the apostle'.

4 There are, however, some mystical views of the person of Muhammad which come very near to 'incarnational' language. See this writer's *Muhammad and the Christian* (London 1984), Chap. 4.

5 The Greek of John 1.1 in the clause, 'and God was the Word', reads *Theos*, not *ho Theos* with the definite article. The point of its omission is that 'the Word' was truly God's self-expression but in no way the forfeiture of the self-expressed. One might compare: 'and music was the symphony'. A symphony is entirely music but there is more to music than the symphonic.

6 'Intelligent intent' is needed here. The Qurʾān is clear that all nature praises God but only man does so with conscious mind. Cf. 17.44: 'All things without exception speak his praise, though their praising eludes your comprehension.'

7 A notable recent example is Fazlur Rahman, *Islam and Modernity* (Chicago 1982), in which he reproaches both those who suppose the Qurʾān to be in no need of responsible interpretation into new times, and those who pretend to bogus new 'readings', supposedly, but erroneously, abreast e.g. of current scientific knowledge. The Qurʾān is a religious source-book and should be read with an alertness both to its nature and to present experience.

8 Perhaps the most notable is the crucial passage in Surah 7.172, where God interrogates all creaturehood, as it were, in the cosmic womb: 'Am I not your Lord?', to which all reply: *Balā*, 'Yes. we so witness.' *Balā* is not only an affirmative, it means also 'affliction', or 'distress', and has been read here as intimating human travail in making the affirmation real.

9 How, for example, should Surah 4.64: 'God sent no prophet but that he should be obeyed.' be understood? What obedience? political? legal? devotional? mystical? Or 4.157 about the illusoriness of the death of Jesus on the cross – a notoriously difficult passage. Or Surah 90 about Muhammad being *hillun bi hādhā-l-bilād*, 'dwelling in this land', or 'a freeman in this city', i.e. exempt from certain prohibitions as to hunting, etc.? Or, again, the passage on which so much turns concerning the right (or duty?) of the Muslim to withdraw allegiance from a ruler he considers un-Islamic: 5.44–9, about 'those who do not judge (*lam yahkum*) by what has been sent down'. Is it political, juridical, spiritual *hukm* which is here in mind? Much turns on the answer. If there are open issues in these more factual phrases, it is much more so in the exegesis of things metaphorical (see the rubric in 3.7).

10 *Commentary on Ecclesiastes*, 3.1.

11 *Midrash ha-Gadol* on Exodus 24.10.

12 Martin Buber, *I and Thou*, trans. W. Kaufmann (New York 1970), p. 158: 'Man receives, and what he receives is not a content but a presence.' See also David Biale, *Gershom Scholem: Kabbalah and Counter-History*, Cambridge, Mass., 1979.

13 See below in the discussion of his literacy/illiteracy.

14 Surahs 12.2; 13.37; 20.113; 41.3; 42.7; and 43.3.

15 Meaning: God, greater, Creator, obey (you, pl.), take refuge (you, pl.), stand in awe (you, pl.).

16 There is a comparable position in the thought of Karl Barth in his discussion of the relation of our human language to the theology, as he holds it, of 'the Word of God'. Cf. John MacQuarrie: *God-Talk: An Examination of the Language and Logic of Theology* (London 1967), 'God graciously confers upon our human language the capacity to speak about himself . . . God makes our human language about him veridical', i.e. truth-saying. pp. 48–9.

17 The case is more fully set out in Kenneth Cragg, *The Event of the Qur'ān* (London 1971), pp. 57–61.

18 'Native' has been taken by some to translate *ummī*, which is to have only part of the clue. When the pagan Meccans wanted to discredit Muhammad's preaching they said he had it from an *'ajamī*, a foreigner. Surah 62.2 gives praise that God had sent among the *ummiyyūn*, i.e. the Arabs as unlettered, 'one of their own number'. See also note 14.

19 G. N. Jalbani, *Teachings of Shāh Walīullāh* (Lahore 1967), p. 92f. Walīullāh's view is in his *Al-Hujjat al-Bālighah*, vol. 1 (Lahore 1979), pp. 220f. See also Muhammad Iqbal, *The Reconstruction of Religious Thought in Islam* (Lahore 1938), p. 171f.

20 See Kenneth Cragg, *The Pen and the Faith* (London 1985), pp. 56–7.

21 One of the early, modern examples of this trend was Syed Amir Ali, *The Spirit of Islam: A History of the Evolution and Ideals of Islam*, London 1922. The subtitle is significant. P. 162: 'In *instituting* prayers, *Muhammad recognised* the yearning of the human soul to pour out its love and gratitude to God.' P. 167: 'In order to keep alive . . . the memory of the birthplace of Islam, *Muhammad directed* that during the prayers the Muslim should turn his face toward Mecca.' P. 171: 'The wisdom of the inspired lawgiver shines forth.' (Italics ours. In each case the reference is to a directive of the Qur'ān, not the personal Muhammad.)

22 See Michael Marmura, 'Avicenna's Theory of Prophecy in the Light of Ash'arite Theology', in W. S. McCullough, ed., *The Seed of Wisdom* (Toronto 1964), pp. 159–78.

23 ibid., p. 161. Al-Juwaynī's thought on prophethood is in line with his 'occasionalism', for which all is directly God's doing.

24 See Annemarie Schimmel, *Mystical Dimensions of Islam* (Chapel Hill 1975), and *As Through a Veil: Mystical Poetry in Islam*, New York 1982.

25 G. von Rad, 'The Confessions of Jeremiah', in L. G. Perdue and B. W.

Kovacs, ed., *A Prophet to the Nations: Essays in Jeremiah Studies* (Indiana 1984), pp. 339–47.

26   *Hastings Dictionary of the Bible*, 2nd edn (Edinburgh 1963), vol. ii, p. 576.

27   Translations vary. The root meaning is God's prevailing.

28   'Affair' is a somewhat pedestrian translation of *amr*, lit. 'thing', 'business', 'matter', with a strong hint of the purposive. Hence our preference for: 'what he has in hand'.

4
Zeal and the Lord

I

'When he [the believer] comes to Me walking, I [the Lord] go to him running.' So, according to the tradition of the great Al-Bukhārī, is the zeal of the generous Lord.[1] Could there be some strange link with the detail in Jesus' story of the returning prodigal, whose father saw him 'a great way off' and ran toward him to shorten the distance and hasten the welcome, reckoning nothing of his rags and squalor? (Luke 15.20). However that may be, it is a sweet tradition. But can we say that it is typical? There is much elsewhere, and in the Qur'ān also, which insists strongly that God is totally un-obligated towards man. There is nothing that may be assumed, still less required, of him. All things remain unpredictably, perhaps inscrutably, locked within the divine option.

If we are to think at all of a divine eagerness we must surely do so circumspectly, lest we offend against treasured Muslim accents on divine otherness, transcendence and prerogative. For, traditions apart, it is precisely these emphases which are zealously guarded and demanded by Islamic theology. Islam is identified by a jealous zeal *for* the Lord, his unity, his sovereignty, his decree and his exaltedness. Our purpose in this chapter is to study some aspects of this 'zeal *for* the Lord', and to discover, if we can, what faith may worthily and intelligently affirm about 'the zeal *of* the Lord'. There must surely be a correlation between the two.

To explore it follows from where we left the two preceding chapters and the logic – as we called it – from creation to theodicy, and how capacities in revelation seemed to point towards something climactic in its own momentum – something which would bring the revelatory activity of God to grips with the evident crisis with which history seems to confront the revelatory will itself, the will of the God who summons us. If believing in revelation at all means a 'liable' God, 'liable' to the human world, then 'zeal' may be a proper word in which to look for the response. Further, the more zealous custodians of revelation are, or will to be, the more they attest a seriousness between

God and man which can hardly be credibly one-sided. There is, thus, a deep truth to be investigated in bringing together this 'zeal for' and 'zeal of' situation, and point in asking what should be learned from it both about 'the zealous God' and what sort of zeal on faith's part is due and right.

II

'God comes running . . .' How can reverence say it, or *taqwā* approve? Yet we must start – resuming all that has been there throughout – from the truth that all theology is about relationship. The word 'God' is, so to speak, a 'transitive' noun, having to do with reality humanly significant. A sound theology will never hold that God is somehow circumscribed in human relatedness so that the correlation present in God's real will to 'need' man is all that there is in transcendence. But we must not so exalt God, beyond and apart from such correlation, as to cut away the ground from religious experience itself, as we do if we affirm of God an absolute isolation and 'indifference'.[2] To deny what we may boldly call the 'liability' of God about man would be exactly to play into the hands of the sceptic who, asked why he did not believe in God, replied: 'Is that not the most charitable hypothesis?' In our human predicament the non-existence of God would be a worthier conjecture than his indifference.

Postively, as we saw earlier, God is 'let be' by us. As the Jewish *Zohar* had it, the unity of God turns upon the prayer of humanity and belongs with 'his holy ones'.[3] *Allāhu akbar* is on human lips. Mercy is registered by *taqwā* as that for which it was meant and where it has being as fulfilment. Revelation, as argued in the previous chapter, proceeds within divine intention and proclaims a divine will which gives, and takes significance, in its human sphere. It means divine commitment, to a degree, in the human response. Pondering capacities in revelation in cross-reference between Christian and Muslim Scriptures, we saw how the prophetic might pass into the filial, the words into the Word, message into personality, and a sending mission into an incarnate presence. If and where it so passes, the content of revelation also passes from the imperative only, to the expressive, from directive to disclosure, from having to do solely with God's will to knowledge of his love. Any such enlargement of its meaning will still be a call to obedience but in the context of a bidding into fellowship.

The point here is not to be categorical about these differing dimensions of revelation, and of Scriptures, but only to see that they are present, contrastedly, within a common theme. They will plainly affect what we can think and believe about 'the zeal of the Lord'. According to Al-Nadawī, 'the holy Prophet said: "God is jealous; his jealousy is aroused by a person indulging in that which he has forbidden."'[4] Islam, it is fair to say, in the language of Elijah, has been 'very jealous for the Lord' (1 Kings 19.10 and 14). Its doctrine of *Tauhīd* is intense; the word denotes not just a stated unity but an insistent one. The reflexive form, 'making one', matches the lively iconoclasm of Islam, its antiseptic quality against *shirk* and *kufr* – those heinous evils of human perversity, which must not be merely thought on but passionately abhorred.

This, one could say, is consistently Semitic. In its own context it matches the Hebraic passion for the divine unity and the urgency of the first commandment in the Decalogue. From Moses through Malachi runs the mutuality of the 'jealous' God and the 'zealous' people. The two adjectives are virtually one and a single root *qānāʾ*, in some usages, has an evil sense, as when the Philistines were envious of Isaac's flocks (Gen. 26.14); or when the psalmist confessed he was envious of others (Psalm 73.3). In such terms the 'jealousy' of God would seem a very strange notion. But the Hebraic tradition understands it as meaning the ardent divine concern for the people's wellbeing and the vigilant divine militancy against all that might harm them from within or from without.

Yahweh, in such context, is credited with strong human emotions. These are undoubtedly in places a clear mirroring of tribal passions and enmities or one-sided partisan readings of events and histories. The Lord 'wraps himself in a cloak of jealous anger' (Isaiah 59.17) on behalf of Hebrew vindication and the routing of their enemies. But that very sense of divine engagement with and for 'God's people' is refined and chastened to become, in measure, the very matrix of the messianic hope. Things which 'the zeal of the Lord of hosts will perform' (cf. 2 Kings 19.31; Isaiah 9.7; and 37.32) came to mean what could conceivably concern a wider world and embrace a deeper task than particularist mercies and privatized reversals of adversity. In that deeper realm 'the zeal of the Lord' may be seen to be the very secret of messiahship as fulfilled, for Christian faith, in Jesus to whom disciples applied the ancient prophet's words: 'the zeal of thy house has consumed me' (Psalm 69.9; John 2.17). So identified, the gospel deriving from Jesus could well be described as the patient enthusiasm of God in love to the world, the point and index of the divine activism about the human scene and sorrow.

Such, clearly, was the New Testament conviction. There, too, the Greek *zēlos* (verb *zēloō*) has the same double sense of the Hebrew. James (4.2) uses it of the one who covets. Stephen in his sermon applied it to the envious brothers of Joseph (Acts 7.9). At least the envious are never 'indifferent', and their sorry 'interests' can be transmuted into the earnest desire that is no longer on behalf of the self but passionate on behalf of others. The transmuting of Saul's vehemence into Paul's ardour is central not only to his story but to all his ethical and pastoral education of the churches. When he writes in Romans 12.13 about being 'addicted to hospitality' he uses the term which once described him as a 'persecutor'. Throughout the Bible there is plainly much to be discerned in the paradox of zeal, and in the making or remaking of zealots. That God may be blasphemed by them, loved through them, that there is a zeal which takes his Name in vain and one that truly names him, are the sharp lessons that emerge. That zeal may be reverently affirmed of God himself is the most mysterious of all. Yet neither Jew, nor Christian, nor Muslim could remain so in denying it.

III

The question, for all our theologies, will be where this engagement of God with our world is dependably identified and how we should understand its consistency with the divine glory and its dependability. Only then can we know the sort of 'zeal' on our part which is fitting to its patterns. We cannot be rightly on behalf of God in contravention of how God is on behalf of us. What Islam calls acting *fī sabīli-Llāhi*, 'in the way of God', is a double formula. It prescribes our theology before it guides our ethics.[5] What *is* the 'path of God' is a question which precedes decision in the path for God.

There was an early Christian practice of commending *bona fide* travelling Christian men and women from one church to another within the recognized duties of hospitality. It was a

practice which had much to do with the growth of local leadership and a widespread sense of community when persecution
– and so enemy infiltration – were factors requiring care and
vigilance and courage. The obscure Third Epistle of John refers
to this kindly 'forwarding' of fellow-believers on their journeys.
'Speed them on their way', says verse 6, 'worthily of God'.

It concerns us all to ask what is 'worthy of God'. When we
do so about our conduct, it can only be as we have done so
about our faith and our theology. What is worthy to be believed
about God and what must be excluded by all right *taqwā* as
derogatory to God? The questions are not easy and prejudice
may well foreclose them so that they are never pressed. We
are all liable to respond to them out of our prepossessions and
these may not readily call themselves in doubt.

Remembering – as we have argued in Chapter 2 – that the
earth is already, in daily experience, a sacrament of transcendence and that whatever we say must be consistent with this
truth of Creator and of creaturehood, and that we are in a
theatre of 'revelation', can it suffice to conclude that God is
not susceptible to assessments, on our human part, of what
is 'worthy of him'? Or do we say that anything is, everything
is, 'worthy' for which he opts and which he chooses? Will it
be fair to characterize Islamic theology, Sufism apart, as broadly
of that latter conviction? None may question him. There are
no human 'rights' where God is concerned. He has his beautiful
Names but in no way do they bind him. His will keeps its
own counsel. The passion of Job, though not his patience,
would be unseemly to the Qurʾān. 'I will work, and who shall
hinder it?' (Isaiah 43.13) is its sense of God's sovereign way.
There are emphases in the Qurʾān which might be read comparably to the comment in the Talmud on the words in Exodus
19.17: 'They stood under the mount'.

> Rabbi ʿAbdimi said: 'This teaches that the Holy One, Blessed be
> he, overturned the mountain upon them like an (inverted cask) and
> said to them: "If you accept the Torah 'tis well: if not, there shall
> be your burial."'[6]

Surah 7.171 records the same incident. Yet, dire choice or not,
the verse is immediately followed by the passage describing
the cosmic, or pre-creation, exchange between the Lord and
the whole human progeny-to-be: 'Am I not your Lord?' with
their response *Balā*, 'Yes, indeed, we acknowledge so'.[7] Does

the divine Lordship *seek* acknowledgement or sharply demand it? Which is to be thought 'worthy of God' of these alternatives? Or should we say that they are not alternatives?

The questions sharpen if we ask whether anything, including creation and the sending of the prophets, is 'necessary' to God. There has generally been a strong instinct in Islam to distance the divine nature from any and every divine attribution, whether of description or action. The latter inevitably 'associate' with us. Yet 'exalted be he above all that you associate' is the steady cry of Islam. Antipathy to the pagan and the pluralist dominates all zeal for the unity. This very zeal for singularity may oversimplify what unity should mean.

There were interesting discussions in the classic age of Islamic philosophy on whether creation and prophethood were in any way incumbent on God to initiate and sustain. There was a tendency among the Mu'tazilites to develop the concept of *lutf wājib*, or mercy which was (in Arabic grammar) *upon* God, the particle *'alā* meaning obligation or duty. These theologians cited the Qur'ān, 6.54, on how God had 'written down for himself mercy' (*kataba 'alā nafsihi al-rahmah*), which could be taken to mean that mercy was not an arbitrary 'option' on God's part, but a veritable commitment. Surah 16.9 said that 'it was upon God (*'alā-Allāhi*) to indicate the right guidance, or show the way', though, here, the immediately following comment says that had God so willed he would have guided *all* of them, with the implication that only some would be so favoured. The notion of divine justice also inspired in some minds the conviction that arbitrariness could not ride with it. So there was a place for 'must' in thought about God.[8] Certain things were 'upon him' as incumbent including the mission of the prophets. According to Surah 8.58–60, he fought their enemies as being also his own. He could hardly not, then, be obligated in their mission.

However, in the main, Muslim theology draws back from these venturesome thoughts about *lutf wājib*, and there is much in the Qur'ān to check, indeed banish, such ideas. In any event, 'God cannot be questioned about his acts' (Surah 21.23). Other theologies, of course, have had their problems at this point. According to Karl Barth in his *Church Dogmatics*, 'God has no need of us ... God knows perfect beatitude within himself ... He could have remained satisfied with himself and with the impassible glory and blessedness of his own inner life.'[9]

The impulses that prompt such thoughts in theologians are understandable enough because of the logical problem of finding the contingent 'necessary' to the eternal. But the consequences to which they lead plunge them into the still greater illogicality of violating the sovereignty of grace on behalf of a sovereignty of freedom. We must somehow understand God as transcending his transcendence, if by the 'transcendent' we mean a 'satisfaction' with immunity. We must return to what is at issue here. For it would leave us with no meaning to 'the zeal of the Lord'. We shall need to reach for some kind of analogy which at once admits of genuine relevance to God of all that we experience *and* his due reality beyond it. Perhaps that of the artist and his art – essentially related in the interplay of fulfilling and fulfilled – is the most apt.

IV

Let us try to move to a wise faith about the Lord's 'zeal' by way of certain further rumination on 'zeal' for him. This can best lead us to the clues we need. A theology that can try to reach a right mind about how to be 'on behalf of God' invoking his Name may hope to be closest to understanding what his Name may be. For there is much zeal which sadly 'takes it in vain'.

It is perhaps odd that theologies of transcendence which most strongly hold that God has no 'need' of the world assume equally strongly that he has urgent 'need' of their zealotry on his behalf. How is it that he who has 'all resources in himself' (*Allāh al-samad*, Surah 112.2) has, nevertheless, to be stoutly defended and asserted by guardians of his cause? Can it be that these are sure of him in a false way – a way which enables them to dominate by doing so in his Name, in effect to use him as the tool of their own supremacy? If so, will not this be the most perverse *takfīr*, or disavowal of God, the more so because paradoxically committed 'for his sake'? The suspicion that it might be so should suffice to give us pause and alert our theologies against themselves. That the suspicion has much ground seems evident if we set ourselves to think a little unconventionally about dogma and iconoclasm, about power and rejectionism and other temptations of the will to be for God. Such temptations beset us all. A vital element in a right zeal has to be its own hesitancy.

Iconoclasm, or hostility to idols, is a lively case in point. Kipling felt he caught the temper of the Islamic *adhān* when he wrote:

> In the silence a voice thundered far above their heads: 'I bear witness that there is no god but God.' It was the mullah, proclaiming the Oneness of God in the city of the Million Manifestations. The call rang across the sleeping city and far over the river, and be sure that the mullah abated nothing of the defiance of his cry for that he looked down upon a sea of temples and smelt the incense of a hundred Hindu shrines.[10]

There *is* an antipathy between Oneness and plurality. But is it rightly read or transacted as an antipathy between Muslim and Hindu? There may be point in divine 'election' into service. But is it soundly realized in apartheid from the Gentile by the Jew? When the perceptive Muslim scholar Al-Bīrūnī travelled in India he certainly heeded the muezzin. But he was also able to appreciate the imagery of the Hindu. His Islamic loyalty had room for the relevance of symbolism and he was prepared to recognize that there could be positive meaning and legitimacy in those Hindu practices which, by the necessities of Muhammad's Meccan vocation, had to be anathema.[11]

The average iconoclast, however, is little minded to emulate this example. One must be adamant against idols and, therefore, one cannot be receptive to imagery or patient to distinguish between worship and veneration. In the name of unity one must hold out against visual representation and fail to see what one's own calligraphy represents. Zeal against idols is likely to miss the fact that one can have the arts without idolatrous reproach and one can be irreproachably free of them and still not have a pure worship. The enmity to form and sign and token, if thoroughly pursued, must take us out of this world, or make a symbol of their seeming absence, or impoverish our imaginations as that which we must consecrate in this sacramental world of our habitation.

A physical iconoclasm, like that of the Quranic Abraham,[12] may be a vital dimension of a living faith, a necesary repudiation of superstition, blindness, mental sloth and emotional bondage. Its activism is all the better for the sense of humour he seems to have retained, and his courage as an emancipator. Without these, and a discerning spirit, the busy iconoclast is liable to find the obvious idols and miss the hidden ones. If

he relies only on axes and hammers and brooms for his demoli-
tions he will leave intact the deeper aspects of all *shirk*, the
unbanished fears, the lingering affection, the reversionary
trust. He will leave intact the subtle idolatries of tribe, or institution, or tradition, or vested interest. Indeed, his very iconoclasm may idolize itself and so falsify the worship which it
ostensibly makes pure. For it is not what zeal achieves but
what it makes of the zealot which must occupy the last analysis.
He may never discover how blunt an instrument he may have
been against the evils he set out to correct. He may never realize
how his ardour has disserved a grateful participation in the
adventure of creation which art, imagination and worship are
set to seek within a world of sense and wonder devised – it
would seem – for just such reverent gratitude.

V

The Abraham allusion may carry the case further in another
sense. For there is much claiming of his insignia. Who are his
descendants? Or, putting the question differently, who are his
emulators? Zeal is liable to make the claimants unilaterally
so – which brings us to strong rejectionism as a characteristic
issue in the cross-reference of faiths. Take the comment of the
celebrated exegete of the Qurʾān, Fakhr al-Dīn al-Rāzī, who
wrote:

> Only the Muslims are true followers of Abraham. If Muhammad
> had agreed to leave in peace people opposed to his teaching and
> who claimed to be followers of Abraham, he would have admitted
> the vanity of his own claim. In fact the dignity of Islam and of
> Muhammad was too dear to God to allow any adversary even to
> claim to be followers of Abraham.[13]

All the elements familiar in the story of religions in general
are here – the will to be monopolists, the assumed necessity
to exclude others from the vital category, the urge actively to
oppose others, failure to do so as proof of disavowal, and the
enlistment of, rather than simply an appeal to, God.

These temptations of religious community are strongly reinforced when they are joined to ethnic particularity or cultural
pride. For these interact with religious zeal, to mutual advantage. When the partnership is politicized the trend to exclusivism is intensified. What is religio-political has then the

sanction of incentives like those which Al-Rāzī is found pleading *and* the implements of state-power or caliphal rule which
the political order affords. There unfolds in the *Sīrah* of Muhammad and in Islamic history the belief that religio-political
alliance is legitimated by God and that the twin elements within
it are rightly aligned. 'Obey God and obey the apostle', was
the steady injunction of the Qurʾān, where it is clear that the
'obedience' is in no way confined to matters of faith and truth
but extends to battle and power. *Fitnah*, or succumbing to temptation, may apply as much to evading military duty out of fear
or love of family, as to giving the lie to the preaching and deni-
grating the faith. 'The day of the criterion' (*Yaum al-Furqān*),
in the origins of Islam consisted, not in the first disciples' accession to faith, nor in any signal occasion of spiritual illumination through the Scripture, but in the notable skirmish at Badr
between Muhammad and the Qaraish which marked a decisive
point in his struggle against Meccan power and prestige (Surah
8.41). The term *Al-Furqān*, significantly, is a title both of the
Book and of a military engagement.

These dimensions – indeed constraining factors – in the theology of Islam from its original history are familiar enough and
do not need to be argued or elaborated here. The present point
is to consider what they mean for the zeal of theology. As
Ignaz Goldziher saw it, Muhammad's appeal to force

> did not fail to colour the idea of God he wished to render supreme
> by military means ... The fashion in which the Lord of the worlds
> reacts to the intrigues of malefactors mirrors Muhammad's own poli-
> tical approaches to the obstacles in his way. His own disposition
> and his own method for combating internal enemies are projected
> on to God who wages His Prophet's wars ... God was thus lowered
> from His transcendental heights to act as the collaborator of His
> Prophet caught up in the battles of this world.[14]

This reading, for Goldziher and others, is made the more significant, and the decision dramatic, by the fact that Muhammad's
early preaching, or *balāgh*, had been wholly characterized by
patience, endurance, noble suffering and steadfastness, totally
uncharacterized by property acquisition, communal advantage
and physical plunder.

Most Muslims would, of course, have a completely different
reading of this history. They would probably agree that the

doctrinal scheme of any religion depends on the historical framework within which divinity is ascribed or invoked. They would claim, however, that the robust realism of the post-*Hijrah Sīrah* of Muhammad grapples rightly – and appropriately to God – with the evils and the hostility manifest in the experience of the pre-*Hijrah Sīrah*. The issue here is profoundly theological. Precisely because it is so sharply drawn between original Christianity and original Islam, its crux is often broached by Muslims in reference to that contrast. Thus, for example, Ziya Gökalp, earlier quoted for the view that the Jesus decision was solely due to Roman circumstance,[15] argues further that by this basic, original decision Christianity in effect disqualified God from things political and effectively 'secularized' the state. He wrote:

> Christianity found a political organisation already in existence and thus it took the matter of organising a government and maintaining laws as matters outside the concern of religion ... By accepting the state outside of religion it was relegating the state to a non-sacred realm. [Otherwise] ... it would have attempted to create one and then it would have regarded it as a sacred being of its own creation. As this government would have been within the religion, and as such a sacred institution, no need would have been felt to establish a spiritual government. If this had happened there would be no duality of temporal and spiritual governments but something similar to the case existing in Islam.[16]

We have already rejected the notion that the pattern of Messiah-Jesus was in any way just an absence of occasion due to Roman power. The question here, for Gökalp and all other Islamic theory, is not simply whether government is 'organized' but how, not whether states and faiths interact but by what criteria, not whether the state is a sacred institution but how its secular, coercive power is responsive to spiritual truth so that it might be known to be a 'sacred' order. Aspects of what is at stake here concerned us earlier. In context now the point is that the uninhibited embrace of coercive force, believed justified by the context of Muhammad's *Sīrah*, worked, by sheer sanction of power, both to establish Islam in unhesitating political terms and to incline Islamic theology to a parallel association of the divine with power and of faith about transcendence with its political expression. The result, further, has been a tendency to give religious zeal unbridled rein or to silence the misgivings

by which, otherwise, it might be tempered and restrained. The
sense of God in this form finds him zealously requiring zeal
– witness the frequent exhortations of the post-*Hijrah* Surahs
to battle array and reproach of the timorous and the pacifists.
It also prompts decisive, and near-sighted, conclusions about
how such zeal should proceed, with what goals and by what
means. It thus tempts the zealous into zealotry and the faith
into a potential absolute in its own right – always 'on behalf
of God'. For power, by its own nature, discredits patience,
and by its own momentum so fears to fail that it may deplorably
succeed. However earnestly or sincerely invoked, it tends to
become self-warranting. The more such invocation is believed
to be for God the more the most ultimate dimension ceases
to be master-judge and becomes instead the ally. Theology is
then liable to think in the same idiom about God himself. It
is not that there are no enemies (of his) to be subdued. The
Magnificat is not silent about the mighty, the rich, the proud.
What matters there is how they are overcome.

VI

Before taking these thoughts into some final theological reckoning, it is important to relate them to the current evidence of
religious extremism on many hands and in many faiths. The
temper expressed by Al-Rāzī in his Abrahamic exclusion zone
speaks from many quarters now. Back in the sixties there were
some who prophesied the complete demise of religion within
a quarter-century. They saw what they called technocratic times
like ours inevitably shedding attitudes labelled ontocratic and
inherited from 'ages of faith' – faith no longer viable in a world
inured to secular human autonomy.[17] The folly of these views
about the demise of religions and how criminally sanguine the
notion they held of the secular future have been evident in
the intervening years. Far from eroding away, religions have
in disconcerting ways displayed their resilience, even if only
in reaction to the sense of threat implicit in confident prophecies
of their demise. Behind those reactions were the sundry factors
those prophets had in mind and which were briefly noted in
Chapter 2.

The fact that the reactions, being extreme and tending to
fanaticism, are the wrong ones does not weaken their psychic

force, their social relevance or their theological entail. Contemporary Al-Rāzī-s exclusifying their possession of their Abrahams are comparably jealous of competitors around the territory they defend as uniquely theirs, be it 'God', or 'truth', or 'salvation', or the 'community-in-the-right'. They do so out of fear for faith both as belief and as identity. They do so, if they are instinctively political, out of anti-imperialism and independence, and when they are theological, out of jealousy for authority, office, continuity, or prestige, or all these together. They are ready for hardness of heart in the protection of the closed mind.

The practical consequences of all such retreat into authoritarianism are the deep concern of the peace-makers, the alert educationalists and the religious mediators in nations and societies beset by these patterns of faith, whether in the tensions of Islam, or Hinduism, or Christianity, or in sectarian fragmentations anywhere. For some, the manifestations of religious fanaticism are such as to call for an effort after global concert of correction, lest what they see as 'licensed insanity' should pass out of the reach of persuasion and control. Such an effort would be analogous in the social sphere to the Brandt Report in the economic sphere – a resolute attempt to get into focus and into correction a vast and threatening feature of our time which, like economic injustice on a world scale, the sanguine or the exempt would otherwise happily ignore.

Such a concert of attention, and the penetration of the nature of religion it would require, might be a highly salutary education of theology, which we cannot here attempt. But one of its lessons would surely be a rediscovery of the subtlety of evil, stemming from an honest reading of the behaviour of religions. How is it, we have to ask, that men can be so magisterially on behalf of God, that religion can legitimate in his Name such unloveliness? It is the paradox in zeal that it makes men fanatical. Just as a proper desire always risks a potential jealousy, so a proper will to assurance becomes an actual captivity to pride and scorn. Precisely because faiths have to do with ultimacy they falsely locate it in themselves. It is a hazard of vocation into which they fall. The sense of divine mandate gives rein, where it should give pause, to things most unlovely – should we not say un-divine? – in human life and mind. These are a habit of enmity, a pride of will, a hardness of heart, and a certain atrophy of mind. It is as though God has been commandeered by his partisans, no longer exalted but rather taken over in a sponsorship that names his Name in vain. Such, as it might be called, is the annexation of God by faiths that have espoused his service and identified his sanction.

VII

The evil in such zeal, if we have rightly seen it, is plainly a factor in what has to do with prophethood as we studied it in Chapter 3. For prophets are clearly foci of zeal, both zeal for what they bring and who they are, and zeal in the resistance they encounter. This is evidently so in the context of the story of Jesus in the Gospel and of the *Sīrah* of Muhammad in Mecca and Medina. Both, within the dimensions of their setting, were confronted by sharp hostility, fed by many of the same factors which we can see in fanaticism today. There was a tenacity, at least until the capture of the city, about Meccan opposition to an upstart prophet, disturbing the traditional paganism of the Quraish and threatening the *status quo* in a commercial capital. The Gospels, for their part, are a history of gathering storm and final suffering, the bitter victimization of Jesus of Nazareth by the Jerusalem he saw as the symbol of all he loved and, therefore, must accuse. Without the zeal of prophethood there would have been no issue in either citadel, in either story. But there was a total contrast between them, in how the precipitating prophetic zeal was fulfilled and how the resistant zeal of recalcitrant society was answered.

It is here that we must return to our study in Chapter 3 about prophethood and, in particular, to the theological decisions of Islam which require Muslims to propose what, in Chapter 1, we noted as a 're-Semiticization' of Jesus on their part and in line with the Qur'ān. That this theme of zeal and the evil of zeal is the right context in which to examine this interpretation may be simply told. It turns on the fact that prophethood, being where zeal is on trial – both pro-zeal and contra-zeal – is, therefore, also where evil, as it were de-neutralized by prophethood's challenge, moves into action and tells its true character.

On this account, the Christian faith has always identified, in what was done to Jesus at the hands of zealous men, an expression of the evil propensity of us all. 'Behold', it said, 'the sin of the world', there in the cross of Jesus. It is this

dimension of the climactic event in Jesus' prophethood which
forbids us to limit his relevance to truth and God simply to
his spoken word, his teaching and his ethics. Rather it requires
us to enlarge it so that it takes in the import of the crisis to
which such ministry led and of the shape of that crisis' resolution in death and resurrection. Such Jesus-prophethood does
not only deepen, as we saw in Chapter 3, from the prophetic
to the filial, from words to the Word, it also deepens from
the hortatory into the tragic, from revelation by things said
to revelation by things suffered. That deepening means also
a deepening in the measure of evil and its zeal – of evil not
simply as a heedlessness of words but a dark defiance of truth,
of evil no longer merely turning from a messenger but crucifying a Son.

It is for these ultimate reasons, within Christian perspective,
that a Muslim case for the 're-Semiticization' of Jesus misreads
what is at issue. It is not that Jesus must be 'restored' to historical Jewishness as his sole context and his due significance. Any
adequate measure of his cross altogether breaks out of such
reduction of the whole and warrants those interpretative forms
which an expanding faith borrowed from the insights of Helle-
nism and the meaning of the Logos. These should be seen
as a wider world, legitimately aspiring and learning to possess
the whole of him, finding the terms in which to do so, within
a fellowship which, likewise, had burst out of the Judaic alone
into the Judeo-Gentile oneness of the apostolic Church.

The Semitic in Jesus is inviolate and utterly secure, in the
Aramaic of his speech, the Jewishness of his ministry, and the
context of his world. It is there, supremely, in the messianic
meaning. There is no messianic without the Judaic. But the
messianic in Jesus achieves a people's private hope in the
people's open grace. The New Testament is shaped by what
was Greco-Roman as the first sector of that translation to the
world.

We have this perspective because of the climax of Jesus' suffering read as for ever indicting religious zeal in a way that
is inclusive of us all. But we have it also because that suffering
suggests a quite disconcerting understanding of how a divinely
true zeal might read its vocation in response to wrong. The
suggestion is in line with the equally disconcerting ideas of
the *Magnificat* which – we may assume – is why Luke the Evangelist decided to set it into the nativity story.

Why is either disconcerting? The reason is in the strange reversal of values implicit both in the Song of Mary and the crisis of Jesus' story. Both have within them the mind of a zeal that reads its task by a radical reading of what it confronts. If true prophethood somehow brings evil into the open by voicing and representing the truth which wilfulness rejects and aims to extinguish, how should prophetic energies respond? Perseverance, not to say loyalty to truth, will persist, as in pre-*Hijrah* Mecca. But sustained iteration of the message may only deepen, as then, the implicit crisis. What then? Reading by the mind of Jesus we have to say that coercion, on the truth's part *via* the messenger, will join the issue, inevitably, on other terms than those of truth alone. Factors of prudence, security, contention, will now confound the stakes, muddy the waters, confuse the parties: they may even vindicate the original rejection as validly a self-defence after threat. They may well entrench it the more sharply. They will certainly sully the original theme. Even if a forcible engagement of the message with the antagonism is physically successful, the victory will not be truth's alone, perhaps not truth's at all.

It was for these reasons, inwardly sensed and obeyed, that Jesus chose to suffer, 'leaving room' (to borrow Paul's phrase, Romans 12.19) 'for the judgement of God', and finding what the 'judgement' was in the cross and resurrection. These were the shape, and the uncompromised nature, of the vocation that had begun in prophethood and been realized in redemption. So the cross became in Christian perspective, not only the measure of how perverse a zealousness may be, but of how its enmity is mastered 'worthily of God'.

VIII

These themes of cross-reference between two theologies bring us back finally to what we should think of God in the light of all we have reviewed. It is clear there is this 'sentness' in his Name, that there is the imperative entrusted to these 'sent ones' summoning mankind to 'let God be God'. It is clear, further, that there is a necessary 'zeal for the Lord' as no more, no less, than the seriousness of his commission. This obligatoriness to go on his behalf and to heed those he sends is inseparable, for us all, from the very meaning of 'God' and the thrust of theology. In creation and prophethood there is a sense in

which we may say he 'comes', urgently, in sacrament and summons, dignifying us in his very demand upon us. Yet, the more
urgent we see these things to be – which is none other than
our confession of his rule – the more uncompulsive we find
they are. Prophets can be, and are, denied their pleas. The
signs of a beneficent Lord can be, and are, ignored in nature.
There is nothing merely self-fulfilling about the claims of revelation upon our obedience. They hinge upon the human will,
and the human will can be monumentally unwilling. There
is a place for human zeal and human zeal is so often quite
misplaced. The purposes of God can be distorted by those who
undertake them. The very custodians of his commands may
invert the situation and make their trust a perquisite and pride.

Is it not clear, then, from our common faiths, that God's
wisdom is human-centred and that God's purposes are human-
linked? Those that might be otherwise are, by the same token,
not within our knowing or our theology, except as reverence
for mystery. The God of faith is the God 'with whom we have
to do' (Hebrews 4.13), and who has to do with us and all humankind. So much is both Islam and Christianity.

By a Christian reading of these clues it follows that we may
conclude that God and coercion do not belong together. There
is evidently great patience in the Almighty. It is not simply
the patience that suffers to be misused by his very partisans.
It somehow also waits for them to discover what they do to
him in their ways on his behalf. This seems to emerge from
all the foregoing in this and the two preceding chapters.

Take the issue of 'sacred' and 'secular'. The 'sacred' has to
concede the distinction, and with it the autonomy of human
life, or else there is nothing to be 'sanctified'. This autonomy
which, distorted, means the 'secular' unhallowed, can only be
so hallowed, not by domination but by consent. That fact indicates how alone the 'sacred' can avail to hallow. Only so is
spirit true to spirit. The more any truth or right is coercive
the less it is religious.

The well-known 'Render to Caesar . . . render to God' passage
in the Gospel (Matt. 22.21; Mark 12.17; Luke 20.25) must be
read in this sense. The words are closely linked with the 'image'
metaphor suggested by the questioner's coin, for which Jesus
pointedly asked. Man, bearing the 'image' of God, his 'representative' in the natural order, is responsible to God for his
whole being and stature. There is no separation of realms. The

whole man, including his political life, bears the image and is tributary to God. What we owe to Caesar, all things political, are within – not apart from – the inclusive loyalty we owe to God. This means that we neither escape God's claims by acting politically, as if politics could take God over, nor leave the political out of the reckoning in the task of being spiritually God's. Being spiritually God's is a close translation of the Qur'ān's own dictum: *Kūnū rabbāniyyīn*, 'Be ye wholly God's men' (Surah 3.79).[18]

It is in these ways that divine sovereignty itself has to be understood in more than static, more than merely judicial, relation to the human vocation. How far we will be from both Bible and Qur'ān if we think of God as some eternal bystander, in celestial immunity from his creation. Were we to think so our very zeal for his transcendence, doctrinally expressed, would have to be seen as a forlorn enterprise, entirely ours, to affirm him. Too often already the sceptic surmises that the Name of God is nothing more than the faithful naming him. Such affirmation, or defence, of God would be hugely ridiculous if not reciprocal to the reality of his relation to ourselves. Atheism, whether as a credal negation or a set of will, is entirely possible. We have to do with a God whose very being, in the sense of human recognition, is left to our consent. Divine being has such a character as to await man's will to love.

IX

But does 'he come running'? Can we go further and say: Divine 'being has such a character as to fulfil man's quest for grace'?[19] Here is the real nub of the question of God: whether there is a reality supportive of the human register of gratitude and responsive to the human search for love. If there is, our worship will not be that of absolute remoteness or unbridled power, for then we would be sycophants, not worshippers. Nor will it be the worship only of all-ordaining law, where being subject would deny our being persons. Exploring in the New Testament what he called 'the disposition of the worshippable', Daud Rahbar wrote:

> The revelation of God in Jesus is the revelation of divine disposition ... the disclosure of a loving, forbearing, forgiving and charitable

disposition . . . Experience of the perfectly loving disposition of God in Jesus Christ is the door to the worship of the true Lord.[20]

Is that Christian persuasion somehow unacceptable to the *taqwā* by which Islam responds to *rahmah*? Need it be? Should it necessarily be seen as unworthy of God, invasive of a due immunity to man? Is God to be thought un-divinely engaged with man in the meanings identified in Jesus as authentically his way with us in the full measure of our need of him? Perhaps the answer has never been more simply put for Christians than by Leo the Great in his Epistle to Flavius.

A condescension of compassion . . . is not a failure in power . . . The form of a servant does not detract from the form of God. There is no unreality in this unity [of God with man] since the humility of the manhood and the majesty of the deity exist in reciprocity . . . The Word performs what pertains to the Word, the flesh what pertains to the flesh . . . The Word withdraws not from his equality with the Father's glory: the flesh does not desert the nature of our kind.[21]

If such be a worthily divine theology, it has brought us from cross-reference to Islam into obligation to all things Judaic by virtue of its ground in Christ.

NOTES

1 Cited in Muhammad Zafrullah Khan, *Gardens of the Righteous* (*Riyād al-Sālihīn* of Imām Nawawī) (London 1974), p. 28.

2 A classicist like Gilbert Murray appreciated that the 'human-ness' of God is essential to any, and all, theism. In his *Stoic, Christian and Humanist* (London 1940), p. 169, he quotes an Arab writer who said that to call God righteous was no less anthropomorphic than to say he had a beard.

3 *Zohar*, 1, 44b, 153b.

4 op. cit., note 1, p. 20.

5 The phrase is frequent throughout the Qurʾān, controlling, for example, both payment in and expenditure from *Zakāt*. Both belief and behaviour have to be 'in the way of God'.

6 Masechet Shabat, 88a.

7 See ch. 3, note 8, and also discussion of the passage by Muslims in, e.g. Kenneth Cragg, *The Pen and the Faith* (London 1985), pp. 24, 119, 172–3.

8   See Fakhr al-Dīn al-Rāzī, *Mafatih al Ghaib al-Mushtahar bi-l-Tafsir al-Kabir*, 8 vols. (Istanbul 1889), V. 432; and wider discussion in Eric L. Ormsby, *Theodicy in Islamic Thought*, Princeton 1984.

9   Karl Barth, *Church Dogmatics*, trans. G. T. Thomson (Edinburgh 1936–81), ii, 2, p. 166; and iv. 2, p. 346.

10 Rudyard Kipling, *The Bride's Progress*. Not the most familiar of Kipling's stories from his India years, but a powerfully ironic tale of a honeymoon tour taking in the ghats of Benares.

11 Al-Bīrūnī (973–1048), of Persian origin, was an eminent scholar, scientist and traveller. His reaction to India can be savoured in Edward C. Sachau's translation: *Alberuni's India*, London 1888 and 1910. See vol. 1, ch. 11 for his allusions to Hindu imagery.

12 He is depicted in the Qurʾān as a breaker of images rather than as a physical progenitor. He breaks statues and when challenged whimsically suggests that in fact they came to blows between themselves (Surah 21.62–3) so that the largest of them smashed the rest. Abraham referred his challengers to the broken pieces to inquire from them! See also Surahs 29.16–26 and 37.83–98.

13 Quoted from S. M. Stern, *Studies in Early Ismāʿilism* (Jerusalem 1982), p. 37.

14 Ignaz Goldziher, *Introduction to Islamic Theology and Law*, trans. A. and R. Hamori (Princeton 1981), pp. 24–6.

15 See chap. 2, note 15, and *Turkish Nationalism and Western Civilisation*, there noted.

16 ibid., p. 216.

17 A forthright example was Arend Van Leeuwen, *Christianity in World History*, trans. H. Hoskins, London 1964. For my part I attempted a rebuttal, at the time, in *Christianity in World Perspective* (London 1968), Ch. 7.

18 See Peter Hinchliff, *Holiness and Politics* (London 1982), p. 5. Hinchliff points out that in five of his works the apologist Tertullian invokes the passage in the sense that the paying of taxes to Caesar is *within* the giving of oneself to God. It is even used as a text about martyrdom in which God receives the fidelity in the death Caesar exacts.

19 John MacQuarrie, *Studies in Christian Existentialism* (London 1966), p. 12.

20 In the *Hartford Quarterly*, vol. 2 (Fall 1961), p. 55. He pleads for a theological sense which does not make rational argument the prior thing but relies primarily on what moves the heart and will. The creativity of a theology depends upon its capacity to meet the soul of any rather than the sophistication of the few.

21 Leo the Great, *Epistola ad Flavium*, 2–4. See E. H. Blakeney, *The Tome of Leo the Great* (London 1923), pp. 26–7.

Messiah and Jewry

5

'He that was to come'

I

Messianic fact may be a theme of lively controversy as to its
recognition or denial. There is no question about the fact of
messianic hope. That its eventuation should be deeply at issue
is eloquent enough of its reality in history as anticipation. If,
therefore, we put 'the coming one' of John the Baptist's query
to Jesus, according to Matthew 11.2, into the past tense, the
words will suffice both Jew and Christian. 'He that was to come'
will stand for everything messianic in Judaic expectation and
vision[1] including even the conviction that 'Messiah' never
comes so that hope, having no 'already', may always be perennial. 'He that was to come' can be read by the Christian as
the glad confession of the identity of Jesus as the Christ. Whatever else divides us we can begin with 'he that was to come'
as a matter of fact and of history. The expectation was real
and really was.

All the anxieties about whether and where in respect of
'Messiah' must be taken back into convictions about whence
and why. Whatever can or does or should obtain about 'him'
belongs in God. Christology is at the heart of all we have carried
forward from previous chapters in 'God and Islam', about
prophethood intensifying into significant biography and about
a human situation where divine Lordship is patiently engaging
with a creaturehood entrusted with divine purposes and meant
for uncoerced response in mind and soul. What we can believe
about 'Messiah' will turn upon what we can believe about God,
the one belief the index to the other, and both involving how
we experience and interpret the human scene. In its deepest
measure the messianic task will be what there must be to make
good a belief in the world-liable God and the God-liable world
– the belief to which theologies of *Magnificat*, the implications
of prophethood and 'zeal', have led us.

Our hope in this chapter is to study what is at stake in the
Judaic-messianic theme, its roots and sequences in biblical history, the Christian confidence about Messiah Jesus and the Jewish dissuasion from it. These demanding areas of scholarship

and mutual tension take us forward in the following chapter into consequences about peoplehood on behalf of God, about election and covenant, the 'Gentiles' and their exclusion or incorporation. These, in turn, leave us, in Chapter 7, with the onus of defining and pursuing a positive relationship of Jew with Christian which strives, in disloyalty to neither, to interpret Jewish continuity and Christian faith-community the one to the other, despite the legacies which attend us all.

II

'Looking for redemption', as Luke's prologue has it[2] (2.38), has characterized the Jewish spirit from Moses to the Maccabees and through all the centuries of the Talmud, however diversely 'redemption' has been understood. The ground of the need for, and hope of, 'the Lord's anointed' lay in that rooted Hebraic confidence that the creation embodied a divine intention and that God was the Lord of history. Faith in God as divinely sovereign over all things, on which all Semitic theism relied, involved a sense of divine relation to them consistent with divine authority. Law, and prophethood to serve it, were clearly part of such consistency and, in the light of their reception in history, some further divine commitment to history, if only *qua* judgement, would seem due to follow. Any theism, as we saw in three earlier chapters, is bound to have this dimension in its thought of God. If it has a retrospect to an act of creative will it cannot dispense with a prospect of creative will to act. Divine agency, in some sense, within events is implicit in divine Lordship over them.

In the Hebraic tradition, however, that corollary of all theism was intensified by distinctive tribal identity and historical memory, whereby God's stake in events was read exclusively in terms of Jewish destiny. There is much that remains mysterious about the sources of the Hebraic interplay of Lordship and peoplehood within which messianic meanings obtain. There is a strange amalgam of who, and whence and where, of the ethnic, the historical and the territorial in their experience. These elements in being and belonging, to be sure, are general enough and in no way strange. Ancestry, memory and soil, with language, make all communities at once human and unique. What is unparalleled about the Hebraic experience of

these denominators is not merely their being celestially credited. Many cultures derived their forebears, their land and
their legend, from the gods. It is that the biblical tradition had
a tenacity and a theme unlike all others. Its Abraham and its
patriarchs were nomads. Its sense of given territory was not
static and natural, but eventful and dramatic. Its memory did
not merely recede into the mists of time and gather round old
haunts and hills; it turned on a trauma of slavery and stood
in the epic of Exodus. They were a people who came to be
who they were, by whence they came and where they attained
and these possessed them of their Yahweh and their Yahweh
of them in a bond of 'chosen-ness' and covenant, sealed in
the mythicized story of Sinai, and perpetuated in the most tenacious collective of which humanity has knowledge.

Some aspects of the price and the entail of this distinctive
self-awareness and the burdens it imposes both for those within
and those outside will concern us in the two following chapters.
The point here is to recognize in 'I will be their God and they
will be my people' the source and condition of messianic yearning. Only if we appreciate its inherent privacy as a perspective
can we measure the radical transformation of the messianic
meaning made in the New Testament. Expectations directed
to God concerning his ends in history were formed and cherished within the retrospect of the Hebraic past and the constraints of the Hebraic present towards the claims of a Hebraic
future. The root-memory of the marvel of the Exodus and the
possession of the land against all odds by a people out of the
wilderness argued both a destiny and a pledged omnipotence
covenanted to it. This furnished a deep well-spring of reliance
when delay or adversity or conscious failure beset their story
or belied their hopes. Sinai and its bond with God dominated
their awareness of themselves and their estimates of times
ahead.

In the broadest terms – omitting here the intricacies in detail
of a tangled study with much scholarly diversity of emphases
– it could be said that Messiahship is the answer due from
God, and for which only God suffices, to the vacancy in history
which waits for it in the pain and perplexity of history's apparent miscarriage if loyally read and lived in terms of divine covenant. When puzzled outsiders asked 'God's people', 'Where
is ... your God?' in respect of vacant, imageless sanctuary,
the reply was that he was in heaven and everything around

on earth was his sanctuary (Psalm 115.2–3). But when taunting
heathen asked it in respect of desolation and defeat (Psalm
79.10), it was for vindication and requital, even vengeance,
that the psalmists prayed from that heaven where God was.
Were there to be no answer to that urgency, no filling of that
aching vacancy; how could God be sovereign and pledged in
faith to them?

Messiah, then, was to be the answer fit for God and adequate
to history. Both concept and confidence wavered and wondered
fearing for the answer lest it should falter or fail, even anxious
lest it should be premature or wanting in the requisites a burdened people variously demanded in their fears and dreams.
Their trauma was the Exile to Babylon, deepening the break-up
of the Davidic/Solomonic splendours, and the demise of the
Northern Kingdom, and bringing into Hebraic experience the
bitterness of a forfeit of the territory and status the Exodus
had inaugurated. Messianic hope became the corollary of everything else in Hebrew faith about God and peoplehood and land
and destiny. Some 'anointed' instrument, agent, or emissary,
of divine provision must be awaited to correct the aberrations
of history and make good the territorial and spiritual realities
of covenant and mercy.

It was natural that hope should draw its imagery from its
own retrospect. David had been the great unifier of the
kingdom, the monarch whose prowess and vision had secured
Jerusalem, and envisaged the Temple. That 'golden age' suggested that a 'son', a 'branch' of David's line and kind, would
renew its glory and security. The kingly Messiah meant a mar-
tial, political saviour, the righteous ruler such as Hezekiah had
been and whose integrity and piety on the throne a coming
one would reproduce.

But the priesthood also had been central to the life of Israel
and Judah and the Temple symbolized all that a right national
future must achieve. So Messiah might be a priestly figure.
Or there might be a double Messiahship to match the royal
priesthood concept in the very being of the nation. Prophets,
too, had their vital role in the story of the past, as seen from
Exile and within it. They had been the mentors, often the
accusers, of kings, and the accusers also of unworthy priest-
craft and ungodly ritual. Perhaps then Messiah would be a
veritable teacher of righteousness, whose authority of word
and character would ensure the Torah-obedience which,

above all else, would be the mark of 'the Lord in the midst'.

Yet this prophet-dimension in the surmises of messianic hope held a puzzling mystery. By its very fidelity and honesty in a setting of frequent obduracy, prophethood had presented a strange image of powerlessness; and how could powerlessness belong with Messiahship? The prophets might well address the courts of power and be counsellors of kings but their vocation to accuse the political order meant that they often incurred its anger. There was among them a tradition of rejection and calamity. Their doctrine of divine requital in adversity sometimes made them seem to be traitors and though the repentance they demanded might well be the prelude to restoration it could hardly of itself ensure it without the political arm which, on one occasion, oddly enabled even the 'Gentile' Cyrus to be named 'the Lord's anointed' (Isaiah 45.1). 'Anointing' for a mission of rebuke, a ministry of words in pain, would seem to be a significance different from 'anointing' to Messianic realism, however shared the single term might be.

Yet perhaps the puzzle of prophethood could hold a disconcerting clue. As suffering became steadily the mark of prophets, and most tellingly of Jeremiah, could it be that a personal travail, bearing vicariously the wrongs of the people, might hold the costly secret of how 'the day of the Lord' might come? What are we to say of 'the suffering servant' of Isaiah 42, 50, 52 and 53, and the meaning of that vision of his 'satisfaction' through the hand of God and the cycle of sorrow? The question is beset with mystery in its own context as well as in the New Testament sequel. The doctrine of the 'remnant', arising from an often disappointed sense that the task of the future might well devolve upon fewer and fewer within an obdurate or listless people, could imply that the messianic hope would live and eventuate only out of loneliness and near despair. If so, such isolation was itself an isolated vision, hardly challenging the explicit assumptions of power and royal-priestly seemliness as alone availing a Messiah from God and proper to Israel.

There were times and situations when the near despair, which thoughts of a remnant and a corporate messianic personality – perhaps even the nation itself in its ideal quality – were set to retrieve, induced instead the apocalyptic Messianism. The godly community amid apostasy must withdraw into austere anticipation until 'the clouds of heaven' disclosed the heavenly figure whose miraculous appearance would alone inaugurate the promised reign. His coming might well be delayed, lest coming before the ripeness of the time, it should pre-date the worst of history's wrongs and so fail their due correction. Thus 'messianic woes' would precede his advent and must be lived through – even paradoxically awaited – to ensure the climax. Such reading of 'the hand of the Lord' might excite a revulsion from its inhibitions and generate a new passion for political zealotry or, by other contrast, a new reliance on Torah fidelity in a day-to-day world one should neither abandon nor defy.

III

To have taken historical bearings of all the foregoing from the first messianic perspective to the time of the Gospels would have been to have its complexities more evident at the price of risking the loss of the central theology which is here our concern. There is, however, one aspect of things messianic which even the briefest of summaries must raise. In what sense was there a universal dimension to the messianic hope? Such a dimension was vital to the Christian welcome to messianic fact in Jesus, and it is clear how that welcome owed much to Hebraic vision. It is important to appreciate how eagerly and wistfully some Jewish measures of Messiah embraced in his benediction the very ends of the earth. Such, for example, was the confidence of Deutero-Isaiah, for whom a salvation restricted to the Hebrews would be to trivialize the grace of God (Isaiah 49.6). Without light to the nations how would Messiah be 'the glory of God's people, Israel'?

Such will for the world was a crucial clue for the Christian future and thus a glad indebtedness. How the hopes of chosen peoplehood can be hopes of, or for, all mankind will occupy our cross-reference in the chapter to follow. There is a fascinating ambivalence within the issue, whether here within messianic hope or, later, within the meaning of a messianic Jesus. Messianic inclusiveness, on the Jewish view, could always bind itself to unyielding exceptionality as its necessary condition. Thus even its most generous self-giving meant a rigorous self-perpetuation. If specialness was on behalf of the human whole, that immunized it from any inward disquiet about exceptionality by taking care, in its own terms, of the one question which might disquiet it, namely: what of 'the Gentiles'? There was still need for discrimination in the very interest of inclusiveness.

Moreover, there were times when the universal emphasis, as for example in the great Psalm 72 about 'dominion from sea to sea', had to do, not with a world's enlightenment, but with a world-wide Hebrew reign of peace and plenty with the nations tributary as vinedressers and ploughmen. Indeed the messianic hope was haunted by what some have seen as the contradictory memories enshrined in the words about 'vines and fig trees'. To be secure beneath them was every man's symbol of national well-being. But there lay within it the gnawing sense that the vines and fig trees of others had been forcibly possessed in the far past of Joshua or similarly regained by later heroes. Uneasiness knew that others in turn, given forceful occasion, could dispossess the Hebrews. Then 'vines and fig trees' despoiled became the prophets' image of divine requital, until, *via* messianic renewal of prosperity, 'Israelites indeed' could come back into their own.[3] In such terms, any sense of the world at large and its relevance to Messiah was essentially self-regarding and its domination a condition of its *pax Hebraica*. It was precisely when fortunes were at their lowest or most critical that salvation was most strongly privatized. As Joseph Klausner, one of the historians of the messianic ideal observed:

> When the political status of Israel was good, its heart was open to receive all the foreigners who would come to join themselves to the people of the Lord. But when its political status had suffered a severe decline and its very national existence was in danger, its heart shrank and became restricted and it began to be fearful of the foreign elements which were striving to devour it.[4]

There is nothing unusual about an open hospitality which has to look to its own capacity to exercise the art and hinge it on its own security. But beneath such honesty lies the still deeper question whether an ethnic and exclusifying collective can ever be what universality asks of those who mean to serve it. A later chapter can face this only after some study of the way in which a Messianism which did break into a de-ethnicized inclusiveness through Jesus was taken, by the Church, to have been achieved in his story.

IV

Messiah according to Jesus – the theme on which we must now embark – whether actual or merely alleged, definitive or indecisive, must be studied against this background with the story as severely condensed. It must be clear that messianic identity is both Who? and How? The person will only be recognizable when what we may crudely call the 'policy' is recognized. The *persona* and the pattern identify each other. Whether Messiah? is a question which will only be answered as the task and the undertaking come together. We must certainly come to Jesus this way in the two shapes of one inquiry. Gershom Scholem, in his monumental study, makes the point in a general, not an explicit, comment:

> As long as it was simply a hope that was projected into the distant future, an affirmation that corresponded to no real experience . . . the Messianic hope remained abstract, not yet concretized in people's experience or demanding a concrete decision. It was possible for it to embody even what was contradictory without the latent contradiction being felt . . . Messianic activity, however, could hardly do this.[5]

What the Gospels believe is that in Jesus things messianic 'correspond to real experience', both in the content of Jesus' teaching and in the climax of his passion. These involve for him concrete decisions which, in turn, evoke and engage concrete decisions about their being messianic on the part of the Church, the community of their recognition. These integral decisions, both his and theirs, take place in a setting of harrowing contradiction in which what is latent becomes explicit and is vitally disclosed in travail and crisis.

The contradictions are familiar enough and stem from all that has just been summarized. The setting in which Jesus lived and moved, from Galilee to Jerusalem, was alive with every form of messianic rumour or surmise – Sadducean worldly realism, zealotry, world-disdaining apocalyptic hope, the Pharisees' sober priorities of Torah loyalty. Expectations, even those of disciples, which could only be fulfilled in being first transformed, beset Jesus on every hand, a fact which perhaps explains his frequent avoidance of the term and his preference for the more enigmatic 'Son of Man'.

But, amid these bewildering contradictions, was there any

'decision' taken – to return to Scholem's word – 'in the concrete'? The decision, the verdict, that 'Jesus was the Christ'
was assuredly taken by the Church. This is not in doubt. There
are those who say that this was the only decision there was.
The Christian Messiahship stands in a *kerugma*, not in an event,
or rather the only event is the fact of the *kerugma*. Messiah-Jesus
stands in the conviction of the Church in a mysterious issue
from his tragic demise, illusory perhaps, compensatory, emotionally intense but not finally warranted by or from Jesus as
he was or how he died. What belief about him history could
warrant for many thus minded is not theirs, or ours, to know
– so tangled and inconclusive is the evidence. What decision(s)
Jesus himself took and whether they could be said to be 'messianic', perceptive historians must forbear to say. The thread of
the story cannot be unravelled, to their satisfaction.

Acknowledging how easily the thread can be lost and how
truly history needs to be perceptive, the conviction here,
nevertheless, is that there was indeed a messianic decision by
Jesus, that it consisted in a conscious response to the gathering
hostility his teaching evoked, that this response was sustained
in filial communion with God and by the light of prophetic
precedent and that it truly generated the cognizance of messianic meaning by which the Church came to be. The prior decision
was that of Jesus, the verdict of his community derivative. It
is every way more credible to derive a Messiah-designating
Church from Messiah-Jesus than to find it in an inventive impulse against all odds and unwarranted in what was prior in Jesus.
There was in Jesus the 'Who' and the 'How' that warranted
the 'Whether' of Messiahship. The faith followed the fact.

That fact-faith situation is, of course, basic to the very nature
of the New Testament. The Gospels are not verbatim reports
or bare registers. They are interpretative portrayals. Their Jesus
is a *persona* within a literary composition drawn from actual
personality. While would-be bare historians (if they can ever
be such) have rightly to ask how the *persona* in the literature
belongs with the personality in the events, if they would be
more than bare historians they have also to ask why and how
the personality should yield, within his most intimate circle,
the *persona* of their composition. For this will be the biggest
fact about the actual history. It is precisely those considerations
about the 'How' of Messiahship which, as we will see below,
dissuade Jewish thought from his recognition, which also

persuaded the disciples and evangelists about 'Who' had been Messiah. In this way the very complexities of New Testament criticism have to be seen within, and not against, the clear decision about both 'Who' and 'How' by which the New Testament lives. Any query, such as those with which study is rightly occupied, asking if the presentation was distorted, has first to ask why it was made. When that prior question is fully faced most other queries take care of themselves.[6]

V

That Messiahship heads into crisis cannot be in doubt since it has to do with God's purposes in a world that is at odds with them. In what way at odds and in respect of what purpose depends on who and how Messiah is conceived to be. There is equally no doubt that Jesus' ministry headed into crisis. Whatever controversies there be, they are not about his being opposed. That the crisis arose from reaction to his teaching and temper is equally evident. It would also seem beyond intelligent controversy that his teaching and character had to do with God's 'Kingdom', with hope and grace, with forgiveness and liberation. These were all messianic themes, however cautious scholarship requires us to be about the terms of the connection. Much of Jesus' teaching could be, has been, paralleled from one school of Pharisees and much else inside and outside the later Talmud. The Christian conviction about him in what we have called the fact-faith situation in no way turns, or needs to turn, on distancing him from things Judaic. Until of late such distancing has been the burden of Jewish comment and estimation.[7] But, for all the intimately Hebraic quality of what he taught, there *were* accents and meanings in which he transmuted or refashioned crucial attitudes in the Judaism of his day. He spoke of God as Father open to all in grace and pardon, rather than as the arbiter of restrictive covenant and a calculus of righteousness. Seeing beyond rules of ritual purity Jesus had a readier mind for the outsider and the fallen. His feel for the outcast or the reprobate in moral terms within the house of Israel foreshadowed a feel for the Gentile outsiders beyond the covenanted mercies. His word proffered a new wine in new wineskins. There was for him a way of redemption, quite other than the elimination of Israel's foes, through a divine openness to sinners.[8]

Whether we call it a christological index or not, there was about his gospel an unmistakable tie with himself, as if the fact of what he was telling of God, and his telling it, and its ground of truth in his assurance about it, and its evident power in human release from evil, meant that 'the Kingdom of God was truly among' his hearers. What might be called 'Jesus' theism' was deeply personal both in its content and its temper with just that interfusing which language about 'sonship' intends. As Martin Buber once remarked: 'If a man has the gift of listening, he can hear the voice of Jesus himself speaking in the late account of the Gospels.'[9] The reference was to the idiom of the Aramaic Jesus spoke coming through the Greek. But characteristic of that Aramaic in Jesus' usage was the divine passive, with its vivid sense of divine action even here and now affirming salvation.

My son, there is One who forgives your sins.
There is One who has numbered all the hairs of your head.
Blessed are those who mourn, for there is One who comforts them.[10]

Jesus behaves and relates, as if he were effectively practising the divine compassion, that it was enfleshed in the ministry to which the reality of it called him.

There is, of course, much else that could be said of how that ministry developed and belonged in time and place. But, holding to the messianic clue so compatible with all the foregoing, we are carried forward to the two further messianic elements of hostility and how it should be faced. This immediacy of the 'Kingdom' in these Jesus-terms was, on several counts, unacceptable because of what it was *not*. It was not nationalist zealotry: nor was it conquering history (whatever that might mean). It was not apocalyptic censure and withdrawal. It had promise and compassion in the present world. It was, moreover, not in all things conformist, nor traditional. Its theme of divine openness and mercy offended those who held rigorously, and perhaps self-bolsteringly, by ritual niceties of synagogue and Sabbath. And, maybe most disconcertingly of all, it was not authorized. Jesus stood outside the schools and the priesthoods and proceeded by the inherent authority of the truths he held irrespective of accredited quotation or official warrant.

On grounds, in the tangle of messianic diversity, of what

he was and what he was not, or, differently phrased, how he was and how he was not, antagomism steadily mounted, fed not only by outright venom but by bewildered prejudice and plain confusion, and counsels of prudence both cautious and callous. It should be clear that there was nothing distinctive in ethnic or religious terms about such emotions of rejection. They characterize all collective mechanisms of obduracy, timidity, prejudice or folly. They constitute what later the evangelist would call 'the sin of the world', endemic, universal, chronic, wherever politics engage with life and religion with challenge.

VI

What was to be done with the enmity? One can hardly deny that it is a messianic question. Should the preacher quit, the prophet abandon his mission, the messenger abort his message? The real prophets had left no such precedent. Should he trim and turn, veer towards a populist pattern, make allies of emerging adversaries? or try to engineer a climax which would precipitate the apocalyptic intervention promised to what, it could be claimed, were messianic woes? How, then, would the messianic consistent with the ministry ever come into its own?

There seems no ground to doubt that Jesus' story headed darkly into a crisis of decision about the gathering rejection, no doubt that he grappled with messianic consciousness increasingly in these terms, no doubt that he sought community with his disciples in the travail of decision. The gospel *in* and *of* Jesus by the constraints of the situation into which it led him would have to become the gospel *by* Jesus in 'the end-thing' which only his decision would attain.

What was it to be? Among all the precedents by which a messianic clue might be discerned, in the measure of the crisis as it was, that of 'the suffering servant' in the later Isaiah would seem alone to be authentic. The line through 'the servant' and the line through Jesus certainly converge in the New Testament. It is both credible and instinctive to believe that they converged in Jesus himself.[11] There are verbal echoes of the words in Isaiah in the sayings of Jesus about the cross. Mark 9.12: 'How can it stand written of the Son of Man that he shall be set at nought?' follows word for word the verdict of Isaiah 53.3: 'We esteemed him not ...' or 'we thought of him as a "nothing-worth"'.

The 'must' in the conversation of Jesus about his suffering is linked closely with a prophetic sense, while 'ransom' recurs in the Isaian and the gospel vocabulary.[12]

It is, in part, the very incredulity such a convergence of idea involved which speaks its authenticity. Suffering as the occupational hazard of prophets was no novelty. But could this be transposed to 'the Messiah'? Any suffering in his case must surely be what he inflicted on Israel's foes. He must be unscathed in order to prevail – which is precisely what the mockers proposed. The cross, as fact, could never be the messianic secret for it totally countered the messianic destiny. Such was the valuation which Jesus quite transvalued.

Nor was this some arbitrary reading, some idle sense of paradox. It was the logic of the renunciation of all other alternatives. More, it was the logic of love itself. The secret of 'the suffering servant' was that evil is not borne away unless it is borne, that evil is not overcome if it is not met and countered in its whole range. If, as many insisted in the 'messianic woes' outlook, Messiah must not come prematurely lest evil postdates him, he must also not come superficially lest evil infiltrate within him. It may well persist beyond him: this is the onus of the Jewish case about 'unredeemedness' to which we come below. But through all such persistence, the principle, the enactment, of its redemption must be thoroughly in hand, known as the messianic secret and achieved in messianic event.

Such principle and such enactment are not present in a purely political Messiahship, vital as politics may be in lesser causes. For what is political and national leaves out of reach the enemies it makes and keeps. 'The suffering servant' healed because by his costly fidelity he ensured truth, mastered evil, vindicated God and released the springs of hope and mercy. By such precedent, deepened by Jesus, we see how in any and every evil situation love must suffer. In suffering it brings the entail of wrong to a stop, absorbs what otherwise would gather evil momentum, and, so doing, commends and transacts the very love of God.

By this light, the whole ministry, teaching and travail of Jesus can be identified as the 'How' of Messiahship and so, *post facto*, the 'Who' of Messiah. The Christian faith lives in such identification. Once made, the identification from 'How' to 'Who' is properly turned around in the glad confession of the 'Who' who knew 'How'. Pattern and person are mutually known.

VII

There are long shelves of books to show that it is readily possible
to put in question this reading of Jesus as the Christ. At every
point there can be alternative readings. We can say that Jesus
was frustrated by his failing of recognition and sought to expe-
dite a compensatory divine intervention by courting arrest. We
can say that he was in fact a political revolutionary who provoked violence and succumbed to it. We can conceive, by contrast, that he was too naive and gentle, caught up in an idealism
all too easily ensnared in tragedy in a world like Caesar's and
the Sadducees'. It may be claimed that he was essentially the
victim of Roman brutality, whether or not abetted by some
Jewish chicanery. Or we can say that there was no Messianism
involved because none is viable on any grounds of God or mankind, messianic promises being inherently ambiguous and their
specifics either elusive or illusory.[13] Or one can say with Rabbi
Heschel that 'history is a circuitous way for the steps of the
Messiah', and cease to try to trace them.[14] This last option would
still leave room for the conviction that the particular history
of Jesus' steps was Messiah's concerted way. However all these
readings may be, there is a sense in which their very presence
in the reckoning leaves us with an act of faith. A Messiahship
somehow made immune from open study, or guaranteed as
if it were not *per se* a theme of faith, would hardly invite to
courage or deserve our trust.

That nascent Christianity received the Christhood of Jesus
as the clue both to God and humanity, and that it believed
it did so by dependable warrant from Jesus in Christhood, is
the crux of Christian theology, with the cross and the resurrection as their sign. What, then, of the painful, searching question
of the Judaic dissent from such conviction? What can we understand about the circumstances of the great state of being
mutually contrary, its constraints and impulses? To what duties
of scholarship, of mind and spirit, do they lead us? What do
we do about the separate continuities, Judaic and Christian,
which perpetuate verdicts of recognition and exemption about
the Messiahship, wonderfully actual or improperly alleged, in
Jesus of Nazareth? In the rest of this chapter some reflections
only, in prelude to the two succeeding chapters in the cross-
reference of Messiah and Jewry.

The Judaic disclaiming of the Christian Messiahship rests on a variety of concerns. Given what we have described, within the New Testament, as a fact-faith situation, the Judaic response was, and is, to disallow the 'fact' dimension. The 'faith' element is undeniable and, as we have said, is vital to the Christian, as indeed to any positive messianic conclusion. Messiahship *per se* stands in recognition. Part of its meaning is that it fulfils hope and hope always has criteria of what it expects. A Messiahship immune from public reckoning would be a contradiction in terms.[15] There have been false Messiahs, most resoundingly of all the seventeenth-century Shabbetai Zvi.[16] Christian messianic faith believed it had the true criteria in the act of acknowledging what it believed to be the fact. To disallow the act of faith is to disapprove the criteria on which it rests. The faith remains intact as something that happened in history but is divorced from 'actual fact'. Instead of the Christian 'fact-faith' situation we have on Judaic ground a 'faith non-fact' situation. The faith was wrong because the fact was not messianic. Being thus returned to the non-messianic fact of Jesus brings us again into all the issues of historical debate just now rehearsed.

On these it is fair to say that Jewish verdicts are as diverse as non-Jewish. Did Jesus claim, or not claim, Messiahship? Can he be implied to have claimed it? Could he have been so without claiming? Jewish scholarship, like any other, is divided about how to handle the Gospels, how to read the relation between the literature and the events. Quite naturally this scholarship cannot disengage from deep emotional tensions arising from factors outside the New Testament. Repossessing in fascinating ways the Jewishness of Jesus, after centuries of disquieted neglect, Jewish scholars have pursued their studies with something of a legitimate *parti pris* as, in their different ways, do Christian and secular academics. The interests of truth and the interests of communities are hard to disentangle. It is not simply facts which are at issue but the very criteria by which they may, or should, be resolved. A welcome to critical scholarship alive to its susceptibilities from community must be the good hope and mutual duty of us all. If we are talking about cross-reference in theology there must surely be mutual reference in other disciplines to common benefit.

VIII

Beyond the fact-faith, faith non-fact, situations as historical

scholarship may probe them, lies a further factor in Judaic disclaimer of the Christian conviction as to 'Jesus the Christ'.
It has to do with universality. Necessarily the messianic
entails the question of Jewry and the rest of mankind. Exclusive and inclusive Messiahship meant an option which any
faith-as-to-fact would bring to the crunch. The 'yea' or
'nay' about the gentile world was crucial to any verdict as to
whether Messiah had been, or should be, identified. And not
only whether his advent would have a gentile reach but
whether their inclusion would be secure and equal or whether
what might accrue to them would be crumbs from the masters'
table. How, further, would messianic inclusiveness relate to
covenant and circumcision? Would an embrace reach out
from Jerusalem to enfold mankind or would wistful nations
have to come to Jerusalem to be enlightened? In a realized
Messiahship what would be the authentic place of the community in which it was realized? How might it relate to its
enlargement?

Sharply nationalist and political Messiahship had its answer
to these questions only by roundly dismissing them. Nor would
apocalyptic Messianism have any time dimension to accommodate them. There were messianic visions which saw the
larger world only as the raw material of Messiah's con-
quests. Or, in the case of Torah-Messianism a necessary selec-
tivity alone could provide the antisepsis needed by a sin-
infected humanity.

The Messiah the nascent Church recognized in Jesus had
a built-in destiny to the world. If the love that bears the evil
is indeed the clue, then Messiah can never be a private saviour,
an exclusive redeemer. The New Testament moves from its
understanding of the cross into a joyful relegation to the past
of the essentials of the discrimination between Jew and Gentile.
'Not for our sins only, but also for the sins of the whole world'
(1 John 2.2), was the conviction of its Jewish leaders as to the
relevance of the cross. There is no doubt that contemporary
Jewry read any such enlargement as a threat and a treachery.
Disclaiming the alleged Messiahship of Jesus, in final perspective, seemed vital to the due and authentic continuity of everything Judaic. This theme leads into tangled questions about
that final perspective – and much else. They are questions better
gathered into the theme of peoplehood and God occupying
Chapter 6.

IX

All that is at stake about 'fact-faith' and 'faith non-fact' – whether reading history or relating to the world – resolves into the fundamental Judaic disclaiming of the Christian Christ on the ground that the world remains manifestly 'unredeemed'. How can the redemption of humanity be said to be achieved, except by a crowd of romantics who have blandly failed to see, or criminally refused to contemplate, the desperate wrongness of the world which Jewry knows too tragically in its own battered and tormented body? Why wrap a legend of victorious love around the gross and chronic evil of all history and pretend we have a saviour and that 'God has reconciled the world'? Messianic actuality must be scorned as a cruel confidence trick unworthy of 'the God of Israel' – if even he is still to be trusted.[17]

Christian theology has here the most urgent of all summonses into relationship, a summons all the more pressing because it rests on a profound misunderstanding. Our first duty is to take the measure of its passion and its vehemence on its own premises and then take on the 'unredeemedness' in the terms in which Christian 'redemption' knows it only too well. This may serve to bring us all to a realism which has disowned both romanticism and despair.

The measure we have to take is everywhere in Jewish writing. Martin Buber's words have often been cited, as quoted by Ernst Simon:

> Standing bound and shackled in the pillory of humanity, we demonstrate with the bloody body of our people the unredeemedness of the world.[18]

In a *Commentary* symposium comes the cry:

> We have been the sin-offering for humanity and we have borne the sins of many. Our very condition indicates in a terrible way our view that man is not yet redeemed. Unredemption begins with us . . . our distinctive gift to mankind?[19]

These, and many other, invocations of Jewish history to disavow redemption must be taken up later as part of the burden of actual relationships today. Here, in the immediate theme of faith about Jesus and Christhood, they merge into the question whether Messiah can ever come, whether the messianic

can ever happen. Or whether an actual, alleged Messiahship
can ever be 'pure' and 'authentic'. 'Unredeemedness' is either
because 'Messiah' was too spiritual or too pretentious. Thus
Gershom Scholem, writing on 'the Jewish categories of redemption within an unredeemed world', avers that Christian
Messiahship 'as a flight . . . sought to escape verification of
the Messianic claim within its most empirical categories by
means of a non-existent pure inwardness'. Thus it understood
redemption 'as an event in the spiritual and unseen realm . . .
in the private world of each individual . . . an inner transformation which need not correspond to anything outside'.[20] Elsewhere he characterizes this as 'a redemption not realised on
earth . . . in soul *and* body'.[21] Such individual salvation 'taking
place now', can have no messianic connotation.[22]

On such a view the messianic hope can never be other than
a hope. Messiah so to speak can never play his hand. In order
that he (or 'the age' or 'the day') may always be awaited, it
or he can never be identified. 'Messianic' means 'futurist'.
Therefore every actual 'Messiah' must be a false Messiah. The
point was very tersely stated by Martin Buber:

> I believe that the world's redemption did *not* become a fact nineteen
> centuries ago. We are still living in a world that is not redeemed.
> We are still looking forward to the real redemption and each of
> us is called to do his part in the work of redeeming the world.
> Israel is the community which retains this purely Messianic expec-
> tation . . . The man who raises Jesus to so high a place ceases to
> be one of us, and if he wants to challenge our faith that redemption
> lies in the future then we go our separate ways.[23]

But, given patience, do we need this sharp concluding rejection
of each other, Jew and Christian? Buber is still speaking of
'real redemption'. But how is it pure, or purer simply by con-
signment to a future we must always await? The Christian too,
emphatically, is 'called to do his part in the work of redeeming
the world'. Realized Christian Messiahship was never said to
be an idle discharge because the redeemer has done all. Quite
the contrary. Paul talked of 'what was lacking in the afflictions
of Christ' (Colossians 1.24) which he must also carry. Repeatedly the letters in the New Testament speak of having 'the
mind of Christ' and 'sharing the fellowship of his sufferings'
(e.g. Philippians 2.5; 2 Corinthians 1.5; 1 Peter 4.13, *et al.*).

It is clear that those who own themselves redeemed must in turn become redeemers, reproducing in their own situations the redemptive principle once for all exemplified in Jesus and the cross. In a strangely anticipatory way 'Take up your cross . . .' is embedded in the gospel story before the cross had been reached by Jesus. This ongoing principle of suffering and redeeming personality, within community of faith, is the perennial pattern, the cross beyond the cross. Far from being an indulgent romanticism, wrapping a halo round an idle self, the faith in Jesus as Messiah meant the utmost realism about redemptions still ahead and the vocation to be part of them.

Such calling to *imitatio Christi* believed itself not only demanded by the great paradigm but truly enabled. It did not hold that Jesus had dealt with all evil quantitatively. That would indeed have been romantic and illusory. One can never already *have* the future and its entail. What faith meant was that he had dealt with it qualitatively, that Messiahship *had* showed its hand, that an encounter had occurred where what could be read as representatively wrong with all humanity had been met and overcome by what could be recognized as representatively Messianic, and that such encounter could be acknowledged as the epitome of what redemption takes. Discipleship to its secret could then be the more conscious, the more adequate, because it could believe itself in possession of the messianic clue, of that power by which in the whole and in the end all evil is redeemed, sacramentalized and sealed in the cross.

Perhaps there is something discernible to interpret this in the nervousness in much Judaic thought about Messiah, to which we have already referred, namely the idea of the 'necessary' so-called 'messianic woes' to precede his advent. These were often thought of as the utmost tribulation of Jewry at the hands of enmity to themselves. But they could also be thought of as the universal acme of evil. Messiah must face the worst and therefore not appear until the worst had arrived. Hence the frequent Jewish confession: 'May Messiah indeed come; but I do not want to see his day.'[24] The same instinct led to the perpetual futurizing of Messiah in the way that we have seen. He could never have finality because history's capacity for evil could never be said to have reached a zenith it might not outdo. On this score – if also on other grounds – realized Messiahship became a contradiction in terms.

What the Christian doctrine does with this criterion is not to think of evil in serial terms, or time-sequence, with an apotheosis necessarily always arguably still ahead (so precluding any feasible Messiah). It thinks instead of evil in expressive, inclusive quality, conspiring as it were to responsive messianic occasion where its essential worst is present and is met in the eminent quality of love. This still leaves us with the reproductive future but saves us from the necessity of being always and only futurist and thereby for ever unpossessed from the past and in turn ungirded for the present because history had held nothing decisive.

The perpetual hope prescript about Messiah has actually led some Jewish thinking into deep reservations about the messianic theme *per se*. Gershom Scholem who knows it so well observes:

> In Judaism the Messianic idea has compelled *a life lived in deferment* [his italics] in which nothing can be done definitively, nothing can be accomplished irrevocably . . . There is nothing concrete that can be accomplished by the unredeemed . . . There is something grand about living in hope, but at the same time there is something profoundly unreal about it.[25]

When hope is only projected without assurance from the past it lacks its most heartening dimension. Some in Judaism would say that this is the burden of an honest realism. With what, for them, is an equal realism the cross has measured, Christians would say that the messianic meaning having been 'done definitively', those who know themselves redeemed thereby have everything 'concrete' to do for that very reason. A redemption by grace is a redemption into hope.

Is 'that which is seen . . . not hope'? Paul's remark in context in Romans 8.24 means that what we have in hand we do not still look for. He does not mean that what we have in hand has no future relevance for which we still look. Hope would only be ended by event, if the fulfilling event were then pure past and did not involve a future, as Christ's redemption does. To have it, is not to dismiss hope as ended like a day gone or a youth passed. It is to kindle hope like a door opened or a pledge begun. In this onward dimension of the New Testament it is right to say that Jesus was Messiah-designate as well as Messiah-actual and only the one in being the other. This future tense, however diversely understood in the trauma, say, of John in Patmos or the 'groaning creation' in Paul's thinking about 'the revealing of the sons of God', kept the Church facing the future but only in the grace that read the past as truly holding the paradigm by which hope received its charter.

How odd to say, two paragraphs above, that for Judaism 'history had held nothing decisive'. Nothing messianically decisive – that, as we have seen, is true. But was there not the Exodus? Is not the gist of Hebraic memory, not to say the deep source of its theology and identity, the fact of that event when 'all our fathers passed through the sea'? The happenedness of the Exodus did not deny the Exodus as expectation. Quite the contrary. 'He brought them out that he might bring them in.' There was hope ahead because there was fact behind. Is it not possible to see messianic event the same way? Indeed the New Testament explicitly does so, speaking of Jesus' 'exodus' at Jerusalem (Luke 9.31) and setting cross and resurrection and Church joyfully within the analogy of the Exodus and 'Christ our Passover' (1 Corinthians 5.7).

In the narrative of Moses' call to his people's liberation in Exodus 3, it would be odd to read the famous words in v. 14 as a philosophic riddle: 'I am that I am.' An enigma would not nerve a reluctant leader nor convey the accreditation of either 'God' or leader (which was what Moses sought in his question) to a despairing, forlorn folk worn down by slavery and sick from hope deferred. No! the words mean: 'I will be there as he whom I there will be.' The God of Exodus is known only in going through Exodus with him. There are no advance guarantees. The proof is in the going. But the great 'I AM' is dependable and when it has happened he will be known *in the event*. Prospect on the nearer side will become perspective on the further side.

The Judaic tradition then in no way excludes divinely definitive action from the sphere of history. It lives by one. It has its own fact-faith equation about the God of 'there and then'. Christian faith sees the 'there and then' of God's Messiah in Jesus as the Christ. It gathers around the cross and hears the Lord say: 'I have been there as he whom I there have been.' Such faith does not romanticize away the unredeemedness of the world but reads it as the measure of the Messiah there had to be.

Peoplehood under God was integral to the experience of the Exodus. So it was also, in new terms, because of the messianic happenedness, as Christianity saw it, of Jesus as the Christ. To community out of event we must now turn.

NOTES

1 Not, of course, overlooking in using the pronoun 'He' the concepts of either dual Messiahship, and a corporate Messiah, perhaps as an 'ideal' Israel. It has also to be remembered that for some 'Messiah' is not a person but an age. Cf. Jacob Agus, 'Messianism is the belief that God will be the ultimate bringer of redemption whether or not He employs a specific person as His agent' (*The Meaning of Jewish History*, vol. 2 [London 1963], p. 470).

2 It is fascinating that Luke, the only Gentile writer in the New Testament, is at pains to include the highly Hebraic material which occupies his first two chapters, where this phrase from his account of Anna is found. His *Magnificat* has clear echoes of the songs of the Maccabees celebrating maternal joy at the exploits of returning heroes, but strangely transvalued by Luke in Mary's salute to the prospect of Jesus. See Paul Winter in *Bulletin of the John Rylands' Library*, vol. 37, no. 1 (Sept. 1956), 'Magnificat and Benedictus: Maccabean Psalms?'

3 The mention of the fig tree in the call of Nathaniel (John 1.49: 'I saw you under the fig-tree'), and the comment about 'an Israelite indeed' echo this idea and suggest messianic expectation as the context of Nathaniel's call. For an interesting discussion of vines possessed from others, dispossessed through others and then permanently secure with no fears or burdened consciences, as a recurrent motif in the Hebrew Scriptures, see Dan Jacobson, *The Story of Stories: The Chosen People and Its God*, London 1983. Also a strong repudiation of Jacobson by Hyam Maccoby in *Encounter*, vol. lxii, 2 (Feb. 1984), pp. 62–7.

4 Joseph Klausner, *The Messianic Ideal in Israel from its Beginning to the Completion of the Mishnah*, trans. W. F. Stinespring (London 1956), p. 134.

5 Gershom Scholem, *The Messianic Idea in Israel and Other Essays* (New York 1971), p. 51.

6 Given, that is, a right willingness for them. It may be well to recall the words of Etienne Trocmé in *Jesus and His Contemporaries*, trans. R. A. Wilson (London 1973), p. ix: 'Most of those who set out to enlighten their contemporaries about the prophet of Nazareth have not the slightest idea of the technical complexity of the preliminary studies which they ought to undertake before ever setting pen to paper. As for those who have undertaken this task of documentation and criticism with the seriousness which it requires, they are rarely brave enough to admit to themselves that the results they have achieved are so complex that their final synthesis includes a great deal of arbitrary simplification.'

7 e.g. Ignaz Maybaum, *Trialogue between Jew, Christian and Muslim* (London 1973), p. 154: 'Jesus has no place in the world of the Jew.' It might be

said that the Talmud began this 'distancing', though its references to Jesus are so slight that perhaps it is truer to say that Jesus was never really encountered by Jewry in general. The Talmud had a negative bias about Jesus through encounter with the Church. He was the illegitimate son of a soldier, learned magic in Egypt, was legally executed, and his body was stolen by his disciples who invented the story of the resurrection. His teachings were evil and he was 'a deceiver of Israel', and Judeo-Christians were 'traitors'.

Foremost in recent Jewish scholarship about Jesus is Geza Vermes, *Jesus the Jew* (London 1974), and *The Gospel of Jesus the Jew*, Newcastle 1981.

Vermes immerses himself ably in the academic issues around the New Testament and sees Jesus as posing no threat to Jewish institutions. But he ignores the crucial interplay between belief in Jesus among his disciples and the understanding of his personality.

8   These points are well and sensitively studied in John Riches, *Jesus and the Transformation of Judaism*, London 1980.

9   Quoted in David Flusser, *Jesus* (New York 1969), p. 38.

10   This 'divine passive' occurs around one hundred times in the sayings of Jesus. The Aramaism was a veiled and reverent way of referring to divine action.

11   C. R. North, in *The Suffering Servant in Deutero-Isaiah* (2nd edn Oxford 1956) traces these parallels convincingly. See also James Moffatt, *The Theology of the Gospels*, p. 149: 'The suffering servant concept was organic to the consciousness of Jesus and he often regarded his vocation in the light of this supremely suggestive prophecy.' On Isaiah 53, H. Wheeler Robinson remarks: 'That which explains the faith of the disciples might with equal justice be used to explain the shaping of the conviction in the mind of their Master' (*The Cross in the Old Testament* [London 1955], p. 101).

12   Among those who are doubtful of this view see Morna Hooker, *Jesus and the Servant* (London 1959); and C. F. D. Moule, *The Birth of the New Testament* (London 1962), pp. 81–3.

13   The alternatives are bewildering. Joseph Klausner, *Jesus of Nazareth: His Life, Times and Teaching*, trans. H. Danby (London 1945), finds Jesus a nationalist, with no concrete plan and frustrated by his people's failure to recognize him. He was crucified through a Sadducean-controlled Sanhedrin lest his pretensions should provoke the Romans and bring Jewish interests into jeopardy. A. A. Kabak (d. 1944) in a major Hebrew novel, *Bamish ol haTsar*, saw Jesus a pensive soulful non-radical, while H. Hazaz (d. 1973) saw him as a non-resistance activist dying as a peace-loving martyr in the tradition of Jewish immolation which culminated in the Holocaust. L. Kochan, however, in *The Jew and his History* (London 1977), rejects such self-immolation in the Judaic spirit and sees the messianic as a cherished memorializing of past redemptions, especially the Exodus. In such inherently Jewish feeling there is little significance in Jesus. Hyam Maccoby, by contrast, in *Revolution in Judea, Jesus and the Jewish Resistance* (London 1973), sees Jesus as in fact Barabbas, a nationalist revolutionary, whom the Gospels misrepresent as opposed to the Jewish religious authorities.

With an anti-Jewish slant the disciples and evangelists turned Jesus into a pacifist and an other-worldly figure. We now have to read the Gospels for the real facts they do not altogether conceal beneath their fantasizing.

14 Abraham Heschel, *God in Search of Man, A Philosophy of Judaism* (London 1956), p. 238.

15 Unless one opts for a 'hidden' Messiah and so withdraws everything into mystery and enigma. The point here about Messiahship being 'open' is not to say that it may not stand in and proceed by criteria which are unperceived by the responding or rejecting 'public'.

16 See the definitive study by Gershom Scholem, *Sabbatai Sevi, The Mystical Messiah, 1626–1676*, Princeton 1973.

17 For this 'proviso' see ch. 7 where the issue of post-Holocaust faith, the meaning of Jewish experience and the significance of Zion/Israel, will come in the context of Jewish/Christian meeting today.

18 Quoted in Ernst Simon in *Jewish Frontier*, vol. 15 (Feb. 1948), p. 26, 'Martin Buber: his Way between Thought and Deed'.

19 *Commentary* (New York, August 1966), p. 120.

20 Gershom Scholem, *Messianic Idea*, op. cit., pp. 1–2.

21 Gershom Scholem, *Sabbatai Sevi*, op. cit., p. 94.

22 See E. E. Urbach, ed., *Types of Redemption* (Leiden 1968), p. 12.

23 Quoted from M. A. Beek.

24 Often said by the faithful in the early centuries of diaspora.

25 *Messianic Idea*, op. cit., p. 35. This awareness of an inability to do 'anything concrete' because one is living in hope makes for a certain paradox, in the same study, when 'concreteness' is alleged as the quality lacking in, and so disqualifying, the Christian messianic.

6
Peoplehood and God

I

The words 'children's children', it has been noted, occur nowhere in the New Testament. In the Hebrew Scriptures of the Bible children and their children find mention almost fourteen hundred times. 'From generation to generation' is the cry of psalmists about enduring truth. The Hebraic sense of God is unfailingly interfused with their sense of themselves as God's from the womb. Divine mystery and ethnic identity are deeply mutual. The worship of the Lord proceeds within an insistent awareness of community. There is God and there are his people in what must truly be described as the most tenacious exchange of bonds known within human conviction. In being Jewish birth itself is belonging: being is to be conceived within the holy 'seed'. The vital conjunction in theology is not, as in Islam, 'God *and* his Prophet': it is 'God *and* his people'.

In what Christians call the New Testament there occurred within this most insistent of all particularities a strange and disconcerting relinquishment of this powerful privacy with God, happening on the part of insiders who had hitherto assumed it loyally. They were moved by the implications of what they were persuaded was the Messiahship of Jesus. Their impulse to feel and to pursue a different inclusiveness in which Gentile might freely share with Jew is the very clue to the newness they discovered and from which their literature drew its name. The sense of vocation and destiny which belonged with their Jewish identity they passionately retained but they saw it, as it were, out of copyright and capable of being shared by all, on the sole ground of faith, without prerequisite of birth or culture. This open peoplehood for God they called 'the Church'.

What, then, of peoplehood and God? What do we say, in our related faiths, about these contrasted patterns of community, the corporateness of historic Israel and the incorporation in Christ? How do we reckon with the implications they hold the one for the other? What might frank cross-reference mean, moving from our study of Messiahship into the Judaic and the

Christian in the human whole as identities within society? The themes here may present a certain parallel to the earlier reflection on the capacities of prophethood. Is there a logic which suggests that just as prophethood arguably moved beyond itself into servanthood and 'sonship', and the 'messenger' become the 'message', so peoplehood in the flesh pointed beyond itself, by its very meaning, to a peoplehood in faith? Can we rightly think of an enlargement of divine employment such as the corporate Church believed itself to be? Or is the peoplehood that educated the world in the privilege of divine employ rightly at odds with how the lesson was learned in the obedience of Messiah Jesus?

That the questions and the emotions they arouse are difficult and lively must keep us alert and sensitive. Some of the more strenuous aspects will come in Chapter 7. The main task here is to explore Judaic self-awareness as identity, the Christian meaning of 'church' and the Jewish response to it. These concerns lead into some reflections on the quandaries of Judaic specialness and of Christian peoplehood and thence into a theology of corporate identity. How can we wisely, truly, credibly, speak of God as 'ours' and of 'ourselves' as 'his'?

II

Claud G. Montefiore, one of the early pioneers of modern Jewish/Christian studies, once cited Paul in Galatians 3.26–8: 'In Christ . . . there is neither Jew nor Greek', and asked whether we could substitute 'In God' for 'In Christ'?[1] It was a telling question. The Christian would answer: 'Yes, indeed!' But he would mean 'God in Christ' – the Christ being for him where God in fact universalizes his grace. Making a point which echoes throughout Jewish thinking, Montefiore saw Paul's as still a conditional universalism.[2] A truly practical universalism, Montefiore thought, would be found without any implied 'abolition of Judaism' or rejection of Christianity, if the formula 'in God' were agreed. There are surely many, in this yet more 'ecumenical' time, who would readily concur.

Yet 'in God there is neither Jew nor Gentile' is exactly what historic Judaism cannot say. For there is, by divine intention, a radical distinction in the relationship of Jews to God and that of all the rest of mankind for whom the term 'Gentiles' is necessary. All humanity is within the Noahid 'covenant' of seedtime and harvest, one in the Adamic creaturehood. It would be inconceivable to think otherwise, since manifestly family and territory, kin and kind, belong within all diversities. There is no discrimination of sunlight and rainfall, night and day, wind and water, except in the vagaries of climate and locale. Philistia, Samaria and Judea have normally the same weather.[3] The New Testament's accent on being 'children of God' by faith implied no disinterest in the human family and the common trust of parenthood.

Not all humanity, however, gathered at Sinai. Only Israel did, in all its generations. The covenant of Sinai was with 'the children yet unborn' (Deut. 29.15: 'him that is not here with us this day'). 'This day', says Deuteronomy 27.9, referring to Sinai, 'thou art become *the* people of the Lord thy God.' Montefiore's formula embodies deeply and hopefully the concern in the quarters he symbolized for a genuine equality of all mankind. Some even indicate an embarrassment that it should not be so. But, conceptually and practically, the otherness exists and is decisive. On all the assumptions of the Hebrew Scriptures through all their vicissitudes from the patriarchs to the Talmud, it emerges clearly that 'in God there is Jew and there is Gentile' radically distinguished.

As we saw in studying the background of the messianic hope in Israel, the components of identity were those of all peoples – ancestry, history, memory, folk-story, territory, and language. That these should be common goes with human creaturehood. It is the meaning the Hebraic mind and spirit gave to their cherishing of these which totally and tragically distinguished them from the rest of human creaturehood. The distinctiveness is sharply reinforced by the reception it has encountered in the human context where even the most assured separateness cannot fail of reciprocity.

If our sense of what it has meant reciprocally is central then the theme can only be explored in a yearning compassion both ways, in respect that is of Jewish suffering and travail and Gentile inferiorization. We shall need to relate peoplehood and God in a way that does justice to the universal incidence of the one, in nature and history, and to the inclusive mercy of the Other, in grace and truth. This will exclude that sheer arbitrary dogmatism caught in the jingle: 'How odd of God to choose the Jews!' – a sentiment which begets other jingles: 'Rejoice! the choice annoys the Goys' (*goyīm* = pagans), or: 'Could God his nod these Jews refuse?' The mystery deserves better than to be trivialized either by bland assertion or cheap banter. God and the arbitrary cannot well conjoin. How, we must ask, did this tenacious quality of Hebraic self-definition arise, to what conclusions does it point as to peoplehood on behalf of God, and into what was it being invited by the New Testament?

III

The first of these questions can only have a descriptive answer. What patriarchal history owes to Deuteronomic prophethood, and both to Rabbinic interpretation, still engages and in part eludes the scholars. But description, as distinct from explanation, centres on tribal identity, sanctioned in history, and nurtured in Torah. All these are seen and experienced as divinely warranted in exclusive sense, whether by *a* God uniquely theirs in monolatry, or by *the* only God unilaterally engaged with them and theirs. This engagement related them to other nations, as émigrés from slavery inflicted, as lawful entrants to territory otherwise inhabited, as witnesses against the heathen, as sufferers from imperial oppressors, as puzzled exiles, and through all these tutors and mentors for the one God because of whom, according to the Abrahamic promise, the nations at large could 'congratulate themselves'.[4] Their developed sense of unique destiny always had that relevance as they saw it to the world in general. In a strange, and still loaded, paradox it was just this *noblesse oblige* which saved them from self-reproach about others while maintaining the reproach implied of others in an abiding exclusion from *noblesse*. Theirs was a sustained insistence on the dictum that 'It is more blessed to give than to receive'. In tragic irony the 'blessedness' of being on behalf of all mankind by such necessary exemption from them has been a frequent travail of distress.

The theme of being Jewish from the womb, of being born to be God's, found powerful expression in the writing of Franz Rosenzweig earlier this century. He had felt deeply the fascination of Christian faith but, in an intense experience in a Berlin synagogue, renewed his Judaic loyalty. Emphasizing that 'Christianity must proselytize', because one cannot be born Christian, he saw the Jew by contrast as 'the product of a reproduction' who 'attests his belief by continuing to procreate the Jewish people'. Whereas Christianity is 'a way' which one must take up by personal faith, Judaism is 'a life' which one possesses by birth in

> the eternal self-preservation of procreative blood ... through shutting the pure spring of blood off from foreign admixture ... Descendant and ancestor are thus the true incarnation of the eternal people, both of them for each other ... We experience our Judaism with immediacy in elders and children.[5]

Though stated starkly and with passion there is no doubt that he voices things Judaic truly. It might be said, of course, that most faiths are an accident of birth, in that vast numbers in every religion have never conceived and certainly never exercised an option to be otherwise. Parents, as Muslims are prone to say, make us what we are. But, at least in the case of Christianity as denoted by the New Testament, there is a necessary 'becoming', a personal exercise of faith before belonging is authentic. Family may be a salient factor but does not of itself constitute discipleship.[6] By the second century, 'the Fathers' and 'Patristic theology' were familiar terms in the Church. But these were in no way 'patriarchs' whose blood stream was the clue to identity. They were mentors in the affirming and defining and commending of the faith into which every generation was invited to enter by its own volition. Paul, according to 1 Timothy 1.2, and Philemon 10, could even refer to Timothy and Onesimus as 'sons' of his (though Timothy was half-Greek), using birth as a metaphor for the fruit of faith.[7]

In the Judaic tradition it is the other way round. This is not to say that faith in the meaning of 'birthright' is absent; quite the contrary. But it is a faith about what is biologically a fact. Peoplehood for God as understood in this Hebraic conviction is 'in full physical reality' which 'goes through history ... as a covenant community completely distinct from all other nations'.[8] The paradox involved here of 'the renegade Jew' who disowns Torah and yet is inalienably within birth-covenant will concern us later. There is paradox in most religion.

Jewish voices have been raised to challenge this reading of a born people of God. Jacob Agus, for example, deplores what he calls Rosenzweig's 'racial mystique ... as unJewish as it is false'. He cites the Judaic welcome to proselytes in the period of the Mishnah and the Talmud but does not reckon with the truth that in Jewish law the self-confessed proselyte has no parents.[9] It seems clear that in the consensus of all the centuries there has been a far greater theme of ethnic privacy in Jewry than a universal openness. Raphael Loewe writes:

> To accept the notion of the divine choice of Israel and of Israel's corollary obligations carries with it certain consequences of ethnic demarcation between Jew and non-Jew. There may be room for debate as to the exact social implications of such demarcation, but about the propriety of ethnical separation itself there can be no argument, unless the terms 'Israel' and 'Jew' – for rabbinic purposes of course synonymous – are to be redefined.[10]

That verdict is echoed in many quarters. Buber wrote in *Two Types of Faith* about Sinai and 'the hereditary actuality of faith'.[11] Ignaz Maybaum quotes Rosenzweig with approval, sustaining him by what Maybaum takes to be the sense of Ezekiel 16.6: 'In thy blood live.'

> No conversion can transform a gentile into a Jew, no anathema can exclude a Jew from his Jewishness. Jewishness has no door through which Jews can get away from their Jewish existence and none which could let gentiles enter the intimacy of the common Jewish bond.

He disclaims, however, that this emphasis on 'blood' is 'racialism' since what is holy is not blood but God's promise. Even so,

> The election of the Jewish people is not a mere belief, a mere doctrine or – least of all – a mere idea. It exists in brute actuality. We can see the actuality of Jewish election at work as we see the dark skin of a negro or the colour of a person's eyes.[12]

The wise student will do well to keep always in perspective the experiences out of which the Judaic conviction of born-specialness speaks and the adversities against which it reacts. But the same wisdom will need to reflect on how far the adversities are reciprocal to the claims. Both cast us back on to the issue as to what manner of people is consonant with the nature of God and the human situation. But there are other aspects of exposition which are necessary first.

IV

The first of these is the concept of 'the Gentiles'. The Jewish impulse to think of humanity inclusively – an impulse which

had many rich manifestations – was somehow always checked
by the belief that it was precisely the pro-human mission which
demanded the separatist privacy. It was as if the Jewish mind
had a built-in mandate to stand apart from the non-Jewish
world as the vital condition of taking note of it. Essential apartness, as it were, had a 'universal' reason. This broadly has
meant that universal humanity could never be thought of without the Jew/Gentile contrast. Salt must retain its saltness if
it is to avail for salty tasks.

Yet if this metaphor is transferred from the ethical to the
communal, from the moral to the 'national', its antiseptic concern (if we may so speak) means an otherness which is also
a rejection, in the form of radically contrasted status and capacity. This is more than the disparities which exist multilaterally
between cultures and races in their several varieties. It is a
unilateral dissociation from *all* others who, by that dissociation
alone, are denominated 'Gentiles'. Is there any other corporate
self-consciousness which requires the whole human family to
be defined by a single contradistinction?

It seems right to trace this sense of things back historically
to the entry into Canaan, where the idolatry of the local tribes
legitimated the conquest, at least as interpreted by the chro-
niclers. The rejection of peoples was within the rejection of
gods. Conversely Yahweh's sole authority married with his
people's victory. The covenant of Sinai itself, though freely
from God's intention, was said by some to have been previously
offered to other tribes and refused.[13] When Israel itself was
guilty of idolatry Deuteronomy (32.21) drew a parallel between
that provocation of the Lord and the people's 'provocation',
by alien people, thus aligning idols with pagans. Thanking God
that one 'is not as these Canaanites or Philistines' is earlier
than thanking God that 'one is not as this publican'. Is it more
dubious in being a matter of race than of character? How subtle
for all of us are our principles of disapproval. Do we have to
assume that only those who are Judaic are also truly monotheist? There have been those who so averred.

It is important always to remember that Jewry saw covenantal
status and election as wholly gratuitous on the part of God.
Deuteronomy 7.7–8, is often cited in this connection. God made
common cause with his people for no reason of their number
or worth, but solely for his love's sake.[14] This sincere disowning
of merit and pride meant, however, that there was an abiding

bond, a mutual contract which bound God as well as people. Both parties had obligations. The divine love was 'disinterested' in the circumstances of choice but not in the intention of will. This conviction as to the unconditionality of election has been the deepest theme and the heaviest burden of Jewish theology. But through all its history from first to last, from Sinai to Auschwitz, it has made 'a people dwelling apart' and a theology dwelling there with them.

There is no need here to set out the several sanctions of Jewishness in contradistinction to 'Gentiles' – the Sabbath, circumcision, the dietary laws and the ritual and social forms of avoidance which either incurred or devised the ghetto. These are familiar enough and, with them, that painful burden the Jew feels of being, perhaps, accepted as human (at least in some post-Enlightenment times) but never truly as a Jew, or being required to choose, as Zionism alleges, between either persecution or assimilation, and therefore never free to be fully himself, to exist authentically without 'gentile' leave. Some of the contemporary aspects of this situation will concern us in Chapter 7. But the fullest reckoning with them all reveals that by a strange paradox the 'Gentile' is necessary to being Judaic. 'We Jews', wrote A. S. Steinberg, 'cannot write them off with the empty and vacuous insult "anti-Semites". Of them we must say: "If they did not exist, we would have to invent them"'.[15] There is much in the cynic's definition: 'The Jew is the victim of the anti-Semite.' Before thinking further into the implications of this dark and tragic paradox of an identity of which inward conviction finds itself vindicated in those who most bitterly oppose and oppress it, we must study how a new interpretation of identity awaited it in the New Testament, how the invitation was regarded and why Judaic peoplehood disallowed the rewriting of the mystery of God in human partnership.

V

That the New Testament lived by a quite radical revolution in how the pronouns 'he' and 'we', that humans might use about God and themselves, would signify is not in doubt. 'In Christ there is neither Jew nor Greek', it declared, in the same breath in which it said 'there is neither male nor female'. This makes it clear that Jewry was in no way being excluded or invited into demise. Clearly the Church was no sexless society like a community of snails. Male and female blessedly persisted. The point of saying 'there is neither male nor female' is that in respect of the fellowship the distinction, still in being, has no significance. Likewise with 'Jew and Gentile'. The Church understood itself as a body in which this most resolute of human distinctions had been quite transcended. Both were equally called into a bond with God and between themselves in which all their continuing identity would find a unity.

There was a sense in which distinction continued as historical memory and contributory gifts. The Epistles still spoke of both categories in the very words which united them. It was not a matter of elimination but of fusion, though – as we shall see – in Jewry's estimate these were assumed to mean the same thing. The coming of both to be one – what Ephesians 2.14 called 'breaking down the middle wall of partition' – was later told in the Creed in the eloquently simple phrase: 'who, for *us men* and for our salvation came . . .' for us humans, that is, comprehending a whole humanity in the confession of the divine initiative, so that no distinctions needed to be stated even in being denied.

This inclusiveness in Christ explicitly suspended the old priority of birth. The 'becoming' of which it spoke was accessible to all and was not 'of blood, nor physical reproduction, nor human generation' (John 1.12). It was also non-territorial. It did not require the land-based character which was the dimension of the Judaic. While Galilee and Jerusalem saw its origins its sense of community was quickly peripatetic, carrying its meaning and its embrace beyond sacred places into the dispersion. Its scattered character was in fact its insignia. There was a sense, further, in which Christ became what the Temple had been in the old dispensation. 'The temple of his body' meant the living organism of those, of any race and colour, who came to be 'in Christ' by faith. This incorporation was as accessibly human as the natural inclusion – as the phrase went – 'in Adam', that is, in the single creaturehood into which common, as distinct from particular, birth ushers us all. The Eucharist, or Lord's Supper, of the new community meant a reach of table fellowship which dietary laws forbade.

These radical new developments in the long alienation of Jew and Gentile owed much to the interpenetration of things Judaic and Greek, Judaic and Roman, in the contemporary world. There were many examples, in the two centuries on either side of the rise of Christianity, of exceptionality negotiating, as it were, with prudent mutuality. But essentially the shape and range of the Christian newness stemmed from the fact-faith about Messiahship studied in Chapter 5. It was the 'How' and the 'Who' as to Messiah, as resolved in Jesus, according to the fact of Christian faith, which generated the revolutionary new beginning. 'Drawing all men' to himself because of 'being lifted up', was how the evangelist understood the mind of Jesus (John 12.32). 'All' did not mean a universally successful salvation, as if the human will had no responsive part and no decision to make. It meant a universally accessible salvation, with none already exempted.[16] The Epistles of the New Testament in their wide incidence constantly celebrate this openness and demonstrate the capacity of 'Gentiles' to fulfil by dint of grace the qualities of character which were the intention of the ancient law. The pastoral life of the Church sought amply to prove that, far from wasting 'pearls on swine', or risking the precious ethic of the Torah among the uncouth, the gospel was in fact achieving – ritual rules apart – the moral vocation of man. It was Messiah crucified who inspired this pastoral expectancy among the hitherto 'unseeded'.[17]

And not only Messiah crucified. What subsequently came to be active in the open, hopeful hospitality of the Church goes back clearly to the teaching of Messiah-Jesus. It echoed at times his very words.[18] The Church translated the moral expectation Jesus had of 'outcasts from Israel' in ethical terms into its own expectation about 'outcasts from Israel' in the ethnic sense. The 'renegade Jew' and the 'righteous Gentile' had long been a puzzle for rigorous theory about 'election'. That apart, there was a strong inference in Jesus' sense of God's effective mercy for publican and prostitute (Jewish ones, that is) as to the same mercy effective for Gentiles. If 'mercy could rejoice against judgement' in the moral case of the former it could equally rejoice against exclusion in the ethnic case of the latter.

So much would seem to be evident from the practice of Jesus, restricted as his own immediate ministry was, for the most part, to Jews and geographically to Palestine. It is not easy to read the Gospels aright on this point. There are restrictive passages and implications which, it might be argued, are the more significant for the fact that a Church might have been minded to suppress them. There are also passages which anticipate worldwideness ahead, which, no doubt, some would want to accredit to the later perspective.[19] Perhaps a more credible commentary on both sets of verses, given the premise of honesty, would be that both are comprehensible within the tensions of Messiahship in process which we have already explored.

When faith in Jesus as Messiah became a fact of the (new) situation it was felt to involve this readiness for the world in an equality of all. What is noteworthy about this conviction was the spontaneous way in which it came about. Though Paul became the main theologian and architect in both energies and interpretation, the initiatives seem to have been those, first, of obscure disciples of Cyprus and Cyrene (Acts 11.20) who remain nameless. Antioch, the city where they did so, itself coined the new name *Christianoi*, to designate that new thing, a fellowship which was neither Jewish nor Gentile but shared between them. The name was uncannily apt, as wit in jest can often be. It fastened on the salient fact within the novelty, namely the Christ and his reconciliation. If it was a pagan intuition which found it odd or ludicrous, Judaic intuition had reactions about an oddness far more disturbing. To these Jewish responses to a Messiah/mankind equation in these terms we must now pass. To see that equation thus through Jewish eyes is to discover its nature still further. It is also to be caught in the most exacting issue in biblical theology. For the question of peoplehood requires us to wonder whether the Bible is truly a unity at all.

VI

It is certainly bound within two covers but the heirs of the Scriptures from Genesis to Malachi found strong inward reasons for finding against the faith-community which belongs from Matthew to the Revelation of John. It is important to realize that those reasons did not turn on what so tragically came to dominate later times, namely responsibility for the crucifixion. That event was always seen as 'the sin of the world'. It was not 'who' crucified, but 'what'.[20] The words of Jesus himself told this (Luke 23.34). Even when the earliest preaching as presented in the Acts narrated the event it was emphatic in that very context about the inclusion of all in its forgiving reach.

It is true that when tensions sharpened over Messiahship, reserved for the Jewish future, or heralded as the Christian present, these created animosity especially over the middle ground of undecided folk, suspected and pressured as either 'crypto-Jews' (because they inclined towards Jesus and the uncircumcised) or 'crypto-Christians' (because they hesitated about the Eucharist and gentile/Torah questions). Such 'hesitants' were the occasion of a tug-of-war which forced latent issues into anxious strife, the more so when 'anti-Jewish' verdicts about Christians deprived them of the protection of a *religio licita* and exposed them to mortal danger. The Gospel of John is plainly influenced by these aspects of a living situation of prolonged and bitter strain.[21]

Through and beneath all these enmities of circumstance, however, the Judaic aloofness from the new Christian option turned on interior convictions which persist into the exchanges of today. Israel saw the Church as disqualified by its deliberate forfeiture of the very categories which 'made' Jewry. It had no ground in 'seed' and 'organic peoplehood'. It had no territorial home. On both counts the very founding principle of Israel was impugned. It was either romantic or pretentious or both to think that community for God could be constituted without the indispensables of the Hebraic heritage, which anyway already existed and were never to be paralleled or superseded. By its faith in covenant and election, Judaism evaluated all else. To take the point of Christianity, then and since, would mean to call in question the very stuff of self-awareness. Such conclusions were reinforced by the belief that the new universality was a pseudo thing, merely substituting a particularism of faith for that of birth. The need for differentiation must persist. It was not feasible either for God's due worship or for Jewry's due fulfilment that the Gentiles should in this Christian way be no more identified as such. The Christian idea of church-community had radically misread the very clue it believed it had inherited, namely corporate instrumentality on behalf of God. That instrumentality necessitated, unchanged and inviolate, the organism which, long ago, it had once and for all acquired. Israel's 'election was God's experiment', and, as such, must be pursued intact.[22]

This cumulative verdict of the Judaic mind about the new departure, the Church, covered the decades when, paradoxically, Jewry both vigorously turned outward to the world and passionately turned in upon its own privacy. The destruction of Jerusalem in 70 AD deepened the exclusivism of the school of Shammai and gave it wider currency in the diaspora. Yet the diaspora had drawn some Jewish ventures of relationship, *via* the synagogue into something almost resembling what, on different premises, the Church became. It is fair to conjecture that the Church took over, or drew off, instincts of outreach Judaism appreciated but failed to maintain, and that by so doing, on those different and seemingly threatening premises, the Church stimulated emotions which ensured its own rejection. If so, the paradox involved only places the Church squarely within the mystery of Jewry's engagement with itself. Was it, figuratively, but in truth, the Gentiles with whom Jacob wrestled at the fords of Jabbok?

VII

If the Gentiles, both as a concept and a presence in the world, fill that role in the drama of Jewish destiny, then the Christian reception of them into a new version of that Judaic destiny made the wrestling all the more tense and passionate. Not least among the strains, if we leave the one analogy for another, was what Gentiles, learning *via* the Christian gospel to be God's people, birth and nation notwithstanding, in fact did with the tuition, precisely in guise of birth and nation, by a wilful arrogation to themselves of a Judaic style 'chosen-ness'. This remains one of the sharpest problems of a cross-reference theology. For it indicates how the plea of election can be suborned in apparent emulation of the Jews, and it also spells the capacity of a gospel of race-and-nation-transcending peoplehood to be overridden by nation and by race.

It is daunting to study how self-styled 'chosenness', distorting both Judaic and Christian conditions of 'election', has generated the most virulent forms of race-and-nation self-assertion. The most evident modern example is the apartheid system in South Africa, so many aspects of which fit exactly into the old Hebraic pattern. There is even the crossing of the rivers in the great trek, emulating Joshua's entry into a 'promised land', where the inhabitants were evil because they were pagan and where rigorous differentiation of races, prohibiting intermarriage, was mandatory. In such terms an assumed destiny of peoplehood under God can go desperately wrong. Yet it was nourished by the devotions which read the Psalms and, with their comfort, also recruited their sentiments of confrontation. With his intense piety Oliver Cromwell did the same. In all such cases the authority of the Christian gospel and *its* peoplehood dimension ought to have vetoed the pride of race and power. Does the fact that it quite failed to make good its inclusive church-concept, or even to have its betrayal consciously understood and confessed, prove the Jewish charge against that concept as sheer 'romanticism'? Does it mean that gospel and Church in the Christian order too loyally held to the heritage it had dramatically revised and too readily assumed the unity of its double-testamented Bible? Or does the whole story merely demonstrate that, where race and politics proceed, religion either connives or withdraws? The history of 'the new world', from Massachusetts Bay Company onwards, with notable exceptions like John Eliot, presents the same features and so underlines the same questions.[23]

There is a still more tragic paradox about the way Judaic peoplehood has been read by others, the tragedy of which has inflicted great tribulation on Jewry itself, namely a perverse transference of exceptionality. Fyodor Dostoevsky suffices for example – the more painfully for his profound insight into grace. In his novels there is a deep antipathy to Jews whom he dubbed *Zhids*, a scurrilous word. Yet he cherished an intense belief in the 'messianic' Russian people. The two intensities were one. The thesis, so deep in the Hebraic, Judaic, Zionist, tradition that there can only be 'one' – single in 'chosenness', took form for him in the insistent exceptionality of Russia, destined to unique vocation in the world. Russianism was, in effect, Dostoevsky's 'Judaism' and it was for this reason Jews had to be despised. Hostility was the psychic necessity in role-displacement. In *The Devils*, a character, Shatov, declares:

> If a great nation does not believe that it alone (alone and exclusively) contains the Truth, if it does not believe that it alone is able and destined to use its Truth for arousing all people to new life and bring them to salvation, then that nation ceases to be a great nation and turns into ethnographic material. A truly great nation can never play a secondary part. It cannot even be content with one of the primary parts. It can only have the very first part ... Every nation is a nation only so long as it possesses its own God and rejects

all other gods in the world uncompromisingly ... The Jews lived for the sole purpose of taking part in the revelation of the True God and to give the True God to the world ... Only one of the nations can call the true God its own.[24]

If that unique nation must be Russia then other claimants, most of all the Judaic which originated exceptionality, must be disallowed. More, they must be denigrated to disprove their claim and satisfy jealousy.

Dostoevsky had a violent predecessor in Ivan the Terrible, whose teachers appealed exclusively to the 'Old Testament' and read it into Russian dominance. Ivan's favourite reading was the Books of Kings. He equated Poles with Philistines and saw himself as warranted in conquest by his people's 'election'. His mentors, called 'the possessors', were opposed by 'the non-possessors' whose appeal was to Jesus and the New Testament.[25]

What should be said when Judaic conviction, however distortedly, generates such borrowing? May the travesty not be pointing to the notion, duly reverent, of plural 'elections' into destiny, of parallel – or at least associable – vocations, not required or warranted to think themselves exclusive? May such a conjecture not find the relativizing secret in a non-racial, non-territorial open peoplehood in the shape of the New Testament Church where vocation would stand, not in pride or right of race, in pride and power of state, in privacies of culture, memory and speech, but in a humanness enabled for the role by grace alone? Is this where the cross-reference of tragic experience points?

By such lights there would still be room for nations and peoples which otherwise are such besotted exclusifiers. The role for them, however, would have to be relative. They could only pretend to emulate Israel's instrumentality for God by renouncing her exceptionality. Abraham Lincoln might then be legitimated where the Dostoevsky of *The Devils* must be laid under anathema. Memorably, Lincoln saw Americans as 'the almost chosen people'.[26] It should, indeed, be not only possible, but obligatory, to read the mystery of landscape, the retrospect of tenancy, the saga of history, the satisfaction of belonging, the trust of 'generation', and the thrill of identity, as divinely given and divinely meant for vocation to the whole. Diversity

need not then be read as threatening, nor the exceptionality
all possess insist that one's own is *the* exception.

This reading can find support in some current forms of Jewish
response itself to the theme of 'chosenness'. For some in Jewry
it has come to seem embarrassing or, at least, capable of 'secular'
interpretation. Elements in the early Zionist movement in the
nineteenth century, represented by Moses Hess, *Rome and
Jerusalem*, and Pinsker's *Auto Emancipation*, were attracted by
'nationalism' in general and read it as the gist of Jewish hope.
When Zionism came into full political being in the state of Israel,
David Ben Gurion insisted that 'chosenness' was really a way
of expressing the inherent virility of the Jewish people. God
had not 'chosen' them, they had 'chosen' God in being a choosing people, i.e. a people resolute in self-help and finding divine
mandate in their indomitable will.[27]

Whatever the idiom, this must mean that the option to be
a 'choosing people' must be open to all. Ben Gurion's
view of exceptionality, unlike the orthodox Judaic view,
brought it out of absoluteness into the sphere of competition. Belief in destiny was simply an asset in the business of
achieving it. God became an ally in the covenant of activism
– a conclusion evident in Ben Gurion's fascination with the
Bible.[28]

Comparable thoughts in a different context guided Simon
Dubnow, historian last century of Jewish intellectual attitudes.
The historical God who directed destiny was for him their destiny's product. The Talmud itself could be understood as the
means to self-preservation. Jewish birth was essentially birth
into a nationality whatever Judaism might mean within it as
a religious commitment.[29] The more Jewish particularism is
understood in this way the more the notion, as it were, 'Gentil-
izes' Jewish peoplehood by reducing the divine 'election' element to human factors which then have to be seen as generic
to mankind. The point for theologians here is really twofold.
Can 'being God's people' truly obtain if it ceases to be spiritual?
Can it be that truly spiritual reality except in 'church' form
divesting itself of what, otherwise, aligns it squarely with historical forces and temptations from which no exemptions are
exempt?

There have been voices this century within Jewry tending
to understand Judaic vocation in such spiritual terms. Thus,
for example, Jacob B. Agus writes:

When we speak of ourselves as being 'chosen' we do so in the sense in which all dedicated, covenanted [*sic*] communities are chosen, i.e. called to serve a high purpose. This doctrine can serve as a useful and inspiring metaphor only if it is purged of all exceptionalist, racist and mystical connotations ... Our affirmation of our chosenness is our way of appreciating the peculiar gifts of our past and of our destiny. In other traditions there are other ways.[30]

Is not that in line with 'the nations bringing their glory and honour into the kingdom'? Admittedly there is the faith-particularism of Christianity in that vision, and to this we come in Chapter 7. For Agus 'chosenness' is 'a meta-myth'. Elsewhere the same writer asks: 'Was Israel chosen as an example or an exception?' His reply is that the answers vary widely. Without conviction of being 'exceptional', there is no vocation. But 'chosenness ceases to be self-critical if the feeling is confined within the boundaries of the people itself.'[31] How it might be extended, through self-criticism, to those outside the boundaries is not clear. Was it not just such self-criticism in the light of Jesus by which the Church broke through the boundary lines – a step which Agus sees as 'premature' with the same prematurity evidenced in regarding Jesus as Messiah?

Contemporary Jewish apologia about 'chosenness' seems, then, to resolve itself into another form of the old issue between 'the land' and diaspora. These take shape as a vibrant nationalism in quest of the re-creation of Zion, and a spirituality variously related to its non-Jewish context and to recovered Zion. In the broadest terms these are Judaism *via* statehood and Judaism as, essentially, religion. In the one case the Jewish self-image is no longer that of total separation from the nations and their ways but, to a degree, of emulation of their nationhood with, perhaps a concession of 'chosenness' elsewhere if virility allows. In the other case, 'election' must be fulfilled in conditions of dispersion, living, as Jacob Neusner has it, 'by truths that could endure outside a single land and culture ... to be created and re-created in every land and language'.[32] If we exclude the mystery of 'holy seed' from that spiritual definition, it approximates closely to the essentials of the Church, given the difference in the 'truths that endure'. It can be said that Jewish experience of this choice about 'being chosen' reflects in important ways the very issues out of which the Christian Church was born. It was defined in stateless spirituality and in will to be present anywhere and everywhere without benefit of heredity and with an equal accessibility to all – an 'anywhere' for 'any who'.

VIII

Our respective theologies of peoplehood for God, despite debts, and mutual constraints, seem to arrive at insoluble disparities. How they might converse and coexist belongs to Chapter 7, with its obligation to other areas of strain. In conclusion here there is one final consideration. It has to do with the fear that the Judaic form of being on behalf of God as 'his people' in the world paradoxically frustrates itself in the very preoccupations it generates. Its perennial concern for recognition – as a condition of its positive role in human benediction – receives perennial rejection, which in turn requires it perennially to resist in order to ensure its task. How does a peoplehood effectively bless mankind if constituted by its very nature to involve a tension predisposing embarrassment or worse rather than benediction and, in the long engagement, engrossing the bearers of the benediction in a constant, tragic concern about 'them that hate us'? The very *Benedictus* of 'the Lord God of Israel', which Christian liturgy has loyally and continuously made its own (Luke 1.68–80), celebrates only because it fears. 'His holy covenant', sworn to their fathers, seems emotionally inseparable from 'the hand of their enemies.' How is 'election' itself to be liberated from the inhibitions it generates both within its ranks and outside its range, to become the liberation, according to intention, of us all? Or is the shape of that vocation inherently undone?

These are puzzling thoughts and some may think them quite irreverent, since they call in question assumptions utterly vital to Judaism and deeply traditional to Christians. No unbelief is meant. Indeed it is just a deep sympathy with the mystery that necessitates the case. For a Jewry at peace with its vocation and set to pursue it unfettered from within or from without would be benediction indeed. The Joseph typology may be helpful here. As Thomas Mann in his great *Joseph and His Brothers*[33] powerfully depicts, there was point in the brothers' enmity, given Jacob's doting on Joseph and Joseph's adolescent dreaming self-importance, all 'the sheaves bowing down' to him, when 'anti-Semitism' broke loose in a Semite family. The brothers' malice, cunning and cruel deception of their father were evils in no way to be excused by provocation. In the event a strange cycle of providence turned it into good. Joseph indeed prospered – not in the prim conceits of youth, but by the stern discipline of adversity and the maturing of his gifts of mind and character. The manifest vindication of his 'chosenness' killed the familial 'anti-Semitism', achieved the promised visions, chastened and retrieved the enmity and rescued the entire clan. Little wonder that Genesis, and the Qur'ān also with intriguingly different details, remembers the Joseph story. And Joseph has sometimes figured in Judaic thoughts about Messiah.

But 'Messiah' has not come. His Joseph-role in the benediction of 'those who hated' remains no more than a custodial hope and, meanwhile, the enmity against the 'favourite' intermittently festers and persists.

There is yet another tragic twist to the parallel. Suffering it was for Joseph, which accomplished the ultimate climax. 'The iron entered into his soul' as 'his neck was put in the irons'.[34] But that suffering, grim and grievous as it was in false accusation, gaol, and hope deferred, did emerge into power and fulfilment. Suffering, however, in the Joseph-people, from the enmity of brothers-Gentile, seems to have no such implementation into its end in the thing achieved. Rather it becomes in all its tragedy a further occasion of the alienating tensions established and reciprocated in the early Joseph scenes. Even to the point of corporate masochism it becomes a perpetuated price of vocation and, from without, a chronic focus of psychic factors of discrimination, given and received. It shapes a situation in which the vocation to liberate seems ever elusive. 'The light to lighten the nations' still waits for 'the glory of thy people Israel'. For 'glory', at least in the Greek sense of '*doxa*', has to be a cognizance as well as a claim.

Judaic peoplehood for God, so long and for mysterious reasons denied this external meed of recognition, and finding instead the withholding of it a trauma of pain, seems to live by the need to survive. It has, for every reason of circumstance and tradition, an instinct to suspect the world, a capacity for being ever under threat, an inability to be reassured. These inhibit what conceptually its 'God-behalf-ness' has the vocation to be. For the world at large is either guilty or unresponsive or sceptical within its spiritual field and this drives the Judaic ever further into self-pre-occupation. Rabbi Dow Marmur, in a painful book, *Beyond Survival*, takes up this theme and analyses the three patterns of insistent prescription for Judaic preservation, namely Orthodoxy, Reform Judaism and Zionism. He argues that only some amalgam of all three – surely an impossible dream – will ensure a right future and rescue Jewry from its own fears.[35] He sees 'the mystical bond' between God and people as entailing 'the neurotic tangle', in which Judaic experience is all too often a burden of frustration.

He is not alone in his acute self-awareness. Gershom Scholem observes:

> Deep, dangerous and destructive dialectics are inherent in the Messianic idea ... The Jewish people have paid a very high price for the Messianic idea – a big question: what price Messianism?[36]

In context he has primarily in mind the false alarms of Shabbetai Zvi, the pseudo-Messiah. But since the messianic idea and the chosen people are synonymous in respect of 'the God's men's burden' they undertake, his remark is in line with the sense we are at pains to understand – the sense of an exceptionality which can neither escape nor fulfil its meaning. A Tunisian Jew, Albert Memmi, in a revealing piece of self-interrogation, described this Judaic comfortlessness at the hands both of Gentile attitudes and Jewish responses. His reflections are a diagnosis of identity which is, at the same time, a quest for rescue.[37]

IX

To conclude any study of peoplehood for God in the terms that the foregoing seems to suggest would be faithless. A sincere theology, Jewish or Christian, is bound to pursue the issues further into the vexing areas of anti-Semitism, the Holocaust, the State of Israel and the tensions – Judaic and Christian – about its significance, the dubious concept of 'parallel' covenants, and the discernible ways in which Jew and Christian can authentically share theology or wisely disagree one.[38] But in all these hopes to relate the 'siege mentality', as Jacob Neusner calls it, must engage a comprehending sympathy. The one point that Jews affirm is that they shall be Jews. Using the personal pronoun, Neusner continues:

> For my part, if I am accepted as a 'human being' and not as a Jew, I do not accept that acceptance. I aspire to no place in an undifferentiated humanity. Take me despite my Jewishness and there is nothing to take. Overlook what is important to me and you obliterate my being.[39]

So writing he phrases eloquently the plea for acceptance which Israel embodies in virile state form as Jewish nationhood (ending *Golah,* or exile as to place) while diaspora Jewry pursues it in the will for non-assimilative presence (making *Galuth* no longer 'exile'). Is it not possible to set the heart of the matter in a Gentile paraphrase of Neusner's plea?

> If I am only accepted as a 'Gentile' I do not accept that acceptance. I aspire to no place in a differentiated humanity if the differentiation is radical and not merely those creaturely things which are natural, cultural and incidental. Take me despite my 'Gentileness' and there is everything to share. Otherwise you locate my being merely in a contrast. I lack 'chosenness'. I exist only in contra-distinction.

In other words, is there not a reciprocal denial of our right to be ourselves, as long as the Jew/Gentile distinction is kept necessary to theology? It is delightsome to discover that when Jacob Neusner, in the same book, comes to define 'life in Torah' it means many things that we can all mean – joy in life, singing, the sunset, celebration. Has the long, deep divide, the siege mentality, the trauma of otherness, really been necessary? Was it not a *Galuth,* an 'out-in-the-world-ness', which in a positive sense under God we were all meant to share? Was it not such a common open humanity, theologically perceived and pursued, without ethnic distinction or landed frontiers, that the Church in genesis from Messiah-Jesus, and because of him, was called and commissioned to be?

NOTES

1 Claud G. Montefiore, *Judaism and St. Paul* (1914), pp. 144f.
2 ibid., p. 145. Montefiore thinks Paul's universalism (which he acknowledges) to have been attained only by 'the abolition of Judaism'. He asks whether there is not a universalism 'won with its retention'. This would mean 'mercies of God . . . not limited by race or creed, by belief or unbelief', p. 143. It is, he says, such mercies in which Judaism believes. This will certainly be true of our common creaturehood, but what of apparently absolute distinction within it to which Judaism would seem to be committed?
3 It is wise to say this because in the lyrical writings of e.g. Martin Buber and Abraham Heschel there is the theme of the uniqueness of the very soil, the rain, the caressing winds in Israel. This cherishing goes back to the Deuteronomic words: 'a land the Lord thy God cares for' (Deut. 11.12). The Torah was for, and only fully obeyed within, the land. In

vol. 4 of his long novel *Ya'ish*, the celebrated writer, Hayim Hazaz, affirms: 'In Palestine the cosmos behaves normally ... Go to the land of Israel, my friend, you will be renewed there' (vol. iv, 55, p. 145). Cf. M Buber: 'This land is called "holy"; but it is not the holiness of an idea, it is the holiness of a piece of earth' (*Israel and the World* [New York, 2nd edn 1963], p. 227).

4　The sense of the familiar promise is active in Gen. 22.18; 26.4; and Psalm 72.17. The nations will bless (i.e. congratulate) themselves in Abraham and his 'seed'. The phrase in Gen. 12.3; 18.18; and 28.14 is: 'be blessed'.

5　Franz Rosenzweig *The Star of Redemption*, trans. W. W. Hallo (New York, 2nd edn 1970), pp. 341, 346.

6　Rosenzweig is one with e.g. Ignaz Maybaum and many other Jewish thinkers writing on Christian relationships in stressing that Christians have to 'become', whereas Jews are 'born'. The theme of being 'born again', which figures centrally in Jesus' converse with 'a ruler of the Jews' according to John 3, must have sounded incredible to Nicodemus. There are indications in the New Testament of the faith of families as such (Acts 16.15 and 1 Cor. 1.16) and there is the fact of infant baptism in many churches. This stands in the conviction that the grace of God does not begin to be true for us when we are old enough to understand. It is a truth about the humanity into which we are born and there to be received. When, in infant baptism, it is received by proxy faith this binds the family's nurture to a Christian commitment through a baptism which is prospective towards personal adult commitment in the confession of personal faith. In this it is radically different from sealing an identity in circumcision. It does not signify that the child is distinguished by fact of particular birth; it affirms the reality of grace for all and sundry once humanly born.

7　This idea of spiritual progeny on Paul's part may be thought the more remarkable in that Timothy's natural father was a Greek. Of the physical parentage of Onesimus we know nothing.

8　Hans Joachim Schoeps, *The Jewish-Christian Argument*, trans. D. E. Green (London 1963), p. 4. Later Schoeps affirms that 'whoever is born an Israelite is a member of the covenant by virtue of his birth'. However, it is only 'he who lives by the Torah and fulfils his duty who is heir to the promise' (pp. 163–4). 'Israel does not need to be redeemed because it has already been elected by God.'

9　Jacob B. Agus, *Jewish Identity in an Age of Ideologies* (New York 1976), p. 280. He cites Jewish welcome to proselytes and denies Rosenzweig's view that 'the eternal people must maintain itself biologically untainted'. On proselytes and parents see also Raphael Loewe, ed., *Rationalism, Judaism and Universalism* (London 1966), p. 134.

10　Loewe, loc. cit., pp. 132–3. Stressing that the Jewish concept of the *goyim* (Gentiles) is bound up with the idolatry of which they were guilty, he considers that there is need for a Judaic re-definition of 'Gentiles' to allow of a sincere monotheism among them. But he sees this need as like 'circum-navigating a rock'. Re-definition of Gentiles, in another sense was precisely Paul's concern.

11 Martin Buber, *Two Types of Faith: a Study of the Interpenetration of Judaism and Christianity*, trans. N. P. Goldhawk (New York, 1961 edn), p. 98.

12 Ignaz Maybaum, *Happiness outside the State* (London 1980), pp. 80–2. He adds that 'Of course, every people is a chosen people . . . but . . .' Elsewhere in *Creation and Guilt* (London 1969), Maybaum explains Ezekiel 16.6 as meaning, during the Exile and being without the Temple, 'live in the Jewish people, as creatures of God' (p. 91). In the same context he contrasts 'the first Christians' who 'stopped living as a people and began to live as members of a church, spirit, not blood'. He notes that in the New Testament the phrase 'to your children's children" does not occur. Cf. p. 121 above.

13 See B. W. Helfgott, *The Doctrine of Election in Tannaitic Literature* (New York, 1954), p. 67, citing Pasik, R. 21, pp. 99f.

14 The reciprocal nature of the covenant is everywhere stressed in Judaism. Hence the desperate trauma of the Holocaust and the mystery of apparent divine 'desertion'. Can there be 'theology after Auschwitz'? Leszek L. Kolakowski, *The Devil and Scripture*, trans. N. Bethell (Oxford 1973), pp. 6–7, misses this point when he satirizes in his ironic style the 'disinterestedness' of divine love as undertaking a protégé with no end in view. He adds whimsically: 'The motive was noble but the effect disastrous. We should count on reciprocity, not charity. We should accept promises only when the maker of the promises knows we can return the kindness.' But, biblically, Israel was the divine protégé in order to be the divine instrument, and divine choosing meant divine binding to preserve and 'partner'.

15 A. S. Steinberg, in A. A. Cohen, ed., *The Jew, Essays from Martin Buber's Journal, Der Jude: 1916–28* (Alabama 1980), p. 170.

16 The context in John 12.20–33 is significant. The saying is in response to word of the presence on the edges of inquiring Greeks, wanting 'to see Jesus'.

17 The curious usage from tennis meaning players not of acknowledged rank may perhaps be permitted in this context. It has an odd relevance.

18 Clear examples are Mark 7.14–19 about 'nothing unclean of itself' found in Romans 14.14. C. H. Dodd remarks in *Gospel and Law* (Cambridge 1957) p. 49: 'It is incredible that Paul was not aware of this saying.' Both Mark and Paul use the same unusual word *koinos*, for 'unclean'. Cf. also Romans 14.10 and Matt. 18.6–7 and Mark 9.42 about the *skandalon* which Paul elaborates with a good Greek word *proskomma*: also the emphasis on being individually accountable to God occurs in Matt. 12.36–7 and recurs in Romans 14.12. Both Jesus and Paul use baptism as a synonym for a self-giving in death (Luke 12.50 and Romans 6.3).

19 Examples are Luke 13.29 about people coming 'from east, west, north and south to sit down in the kingdom of God'. Also Mark 14.9, where the incident of the women anointing Jesus would be told 'throughout the whole world'. Some, however, do not read these and similar passages as envisaging a *gentile* 'width' of the world. See discussion in Joachim Jeremias, *Studiorum Novi Testamenti Societas*, Bulletin iii (Cambridge 1963), pp. 18–28.

20 The Jewish writer, Ellis Rivkin, is of this mind too. See L. Edelmann: *Face to Face: A Primer in Dialogue*, 1967.

21 For example, Chapter 9 with the blind man cast out of the synagogue, his parents unwilling to 'get involved', and the tense, timorous quality of the man's allegiance. For some discussion and further reference see A. E. Harvey, *Jesus on Trial, A Study in the Fourth Gospel*, London 1976.

22 Leo Baeck, *This People Israel: The Meaning of Jewish Existence*, trans. A. H. Friedlander (New York 1965), p. 141.

23 See *John Eliot's Indian Dialogues*, ed. H. W. Bowden and J. P. Ronda (Westport, Conn. 1980), for a fascinating measure of the encounter between Puritan theology and 'Indian' culture in the Boston Bay area of the Massachuset tribe in the early seventeenth century. Eliot's efforts were undermined by the obduracy of white settlers for whom trade and suspicion were more powerful than ventures in universal grace.

24 Fyodor Dostoevsky, *The Devils* (or *The Possessed*), trans. A. R. MacAndrew (London 1962), Part II, Chapter 7. See A. S. Steinberg, in op. cit. note 15.

25 James H. Billington, *The Icon and the Axe: an Interpretive History of Russian Culture* (London 1966), p. 75.

26 President Lincoln, addressing the New Jersey Senate in 1861: 'the Almighty, of this, his almost chosen people'. One might compare Herman Melville, *White Jacket* (London 1850), p. 189: 'We Americans are the peculiar chosen people – the Israel of our time: we bear the ark of the liberties of the world.'

27 David Ben Gurion, *Recollections*, ed. T. R. Bransten, London 1970.

28 *Ben Gurion Looks at the Bible*, trans. J. Kolatch, London 1972.

29 Simon Dubnow (1860–1941), the Jewish historian, believed in diaspora nationalism with cultural autonomy, wherever Jews found themselves.

30 Jacob B. Agus, *Jewish Identity in an Age of Ideologies* (New York 1976), p. 324.

31 Jacob B. Agus, in *Journal of Ecumenical Studies*, vol. 6, no. 1 (Philadelphia 1969), pp. 18–36.

32 Jacob Neusner, *Stranger at Home* (Chicago 1981), p. 181.

33 Thomas Mann, *Joseph and His Brothers*, trans. H. T. Lowe-Porter, London 1978 edn.

34 The usual sense of Psalm 105.18 in its recital of the Joseph saga is the steeling of the soul by adversity. But the Hebrew can quite well bear the literal sense of the neck (*nepsh*) in the prisoner's collar.

35 Dow Marmur, *Beyond Survival; Reflections on the Future of Judaism*, London 1982.

36 Gershom Scholem: *Sabbatai Sevi*, op. cit., p. xii. See Chapter 5, note 16.

37 Albert Memmi, *Portrait of a Jew*, trans. Elizabeth Abbott, London 1963.

38 A double obligation well exemplified in Eugene B. Borowitz, *Contemporary*

Christologies: A Jewish Response (New York 1980), a study by a Reform Judaism scholar of six recent Christologies selected by consultation with the American Theological Society.

39   Jacob Neusner, op. cit., pp. 31, 45, 105.

7

The Tent of Meeting

I

Marc Chagall is among the most eminent of Jewish artists this century in oils and in stained glass. What significance belongs to the fact that so many of his paintings centre on the crucifixion?[1] What does the repeated subject mean and how should it be read? There stands Jacob's ladder; weeping patriarchs in clouds above lament the scene of a burning synagogue; an overloaded boat of refugees drifting perilously; a man with a placard *Jude* on his breast and a forlorn rabbi clutching to his bosom a scroll of *Torah*; while the face of Jesus takes all wistfully in, his loins covered with the prayer shawl. Is the painter suggesting that the sorrows of Israel somehow meet in the travail of Jesus?

The theme is one to which we will come only at the end of this chapter, having, through most of its course, occupied ourselves with other formulated patterns of Judeo-Christian meeting. The image of 'the tent of meeting outside the camp' (Exodus 33.7–11) can serve our purpose well. Admittedly in those original days it was within range only of the tribes of Israel. But if we have licence to extend the reach of access there are points to which Gentiles can appeal. Unlike the Tabernacle 'in the midst of the camp' (Exodus 40.34–5) 'the tent of meeting' stood outside. Therein it was symbolic of the nomadic vocation which, at least in the retrospect of interpreting historians and thinkers, represented the primal age of Judaic derivation and decision. There may have been anachronism in the thinking of the interpreters. But it is to primal meanings that meeting must repair.

Further, unlike the Tabernacle, 'the tent of meeting' was available to every Israelite. The divine presence, summoning and halting, hovered there. To consult with Yahweh each and all had to proceed beyond the tents of their own encamping – a fair hint of our need now to transcend things merely communal and partisan. The prophets sometimes looked idyllically to that early quality of nomadic faith and pristine vision, to call Israel back from the accumulated compromise and jadedness of later times. Perhaps, then, it may also serve to take us now out of fixity and prejudice into a readiness to meet with God outside our entrenchments, our habitual haunts of controversial familiarity. 'I will make you live in tents again as in the day of meeting', Hosea has Yahweh say (12.9), and the reference is to the halt in Sinai when the people and their leader were still only discovering themselves. There is much in the implied mutual rejectionism of Jew and Christian which makes 'the camp' a sharply pointed imagery. 'Outside the camp' was where writer and readers in the Letter to the Hebrews (13.13) found themselves summoned to go in their obedience to Christ. Loyalty to Judaism has meant long estrangements from the solidarities of the gentile world. Furthermore, the divine *Shechinah*, or 'Presence' (from the cognate Semitic root for 'dwelling'), or 'God with his people', became a paradigm for the first Christian theologian on the Incarnation, the John of the Fourth Gospel: 'The Word . . . tabernacled among us and we saw his glory, full of grace and truth' (John 1.14). May it not be, then, that this mysterious 'tentedness' of God with people, or in personality, affords us the surest clue of imagination in facing the implications of all we have already studied about Messiah and community?

II

We begin where Chapter 6 concluded and the psychic preoccupation of Jewry with guarding, cherishing and perpetuating its identity. Everything, somehow, is grist to the mill of apprehension as to its reception, or more likely its denigration, in the world. The Judaic mind, inevitably, justifiably and, it would seem, incurably, responds to all else in terms of anxiety for its due acknowledgement. To take this situation generously and perceptively is surely the beginning of all wisdom. As so much serves only to accentuate it, the first necessity is to hope to allay it, if not set it at rest. One might almost paraphrase Augustine's famous words and hear them say: 'O Lord, thou hast made us for thyself and our hearts are restless till all know and see it so.' It is just those Christian themes about Messiahship realized in Jesus and the Church as an open people for God which most acutely kindle to vigilance and pain the vital impulse of Jewry to secure a threatened psyche. And there is so much else in history stemming from these themes which accentuates anxiety. How then can we properly meet in terms which only minister to the ancient unease? How can Christians be themselves in Jewish meeting and yet allay the perennial disquiet? If there is any positive answer it must at least begin with the mental preoccupations as they are and not as it might be wished they were.

Commenting on Vera Brittain's *Testament of Youth* with its dark cycle of war and tragedy, Alistair Cooke – hardly a writer to reach easily for a religious perspective – fell back upon a sentence from *Punch* about her portrayal of the travail of 1914–18:

> It is impossible to condemn a nursling of nineteenth-century materialism for having failed to improvise a creed which should see her through the shattering of her world.[2]

Whether a 'creed' is ever 'improvised' to survive a 'shattering' we may well dispute. For those that matter are not improvised. What is unparalleled about *fides judaica* is that the shattering and the creed have been inseparable. The tenacity of the conviction about election has been the companion of adversity, the target of antipathy. These, in turn, have tempered and toughened the interior experience of the mystery that excited them. It is not simply that Jewish courage is at stake in Jewish fidelity. That is true of all belief-loyalty. It is that somehow all that doubts or counters the Judaic faith from outsiders entails for those inside not merely an issue about meaning but a menace to existence. Themes are not merely conceptual and doctrinal and certainly not academic, but deeply existential. Such, no doubt, is the case with all religious conviction, but nowhere so intensely as with Jewry. For at the heart of their faith is a distinctive thesis about themselves, not simply as believers in this or that, but as bearers of a distinctive destiny which demands recognition not only as a doctrine but as a divine prestige. The truth-relationship which is present between all religions in respect of content, whether akin or contrasted, becomes uniquely in the case of Judaism a status-relationship and as such never possessed satisfactorily in the absence of its recognition. The Jew, in the phrase of Arthur A. Cohen, can 'never desist from his own reality'. For, to do so, would be 'saying No! to God'.[3] An ethno-theology necessarily unites credal conviction and psychic existence so that issues for the former become crisis in the latter. The world, whether of faiths or of society, is then seen and experienced in terms of *adversus Judaeos*. The result is a sustained anxiety for acceptance which takes the form of an inherent defensiveness. Involvement with humanity in benediction entails continuing apprehension and exemption.

III

Our first obligation is to take this deep paradox as the irreducible fact of the situation, the necessary condition of all else. There is space to explore it further only briefly in three areas as a prelude to reflection on how Christians in this century have responded to its pathos and yearning. The three are Zionism, the Holocaust and the tradition of Judeo-Christian encounter since the New Testament. Each of these makes massive demands on patience, sincerity and discipline of mind.

The century or more of modern Zionism enshrines the tension within Judaism as tellingly as any other cycle of events in its long history. On the one hand a tremendous achievement surmounting enormous odds, an arduous and successful campaign for statehood and political salvation efficiently concluded; on the other a bitter encounter with rejection and hostility – a hostility entirely predictable and justifiable in all the given facts of the situation but inevitably read, and countered, by Israeli interpretations as just another phase of the interminable anti-Semitism incorrigibly practised by an all-hating world, a Palestinian version of a universal antipathy. Thus Jewry is tempted by its most splendid modern triumph into new reaches of the pride of exceptionality and the tragedy of its misreading.

The Zionist is sure that the misreading is wholly Arab. He has no mind to seek an interpretation other than his own, despite the sharp cleavage in the self-awareness of Judaism that resulted from incipient Zionist propagation in the early days of the Zionist Congresses and, indeed, until 1967. For him the logic against diaspora as vocation was incontrovertible. The return to Palestine was divinely legitimated by every right of unrelinquished possession, by historic title and religious necessity. On no count of justice or ethics should its propriety be challenged. Had the existing inhabitants not perversely resisted, inept as their politics and patterns have been, all could have been peaceful and innocent, a colonization by consent of the natives. Though, in the event, war and struggle have occurred, and the Israeli prowess has succeeded, this should

not be read as any *de facto* acquistion by conquest. The appearance of 'conquest' is wholly due to the reactions of those who
did not admit the right of Zion.[4]

This reading of events can only seem, from the other side,
a gross misreading both of what occurred and why. The 'innocence', so sincerely desired and naively assumed by *Hibbat Zion*
and other pioneer visionaries, was, and is, illusory. The inhabitants were certainly there, outnumbering the Jews present in
the eighteen-eighties by twenty to one. Theirs, too, however
despicable by some Zionist disesteem, was a territorial love
rooted in peasant tenacity and a long sense of ancestry. Do
not all races find their unity from a mythology marrying them
to rock and hill and soil? This Palestinianism is not a pseudo
thing, a pale reflection of Israeli land-love, a false and foolish
gesture of imitation. It is a genuine passion, proven, like Jewish
diaspora, in adversity. It is fair to say that all the logic of Zionist
argument – the necessity of statehood *via* territory of one's own,
inauthenticity outside it, the sense of self-negation in exile –
belongs equally to the Palestinians in dispersion. They have
shown in deep suffering their ability for the definition of nationhood which runs: 'A nation is any people believing themselves
to be one.'[5] Is that anxiety-to-be on the part of a tragic Palestinian people to be answered, in effect, from within a successful,
but still embattled, Judeo-Zionist anxiety-to-be, merely by
something like the counsel of old Caleb according to Numbers
14.9: 'The people of the land are bread for us . . . and the Lord
is with us.'? And if they, politically, have stupidly all along
played into our hands are we the less to blame? Should we,
in a word, be reproached for winning?

Though political Zionism, in its early decades, caused acute
disquiet throughout Jewry as a dangerous ambition or a dreamy
illusion, the renewed experience of antipathy which its success
has occasioned, has largely united Jewish sentiment in its
favour. Success normally succeeds and, when tinged with
admiration and shared congratulation, is the more attractive.
But it is clear to the perceptive within Judaism and beyond
that it would be false to read Palestinian resistance to the *fait
accompli* as yet another cycle of *adversus Judaeos*. Insofar as Zionism is a bid for normalcy and acceptance, in very human –
even Gentile – terms, the form and history of the bid have
themselves ensured its inner frustration, whatever may be its
external and irreversible success. The long and costly story of

Zionist accomplishment – so resounding had it been attained in an uninhabited vacuum – proves to be yet another price paid for the paradox of Jewry. The psychic preoccupations persist, all the more tragically, in the very context of the supremely resolute and decisive attempt to end them.

That outcome, self-entailed as it was, does not – within Judaic prescripts – make the Zionist aspiration ill-judged. On the contrary, suspected and decried as it was by many in Jewry until it prospered decisively,[6] it sprang from deeply instinctive, some would say impeccable, Judaic logic. 'Host nations' – as the term went – faced Jewry with two alternatives, both of them finally intolerable. These were either implied and creeping assimilation, or persecution. The latter, so grievously renewed from time to time, meant an endlessly precarious existence, a ghetto life forever at the mercy of fickle and hostile Gentiles, capable of the most brutal savagery. If Jewish 'provocation' was so perennial then Jews must abstract from an alien world and betake themselves to where they would be 'hosts' to themselves in the promised land. Thus Jews would themselves achieve on behalf of Gentiles the final solution to the 'Jewish problem'. Persecution would be past and over.

But in the 'liberal' world post-Enlightenment society only tolerated the Jew on the implied assumption of his low profile and the ever-present 'threat' of assimilation through laxity in dietary laws, inter-marriage and Gentile dominance. This tolerance was, anyway, never guaranteed, and at best made Jewish existence somehow inauthentic. There were deep implications here about the very nature of Judaism, either as a religion or as a *volk*.[7] But in Zionist logic, liberal society could be as lethal to a pure Judaism as persecution. Auschwitz and Oxford, according to one Rabbi, were comparably a menace to Jews.[8] The only final security for diaspora Jewry would lie in a Jewish statehood which would be a refuge for the persecuted, a symbol for the scattered and a bastion ensuring the only sort of mutual respect this world understands, with teeth, if need be, to enforce it. Thus the argument for the Israel that was to be.

It is important, therefore, to see the will for Israel-to-be as springing directly and logically from the ghetto and the Enlightenment, those twin forms of modern Jewish existence, both arising, diversely, from within Jewish self-interpretation and diversely required by the verdicts such interpretation reached about diaspora and destiny. But it is equally important

to see that political Zionism, by this logic, was *not* seeking in
the Arab East a re-location of 'host nations'. A Palestinian one
might well have been kindlier than some European ones. No!
the aim, unequivocally, was the end of host-nation risks by
the achievement of *Der Judenstaat*. It is this plain fact, however
concealed in the tortuous evolution of actual events, which
makes it clear that political statehood was mandatory from the
start, that bi-nationalism was never a Zionist possibility, and
that large human displacement to ensure Jewish majority population was implicit. When the day ends, the end, indeed, is
known, but essentially it was there from the beginning unless
Zionism was to reverse all its logic – a logic drawn from a long
retrospect of history. Zionism, then, sprang authentically from
a deep reading of the Jewish past. There is nothing, therefore,
extraneous in its Middle Eastern experience, but only another
cycle of the same haunting paradox. The context confines and
disallows the State, just as it did the ghetto. The difference
lies in the resilience of fire-power and political finesse and the
sense of never again humiliation. But that difference does not
leave the soul at peace or the world at rights.

There is a happier irony about Zionism. For all its calculated
effort to make good exceptionality and pursue a determined,
sometimes defiant, 'auto-emancipation', it has been involved
and indebted, within that very enterprise, to factors and attitudes in the wider world. It has been willy-nilly party to the
truth that no total self-sufficiencies are feasible in this world.
There have been many outside Jewry but among its dispersed
habitations who, whether out of sentiment, admiration, Christian faith, biblical associations, or general goodwill, have fostered the making of Israel. Directly, or indirectly, *via* Jewish
liberties in the diaspora, non-Jewish humanity has contributed
massively in circumstance and sacrifice to Zionist achievement.
The issue of the First World War, when Zionism itself sometimes hedged the bets, and more vitally the ultimate allied
defeat of Hitlerism, were fundamental to Jewish hopes. The
Balfour Declaration owed much to biblical sentiment in Welsh
and English circles. The vision, drive and tenacity were wholly
Jewish but the occasions and resources by which these were
fulfilled were owed elsewhere. J. L. Talmon, the Israeli historian, observed:

No Jewish historian, whatever his evaluation of the various factors involved in the restoration of Jewish statehood, can ignore the fact that Zionism would never have had a chance for success if centuries of Christian teaching and worship, liturgy and legend, had not conditioned the western nations to respond almost instinctively to the words 'Zion' and 'Israel'.[9]

Politicians and fighters, like David Ben Gurion and Menachem Begin may be less minded than historians to concede that there is such positive relation to humanity at large. But the more Zionism itself can be seen to be not altogether self-sufficient the more things Judaic may be released from the intense preoccupation we are discussing with their survival as divinely *sui generis*.

But, overwhelmingly, the circumstances of Israel's establishment and of the Jewish measure of mankind are dominated by the Holocaust, a concentration of evil which fulfils all the worst fears and presents Jewry with an almost insurmountable dereliction of faith as to their human meaning, even faith as to the reality of Yahweh and his 'covenant'. For some, it makes theology after Auschwitz inconceivable. It devastates all those positive dimensions that might have encouraged a grateful Zionism and silences all voices of hope that will not, or cannot, take its measure of despair. There is no relationship with Jewry that can ever avail which does not live this desolation in Jewry's terms. How to do so without yielding to another despair about ever serving Jewish travail and Jewish peace is the hardest vocation of those who are not Jews. Where can such honesty begin? For the Holocaust defies all norms of reckoning.

IV

'Were hatred a solution', wrote Elie Wiesel, 'the survivors, when they came out of the camps, would have had to burn down the whole world.'[10] From a most eloquent and influential Holocaust survivor and memorialist, the saying has a double significance. It captures the intense quality of angry pain haunting the spirit of all who wrestle with the appalling toll. But it also suggests, perhaps unwittingly, the fact of human solidarity where the ultimate realism must come. 'Burn down the whole world' – then it must be true that the horror of the Holocaust reaches back and down into the inclusive tragedy of mankind. Elsewhere in Wiesel's *The Oath*, a narrator says: 'Every truth that shuts you in, that does not lead to others, is inhu-man.' [11] To have been 'shut in' by the Holocaust is the desperate experience of the Jewish soul. It is the most isolating event of all time, the unspeakable proof of exceptionality, the most brutal victimization of any people known to history. Must it not end all theodicy, annul for ever the trustworthiness of God, the God of whom it is said that 'He chose the Jews.'? Is it not the manifest end of all covenant, consigning the Christian notions of forgiveness and redemption to an extinction for which there can never be an Easter? It disqualifies for ever any gospel of the cross.

Any will, however reverential, to see the agonies of Europe in the thirties and forties more inclusively at once assumes for Jewish souls the shape of a conspiracy. It will not do to observe with Albert Camus that some seventy million perished or suf-fered total desolation through war and persecution in the first half of this twentieth century.[12] Not to isolate the Holocaust totally from all else would be to give a posthumous victory to Hitler by seeming to mitigate the uniquely horrendous uniquely undergone. Lest the horror should ever undergo the blurring of distance and forgetfulness or just the weariness that will not bear its truth, it must be forever kept in mind and not suffered to fail of the grim perpetuation from which history might otherwise absolve the generations then unborn. Only such tenacity of memory does justice to the six million, herded, defiled, massacred, eliminated, in bestial genocide.

It is this awful 'truth of the Holocaust that shuts in' the heart of Jewry. A history so daunting, a desperation so unparalleled, could have no other sequel than a burden of responsibility for ever unrelieved – responsibility to the dead to give them 'a place and a name', responsibility to the world to remind it for ever of how grimly the good earth holds in its chemistry the ghastly perversity of mankind visited upon a single people. This is the spectre of horror and psychic oppression haunting the survivors and their heirs. It acts as a perpetual compulsion to existential otherness. To have been so monstrously 'willed against' by history and humanity is to be fated to remain, as it were, instinctively and irreconcilably on guard against the world. For the rest of mankind this becomes, in turn, the search for conscious solidarity with this most tragically introverted of communities, in all the forms which such authentic solidarity has imagination and humility to take.

When this Judaic sense of post-Holocaust burden is passionately linked with the fact of the State of Israel as the one realist
comfort the sense of apartness is intensified. Modern Zionism,
of course, predates the Holocaust by more than half a century
and its logic owes as much to Jewish distrust of enlightened
'liberalism' as to the experience of pogrom and ghetto. But in
a foreshortened perspective this is often forgotten and Holocaust and Israel become as Gethsemane and Easter to the Jewish
mind, only that the Holocaust beggars all such comparison and
Israel is a far surer, better fact than any Easter in its rugged
concreteness. The fusion of thought became very evident in
the reiterated theme of Menachem Begin's speeches in the summer of 1982, associating the all-out attack on the Palestinians
in Beirut with the bunkers in Berlin where Hitler was finally
cornered and doomed. Perhaps there was in that reading of
events, however dissimilar the situations, a victor-ex-victim
instinct to avenge the past. Certainly young Israelis of a later
generation no longer need to ask, when told of the Holocaust:
'But where was our Army?' The resolve: 'Never again', yet
the dread that it might be again, together intensify and concentrate the defiant yet inwardly restless conviction of singularity.

It is a set of mind so entirely comprehensible, so indelibly
written into the psyche, so historically rooted in adversity, that
it is almost impossible for the outsider to relate to it with any
healing intention, any authentic care. This is the more so since,
as outsider, he is in some way inculpated as part of that world
which justice would be required to 'burn down', were requital
made. Some outsiders try to escape into a pseudo-innocence,
to minimize what minimizing only aggravates, or passionately
identify with the utter vulnerability of those unforgettable victims. These reactions involve historical issues, some of which
we must ponder shortly. But all of them either miss or distort
the hope and the cost of healing.

For healing can come, neither in forgetfulness nor in the cherishing of pain and memory. It can come only in the awareness
of human solidarity and the freeing of the shut-in spirit. Elie
Wiesel is right. We must belong humanly with others if we
are to accuse 'inhumanity'. His very writing, with that of many
perhaps less compelling, is an appeal to wholeness, to others.
Singularity of suffering truly measured returns us back to a
human whole. There is no such thing as a literature of despair.
For a literature believes, appeals, affirms, awaits response. To

accuse is to assume there is an 'ought' in being human. The sense of the absurd, the blasphemous, the unspeakable, can only obtain in the reality of the responsible, the just, the compassionate. To deny these meanings is to have no complaint. Unless there is an entrustment to man, a goodness meant to be willed, the 'problem' of evil, however heinous, evaporates. It is merely what transpired. It has to be seen that the enormity of the Holocaust and the passion that palliatives, denials, excuses, and oblivion must be vehemently repudiated, alike demand a liable world, an authentic humanness. Only then is the crisis present, is the crisis understood and the sense of outrage consistent with reality.

This sense of human solidarity both in evil and in good in no way exonerates the guilty. But it does require that the Holocaust be condemned within a perspective that sees it in totality. The enormity of Nazism reaches back into the crimes of Versailles and these, in turn, into the desperate miseries of 'the Great War', and these again into the far past of European culture. In his perceptive *Autobiography*, Edwin Muir remarks of the young Gestapo soldiers:

> It suddenly came into my mind that they had been bred by the First World War. They had been children in 1919 when Germany was so wretched, and young girls and boys sold cocaine in the streets of Berlin and gave their bodies to anyone for a free meal.[13]

Such openness to the whole past and to a wide world is the only quality of justice to climactic sufferers. Or, as W. B. Yeats had it in the Irish context, evils start far back:

> Great hatred, little room,
> Maimed us at the start:
> I carry, from my mother's womb,
> A fanatic heart.[14]

To fear such considerations are a cunning apology is only to corroborate how urgent and authentic they are by measuring the entail which retrieval must face.

It is sometimes asserted that to look for redemption in tragedy is merely to encourage acquiescence in death, the death, that is, of others. For it is the living who survive to 'interpret' the suffering this way. So doing are they not glorifying a passivity when they should be demanding retribution? Are they not merely being generous with deaths not their own? If this way is then attributed to God, as in the Christian understanding of the cross, is not the eternal justice thereby atrophied? Is it not sounder, in the light of the Holocaust, to exclude God altogether and to assume the whole Judaic covenant an empty mockery? That would, indeed, be a posthumous victory for the Nazis and, more terribly, it would make acrimony the only voice from the dead.[15] 'In all their affliction, he was afflicted', said the prophet (Isaiah 63.9), 'the angel of his presence saved them' – the truth which Christianity ripens, as it believes by authority of Jesus' own suffering readiness, into the saying that 'God was in Christ reconciling the world . . .' (2 Cor. 5.19). It is almost a commonplace of Judaic thinking about 'Messiah' that, if he exists, or is to come, he is as much dependent on us as we are on him. In that event all occasions of evil must be his field, and ours. The more absolute the arraignment of evil and the more cosmic its dimensions of guilt and horror, the more imperative and unfailing 'the angel of his presence'; unless we are to fall back upon a despairing atheism which will also silence our indictment of the cosmos.[16] That will be a very raucous silence. For, no longer crying shame and hope because it is no longer trusting God, it will cry only spite and wrath and so betray the dead anew.[17] It is only the will to redemption that saves us holding our faith negatively, being as it were Jews only to defy the anti-Semites, or saying, as did Elie Wiesel in a mood of isolation: 'All I knew of Christianity was its hate for my people.'[18] The pain in his autobiography only makes the more telling his will to relate – the costly relation which prompts Robert McAfee Brown, interpreting his thought, to say: 'Jewish theology is human relations.'[19] To realize what price of pain, not to say paradox, is in that conclusion is to be committed to a Christian theology of Jewish relations in a human whole. But first, what of this perceived 'hate for my people'?

V

The onus for traditions of hostility has to be mutually faced. To commend, as we have done, the openness which can recognize and surmount its own shut-in assumptions, is to require of ourselves what we await from others. The Jewish perception of anti-Semitism and its Christian associations requires it of us, and of our theology, more intensely than any other field of cross-reference. It is necessary to carry forward into its demands the points already made in Chapter 6 about the differing peoplehoods to God on which the two faiths proceed. The first prerequisite is to renounce and resist two contrasted distortions. The one is exoneration, the easy echoing of the sentiment voiced by some Jews themselves that they cling too much to a querulous accusation of the world and should cease 'trading on their wrongs'. Such a cheap ignoring both of history and of heart would be utterly unworthy, a blasphemy against both God and man. The other distortion is the false and magisterial incrimination of all Christianity from the New Testament onwards which some Christian voices, in a passionate partisanship with Jewry, have made. 'Anti-Judaism', it is said, 'is the left hand of Christology'.[20] 'The Nazi final solution was no more than a logical application of historic Christian attitudes and demands.'[21] 'Contact of Jews with the Christian Church is an insult to Holocaust victims.'[22] 'Was God really serious about making all things new in Christ when Calvary could lead to the crematoria of Auschwitz?'[23] These are all wild and facile dicta, prompted perhaps in some cases by excess of zeal or passion but quite wanting in the discipline of either spiritual perception or intelligent scholarship.

There is one other aspect relating to anti-Semitism which needs to be noted with care, namely the charge that there is no distinction between anti-Judaism and anti-Zionism. The two are frequently bracketed in one with anti-Semitism. It may well be that some ill-wishers utilize the Palestinian exile as a means to generate hostility to Jewry as a whole. But to see the reproach or rejection of Zionism as *ipso facto* anti-Semitic, or anti-Judaic, is dishonestly to ignore two evident facts. The one is the vigorous anti-Zionism within Judaism itself; the other is the deep, legitimate claim on justice which the Palestinian tragedy holds against Israel, for displacement, suffering, homelessness and death.

That Judaism is by no means unanimous or at ease about Zionism is plain from the Zionist story. Even as late as 1963, Jacob Agus was writing, with wry satisfaction: 'Even now . . . the Zionist philosophy is slowly receding, allowing the dynamic equilibrium of Judaism to reassert itself.'[24] That he was wrong in his prognosis does not mean that he was wrong in his distinction. There is even a sense in which, in its campaign, Zionism itself approved the anti-Semites in echoing *some* of their strictures against diaspora Jewry. Zionism represents a crucial decision within the bosom of world Jewry about what its nature is – a decision deeply resented, suspected, disavowed, by significant Jewish opinion and loyalty committed to something like the church-concept of spiritual community (though without the trans-ethnic openness). To see Judaism and Zionism, therefore, as equatable, and hostility to the second as anathema on the first, is either stupid or malicious.

This is the more so when hostility to the second has within it sharp grievances which Jewish love of country and bitter knowledge of exile and its tribulations should make Jews the first to understand. Despite the understandable yearning of Israel for a verdict of innocence, despite the irrefutable warrant to possess with which Zionism believes itself armed, there is no honest denying the enormous human cost to Palestinians and Lebanese of the insertion, historically, of the modern State of Israel into their geographical context. Those wrongs are not to be ignored, or scouted, as far as any Christian reading of theology is concerned, by arbitrary divine *fiat* or doctrines of heavenly partisanship. The Christian gospel is committed to an understanding of prophecy and of God in Christ for which moral criteria are paramount and in which a divine embrace holds all peoples in an equal accessibility to grace and hope.

VI

Having resolved against facile partisan verdicts either excusing anti-Judaism or confusing it with anti-Zionism, how ought a search for 'the tent of meeting' to grapple with the long legacy of anti-Semitism and of Jewish suffering at its hands – a search, that is, striving towards a hope honest about the past? Before coming critically to the idea of the two covenants, what of the New Testament itself as the actual, or alleged, source of anti-Semitism? What, beyond it, because of it or despite it – as the case may be – of the long and bitter centuries of enmity and contention? How may we negate the negation of the mutually hostile position tersely put, for example, by Eliezer Berkowits: 'Judaism is Judaism because it rejects Christianity and Christianity is Christianity because it rejects Judaism ... All we want of Christians is that they keep their hands off us and our children.'[25] There are other voices disputing the theme of a Judeo-

Christian tradition[26] as something that has no real existence.
For these thinkers the New Testament is the final reason for
mutual negation.

What shall we say of it, and in particular how may it inform
and sustain us positively in the will to get beyond reciprocal
negation? There were inevitable tensions about the Christian
claim to Messiahship, the mystery for such persuasion of Jewish
non-acceptance, the issue of Judaic status and continuity given
the incorporation of Gentiles, the continuities of Torah and
synagogue, Paul's tortured logic about a temporary 'blindness'
in Israel in order to let in non-Jews.[27] With these, and much
else, at stake there were sharp personal tensions, emerging
very clearly in John's Gospel, between two communities –
themselves not uniform – over the frontier between them and
those so-called cryptic souls who became suspect to both sides
for their hesitancies about table fellowship or their indecision
about topics which the purists saw as vital.[28]

To have those tensions in perspective we must keep ever
in view the fact that the New Testament has no finally rejectionist attitude to Jews. Its authors, with the exception of Luke,
were Jews themselves. The sharp denunciations recorded in
Jesus' preaching, as for example in Matthew 23, have to do
with moral and spiritual features, to which all establishments
are liable. They are not a 'diabolizing' of Jews ethnically or
racially. Indeed their tone is very much in the tradition of the
Hebrew prophets and their content has to do not with Torah
as such but with its abuse. It was as custodians and not as
'Jews' that Jesus remonstrated with them. It is fair to see in
the intense pastoral preoccupation of the apostles, as mirrored
in the Epistles, a concern to reproduce in gentile life and culture
just those qualities of integrity and discipline for which torah
existed and which Jews feared would be jeopardized by Gentile
fellowship. It would be wrong to read in Paul's Gentile priority
in mission any final repudiation of his own people. It was,
rather, an enthusiastic fulfilment of a Jewish will to embrace.
The offertory to Jerusalem, which took Paul into imprisonment,
is the clearest index to a continual bond with his own. No
diabolizing here.[29]

It is sometimes said that the New Testament yields evidence
of a deliberate denigration of Jewry in order, for tactical reasons
in the early Church, to exonerate the Romans whose favour
required such ingratiation. It is odd, in that event, to realize

that the Creeds refer only to 'crucified under Pontius Pilate', and never attribute the cross to Jewish responsibility. Indeed, even the reference to Pilate is 'under' (i.e. the regime of) and has a primary purpose, not to incriminate but to attest the historicity. Where preaching in the Acts links the death of Jesus with the Jewish establishment it promptly also embraces them in an inclusive grace. The New Testament, as we have seen in Chapter 6, cannot be absolved of interpreting Jesus-Messiah as intending a whole world. But it does its utmost to win Jewish misgivings from the fear of such obedience and gives them always the priority in its commendation. That misgivings finally prevailed and became irreconcilable has much to do with contemporary events. That a Rubicon was crossed is not in doubt when the Church became almost exclusively Gentile. But the boats were there for all to cross. What faces us now, in this late twentieth century, is not served by mutual negation of what then transpired. Rather it invites us to discover how to meet in the reality of the long, bitter, resolute, positive experience of those who recognized no Rubicon and regretted those who did.

That task is crippled by the tragic legacy of the centuries between, by the distortion at Christian hands of things Judaic, by the notion of diaspora as a punishment for 'deicide', by prolonged disparagement and active persecution of the Jewish people, by the cruel instigation of that desperate sense of loneliness and identity-anxiety noted earlier, and by Christian pride and ostracism responding vulgarly and blindly to the Judaic exclusivism of kin and ritual. That there is here a bitter legacy, the documentation of which in some quarters remains a continuing exercise in polarization, only makes more imperative a genuine will to own it for what it is and to press on towards that positive mutuality which, having it always in soul-grief, may yet repair and redeem it.[30] But is the now popular thesis of the two covenants the authentic way to do so?

VII

Developed from the Jewish side by Franz Rosenzweig and from the Christian by such writers as James Parkes, with Paul Van Buren as a recent recruit, the two covenants theory suggests that Christianity should be seen as the extension of God's grace to Gentiles. Jews are not within the 'new covenant' because they are already covenanted with God. It is possible for Jews, on this view, to recognize and approve all that the Church believed itself to be on the condition that it is seen as non-inclusive of the Judaic peoplehood. Jews are 'people of God' by birth and do not have to 'become the children of God' by being 'born again' as Gentiles do. Belonging already in God, the gospel cannot involve them. For to suppose it doing so would imply that God had reneged on Sinai and would disqualify the ancient status. But for Jews to argue from this the non-reality of everything Christian would be to fly in the face of an irreducible historical phenomenon, the *de facto* reality of Jesus-Messiah in the sense of Christian conviction which, no less than Judaic self-understanding, is a fact of the human situation, and which, incidentally has been responsible for an amazing mediation to the world of things Judaic – psalms, ethics, norms – that it would be churlish to deny or decry. Jews could acknowledge this actuality as an admissible form of monotheism for non-Jews. Their own identity need not be affirmed by rejection of a Christian Messianism and all its worldwide implications so long as they maintained their own exemption from its relevance. In this generous way Jews could approve Christianity without Judaic compromise.

Christian sponsorship of this thesis reciprocates by reading the gospel in the non-inclusive terms which it requires. James Parkes gives to his advocacy of parallel covenants and Jew/Gentile otherness a dimension which turns on a doubtful formulation. In some ways it is analogous to the case developed by Martin Buber in *Two Types of Faith*.[31] Parkes sees Judaism, with its intense community consciousness, symbolizing the concrete role of society, in contrast to the Christian concern with the personal. The Jew is born, the Christian is made. The one lives in orthopraxy, the other by orthodoxy. In the one case the whole of one ethnic people is chosen, in the other a conglomerate of 'church'-form involving individual recipients of grace. It would be inappropriate to see the former among the latter. The multi-cultural accessibility of Christianity is safeguarded by doctrine *via* the Incarnation. Resting on individualism it has to secure itself by dogmatic Christology – a Christology which fulfils for Christians what election does for Jews. Both are authentic and disparate. Christians can be united with Jews only by separation. On this count it was actually necessary for Jews to reject Jesus as Messiah. It would have been their treachery to concede him as such. But this need not deter them from allowing, indeed, welcoming, the Christian way to God through Christian Christology, while their self-exemption from it implies no invalidity for Gentiles.

Parkes' thinking throughout was inspired by a passionate concern to repudiate and eliminate anti-Semitism. He sought to make all relationships positive by taking both Sinai and Christ as divine events. Neither faith should judge the other 'by standards to which in the divine purpose it was never meant to conform'.[32] 'The relations between Sinai and Calvary are basically those of creative tension arising out of the dual inheritance of humanity',[33] i.e. the duality of the societal and the personal.

A variety of other Christian thinkers have espoused these broad principles of distinction. Some among them, like A. R. Eckardt, have gone further in revising the gospel in the light of the Holocaust, requiring, for example, that the doctrine of the resurrection be expunged from the gospel: 'That Jewish man from Galilee sleeps now . . . with all the disconsolate and scattered ones of the murder camps . . . But Jesus of Nazareth shall be raised.'[34] Jürgen Moltmann insists: 'For a Gentile Christian . . . there is nothing more positive for his salvation than a Jewish No!'[35] Each must go on believing in their own hope, their own faith, separately, in disparate futures until the eschaton.

There is in all this what German calls *Standortgebundenheit*, the state of being standpoint-bound. What shall we say of it from within either community of belief? There are Jewish writers who demur strongly from it on Jewish grounds. It has, for example, to be realized, *pace* Buber, that Judaism is intensely personal and that there is a strong societal dimension in Christianity. The distinction Buber makes between *emunah* and *pistis*, Hebraic trust/faithfulness and Christian 'believing-that', is wrongly categorical. There is Hebraic *pistis*, witness Maimonides, and there is Christian *emunah*, witness, for example, William Temple's *Christianity and the Social Order*.[36] In neither faith can 'believing-in' be free from 'believing-that'. Further, as noted in Chapter 6, even if there is something metaphysical about Judaic peoplehood making it divinely *sui generis*, it remains true that all peoples have their histories, memories, myths and mountains. As David Hartman remarks:

Other people have their own Egypts, their own deserts, their own

Sinais, and each builds from his own. I have no criteria as to what
is not to count as a person's Egypt, or Sinai or desert.[37]

The Church in its universal access principle does not exclude
the societal particularities of every culture in inviting them all
to share in Jesus and the cross the foundation-order of a peoplehood that incorporates their rich diversity by relativizing their
ethnic prides. In this light James Parkes' distinction between
Judaic societal and Christian personalism, however laudable
its motive, looks highly forced and artificial.

But more importantly the two covenants theory totally alters
the New Testament perspective. Jacob Taubes among Jewish
writers has seen this clearly.[38] It amounts to a rewriting of 'God
so loved the world' so that it reads: 'God so loved the Gentiles'.
It makes havoc of the dictum: 'In Christ there is neither Jew
nor Greek.' It perpetuates and entrenches the category of 'Gentiles', which the Church was born to transcend. So doing, it
ultimately undermines its own motive of relatedness by under-
writing in a new form the age-long exclusion and exclusivism
of the Judaic tradition. It is still saying to Jewry: 'You are not
included.' In that stance it surely transgresses the meaning and
openness of Christ. So to conclude will still leave us with the
duty of understanding what is affirmed in Jewish continuity,
and it will require us to reckon with that Judaic reality more
fundamentally precisely because we have not accommodated
it in a manner uncongenial to itself and inconsistent with our
sense of Christ. To this we will shortly come. Can we rightly
come to it, unless we hold at least in hope to the mystery of
what the Church was meant to be, and the vision of a human
incorporation where diversity could be benediction because it
was all controlled and conditioned by a humanity at one in
grace? Has the Christian any warrant to exempt from grace,
as urgent and as generous, any in God's creation? Let old John
Donne say:

> It was so to the Jews and it was so to the Gentiles too ... Christ
> hath excommunicated no nation, no shire, no house, no man: He
> gives none of his ministers leave to say to any: 'Thou art not
> redeemed': he gives no wounded nor afflicted conscience leave to
> say to itself: 'I am not redeemed.'[39]

We are back full circle to the unredeemedness which, for Jewry,
disqualifies as romanticism both the gospel of open grace and

the Church which supposedly embodies its community. If we take the Jewish will to non-inclusion in what Christians say can only be itself in non-exclusion, if we insist on wanting the unwanting because they can never rightly be unwanted, are we all simply locked in standpoint-boundness? If not the two covenant theory in some form, what then? Or can its intention be reshaped to a better reconciliation? [40]

VIII

It may be useful to recall that in the early Church there were those who understood themselves to be both Jews and Christians. The virtual gentilizing of the Church by the second century was due, in large measure, to circumstances of history which tended to extinguish, or at least to obscure, what such a reconciliation might have been. Was the result a case of a losing side passing into a silence we cannot now interpret? Be that as it may, we must now think and act in the real present of our time. Some thinking on either side will remain irreconcilable. Some, mainly on the Christian side, will be urgent for understanding but with some compromise of interpretation. Others again, the cynics, will see the whole effort after dialogue only a sign of Christian weakness in face of secularity. Others, too, in Jewry will maintain a traditional disinterest in Jesus, despite the recent efforts of notable Jewish scholarship to repossess him. The Jesus of Christology, the aloof ones feel, is an essentially Aryan Christ for whom the only right Judaic stance is their aloofness.

But these are the negative postures. A perceptive Christianity can surely acknowledge the continuing authenticity of Judaism, first by heeding carefully the deep reasons for Jewish dissuasion from the Christian Messiah and then by realizing how far the cares of these, when discerned faithfully, have the New Testament with them. In preface to a final conclusion about this 'tent of meeting', it is fair to make two points. The first is that what the Christian sees as the validity of the Jewish past, as historical preparation for Christ, need not be thought to be forfeited because Jewry withheld recognition of such fulfilment. The debt remains and Christianity has always witnessed to it gratefully by its desire, at some cost, to see the Hebrew Scriptures as its own. This tribute of debt may offend some

Jewish thinking. But Christianity's debt to what it calls 'the Old Testament' *need* not turn into umbrage, still less into hostility, because those to whom it is owed failed to accept the Christian version of what their significance had been. On the contrary, the sense of Christian roots in Hebraica ought to relate Christians expectantly to fruits of those same roots in the ongoing spirituality they have sustained since the Christian vintage was drawn off.

That view finds corroboration in the second point. Does not the mystery of election stand – like all religious meaning – in the conviction that it is so? As long as the Jewish spirit holds authentically and tenaciously – as it does – to the faith as to covenant does not covenant abide? Faith is not to be thought unilaterally renounced by the God on whom it relies. Believing, in this mysterious sense, makes it so. Judaic covenant is, and always was, established in the experience that made it so, *via* the interpretation that experience received. Facts of belief are facts – of the situation. It is no part of Christian or any other relationship from without to devalidate what is only inwardly possessed. We have no exterior criteria by which ever to say: It is not so. In this context the 'truth-for' situation as it applies to others has to become, for us, a 'truth-of' acknowledgement as far as they are concerned. It is only by such a mutual posture that we can hope, together, to undertake the still urgent search for the several outward relationships of truths inwardly possessed.

These two considerations could not stand in themselves without what, further, we can discern when we bring together the ultimate grounds on which Jewry exempts itself from Christianity and the New Testament content of faith. If Messiahship, as Buber requires, is 'a process which passes through men in suffering and hiddenness',[41] may not that be a view of messianic community, as the apostles knew and told it, without excluding the messianic personality? Were we to argue that messianic self-disclosure, as Buber does, is a contradiction in terms, would not this mean that the messianic *per se* must be unimaginable? The New Testament's gospel is not 'encroachment from the beyond' as if all hope was ended and history 'tied up and its door shut'.[42] On the contrary, the New Testament is full of the thought of 'the God of patience', only it sees the clue to that patience realized in the cross. But the future is there, requiring the messianic conformity of all disciples, the Christ-already being the pattern, not the climax, of the Christ-to-be. In that sense the divine travail remains.

To think these kinships of mind is not to revert to a bald two covenants position. It is, rather, to think towards the approximation of what Christians believe and what Jews in that context wish to hold in reservation. The two need not be far apart. For the reservations belong with the meaning from which, institutionally, they refrain. Arthur A. Cohen writes:

> Israel must soften its heart before the historical happening of the life and death of Jesus for the sake of those who affirm it to be more than history; but, likewise, those who believe in Jesus as the Christ and in their belief know its truth for themselves must understand what is affirmed in Jewish disbelief.[43]

On such terms there is no doubt we both possess and retain our share in God.

A most eloquent exponent of this sense of things was the late Rabbi Abraham Heschel. Saved from Warsaw after the Germans arrived there, he lost his whole family. Yet, as Neusner observes, the word 'Holocaust' scarcely appears in his many writings. He understood that 'retaining our share in God' lay in the travail of hope, knowing ourselves to be, as creatures, God's stake in history, whose task was to vindicate him. In that task Heschel found, *via* the prophets, the central clue of divine pathos. There was a *unio sympathetica* between God and his prophet-servants. These could know that their suffering was divinely shared. Heschel's was not a voice of which many Jewish scholars and activists approved.[44] But the Judaism for which he spoke and God as 'the most moved Mover' has the same soul as the theology which fashioned the New Testament Church. 'The tent of meeting' is not reached through two covenants that leave us in the mutual otherness they seal but rather in the single conviction of the 'divine earnestness about our life'.[45]

Does 'divine earnestness' about us seem a rather elusive conviction, even a nebulous wistfulness? The intensity it implies, both as to God and in ourselves, may be thoroughly biblical. But can it be more than *our* will to think it so? To what shall we point as 'earnestly divine', in the sense not only of ardour but also of the *arrabōn*, the surety, of which the New Testament wrote?[46] Christianity lives by the answer which realizes it historically and presently in the Christhood of Jesus. It holds that

answer in trust in the vocation to open community in its meaning – a community called to endless patience with the reservations that doubt either its credentials or its sincerity. But this
Judaic criterion of 'divine earnestness about our life' is the one
which it would most desire to be found to satisfy. The Jewry
which requires it proceeds from that very sense of the divine
which Christian faith in Jesus as the Christ substantiates in
event and in life. We do not share the eventuation: we are
one in the sense of God.

'Divine earnestness about our life' has an odd sounding ring
in India.

NOTES

1 The following are examples: *White Crucifixion* (1938), *Crucifixion in Yellow*
(1943), *The Yellow Christ* (1945), *Descent from the Cross* (1947), *The Crucified
of the Bridge* (1951).

2 Alistair Cooke, *Masterpieces: A Decade of Classics on British Television* (London
1982), p. 203.

3 Arthur A. Cohen, *The Myth of the Judeo-Christian Tradition* (New York 1970),
pp. 87 and 33.

4 Perhaps the most notable statement of Jewish particularism and justifiable
'non-conquest' is found in Martin Buber, *Israel and Palestine, the History
of an Idea*, trans. S. Godman (London, New York 1952), pp. 48–50: 'If the
peoples come and reproach Israel saying: "You are a people of robbers:
you have conquered the lands of seven nations", Israel can point out
to them that its God created heaven and earth . . . He can apportion land
to whom He wills. "According to His will He gave you the land and according to His will He has taken it from you and given it to us." This does
not mean at all that all invasions of other lands are to be considered equally
justified because they are willed by God, or even that all acts of violence
of one people against another people are justifiable. The essential point
is that Israel heard the will of the Lord of the world . . . and conquered
the land in the perfect and well-founded faith that it was accomplishing
His will. With however little or much right in each case the nations can
accuse each other of being robbers, their charge against Israel is totally
unjust, for it acted under authority and in the confident knowledge of
its authorisation. The revelation, the faith in it, and the action following
from this faith, are what differentiate Israel from other nations, not merely
"religiously" but historically . . . No other people has ever heard and accepted the command from heaven as did the people of Israel . . . Where
a command and faith are present, in certain historical situations conquest
need not be robbery.'
      One may compare the comment of R. J. Z. Werblowsky in *Peoples and
Conflict in the Middle East: A Preliminary Report for Study* (New York 1973),
p. 107: 'Israel is a fact . . . a fact that exists by right of history and not

by right of conquest. The conquest was incidental, forced upon the Jews, though – *post factum* – its importance can hardly be over estimated.'

5 A dictum owed, I think, to Professor Ernest Barker. My responsibility to current political themes as far as 1980 I tried to fulfil, at greater length than is here possible, in *This Year in Jerusalem*, London 1982.

6 The success of Zionism, especially since 1967, makes it difficult for new-comers to the history to realize how heavy were the odds against the Zionist idea in its early form and how uphill its propagation was in face of fears for diaspora Jewry whose loyalties to the countries of their residence might become suspect. Zion seemed to many a chimera, a false vision, a betrayal of the vocation of Jewry to be 'among the nations' for God's sake. See note 7.

7 The Zionist doctrine that *Die Juden sind ein Volk* was read by many anti-Semitic agitators to mean that Jews could never be truly part of a European nation. Nahum Goldmann in 1920 declared that Judaism could have nothing in common with Germanism and was taken by some to mean that there were two nationalisms which could not accommodate each other. This was the implication of a nationhood elsewhere, as the true *Volk* centre of Jewish loyalty, which made non-Zionist Jews apprehensive and gave fuel to anti-Semitic arguments.

8 Dow Marmur, *Beyond Survival: Reflections on the Future of Judaism* (London 1982), p. 36.

9 J. L. Talmon, *The Unique and the Universal* (New York 1965), p. 72.

10 Elie Wiesel, *Legends of our Time* (New York 1972), p. 233.

11 Elie Wiesel, *The Oath* (New York 1973), p. 73.

12 Albert Camus, *The Rebel, An Essay on Man in Revolt*, trans. Anthony Bower (New York 1956), p. 3, Introduction. In the closing stages of the Great War and its aftermath in Turkey the Armenian people suffered a genocide, fewer in numbers but even more lethal in proportion. But reference to it is uncongenial to writers on the Holocaust. One might equally well imagine the Gregorian Church pondering the possibility of theology after Musa Dagh, or the legitimacy of Negro Spirituals being repudiated in the light of the real facts about the Slave Trade.

13 Edwin Muir, *Autobiography* (London 1954), p. 262. Earlier he describes the young distraught nature worshippers, the *Wandervogel* of Dresden, carrying guitars into the woods. 'The War had made them poor and wak-ened in them a need to be with harmless, unwarlike things like trees and streams and to move freely through peaceful spaces. Most of them, I have been told, were carried away later by the gospel of Hitler. They had nothing but simplicity . . . to protect them against him' (pp. 202–3).

14 W. B. Yeats, *Collected Poems*, Definitive edn (New York 1956), p. 249, 'Remorse at Intemperate Speech.' 'Out of Ireland have we come.' One might also recall the line: 'In the lost boyhood of Judas Christ was betrayed.'

15 Echoing a line of Edwin Muir's about 'hatreds thrust upon us by the acrimo-nious dead'. But it is we, the living, who make them so, if at all, by the

spirit in which we hold them in our souls. See Muir's 'The Wheel', in *Collected Poems*, p. 105.

16 Elie Wiesel in *The Jews of Silence* (New York 1968), writes, in part, about the unconcern of some Jews in the dispersion about the plight of other Jews. His whole writing is a sustained protest against *all* silence in the presence of history. Hence the case here that silence must overtake all reproach, however clamant, in the absence of those ultimates about man and God in which alone reproach has meaning.

17 cf. the remark of Elie Wiesel in *The Jews of Silence*, p. 82: 'For want of better teachers it is the anti-Semites who are making them Jews.' 'We are Jews for spite', one student told him.

18 Elie Wiesel, *A Jew Today* (New York 1979), p. 5.

19 Robert McAfee Brown, *Elie Wiesel: Messenger to All Humanity* (St Louis 1983), p. 141.

20 Rosemary Ruether, *Faith and Fratricide: Theological Roots of Anti-Semitism* (New York 1974).

21 A. R. Eckardt, writing in E. J. Woods, ed., *Jewish/Christian Relations* (1976), p. 48.

22 Eliezer Berkovits, writing in *Judaism*, vol. 27 (1978), p. 325. See the same writer in F. E. T. Talmage, ed., *Disputation and Dialogue: Readings in Jewish/Christian Encounter* (1975), pp. 284–95.

23 H. J. Cargas, ed., *Where God and Man Failed* (1981), p. 65. The writer is J. K. Roth.

24 Jacob B. Agus, *The Meaning of Jewish History*, vol. ii. (London 1963), p. 447.

25 In F. E. Talmage, ed., *Disputation and Dialogue: Readings in Jewish/Christian Encounter* (New York 1975), pp. 291 and 293. The writer is Eliezer Berkovits. He sees Judaism as totally self-sufficient and the notion of a Judeo-Christian tradition as fantasy. Dialogue is an immoral attempt to whitewash a criminal past.

26 Notable among them Arthur A. Cohen, op. cit., note 3 above.

27 It seems clear that Paul felt intensely the burden of Jewish non-acceptance of Jesus as Messiah. He lived the issue rather than merely studied it. This explains his passionate desire to retain both conviction as a Christian and hope as a Jew. Hence the thesis of a temporary 'blindness' to make room for the Gentiles. It is as if he turns a spiritual tension into a time-sequence and imposes a dilemma on a calendar. When in Romans 9–11, and Galatians 4 he wrestles with the question he uses Midrash-style arguments where his metaphors about vines and grafting, heirs and wards, are curiously complicated and it is not clear who is being grafted into what. Despite what commentary has done with these passages since, one thing is clear, namely that Paul's love for his own people is paramount. Were it not so he would have had nothing to resolve.

28 See Chapter 6, note 21. The frequent reference to 'the Jews' in John's Gospel, we need to remember, is being made all the time by Jewish folk, e.g. the parents in 9.22, are described as 'afraid of the Jews', being Jews

themselves. The designation, then, is not an inclusive or ethnic one, but refers to that aspect of society which, in the Gospel's context, symbolized hostility. It is perhaps a measure of the enmity that, in John, when the authorities refer to Jesus they do not use his name but, disparagingly (?) speak of 'this man' (9.16, 24; 11.47; 18.17).

29   A term used by Rosemary Ruether in her insistence that there is nothing but denigration for Jews at Christian hands, *Faith and Fratricide*, cf. note 20.

30   Jules Isaac, in *The Teaching of Contempt*, trans. H. Weaver (New York 1964), traces seven areas in which he grounds his definition of Nazi anti-Semitism as 'a secular radicalization of the anti-Jewish impulses of historic Christianity'.

31   Martin Buber, *Two Types of Faith, A Study of the Inter-Penetration of Judaism and Christianity*, trans. N. P. Goldhawk (New York 1961), in which he makes a stylized distinction between Judaic faithfulness and Christian 'credalism'. It is remarkable that so perceptive a thinker, to whom Christian theology owes much for his personalism and his interpretation of the Exodus, should have so sadly misread the Christian ethos.

32   James Parkes, *The Foundations of Judaism and Christianity* (London 1960), p. 201. See also his autobiography, *Voyage of Discoveries*, London 1969.

33   ibid., p. 200.

34   A. R. Eckardt, *Elder and Younger Brothers* (New York 1967); also *Resurrection and Holocaust*, Israel Study Group (New York 1978), p. 13.

35   In *Jewish Monotheism and Christian Trinitarian Doctrine*, A Dialogue by Pinchas Lapide and Jurgen Moltmann (Philadelphia 1981), trans. L. Swidler, p. 89.

36   William Temple, *Christianity and Social Order*, London 1942.

37   David Hartman, in *Immanuel*, no. 6 (Jerusalem 1976), pp. 79–80.

38   Jacob Taubes, in A. A. Cohen, ed., *Arguments and Doctrines: A Reader in Jewish Thinking in the Aftermath of the Holocaust* (New York 1970), p. 409

39   John Donne, *Sermons*, ed. E. M. Simpson and G. R. Potter (Berkeley 1953), vol. vi, Sermon no. 17, p. 344.

40   The theme of conversion, obviously germane to all this discussion is deferred – for reasons which will then appear – to the concept of Hinduism and Chapter 10.

41   Martin Buber, *The Origin and Meaning of Hasidism*, being vol. ii of *Hasidism and the Way of Man*, trans. M. Friedman (New York 1960), pp. 110–11.

42   Andre Neher, *The Exile of the Word*, trans. David Maesal (Philadelphia 1981), p. 190.

43   Arthur A. Cohen, *Myth*, etc. (note 3 above), p. 41.

44   Abraham Heschel, *The Prophets*, New York 1962. It is right to note that there are many voices in Jewry disapproving strongly of Heschel's faith as to divine pathos. Eliezer Berkovits, for example, sees Heschel here as having fallen into a Christian heresy. God, being perfect, cannot 'need' man: 'A God of pathos has no basis in Judaism.' Leon Roth, too, sees

it running counter to the basic assumptions of Judaism. See M. Vogel, *The Death of Dialogue and Beyond* (New York 1969), pp. 173f. Both Judaism and Christianity are widely diversified. It would be impossible to relate all to all: but of some to some the kinship stands.

45 Abraham Heschel, *The Earth is the Lord's* (New York 1950), p. 83: 'Our existence is never in vain. There is a divine earnestness about our life. This is our dignity ... We are God's stake in human history ... The time for the Kingdom may be far off, but the task is plain – to retain our share in God in spite of peril and contempt.'

46 See 2 Cor. 1.22; 5.5; and Eph. 1.14. *Arrabōn* is a Hebrew word in Greek letters and denotes that part of a price paid in pledge of later fulfilment of the rest in order to clinch a transaction. In the passages noted it refers to the present activity of the Holy Spirit as surety for the final redemption, or 'inheritance' (itself a word which attests the open-peoplehood for whom a 'kin' term can be used despite the absence of literal kinship). It is not suggested here that there is any linguistic connection between 'earnest' as adjective, i.e. 'ardent' or 'serious', and 'earnest' as noun, i.e. 'pledge'. But that does not deprive us of the aptness in the double usage here.

Christologies and India

8
'Is Christ Multiplied?'

Paul's question was the contrary: 'Is Christ divided?' (1 Cor. 1.13). It expected a resounding answer: No. The partisanship of particular ministers, which was the concern of his letter, had no place in the unity of Christ. Christ alone had suffered for each and all. His alone was the name of the common baptism. Jesus was Lord of a single fellowship in which he belonged to any only in belonging to all. 'You are Christ's', Paul told his readers, 'and Christ is God's' (1 Cor. 3.23). There is no division here.

Is there point, then, in reversing the question to ask about plurality. 'Is Christ multiplied?' – what might the question mean? Was not the confession that 'Jesus is *the* Christ' the very nerve and fount of Christian existence in the New Testament? When the first Church said, as it so loved to do: '*Our* Lord Jesus Christ', was there any implication that the possessive pronoun might be used by others for some other Christ? Could that term have a different or competing currency? The 'our' was indeed open, as wide as the world. It was not restrictive as to possessors: it was only restrictive as to the one possessed. The whole world might join itself to the collective relevance – this was the dearest ambition of the users – but with no thought that the criteria of Jesus' being 'the Christ' could be any-how, or any-where, or any-when, variable or several. To confess 'Emmanuel, God with us', could, and should, mean an ever multiplying community of his recognition but not, surely, a diversity of what or who was recognized in incorporating love and faith.

Yet those who say: 'Us', are everywhere multiple and distinctive, being made so by those sanctions of nature, tribe, culture, language and memory which, we say, are rooted in the created order and must, therefore, derive from the Creator's purpose. Could it be, then, that there are diverse and plural ways in which the 'with us' about God is realized and fulfilled? Could what Christian faith acknowledges as the Christ-Event be differently the Christ-Idea elsewhere – the focal point of reference

for the transcendent? To speak vaguely and elusively about
where eternity meets time or about a 'Jacob's ladder' – so to
say – where the mystery within religions is transacted conceptually or symbolically will be a long way from the specifics
of Christian Christology, and we will need to ask why such
diffuse themes should want, or receive, the Christ-language.
Nevertheless such wider Christologies, however remote from
the messianic actuality as known to the New Testament, do
find currency and expect attention from theologians who
believe they have in trust the true 'Emmanuel'. Indeed, there
are theologians ready to dissociate Christhood from Jesus in
any singular sense. Thus a writer in *Concilium*:

> The totality of the Christ is not Jesus and cannot be contained in
> and limited to him.[1]

What this diversification of Christology might mean it is the
task of this Chapter to examine and interrogate. The issue follows urgently from the theme of the preceding section about
Messiah and Jewry, just as that section developed here from
within the area of God and prophethood and, thereby, of Islam.
The messianic theme was traced in Jesus, in the decision within
his ministry, and the first Christian community's realization
of that messianic decision and their experience, because of it,
of a new peoplehood under God. Such messianic actualization
by Jesus as the Christ was heralded by Jewish faith and by
Jewish initiative interpreted as transcending Jewry to embrace
mankind. But the mainstream Judaic verdict withheld such
recognition and refused enlargement. For Jewry at large the
messianic question remained puzzlingly, tragically, even permanently, open. Meanwhile the Christian sense of an accomplished Messiahship in Jesus' terms ripened into a
Christology, moving from and with the messianic deed into
a faith as to the messianic person and how he should be understood in relation to God, to the God disclosed in the messianic
decision which, for Christians, had determined the messianic
meaning. Christology had to do, in this way, with the art of
being Messiah – which takes us to Gethsemane – before it had
to do with the defining of Messiah's being – which takes us
to Chalcedon and beyond.

   That realm of Christology, from doing to being, from act
to essence, and with it the continuing messianic issue, Judaic

and Christian, is familiar enough. But can Christology be extended into the plural outside this Semitic field of the *Mashiach* vision which belongs so singularly with the biblical heritage? Will it be warranted to use the Christ-theme for vaguer aspirations, legends, ideals – Asian or other – which have symbolic currency and may be seen to play the central role in other faiths that the Jesus-dimension (if we may so speak) has for Christians? A central role, indeed, Krishna plays in the *Bhagavad Gita*, the most loved literature of Hinduism. Will the mere fact of centrality, irrespective of the theme in the 'central', make him, as it were, another Christ?

This is the kind of question we have to face in taking Christology into the plural – as it is undoubtedly, if bewilderingly, taken in our time. No Christian cross-reference can be alert or adequate if it does not reckon with faiths and forms which want to possess Jesus on their own terms, not ours, and which see an 'identity' of the Christ wider than our 'identification' of him. To that distinction between inclusive 'identity' and different 'identification' we will return. Christology, so the challenge runs, can be culturally ubiquitous. The Christ-Idea must be de-monopolized, and Jesus with it. However we see it, the salvific, the redemptive, the divine-human, the mediatorial, must be taken out of Christian copyright.

India stands as the best representative of this demand. By aiming for some mental sympathy with the Hindu/Indian milieu we can most usefully face the pluralizing of Christologies. There is a long Hindu tradition of absorption, of non-distinction, of revering reverence *per se*, of tolerating all but intolerance. This is not to say that Hinduism spells an unconditional hospitality. Quite the contrary. It is as tenacious of those who want to leave it as any other '-ism'. It can be sharply exclusive about its non-exclusivity. It has anathemas but reserves them for anathema. It wants to be rejectionist only of rejectionism. Thus it was a Hindu instinct both to welcome Jesus and to detach him from the Christian context of his historic meaning and, indeed, from the Jewish context of his story. Many Christian theologians within India, both Indian and expatriate, have wrestled with, and aspired to, a Hinduized Christology.

The principle of reverence for reverence means that one may give one's own imprint to one's borrowings. Is it not the host who decides how he will entertain his guest? And 'entertain' is a nicely balanced word, suggesting both courtesy and control.

Can this 'entertainment' happen in Christology and, therefore, also in theology? Was there, we might ask, any point, even within basic Christian definitions, when it did *not* happen? If what we like to think to be definitive Christology was not free of cultural determinants, may not other cultural determinants have their place? Need these imperil whatever the 'essential' is which abides through *all* cultural contexts?

It has often seemed to India-lovers that India has a special vocation in this cause. Do not Greece and India, as it were, divide the world between them? – not 'chosen' in the manner of Hebraic understanding of 'the jealous God' and divine election, but manifestly mentors of mankind. Greece had her role in Christology in the Fathers and the Creeds and their legacy is with us still. May India not covet her own role in Christology? We must look at the ideas of those who think so.

II

Their ventures raise two deep issues which must occupy Chapters 9 and 10 below. But it will be well to set them down here for their bearing on the present theme. They are the question of history and the question of conversion. If there are to be Christologies apart from the Christ as Jesus they will be dispensing, to greater or less degree, with the historical actuality from which the very term derives. The Hindu mind, in poetry, legend and symbol, is very ready to dispense with the historical. *Māyā, karma* and *brahmavidya* proceed upon illusoriness where specifics of time and place dissolve into indistinction and myth or fantasy may serve equally well. Meaning does not need to happen. Christian Christology, however – for all its internal debates – is committed to history and history is a great particularizer. It ties meaning to times, persons, places and situations. If we relegate history to the margins we may attain a totally mythical Christology with no duty to event, whether quest or inquest.

Further, plural Christologies suggest plural contexts of salvation, whereas Christianity is traditionally conversionist. It seeks allegiance and desires to incorporate. Its insignia are faith, confession and baptism. To 'make disciples of all nations' was the mandate of the apostolic Church, while the Hindu instinct, on which Gandhi, for example, firmly insisted, sees migration out of religious identities as foolish or worse. What implications, then, arise for Christian theology about what has to happen in the soul, if Christologies are truly multiple? Has what Christians call 'the work of grace' in souls effectual channels as disparate as the Christologies? If not, how are they Christologies in fact? If so, in what do their means of grace consist? In the context of these questions in Chapter 10 it will be wise to revert to an issue remitted from Chapter 7 as to whether Christian faith should renounce or relinquish its open hospitality and its rite of baptism. These are large questions.

III

It may help to clarify if we indicate what is *not* meant by plural Christologies in this context. We need not go to India or seek acclimatization in Hinduism in order to study varieties of christological thought in the mainstream Christian tradition. That these are already 'plural' we must honestly concede. Plural, too, are the interpretations of Jesus which are antecedent to Christology or which forbid Christology altogether. These are important areas of our duty which we must here integrate into a still larger intention. That intention is to explore 'ideas' of what might be 'Christic' by a greatly elasticized notion which is ready to detach radically from New Testament norms (for all their being in debate) and extend to whatever seems religiously significant on the 'same' behalf. The burden of Christian cross-reference into such alleged 'sameness' must be felt for what it is – not lightened by easy sentiment, nor shunned by zealous rejection that has not stayed to wonder why the Christ should be wanted, ourselves apart, for others' purposes. We have to face, for example, whether the revelation to Arjuna in the *Gita* of Krishna, erstwhile charioteer, in the blinding splendour of divine majesty is in any sense a Christ-experience.

However, sharply different as that issue must be from any within New Testament parameters, it will be well to begin from how plural Christian Christologies already are. For it is, in part, just this plurality which has inspired, or instigated, the wider, wilder concepts we have to study. If history, as Christians stress its significance, can be so fruitful of interpretation, perhaps ideas and ideology can take them further, and out of history altogether. If historicists are not agreed perhaps they can be muted. Or at least their disquiet may be ignored. In any event the grounds for historical resistance to the fertility of Indian, or other, imagination will be weakened precisely by their inability to be in themselves univocal. We defer to the next chapter the vital question of the constraints which a Christian loyalty to history can reasonably require of those who want to recruit it for themselves. That will mean asking what the Christ-happening really, truly, was, though the answer is in part implicit already in preceding chapters about Messiah and Jewry. In this chapter what is important first is a lively appreciation of why this enlarging, diversifying or naturalizing of Jesus and of things Christic emerges within other cultures and in India in particular.

IV

There would seem to be two factors present. The one is the contemporary sense of nationality and the cultural identity which anciently sustains it. The other is the kindling of mingled attraction and perplexity which belong with sensitive mission across such identities. Mahatma Gandhi and C. F. Andrews, close associates as they were, are telling examples in either case.

All peoples except the Jews are involved in the puzzle of their place in an economy of grace which has its messianic matrix in just one historical context and that a context passionately particularist. Many identities, of course, the Irish, the Italians, the English, the Russians, have long forgotten (for emotional purposes) that their faith reached them from alien hands and through alien speech. Their histories, as it were, have long since digested things Christian into themselves. With tiny exceptions it was not so with India, and in modern times the Christian Christ was associated closely with imperial presence and alien power. The counter – and, though counter, very positive – assertion of Indian-ness (and inevitably with it of Hinduism) posed deep emotional questions about the 'housing' of Christian faith in non-Indian idiom and aegis.[2] That countering was evident throughout in Gandhi's leadership and campaigns and underlay his vehement repudiation of 'Christian' conversion. His spirit was deeply and staunchly sustained by Hinduism in its positive quality, but he operated in a context of political resistance and Swaraj. Religion was his ally as well

as his inspiration. There was a political legitimation and, therefore, a political criterion in his religious judgements. Within
these Christianity was both profoundly recruited and firmly
excluded. The Sermon on the Mount was authentic but baptism
was *verboten*.

We must, however, pursue these political concerns with
identity into much deeper areas of the spirit. They have to
do with what, allegedly, is the most vital thing, namely the
divine gospel, being indifferent to, and oblivious of, the culture
which defines you. Being Judaic-messianic in its vintage it had
no need of the Vedas or any other treasured source in *your*
heritage. It presents itself to you out of foreignness as if to
imply that its only use for you is your acceptance. How this
aspect of the gospel affected at least one Indian theologian,
Vengal Chakkarai, we will note in the chapter following. It
has to do with how history in the Incarnation relates to before
and after.

Here, the concern has to be expressed in terms of place as
well as time. Where, if at all, was India in the 'preparation
of the gospel'? The fact that Englishmen may have reconciled
to a non-place – with some subsequent compensations – should
not forbid the question to Indians.

Indeed, there have been 'Indians' elsewhere who asked it
pointedly and their query may serve to make the point. In John
Eliot's *Discourses* he records a Massachuset 'Indian' asking: 'If
this faith is so true why was it not given to *our* ancestors?'[3]
Comparable interrogation of missionaries is reported from
Africa, Oceania and almost every other field of mission. The
ultimate revelation, urgent of acceptance, comes only belatedly
to inform. Why could it not originate where one is oneself at
home?

A universal gospel cannot ignore this question or dismiss
it with impatience. For the sense of one's importance to it is
a first accent in its presentation. Arriving, it welcomes all; but
its arrival is wholly foreign. Such is the experience of most
of mankind, who have, as it were, no founding 'place' in the
good news of God.

It is easy, of course, to respond that an originating particularity is inescapable. And it may be true that accepting only to
receive is part of humility, a posture of pure gratitude that
leaves no place for query. Yet are we not also meant to be
humbly grateful for identity and to bring its 'glory and honour'

into Christ's Kingdom? Can these be only *post facto*? Are the antecedent hopes which Christhood is claimed to realize only Judaic in their character and their definition? Are other literatures and dreams not in some way 'messianic' in their own idiom, so that a universal Messiahship may be seen to belong with more than Judaic prophecy and belong in a manner recognizable by their own lights? These, plainly, are difficult questions. But if we Christians are seriously concerned, in the present, with other faiths and peoples, we cannot dismiss their past or be heedless when they ask: 'Why did God leave us so long in the dark?'

It is not only national, cultural and religious factors which arouse these thoughts in Indian or other minds in the encounter with Christians. They trouble missionary spirits also. For they cannot be separated from the will to identify and understand. The effort to take the gospel must incur the heart-situations which taking it involves. Those who have come close to India by long residence and study have found themselves wanting to share the perplexities that beset the Hindu mind at the otherness, the exclusivity, the privacy – as they see it – of truth which characterizes the Christian tradition. Does missionary experience in this sense inspire or warrant a refining of missionary vocation, a sharing of the local travail about the old in the very appeal of the new?

Charles Freer Andrews (1871–1940) was the outstanding example of this capacity to translate the logic of Christian mission into the terms of a Hindu, Indian sympathy. With him obedience to Christ came to mean a relinquishment, first of his official missionary auspices, and then of his Anglican orders. But these were the context through which he found his close identity with Indian aspiration for freedom, his vocation to assert the truth of British obligations in the surrender of empire, and his obedience to all he owed to Jesus Christ. There were those who suspected or alleged that he had almost, or actually, Hinduized. To refute them he added a codicil in his will that he wished to be buried, not cremated, lest the latter should be taken as a token that he was at heart Hindu. There was never a question about his heart-loyalty: the only issue was the pattern of its translation.

It is fair to say that Andrews, with his rare gift of friendship and his deep suffering, both physical and mental, was content to leave aside the claims of theological intellect. Where he saw a self-giving love, an openness to forgiveness, a will to atone, he found Christ-association. Jesus was for him 'the prince of Satyagrahas'. Jesus' being 'the Son of Man' meant that as 'an all-embracing sacrament Christ must be seen and revered in all' mankind. He lived by the conviction, in the words of his undergraduate teacher, Bishop Westcott, that 'nothing truly human can be left outside the Christian faith without destroying the very reason for its existence'. He was content to abandon the subtleties of conceptual theology which had once been important to him, in order to possess 'the human in Christ which is also divine' and when he saw 'this divine beauty, truth and love in others also . . . to relate it to Christ'.[4]

This did not mean that his friendships into Hinduism were undiscerning. Of Advaita Vedānta, he wrote that a Christian 'will never accept as finally satisfying a philosophy which does not allow him to believe that love between human souls may be an eternal reality'. But he grew increasingly disinclined, under the influence of Gandhi, to seek recruitment into Christian faith *via* baptism. He aimed to ensure that no one, by his ministries, came into Christian faith except by irresistible conviction. He did not approve Gandhi's demand that all converting be proscribed, as if there was nothing dynamic in religious encounters. The notion that all religions are alike or equal was idle folly.

Yet 'the atonement', he said, 'must be widened out far beyond a single act of Christ, however representative'.[5] He liked to think that seeds of Christian teaching had earlier been sown in India to explain the *Bhakti* school of devotion which so appealed to him in Hinduism. He wrote:

> I am beginning to understand from history that Christianity is not an independent Semitic growth but an outgrowth of Hindu religious thought and life besides . . . Christ appears to me like some strange, rare, beautiful flower whose seed has drifted and found a home in a partly alien land . . . Christ, the Jewish peasant, lived instinctively, as part of his own nature, this non-Jewish ideal of *ahimsā* which is so akin to Hinduism. He had the universal compassion, the universal charity, as marked in the agony of crucifixion as on the sunny Galilean hills.[6]

So, as with Paul, 'the necessity (of witness) was laid upon him' but within 'a precious element of goodness which we can all hold in common'.[7]

The need for Christian mission to reckon positively with another culture's place and past was pursued in more rigorous terms than those of Andrews by Alfred George Hogg (1890–1954), his contemporary and President of Madras Christian College, where he taught philosophy to Sarvepalli Radhakrishnan.[8] A keenly intellectual theologian, Hogg nevertheless distinguished between 'faith' and 'beliefs', soul-attitudes and mind-formulations. He held that the trust of communication could only begin in a positive relation to Hindu religion. This was so, in his view, even where contrasts were most painful. One such area was the theme of *karma*, as the entail of suffering which excluded the possibility of redemption, divine or human. Responsively, he interpreted the ministry and passion of Jesus as pioneering and creating a community of love capable of bearing the common *karma* (thus no longer inexorably private) of humanity. He held that this achievement – as the messianic for the *karmic* – could alone have happened from and through 'the God', as he put it, 'who must needs be in Christ Jesus'.[9] In this way a Hinduism, essentially crippled because the Hindu idea of God had never been moralized, might find its own vision of the human lot christologically transformed.

There are numerous other examples that might be cited of a missionary theology wrestling with the duties inseparable from a proper register of the sympathies without which mission is itself betrayed. This need not obscure the other truth that impact happens by force of contrast and surprise, even condemnation, by the sheer otherness of what is heard in the gospel. But it is only the interpreter, not the antagonist, who introduces the revolutionary factor. It is the missionary experience of some that – to speak formally – Christology ceases to be singular when it is understood.

V

Such, at least, would be the verdict of a writer who – as confidently and as bewilderingly as any – affirms a multiple Christology, Raimundo Panikkar (born 1918). With his double birth heritage of Hispanic Catholicism and Hinduism and his studies and teaching in places as diverse as Barcelona, Varanasi, Munich, Rome, and Santa Barbara, he is well endowed to grapple with the mutual bearings, as he sees them, of Christology

and Hinduism. That his writing is elusive, sometimes exasperat-
ingly obscure, must not be allowed to provoke readers into
an easy charge of syncretism, not at least until they have wrestled because of him with the question whether, or why, syncretism is a thing of reproach. If quest, rather than creed, is the
ultimate loyalty, then syncretism, precisely by trespassing across
religious monopolies, may be a condition of loyalty. Either way
it may be well to avoid pejorative words and be critically alert
for the intention, beyond the form, of the case being made.

At risk of focusing unduly a thought that is often diffuse
in Panikkar – a characteristic commendable to the Hindu –
Panikkar's Indian Christology may be studied *via* the distinction
he makes between identity and identification. Christhood is
an identity wider and larger than the identification of it which
Christians find in Jesus. The Jesus of Christians, for whom
the particular history is vital, is their identification of Christ-
identity elsewhere, outside the historical particular that belongs
with Jesus. Thus it is right to say: 'Jesus is the Christ', but
it would not be right to say: 'The Christ is Jesus' – at least
not restrictively – since, in the second sentence, the subject
is more than the predicate it receives. To illustrate outside
Panikkar, one might truly say: 'The symphony is music', but
not: 'Music is the symphony'. For there are many other forms
of music than the symphonic.

Panikkar is thus inviting Christians to think of a Christhood
identifiable, to be sure, in Jesus but diversely identifiable Jesus
apart. If we ask why this other-than-Jesus Christology should
be so named he explains that he speaks throughout of 'Christ'
because it is the word used by Christians, but in the Panikkar
usage it ceases to connote the Christians' Christ. The Christ-
term then becomes almost a synonym for whatever in religious
experience explains, transacts or mediates the relation between
God and world. God is 'the "to Whom?" of our search' and
Christologies the answers by which we live.[10]

This is the meaning of the hidden 'Christ' of Hinduism, a
faith offering to Christians 'the authentically Hindu gift of a
new experience and interpretation – a new dimension – of 'the
mystery of that reality for which Christians have no other name
than Christ'.[11] If we ask why this mystery we all share should
not be called 'God' rather than 'Christ', Panikkar replies that
each faith must use its own concepts to denote the ground
where religious existence belongs. His assumption is that such

ground is essentially identical and therefore appropriately denoted by our vocabulary which speaks of Christ. His belief is that what the Christ-language signifies for Christians cannot be valid if it is held valid only for them.

Thus Panikkar can speak of many Christs, not by abandoning history in the case of Jesus, but by claiming that historicity is not essential. He does not imply that the author, for example, of the *Brahma Sūtra* thought explicitly of Jesus as the goal of *ista-devata*, or devotion. Nor is the Christians' Jesus the *Ishvara* of the *Vedānta*. Identities here are not subject to historical considerations. The necessity of the historical is simply a requirement for Christians in *their* Christ-identification and should not dissuade us from thinking Christologies otherwise. To require historicity is simply to presuppose the Christian concept of Christhood.

The point at issue here we will resume again in Chapter 9 in a different context. Panikkar believes that the Johannine concept of the *Logos* arguably sustains him. The *Logos* is 'made flesh' and that, *a posteriori*, means the Judaic, biblical, Galilean idiom. But what of the *Logos a priori* 'before the foundation of the world'?[12] Need we conclude that the eternal Word is unilaterally characterized by the accidents of time and place which belonged with the incidence of being 'made flesh'? On that ground may not the Christ-Idea be disengaged from the Christ-Event? If so, then the identity of Christ must transcend, while still possessing, that identification by which the New Testament confesses it. We may locate in Hinduism the living presence of the mystery which Christians call Christ.

We may still be left wondering why the New Testament term should be used for mystery so elusive. It is as if a Christ of concept or of contemplation is replacing the Christ of actuality, with a readiness to equate the two by dispensing with the event-character which in Christianity defines it. Panikkar seeks to commend his position to his Christian readers *via* an analogy about 'real presence' in the Eucharist.[13] The sacramental situation in Holy Communion de-literalizes 'the flesh' we eat. Spiritual perception likewise de-historicizes Christology. 'The night in which he was betrayed' is perpetuated only sacramentally in Holy Communion. So Christhood is universalized only contemplatively. The 'real presence' is there, history apart, in the mystery of every faith. Beneath the Buddhist's compassion or the Muslim's surrender is the 'who' of Christian *agape*.[14]

But do we not have to ask about the specifics of that Christ of history whom sacramental *anamnesis* explicitly recalls? Are we to see the historical dimension in the Gospels as some kind of transubstantiation by which the eternal reality is made perceptible to our senses? Is not the Incarnation itself the sacramental situation in which 'the Word is made flesh' in divine self-giving? Panikkar takes the Christ of history as only one construct for a mystery hidden otherwise elsewhere. The history, then, is like the 'bread and wine' of what is more than they.

This use, on his part, of a puzzling analogy about 'real presence' has a parallel in his invocation of Paul's argument on the Areopagus. Panikkar quotes Paul's words: 'Whom you in ignorance worship, him I declare to you' (Acts 17.23), and uses the identity-in-distinction there to sustain, as he sees it, a discernible identity between Jesus as Christ and Christs many.[15] The 'unknown' deity of the pagan altar and the 'known' God-in-Christ are one identity (in the logic of Paul's words) in differing identification.

Panikkar, like many in the inter-faith field, pleads the ecumenical precedent among Christians.[16] What has been done to bring Christians together, abating prejudice and ending mutual recrimination, has to be achieved in the much wider arena of religions in general. He is not deterred by the thought of how evidently sharper the issues are when one passes from tensions within one faith to those between many.

It is possible to reject Panikkar's thought as simply self-warranting, even tautological. Thus, for example, he writes:

> Christianity and Hinduism meet in Christ: Christ is their meeting place. The real encounter can only take place in Christ, because only in Christ do they meet ... Christ is there in Hinduism but Hinduism is not yet his spouse.[17]

It is easy to ask, impatiently, What has he said? But criticism which stops short of facing his premises will not have the measure of his positions. Both derive from the effort to think Christology from within Hinduism. The objections which arise very naturally from Christians as to how all is to be squared with Jesus of Nazareth cannot be intelligently pressed as if Hinduism was not what it is. Panikkar is trying to see Christhood as Hindu presuppositions require him to do – free of necessary historicity and incarnationally interpreting dimensions more than the Judaic. In objectified belief, he says, we are all what we are. In contemplation we may participate beyond ourselves. Or we may do so if we are among those, not the masses, who can experience a unity in religious traditions which, objectified in beliefs, are sharply distinctive.

Panikkar illustrates what this cross-participation might mean by an exploration of *karma*. In this he asks radical things of the Hindu as well as the Christian. The former must concede, and appreciate, that there *is* historical dynamism as opposed to Hindu apathy and determinism. He must also un-think re-incarnation as not integral to *karma*. *Karma* may then be read as 'excluding the private owning of one's life', and affirming 'the cosmic solidarity of the whole creation . . . the irrepeatable value of every act . . . which never remains barren or without effect'. That there is no escape from the karmic law may be read as there being no exemption from inter-relatedness. As such it is 'the very co-efficient of creatureliness'.[18] May not this bring us near to the Christian sense of being 'in Adam'? Further, 'the Lord of *karma*' is also within *karma*, for if 'he' were outside it 'he' would no longer be its Lord. May this, then, serve to explain the Christ-principle of suffering within the entail of collective humanity? Might this be a Christology, by Hindu lights, discernible yet disengaged from the particulars of the Jesus-story?

If *karma* in this way can be seen, or made, to mean a responsi-bility to the whole earth, embracing human and divine, we are still left wondering how the divine 'stake' in the human whole thus 'bound in the bundle of life' is fulfilled and where, and how, redemption happens. Are we not still in need, for all the enterprise of dialogue here, of the actual redemption by the cross-measure? Is that how the historical indifference of *karma* yields to the historical in Jesus?[19]

Yet, if it is thought so to do, this, on Panikkar's showing, would obtain within a pluralism which could just as well dis-pense with history. Elsewhere, in an ugly term, he pleads for 'the de-kerugmatization of faith', by which he means not requir-ing exclusive formulae (beliefs) which inferiorize or contradict the different belief-language of faith elsewhere, such faith being essentially one reality. 'Religions', he declares, 'are equivalent to the same extent that languages are translatable and they are unique as much as languages are untranslatable.'[20]

VI

Christology and India are vastly larger themes than a single writer can exemplify however generously summarized. But *The Unknown Christ of Hinduism* in its elusive boldness is as useful a manual as any for the measure of theological cross-reference in India. It has provoked both Hindus and Christians. Some among the former resent what they read as the old 'fulfilment' nexus between Hinduism and Christianity. Thus S. Dindayal writes:

> One may rightly assume that it is the unknown presence of Krishna and his liberal teachings that are working among a small minority in the Church, causing rebellion against authority and seeking more freedom.[21]

M. M. Thomas's *The Acknowledged Christ of the Indian Renaissance* gives the riposte that the title suggests.[22] Our present duty, against the background of *The Unknown Christ*, is to take brief note of how Christs-many may be claimed in the Hindu setting.

The 'I' who is 'born of his own power', comes, according to the familiar story, to take birth age after age, whenever there is an uprising of lawlessness. Then eternal Law is confirmed and men of right intent are delivered, and evil-doers brought to nought. Every path men take to the Lord is the Lord's path. He is theirs in the way of their search unto him. *Brahmavidya*, or knowledge of the supreme and union with the absolute Lord, is the heart concern, the religious goal, of Hindu India. May this yearning be understood as 'a Christ of intent'? Is Christianity somehow 'religiously underdeveloped'[23] if it wants to insist that Christhood can only be identified and denoted within the prescripts of the Judeo-Christian tradition? In Rāmānuja's *Brahma Sūtras* the soul reaches out in love towards God. Sankara's view of the *Upanishads* celebrates a non-dualist theme of the Godhead present to the human soul. The *Gita* resonates with the theme of wondering *bhakti* devotion whereby the soul is held in saving awe and adoration.

Can we reckon such Hindu devotion and the deliberate self-disciplines which undergird it as a partaking of Christ, the Christ who said: 'I and my Father are one ... You in me and I in you'? If we insist on history as a *sine qua non* of the Christ shall we be imposing what is a necessity to us, in our Judeo-

Christian tradition, upon a mind-soul order for which time cannot avail for the eternal, being itself the sphere of *māyā* and illusion? Alternatively, if we relinquish a definitive historical to accommodate the Hindu 'Christs' how will we exclude the lurid Puranic tales or the antics and lusts of the other Krishnas, where what is quite nugatory of a true *bhakti* lurks within the imagination from a 'history' our hospitality accepts in the absence of anything decisive to banish them? Or do we conclude that because these, too, are unreal in *māyā* their degrading presence in image and symbol can duly coexist with Jesus of Galilee and of Gethsemane?

Deferring, as agreed, the examination of the history theme, we may ask whether we can understand transcendent reality under a diversity of manifestations which have a unity from within, in respect of their one source, and a diversity from without, in respect of their form? Does the concept of the ineffable avail to contain the otherwise irreconcilable? Or, as the *Gita* is interpreted to mean, can the supreme reality be pure Self, totally detached from all action, unconcerned and indifferent, yet *also* cosmic reality, by nature involved behind and in the perceptible world? Or, again, would it be right to see the *Gita* as the attempt of its unknown author to introduce an ethical and social dynamism into Hindu mentality without openly violating the philosophy of *Brahmavidya*? In that case, all that is most attractive about *bhakti* and *vidya* in the poem is in tension with the orthodoxy about the transcendent which it prefers not to disturb or revise. Religious literature which is responding to a crisis situation in its time and place need not be held to theoretical consistency. By that proviso, the *Gita* might be read in terms of this intention and not of all that might be implied from its entire content.

Even so its call to the realization of the human meaning belongs squarely within the caste system. Arjuna is a *kshatriya*, a member of the warrior caste. His *dharma* duty may enjoin detachment from self-interest, but it requires conformity to its own assumed prerequisites of battle and strife. Its solace is that mortality inexorably overtakes both slain and slayer alike and with this single scythe cuts through all the misgivings which the will to peace has raised. Does disinterest justify whatever is disinterestedly done? Or must we not move on from the detachment which seeks no (personal) merit to the repudiation which admits no (moral) wrong? Action and renunciation may be compatible, as the *Gita* teaches (Book V), within *dharma* so conceived. But outside it, must it not be asked whether renunciation must not include actions wrong in themselves as well as private interest in the fruits of them? Can the criteria of action and commitment to it be only those of a conformist's attitude and not also – and more – those of substance critically weighed?

These are some of the questions which press for answer when we endeavour to move with and from the *Gita* towards a Hindu based Christology. If we seek it in the transforming vision of awe and glory Arjuna experiences in the climax of the poem the parallel may seem authentic. There could be a genuine sympathy between *bhakti* and *vidya* in those Hindu terms and 'Christ in you the hope of glory' of the New Testament. But we are left asking whether it matters that knowledge and devotion thus compared relate to any claims of conscience in the living world. As a poem, the *Gita* is celebratory in mystical vein. As a letter Colossians is immersed in daily life. The latter's 'Christ in you' concerns the pressures of society and the calling to personal holiness. Could the contrast be a clue to what is disparate in the 'Christologies'?

It is noteworthy that Krishna at the outset of the *Gita* is Arjuna's charioteer. There is lowliness here, realism, service and – by these – proximity, nearness, presence. These are all marks of the Incarnation also. The ultimate intimations of majesty spring from a station alongside. This is the way of Christology. But 'chariot' and 'charioteer' to a *kshatriya* bring no challenge to his identity or his function as a warrior. They come to him in the guise of his own assumptions: they are confirmatory of all that he assumes of himself and of his role. Indeed, in the *Gita* their precise function is to bolster and fortify those assumptions against the inner doubt in which we find Arjuna when the poem opens. This is not the way of Incarnation. As celebrated in *Magnificat* it sharply rejects and overturns existing norms. It does not steel the will to courage in a fated world but to expectation in a transformed one. Any sympathy to equate the final splendour of the *Gita* with a Christology in terms, for example, of the Fourth Gospel,[24] or of Revelation in Patmos, must take pause from these earlier contrasts. The clue to the glory is in the guise of the humility.

The Jesus from whom Christology derives does not admit of the sort of analogy present in the charioteer-to-*kshatriya* tie.

It might indeed be possible to say that he has become so in the tradition of some Christianity. It is in fact the burden of liberation theology, for example, in Latin America, that the Christ of the Creeds and the ecclesiology around him have buttressed and confirmed the vested interests of exploitative economies and blessed political oppression. In that sense *some* Christologies come where interests are and give us warrant to pursue them and even to allay our doubts.[25] In this sense a certain parallel is uncannily close. But that concerns an aberration which a true Christology impugns. The Krishna/Arjuna, charioteer/*kshatriya* association in the *Gita* serves rather to illustrate what Christology so differently confesses. The kindred circumstance of lowliness and the final glory of transcendent wonder have between them a very different story.

Circumstance in Jesus had to do with 'the servant' who healed, who taught, who prayed, who lived – as his disciples came to believe – messianically, who suffered and died, who 'entered into glory' only out of the travail of ministry and the mystery of resurrection. This Christology, incipient before it could be confessed, was not in sanction of a *māyā* stance, a karmic necessity, a caste-shaped duty. It 'opened the kingdom of heaven to all believers' by breaking open the old norms of race and righteousness. It happened not in the way of celestially confirming with lyrical beauty the dispositions of a static philosophy which was the achievement of the *Gita*, but by a liberating grace availing to all through the self-giving of love in the drama of a representative encounter with human evil.

VII

Deferring, as agreed, the dimension of the historical in this alignment of gospel and *Gita*, does this moral aspect, the contrast in how they join the lowly coming with the sublime disclosure, mean that there has to be some sort of protective jealousy to defend the contrast? No! indeed. There *are* Christologies at once rebuked and yet proven by the definitive Christ-Jesus. It may help to consider them if we reverse the distinction earlier cited from Raimundo Panikkar. He spoke of a Christ-identity wider than the Christ-identification Christians affirm in respect of Jesus. Suppose we make Christ-Jesus the 'identity' and say we perceive 'identifications' of him in other figures in other

situations. As in Panikkar's reverse usage, these 'identifications', though validly made, will not be complete. Yet, albeit
partially, they do have something of the Christ-Jesus 'identity'.
We will not then be pluralizing what is definitive but acknowledging where its definitive quality finds expression or oper-
ation elsewhere. The decisive divine action Christianity affirms
of Christ-Jesus – 'God in Christ reconciling the world' – holds,
but the principle which made it so may be elsewhere exemplified. Cross-reference into India would seem to bring the course
of thought round to the same point, in this context, as the
Judaic anxiety about the unredeemedness of the world. The
earlier analogy of music and the symphony, used in relation
to Panikkar, will not avail us here. We could not then say:
'Music is the symphony' in any restrictive sense, because
'music' was an incorporating predicate about 'the symphony'.
In this context it will be wiser to take some analogy from
literature in which we might say, for example, that Keats
yearned after a Shakespearean quality or that Dostoevsky
possessed one. Writers may be compared to Dickens while
Dickens remains incomparable. That which is personally denominated, as here, is never plural: its character may be plurally
recognized.

In *Concordant Discord*, R. C. Zaehner notes the Christ-like-
ness of Yudhishthira, 'king of Hindu righteousness and capable
of deep compassion', a servant of the servants of God who
in meekness condemns evil and gives up all his possessions
for the welfare of his friends.[26] There is much laying aside of
sovereignty and taking of the mendicant's role in Hindu mythology of Rama and Krishna. The christological dimension may
be attenuated and, indeed, compromised by other features
which a concern for ethics and history would necessarily deplore. But is it not precisely part of the messianic meaning that
it should generate its own imitation and be also the measure
of what the imitation lacks? Each ministry is vital to the other,
while a blank repudiation would serve neither. It is just in being
altogether distinctive that Christ-Jesus makes the Christ-
measure a universal criterion to be invoked.

It has often been said in the plea for plural Christologies
that there are diverse manifestations with a unity from within,
that the transcendent can never be exclusively appropriated
because encounter is in the way of our search and search is
always culturally plural. It would be in line with these thoughts

to plead also – to use a crude formula – that Christology is about a 'what' not a 'who'. Not 'whom' but 'what' would certainly fit the pluralists, subduing the instance to the norm, reading the norm in the diversity of instances. Christology would then be – as we have seen – the norm and Jesus an instance.

Let us accept the 'who' and 'what' formula. It has point. But it is a logic which can be turned on its head, as we do here. For we must say that 'who' and 'what' cannot be well served by this sort of distinction. The one defines the other. As we saw in Chapter 5, the messianic is both person and 'policy', both action and pattern. To know 'how' is to know 'who', to know 'who' is to know 'how'. For the whole issue, the enigma, some would say, is where the twin recognitions of identity converge into conclusiveness. It would be arbitrary to suppose that a 'how' to enable recognition of a 'who' is more to be assumed than the reverse. Plural Christologies of Hindu provenance presume that there is a 'Christ-principle' which needs no concrete definition, whose incidence nevertheless can be variously identified. Plural Christologies of Christian order will hold to the 'Christ-principle', a concrete 'what' and 'who' inseparably one in Jesus and the cross, which may then be discernibly reproduced in other lives and cultures thanks to its once-for-all incidence in the there-and-then of what Wilfred Owen called 'the maps of Golgotha'. If it be said that this is a joining of 'what' and 'who' which is arbitrary, the response must be that unjoining them, no less arbitrary, would be to leave Christology itself altogether conjectural, a concept lacking in both origin and credential.

This brings us to the role of the historical. It will be right to note in preface how this convergence of 'who' and 'how' in Jesus leaves ample room for that central role of the imagination to which all Asian religion pays tribute. So much in all faiths is not conceptual, still less cerebral, but belongs with symbol, rite and culture. Jesus-Christology is well able to home itself in every context and so to meet those considerations which we earlier examined, both in eastern hearers and in missionary-comers, having to do with love of land and people. There is an almost universal art in celebration of Christ's nativity. His passion, too, for all its there-and-then-ness in the Roman idiom of ignominy, translates into every imagination. The Mediterranean confinement of so much interpreting theology is no necessary pattern for the interpretation in the arts. In that sphere C. F. Andrews was sound in his confidence that Jesus belongs in India by right and not by importation. To proceed with reflections about history will be to ask how that confidence can also find theological expression.

NOTES

1 Paul Knitter in *Concilium*, ed. M. Eliade and David Tracy (June 1980), 'Christianity as Religion, True and Absolute', p. 18.

2 This predominant association of Christianity with the British Raj as far as the nationalist movement was concerned does not overlook the ancient Christian Indian presence from near apostolic times. See Stephen C. Neill, *A History of Christianity in India*, vol. i, Cambridge 1984.

3 See Chap. 6, note 23. 'Why did God leave us so long in the dark?' is another form of the question.

4 B. Chaturvedi and M. Sykes, *The Life of C. F. Andrews* (New York 1950), p. 235, from his paper: 'Why I am a Christian'. On Andrews, see also Hugh Tinker, *The Ordeal of Love*, Delhi 1979.

5 ibid., p. 111.

6 ibid., p. 102.

7 ibid., p. 310.

8 A. G. Hogg's writings include *Karma and Redemption*, London 1911; *Redemption from this World*, Madras 1922; *The Christian Message to the Hindu*, London 1947.

9 *The Christian Message to the Hindu* (London 1947), pp. 82–6.

10 *The Unknown Christ of Hinduism*, rev. edn London 1981, p. 168.

11 ibid., pp. 4–5.

12 ibid., pp. 162–5. He writes that it 'cannot be within the compass of this essay' to discuss the issue implicit here in confessing 'the Word made flesh' yet finding in the Logos before the flesh an implication of some significance in distinction. We might ask 'How is the Word truly made flesh' if its prior significance has to be reserved in this way? Then has the Incarnation of the eternal Word truly happened?

13 Yusuf Ibish and Ileana Marculescu, ed., *Contemplation and Action in World Religions*, Washington 1978. Panikkar's paper is 'Action and Contemplation as Categories of Religious Understanding', pp. 85–104. He has a similar use of the Eucharist analogy in *The Unknown Christ*, pp. 2–5.

14 Ibish, op. cit., p. 97. One might cite a comparably sanguine view in Bede Griffiths, *Christian Ashram* (London 1966), p. 100. 'They will learn to discern Christ as the true fulfilment of all the ideas which are contained within them and which only receive their full meaning when they are understood in relation to Christ.'

15 *The Unknown Christ*, p. 168. Panikkar cites *Rigveda*, X. 121, 'What God

shall we adore with our oblation?' as parallel to Acts 17.23. The problem comes in shifting the exploratoriness from 'God' to 'Christ', in that the latter is Christianly understood in precisely the opposite sense, namely as God-commended, inclusive disclosure of the Eternal, so that worship may *know* its theme, its source and goal.

16 Ibish, op. cit., p. 100. This progression from the ideals and lessons of inter-Christian relations to inter-religious relations is often invoked as proper and feasible. See Bede Griffiths, op. cit., p. 98.

17 *The Unknown Christ*, pp. 6 and 17.

18 Ibish, op. cit., p. 94.

19 ibid., pp. 94–5. It would seem impossible to fit the messianic meanings of initiative and grace into the karmic pattern of necessity which involves *karma's* Lord within *karma*.

20 R. Panikkar, *The Intra Religious Dialogue* (New York 1978), p. xxv.

21 In *Bookshelf* (November 1970), p. 25.

22 Madras 1970.

23 Klaus Klostermaier, *Hindu and Christian in Vrindaban* (London 1970), p. 29.

24 Bede Griffiths in *Return to the Centre* (London 1976), makes this kind of equation whereby, for example, the meaning of John 17.23: 'I in them and thou in me that they may be perfectly one' is read as the merging of individual consciousness into the *advaita whole* (pp. 32f.). What we have in Christ is absorption into undividedness, and 'that God may be all in all' (1 Cor. 15.28) means 'that God may be everything to everyone' (p. 51).

25 Theology, especially systematic theology, as a wilful escape from obedience to God, the sense that dogma is used simply to sanction and legitimate our economic interests, is a passionate theme in e.g. Jose P. Miranda, *Marxism and the Bible*, trans. John Eagleson (New York 1974); and Jon Sobrino, *Christology at the Cross-roads*, trans. John Drury, New York 1978. In that sense a Christology might be likened to a Krishna validating an order of things, an economic system proper to us.

26 R. C. Zaehner, *Concordant Discord, The Interdependence of Faiths* (Oxford 1970), p. 35.

9
Jesus Singularly Christ

I

The Christian religion, based on belief in the risen Christ, emerged
... with a rapidity that must be staggering to any historian. This
might be more easy to explain if Jesus during his lifetime had adum-
brated more of the faith than he did to the disciples, who remained
uncomprehending until, shortly after the Crucifixion, some sudden
illumination enabled them to fit everything into place ... in the
years (and indeed in the weeks, no doubt in the few days)...[1]

So the Cambridge historian, Herbert Butterfield, pondering the
crux of the Messiahship of Jesus *and* the emergence of the Christian faith and church. With a sound historical instinct he takes
the cross and the faith-community to be one eventuation, the
fact of a happening becoming the fact of an experience.

It is this actuality of the Christian Christ which we now have
to study. The proper openness of the preceding chapter obliged
the course of thought all the time to a sort of 'Yes, but ...'
lest multiplying 'Christs' should somehow do violence to meaning or blithely neglect the frame of historical reference to which
the coveted term belongs. For the fact remains that, however
far the desire may go to disengage Christhood from the necessity of Jesus, it is, none the less, the Christian Christ where
the 'suchness' is.[2]

This is the intention in the 'singularly' of the chapter heading.
It might perhaps, in line with Chapter 8, employ a question-
mark. But let it stand just affirmatively, with the double import
of the word.[3] The Christian Christ, after all, is the only one
there historically is. The Judaic Messiah is either awaited in
messianic futurism, or spiritualized in Torah loyalty or ideal
nationalism.[4] Jesus, we may fairly say, is only available as a
historical figure, for Christhoods other than his own history,
because that history makes him so in its own New Testament,
than which there are no other sources to do more than help
sift and read the Christian ones, marginally. Without the Christian Christ in singularity there would be neither term, nor
figure, nor image for associationists plurally to discern or love

or follow elsewhere. *Imitatio Christi* may have its own ways, even whims, and Christians should not complain – for they are witnesses and servants, not proprietors. But *Iesus Christus* apart, where were the *imitatio*? If this, it be protested, is to misinterpret what the plural Christhoods mean, it will be for their advocates to explain their desire to share the word. Our concern here is to inquire what the singularity of Jesus as the Christ requires of a Christian fidelity responding to 'Christs other'. It must also be to face, within the Christian parameters of the New Testament, those instincts, so characteristic of India, which by concepts of *brahma* and *avidya* and *māyā* deny all singularity as illusion upon illusion. It will also be to ask why, nevertheless, they want the idea of 'Christ'.

II

But thus to take one's stand on 'happenedness' is to incur all the issues about history. In the case of the New Testament they are formidable and manifold, both served and disserved by the volume of the research which has overlaid them, frequently pursuing minutiae at the expense of perspective. In its clear consensus, without which it would not be the document it is (indeed, would not *be* at all), the New Testament expresses the fact-faith situation we have seen in Chapter 5. It makes central in its gospel form the person and teaching of Jesus as that which alone explains and generates the community out of which it is described. In its Epistles it bears witness, by its corporate fellowship and ethical concern, to antecedents in Jesus which must, therefore, be read to have been of such a sort as to issue into that which confesses them. We have to comprehend a Jesus sufficient to have had such issue as the Church became, with his passion as the crux of it: and we have to realize the New Testament as the clue to who and how we must see him to have been. It is this inter-relevance of Jesus-story in its happening and the church-story as a-there-fore-happening which historical perspective teaches. It may be lost upon more minute studies that have not seen that the criteria of the event are only in the whole.

There is nothing unique in this situation. It is a quality of all significant record of events. Event is only told out of the experience in which it was registered and such experience itself is the matrix of the significance which it tells and, therefore,

the clue to the event *per se*. There is what happened and what
what happened meant. Without the latter, noted, pondered,
stored and probed in mind, the former never becomes history
and is, as it were, unhappened into oblivion. It is thus the
historian who 'makes' history, given the 'history' (as yet unre-
corded) which makes him historian. This process has a cumulative character. Sifting and interpreting become feasibly more
neutral as events recede. But where they pass – as they do
in religion – into the possession of memory that lives by them
in communities that celebrate them, this existential sense of
them perpetuates, to a degree, the existential shape of their
historical character. This, then, exercises a prerogative over all
'development' by which the future transmits them. Moses and
the Exodus are the most evident example from the Judaic tradition. The Passover is a fact-faith, event-experience reality,
which became, so to speak, a property of identity, making what
it was made by.

It is emphatically this way with what Christians call the
Christ-Event. It is vital that we see and apprehend its inter-
quality turning upon *both* Jesus in his significance *and* the founding 'Christians' in their faith-receiving of him. The central fact
of gathering official hostility to Jesus within his ministry is not
in doubt. It was in line with long prophetic experience. There
is nothing mysterious or inexplicable about the several factors
which set authority, popular expediency and ordinary human
obduracy, against him. That the ensuing confrontation entailed
deep anguish and mortal danger cannot credibly be denied.
Nor can the fact that Jesus did not flinch from it, indeed courageously faced it into climax. That this inner decision as to a
suffering vocation stood in Jesus' reading of the messianic secret
seems reasonably to follow. It was certainly so in the conviction
of the Church – the Church which joined everything it became
in teaching, ethics, liturgy and human reach to that conviction
as its source, ground and warrant. It was in terms of that conviction that it wrote the Jesus-story.

To conclude, as we must if it did not belong to Jesus, that
this 'history' derived (by way of origin, not of recognition) from
the 'genius' of his followers so that it became theirs about him,
not theirs through him, is to have the incredible at the heart
of a transforming wonder. To think it their blundering reversal
of shattering tragedy by a self-persuasion which somehow
countered all their traditional, now ruined, ideas of Messiah,

and to suppose they achieved this *volte-face* from dereliction
to assurance without authority from the manner of Messiah
Jesus had willed to be, would seem a strange conclusion. It
would be guilty of ignoring Easter – Easter as the pivot of the
disciples' realization of Christhood, Easter as the culmination
of the fact that it truly belonged in Jesus.

The bond between a Jesus-decision and a church-awareness
is the point of the authentic. The two are mutually confirmatory.
Their being so stands within the event-experience situation we
have noted as characteristic of all significant history in the
double meaning of happenedness as fact and happenedness
as record. It might be possible to read Jesus' movement into
Gethsemane, and his death beyond it, by other lights than those
of messianic decision for bearing evil as the cost of its redemption. It might be possible to suggest a wilful forcing of the
divine hand by structuring a crisis out of which divine rescue
would become suddenly crucial. Judas himself may have
schemed this notion to induce the vigorous action the lack of
which he deplored. It would be possible to suggest that Jesus
made a violent end inescapable by his words and deeds concerning the Temple and that the authorities found his disturbing person expendable and he was too crass, too obstinate,
too naive, to escape them. It would be possible to find in the
crucifixion the violent fate of a failed Zealot. Language about
'the cup my Father has given me' may be read as the reading
backward of what was later held so. Indeed that last possibility
cannot be categorically excluded from anything in the Gospels.
It would hardly be a faith-response on our part if we assumed
that everything was under guarantee, as if any history – and
much more faith – were a matter of mathematics. As Browning
had it:

> You must mix some uncertainty
> With faith, if you would have faith be.[5]

But when, with due reservation of mind, you have supposed
any or all of these things, you are still left with the fact that
the mind of the first Christians disallowed them, and, in their
own positive identification of the messianic, had in possession
'the mind of Christ'. Had they in fact distorted him in what
was emphatically their own coming-to-be who they now were?

There is no mistaking their identity and their accrediting it
to Jesus. It took them into a new unity with mankind, breaking

down the most tenacious of human frontiers – that dividing
Jew from Gentile. It took them, in their Jewishness, into new
dimensions of theology by which they cried: 'Worthy is the
Lamb.' That sense of 'the Throne' which was 'God's and the
Lamb's' meant that they recognized in the love that suffered
the index to the sovereignty behind all things. That Jesus had
achieved the messianic meaning, by cross and resurrection,
lay at the heart of all their moral passion. They proposed to
transform the inward man by grace of 'the mind of Christ'.
They were liberated into a redeeming existence by virtue of
a redemption, happened in Jesus.

Their *kerugma* was a fact, a reality *per se*, but not, as some
in New Testament scholarship have supposed, sufficiently to
itself, so that one might say: 'The real Christ is the preached
Christ.' Or that the gospel lay in being believed to be one.
Such dicta rest on *a priori* philosophies of existentialism and
on a total pessimism about the history of Jesus. But that same
pessimism fails to reckon with the degree to which the *kerugma*
of the apostles (thus made the only fact there is) must be said
to disallow it. For that *kerugma* could not have emerged nor
have been the thing it was without the antecedent in Jesus
which, on such negative view, it cannot now be trusted to tell
us. This is not to say – as already conceded – that the gospel
portraiture from within the world of the Epistles is in no need
of historical scrutiny. It is to say that all such scrutiny must
intelligently begin and continue within the awareness that there
was a history yielding the Jesus of the *kerugma* and that the
kerugma must remain the primary evidence for its overall thrust.
This brings us back to that reading of Jesus which takes him
as authentically fulfilling Messiahship, by his own acceptance
of the suffering pattern his ministry presented to him, in the
very terms in which the Church so confidently preached him
– a confidence discovered *post eventum* against all the odds of
their desperate extremity of prior confusion.

The point is important in the context of our concern about
plural Christs and the role of history. If, in the Bultmann manner, we may regard the real Christ as the preached Christ,
then it might be argued that any preached Christ becomes a
real one. The way is then open to leave history behind and
Christ-ize any religious theme or fantasy where we choose to
locate a mystery. Untethered to event such thought-Christ-
hoods might arguably be likened to a New Testament *kerugma*

detached from what happened as event and exclusively located in what happened as experience. All sincere experience could, in that sense, be claimed as Christic, if it chose to use the name. *Kerugmas* might in that sense be self-generating.

That way, of course, lies precisely the gnosticism against which the New Testament and the apostolic Church set themselves so firmly, insisting that Jesus was 'come in the flesh', and, credally, that he was 'crucified, dead and buried'. Docetic notions about mere 'appearance' in the crucifixion and/or, historical unreality around 'the Word and the flesh', may have left a certain type of Christology intact. But they vetoed the basic Christian theology of 'God in Christ reconciling the world'. That theology affirmed the historical actuality of the living Jesus, born, serving, resolving, dying and alive for evermore.

III

But, if the very writing of the Gospels and the communal ethicism of the Epistles witness to a Jesus who was Christ within a history, could the apostolic faith, purporting to be the living register of that history and the authentic future of what its past had been, have arisen unwarrantably from other sources through which it then refracted what it decided it had been? The question deserves consideration if we are committed to history and, in that commitment, believe there is valid index, both ways, from Jesus-story and church-faith.

It is here, of course, that for many critics conjecturing notions of dying-rising 'saviours' come to hand from the pagan classic world, Osiris, Adonis, Attis, Mithras and the rest. Could these, with their coterie of cults and memorial feasts, their rites and mysteries, have tempted the first Christians into some compensating, imitative apotheosis of the stricken Jesus? Thus detached, or better retrieved, from the historical he might be available on other continents to provide one 'identification' of a wider 'identity', with India instinctively fertile in the cause. His 'history' then would be neatly rescued from Semitic particulars and happily domesticated anywhere.

But the sense of Jesus in his Christhood being fitted, by Jewish disciples in the Palestinian milieu, into such a pattern has nothing to commend it to serious consideration. Paul's teaching of salvation, too, is radically contrasted with such mythic figures. As A. D. Nock observes:

> A general atonement by a redeemer is not Hellenistic. Attis, Adonis, Osiris, die, are mourned for, and return to life. Yet it is nowhere said that *soteria* comes by their death. *Soteria* of a sort may come from their return to life or from the assurance that they will do so in due season ... The deliverance is a deliverance in harmony with the god's deliverance, not a deliverance brought by his sufferings ... From this to the self-oblation of Jesus, as it was preached, is a perceptible distance. The key to the Christian doctrine is given to us by Jewish conceptions alone.[6]

We can, therefore, no more defy the constraints of New Testament Christology on behalf of Krishna than on behalf of Osiris. If India is to orientalize Jesus and Christhood it must be within the terms of the event-experience as the integral 'happening' by which meaning came about, as both fact and perception.

Before seeing how some Indian theologians have done this, it is germane here to note how the New Testament confidence in Jesus' Christhood survived the delay of the *parousia*, a delay so prolonged that it ceased to be so described. The hope of Christ's appearing, with the cosmic 'fruits of his redemption' was a proper dimension of the accomplished Christhood of the cross and resurrection. To 'see not yet all things put under him' was to be in the real world. It was also to be in hope. But the 'not yet' was capable of being renewed through passing years by virtue of 'but we see Jesus, crowned with glory and honour'. Time's forward movement, while still a realm of hope, could in no way undo what time, thus receding, was seen to have decisively contained. If the way *parousia* had been understood entailed disappointment of hope in those terms, this in no way disqualified either the redemptive history or the faith that cherished it. It is surely right to see in this how crucial, definitive and resilient that history was, as the there-and-then of event and the here-and-now of experience. If we ask about the actual 'future' Jesus has entered into *via* the centuries it has been that of his Christhood as the New Testament first greeted and declared it, as 'the earnest of the inheritance'.[7]

The Eucharist is the clearest expression of this truth as it is also of the interrelation between Jesus in his ministry and the Church in its faith. For in 'the bread and wine' of the upper room Jesus clearly focused his travail, as he perceived it, on the redemptive principle. Remembrance was centred on suffering, not on teaching as such. Nor was it 'remembrance' concerned with facts which were unforgettable but instead about meanings which must be paramount. That Last Supper did not have to do with *whether* Jesus would be recalled but with *how*. It was not a device to prevent oblivion but a sacrament to transact redemptive love, once for all enacted and perpetually to be reproduced. 'Do *this* in anamnesis.'

It was in that sense that the apostles fulfilled it. Their whole worship came to revolve around that reading of Jesus which Holy Communion involved and did so in the confidence that it was Jesus' reading also. It is, of course, possible to say that it was the Church which inaugurated the Eucharist as the index to its mind and then attributed it back to Jesus. But that conjecture incurs all the contrary considerations already noted in the overall context in which it must be placed.[8] The gospel in Acts and the Epistles leaves us in no doubt about 'the breaking of the bread' as the sign of community. How Jesus 'took, and blessed and broke and gave ...' was a key memory of his ministry. The bond between community and ministry would seem to be complete, the sacramental theme of the unity between event and experience.

IV

From this ground of conviction about the Christhood of Jesus as real and actual in history and generating a (church) history for which it was real and actual, it is time to turn to some representative Indian thinking which starts from a controlling sense of this actuality but aims to formulate its significance in terms that differ from those of western, Greek, Chalcedonian language and ethos. This may be prefaced by the thought that the actuality of the cross faces the rawness and realness of human evil with more authority than mythical figures could ever do. Fantasy 'saviours' may intrigue the imagination; they are no match for the real intrigues of evil in the actual world. The notion of *māyā* is no remedy. It is only the illusion of no encounter, and illusion is simply a device of evasion.

No less a vintage Hindu than Mahatma Gandhi could serve as our most eloquent witness for the necessity of history rather than myth. Certainly the British Raj could not have been ousted by notions of *māyā*. Gandhi felt himself strongly addressed by events and these evoked from him action in response. There was for him a relevance in present history not to be heeded by dreams of unreal heroes. Within *lokasamgraha*, or concern for social change, he insisted that *dharma*, or religious 'duty', had to be re-read by each generation for itself. History mattered. Hence the burning of foreign cloth, the campaign for hand-loom spinning, temple-entry for *harijans*, and the salt marches. 'I saw that nations like individuals', he wrote, 'could only be made by the agony of the Cross and in no other way.'[9] In grappling with caste and communal antagonisms he was acutely aware of the need for integrity about facts and was adamant about honesty in reporting.[10] To redeem situations entailed the anguish of knowing them for what they were.

It was precisely this sense of history as action which provoked him to say: 'It would be a poor comfort to the world if it had to depend upon a historical God who died two thousand years ago.' Poor comfort indeed, if relegated to pure past, and equating 'historical' thus with some museum. The real sense of the actuality of Jesus as the Christ, by which the Church lived and lives, is better captured in Gandhi's other observation: 'Do not preach the God of history, but show Him as He lives today through you ... I may suggest that God did not bear the Cross only nineteen hundred years ago, but He bears it today.'[11] It is 'the God of history', and only he, who lives through the centuries of New Testament loyalty. Not to 'preach him' would be to preclude the very pattern which demands emulation. Gandhi is eloquently pleading for what might be called a Christology of action, of present action. Such action, however, has its embodiment (Christians would say its Incarnation) in a personal 'definition', i.e. in a history, happening in time and place, where its register in discipleship and *confessio fidei* was an abiding happening also. What Gandhi sees as irrelevant – indeed unfortunate – is the development of a Christology of action into a Christology of being, taking Christhood, as it were, out of Gethsemane and into Chalcedon, away from 'It is finished' into 'He is debated'. That development was well intentioned. For it had to do with the ability to believe in the action as truly that of 'God in Christ'. But to be recalled to the garden and the travail, from formulae and conference, is surely right. It certainly restores us to history as the crucial factor for which myth and legend and idea can in no way suffice. In this conviction many Indian theologians are heartily with Gandhi.

V

Most Indian Christian theologians insist that they are not merely acclimatizing the gospel in India but seeking a genuinely Indian interpretation of Christianity. It is noteworthy among leading Indian Christian theologians that while making a serious bid to revise orthodox Christian ontology they hold closely with the history of Jesus, with what one of them describes as 'the raw fact of Christ'.[12] They would have little sympathy with the sort of question asked by Henri Lubac at the time of Vatican 2: 'If the great Councils had not fixed once and for all Christological Orthodoxy, what would Christ be for us today?'[13] Their answer would be: 'Much everyway.' For the Christ of action abides as the focal point alike of faith and hope.

This stance is part of a reluctance, in many quarters in Indian thinking, about the institutional Church. But it belongs squarely with the impulse to believe that India should not be tutored by Greece in its Christian *credenda* but must enshrine its credal expression of the Christ in Jesus in its own idiom. It also believes that it should not be in exclusive fee to the Judaic in the terms by which it understands and interprets the reality of 'God in Christ'. This unreadiness for a Hebrew monopoly of the determinants of Christian vocabulary must surely be seen, by those in the West who take the biblical Canon with a completely unquestioning submission, as properly part of any genuine faith in Christian worldwideness. The faith cannot truly belong to the world while entrusting its expression to a highly idiosyncratic set of images and mental forms.

The Epistle to the Hebrews is a case in point. Its thought is of a deep and powerful quality and some of its phrases echo resoundingly through Christian tradition. But it is grounded in imagery of tabernacle and temple and tribal lore which remain opaque to Hindu intelligence where they are not indeed revolting. Blood, to Jains, far from 'cleansing' can only defile. The point about Melchisedec, 'king of Salem', and his tithes from Abraham is remote and elusive, if not arcane. It does not carry meaning to those outside the original readership or those not serviced by a recondite scholarship. It has to be taken on trust and, as such, obscures what it should illuminate. Or at least its obscurity prompts the loyal question whether there are not 'Melchisedecs' in other lore and mythology with equal potential to recruitment. Is the institution of the Canon fair in giving exclusive, favoured, even tedious, currency to one 'hero' out of Genesis? There is much else in the Epistle to the Hebrews to mystify the Asian reader, to puzzle rather than to educate the soul. *Argumenta ad homines* are fine, if we change them with the *homines*. Otherwise the very principle which justifies them becomes their condemnation.

Where a feeble sense of how wide the world is dulls the force of these questions there may be a total failure to realize the degree to which our Christian gospel has been dominated by metaphors liable to mislead when transferred outside the culture of their origin. The 'price' metaphor, for example, has been a danger to doctrine whenever it was lifted out of a context where 'price' was 'paid' *for* but in no way *to* (as in vigilance being the price of liberty, or risk the price of adventure), into a mercantile mentality where commodity always had a seller if there was a buyer. The meaning of atonement was travestied when Messiah-Jesus was understood somehow to have 'bought out' the devil. Imagery from animal sacrifice, so prominent in the Hebraic heritage, can easily disserve when it is crudely pressed. There is nothing less like a lamb than the lamblike Jesus in Gethsemane, in that no animal ever comprehended in its victimization the reality of volition.

The western Christian needs only intelligence and not a journey to India to alert him to these pitfalls in the trust of the cross. The point about a theology in and of Asia is that it has its own experience of them and must not be willed into any suppression of what is at stake out of a mistaken loyalty to a geographically partial background. On the contrary, Christian expression that is genuinely embracing the world – its own world – must belong there truly and responsibly. When this responsibility leads us back into the final referent for such Christian expression *per se* it is to 'Messiah according to Jesus' that we are led. We come back to the singularity which alone requires and enables the responses to time and place and people in their due diversity.

VI

It is illuminating to see how referral and response – the one to Christ-Jesus, the other to India – came together in the thought of a perceptive and representative Indian theologian, Pandi-peddi Chenchiah (1886–1959).[14] An able lawyer and a Chief

Judge, he was a Christian from boyhood in a first generation family. But Hindu sympathies figured strongly in his expression of Christian thought. He did not write systematic books but preferred the medium of articles in the secular and Christian press. His mind moved from quite different points of departure from those of Hebraic tradition and Patristic theology. He began, in the phrase already quoted, from 'the raw fact of Christ' – a dictum echoed, no doubt quite unconsciously, in the often quoted phrase of Herbert Butterfield: 'Hold to Christ and for the rest be totally uncommitted.' [15]

But what do we identify as 'the raw fact'? Chenchiah used the word 'raw' to exclude what he saw as the over-formalized, intellectualist, definitions of Nicea and Chalcedon. He wanted to return to the historical, to the messianic. But the messianic, for him, was not quite that of our Chapter 5, with its emphasis on messianic definition against the background of the hope of history. Rather it lay in the historical character of Jesus as man in Christhood. The messianic dimension was measured in an inward sense. This corresponded with Chenchiah's instinct to start in his faith from the human end. Jesus, as he had historically been, could be identified with a new quality of human existence, evident in life and ministry and self-oblation. So identified, the Christ-reality could pass into each of us, making us 'Christs' 'after his image'. Such experience (*anubhava*) did not dispense in any way with the historical Jesus: it inwardly possessed reproduction. Chenchiah saw the manhood of Jesus as the clue to how God stood in relation to man. He did not think of the Incarnation as 'episodic' – a danger to which orthodoxy is liable – so that we have in mind, as it were, an episode in transcendence, a 'visitation' that came to an end. Rather, leaving aside the interests of metaphysics so prominent in traditional categories, Chenchiah interpreted Jesus as 'the man without *karma*', 'the new humanity', a genuine mutation (to use a secular term) in which by faith we might all participate.

With this theme of 'Christ in you, the hope of glory', Chenchiah's Christology moves away from a sacrificial view of the cross. Metaphors drawn from that context he sees, in line with our earlier general observations, as 'an attempt to reduce Jesus to the ideology of Judaism'.[16] His phrasing here is vague and unfair, inasmuch as Judaism, especially in Talmudic form, no longer has sacrificial focus. His comment intends the Old Testament tradition of the *cultus*. His view of the Incarnation reads the 'Sonship' of Jesus as defined in the newness in which the divine is humanly disclosed and by which in the direct contact of faith we may become 'partakers of the divine nature'. Phrases such as 'of one substance with the Father', while safeguarding what it was important to safeguard by criteria so concerned, do not suit or satisfy Chenchiah with his different concern for the Christ of *our* experience. 'Belief that' will be formulated in ways important to the 'believing's' perspective; 'identity with' Jesus centres on the share we have, by faith and the Holy Spirit, in that 'fusion' of the divine and the human which happened in the Christ and avails because of him for all whose being is open to his incarnate presence. Jesus, as 'God the Son', is the prototype of the new creation, the fruition of that divine purposiveness which undergirds the physical creation. Jesus exemplifies and bears the final destiny of the cosmic whole.

The Indian impulses in this thinking are clear enough: the need to motivate and sustain the forward movement of Indian political fulfilment and its social struggle; the sense of a *yoga* of the spirit; a will to escape from the incidental *avatāra* of the Krishna style, by faith in a once-for-all, ever-continuing Incarnation; and confidence in a new order here and now ours in the Christ who breaks out of *karma*, 'firstborn of the new creation'. Chenchiah's theology draws deeply from the New Testament while exercising a radical freedom to differ from accents in its authorship. He is not intimidated by canonical status. There is a futurism in his view strangely akin to that of De Chardin. 'Christianity comes to us as a seed not as a tree.' [17] Historicalness in Jesus is paramount, but is constituted by the actuality of his consciousness of the divine which his ministry involved and which underlay his whole teaching and his transcendence of the ego-centred institutions within which he moved and because of which he suffered. Chenchiah always insisted on the phrasing which runs: 'Jesus is God the Son', not 'Jesus is God', [18] so that the radical transcendence of the gospel is preserved.

Chenchiah was tempted into metaphors about 'the new birth' which were dangerously biological in the analogy employed. He was highly critical of church concepts in general and of much in Indian Christianity in particular. Institutionalizing displaced the central inward experience: church-discipline and community-structure did duty for inward Christhood. His own sense of inward certitude made him critical of the need for security which church authority and scriptural reference supplied for others. His theology was in no way an attempt to point forward to Jesus from Hinduism – the 'fulfilment' idea: rather his concern was to build bridges from Jesus to Hinduism. It was, for him, the same about Judaism. Jesus had his own messianic 'mind', as we have seen. Judaism did not recognize his criteria and when Matthew, for example, later wrote into his Gospel citations of Hebraic 'fulfilments' these were subsequently discerned and never, in respect of Jesus, corporatively operative from within the old tradition. Similarly it would not be Hindu clues which would arguably point to Jesus: rather the movement of witness would be from him to them. Chenchiah firmly believed in the singular Christ, but he believed that Christhoods were eminently comprehensive of the hopes of Hindus.

VII

'We can no more think of God without Jesus Christ than we can think of Jesus Christ without God.'[19] Hardly a satisfactory formulation since 'think about . . .' is so vague a use of language. Yet in instinct it is one with the historic Creeds whose intention was to confess 'God in Christ' and Jesus-Messiah as the 'particular historical figure through faith in whom God is established to be God'.[20] Vengal Chakkarai (1880–1958), another seminal figure in Indian Christian thought, saw 'the fact of Christ' as the core of faith, the faith he embraced at the age of twenty-three. Like his contemporary, Chenchiah, of Hindu birth and a lawyer, he saw the historicalness of the gospel in Jesus as paramount, and the theme of personal *anubhava*, or 'experience'. Unlike Chenchiah, he set out his thinking in two major works, *Jesus the Avatar*, and *The Cross and Indian Thought*.[21] In the former he invited a dangerous misconception, but excluded it with the emphatic article. The significance of Jesus *might* be comprehended under the Hindu term *avatar*, but only by the utter contrast of its singular nature. The Christ-Event enshrines, *via* the messianic achievement of Jesus what must be understood as the Christhood of God.[22] Jesus is, as it were, the removing of the veil so that we look upon the face of God. The long tradition of *bhakti*, or soul-devotion, from Hindu religion, can then take over in the heart's recognition of 'the light of God's countenance'. Chakkari revels in Hindu terminology in Christian connotation.

Soul-love to Christ turns on the realization of the self-oblation of Jesus in the suffering of the cross, a *kenosis* arising from a completeness of communion with 'the Father'. What is distinctive about Chakkarai's emphasis here is the way he treats the 'before' and 'after' of the Incarnation. Jesus, in historicalness, is a parenthesis between pre-history and post-history. The human immediacies have to be seen, at the ascension, as transcended in both directions. There is a universalizing of what had necessarily to be particularized in the very context of Incarnation. But the Christ whom we have come to know as divine in Jesus must be understood comprehensively of all that is antecedent in every culture. He cannot rightly be confined to a Hebraic ancestry or made the prisoner of categories, albeit biblical, which would monopolize his interpretation.

Likewise, in the onward sense, the Incarnation means a dynamic and continuing force, or presence, in the indwelling Holy Spirit within the believing fellowship. As in Chenchiah the accent is not on what can be said on how to formulate a doctrine of 'the two natures', but rather on experiencing the oneness of soul with the living Christ which Chakkarai links with the great ideal of the Vedānta, the discovery of oneness. He finds *advaita* 'wrought on the anvil of the life of Jesus'.[23] The analogy is curious and some would find the term stretched over a radical distinction. But that is the measure of the task of cross-reference. Chakkarai wants to believe that the goal of non-duality, the awareness of the human *atman*, or soul, in oneness with *Brahman*, or ultimate reality, is realized within the love of Christ, received and returned, as the end of *māyā*, or illusion. The problem remains whether what is overcome is an illusion of self as physiological privacy, or the illusion of self as a proud self-sufficiency. This urgent distinction we shall find awaiting us in the encounter with Buddhism as a religion which broadly identifies the two, making any salvation of the self as self impossible. In Chakkarai's theology of *atman* and *bhakti*, *Brahman* is no longer absolute in any sense which would preclude the outgoing love implicit in Christ's Incarnation. He is not to be reproached, however, for seeking a Hindu frame of thought by the fact that its original implications may have been elided. Did not the New Testament writers do the same with the Hebrew and Greek 'baptisms' of terminology? Do we see these as somehow more congruent only because they are more familiar and a Canon has sanctified them?

In his confidence that *bhakti* through Christ *is* experience of community in God, Chakkarai relies on the understanding of the Holy Spirit. There is at least consistency here. For the rubric which would forbid the use of *advaita* language to Christian soul experience would also exclude those dimensions of theology which the theme of the Holy Spirit expresses. Here we come upon the Johannine emphasis on the 'proceeding' Spirit, that energy of divine action within the soul which implements and makes operative the energy of grace present in the suffering love of the cross. Chakkarai here recruits the Hindu term *shakti* (power). Through and beyond the terms familiar to biblical 'sacrifice' as the sphere of forgiveness, he understands the cross as a well of power flowing in heart transformation wherever it is received.

Thus Chakkarai's Christology is grounded in a firm conviction of the singularity of Jesus as the Christ. But there is a clear 'Hinduizing' on his part of that otherwise quite un-Hindu accent on the historical, from Galilee to Gethsemane.[24] He reads New Testament *kenosis* as a self-emptying on the part of Jesus which, in its ardent moral quality and reach, constitutes also an ontological union with God. The 'egolessness' which Chakkarai identifies in Jesus in his Christhood has to be read, he insists, as the proof and meaning of his incarnate divinity. In these terms western Christology, with its anxious formulae about 'the two natures' and the 'one substance', has been wrongly preoccupied with conceptual questions which have been, and necessarily, left behind in the actuality of a self-oblation in which the very personhood of Jesus was given up into the divine will. Why, then, should our thought be busy striving to define the mystery of the personhood thus willingly yielded?

By the same token those who receive Jesus as the Christ in *bhakti*-discipleship will no longer be concerned for their personhood – in the way that much Christian intellectualism has been in its unease about Hindu and Buddhist 'emptiness' or *advaita*. In Chakkarai, it is as if a profound Christian moralism, in both the Christ and the self, remits, or simply removes from anxious relevance, those problems of personhood which dominate traditional Christian thinking both about Jesus as God and Son and about the believing self. Chakkarai thinks of the exalted Christ as belonging to all cultures by virtue of that achieved egolessness of the cross, which ascension vindicates and enthrones, and by which Jesus ceases to be merely Hebraic, Galilean, or the conceptual property of any single culture. In this sense the Incarnation had its necessary historical incidence, speaking Aramaic, summoning fishermen, and hallowing bread and wine. But by the nature of Incarnation itself, the accomplished cross and resurrection leave behind the incidental and the circumstantial in the inclusiveness which cannot fail to characterize one 'who was made man'. The Canon and much theology, however, have persisted too long and too timidly with the incidental as if it had not yielded the universal.

It sometimes happens that theology finds its besetting questions not answered but rather differently asked. Other studies undergo the same experience. The old question: 'How is God made man?' took the western Fathers (all of them west of India however, otherwise, eastern) into all the issues from Nicea to Chalcedon and beyond. Indian theologians, as here in brief in two representatives, let the basic query of their Hindu context, which has to do with selfhood and its puzzle, suggest a Christology in which Christhood is thoroughly historical and, for that very reason – being the history that it was – also the very incidence, in moral disclosure, of the being of God.

VIII

'Why not the philosophy of our land . . . more Christian than Alexandria?', asks Chakkarai.[25] He and Chenchiah in broad consensus represent a deeply Indian verdict on Christology. The clear emphasis on historical singularity is unmistakable. *Māyā* and *karma*, far from inviting into indifferentism, or unreality, supply terms of contrast by which the Christ-Event can be apprehended and its measure understood. The cross, within the meaning of the incarnation, becomes, for these thinkers, the focal point, the central crisis, of what *vedānta* seeks, namely oneness with ultimate Being. But this mystery of 'the love of Christ' is not allowed to stay as the enigma of metaphysical curiosity or philosophic discourse. Belonging as it does with an inclusive act of moral self-oblation within the divine compassion – by which alone human history can feasibly contain it – it becomes, in its once-for-all historicalness, the inflowing energy of grace by which what it discloses as the Christhood of God is present and active in a 'Christification' of those who receive it.

The *Gita* tells that the Lord of majesty manifests himself in any form desired by the worshipper. That, as Chakkarai puts it, is 'the spirit of accommodation of the Hindu genius'.[26] Those incarnations occur, discharge their task and terminate. *Bhakti* is kindled by the very fact of their being congenial to the devotee's context of mind or circumstance. May we not say, by contrast, that the Incarnation within Christhood centres, not in a religious option of ours, but vitally in the heart and marrow of our human wrongness and despair. It is the cross which divinely discerns, identifies and accomplishes what Incarnation has to be and mean, if the divine ultimacy is to be truly known in deed. It is not by prescripts of religious aspiration born of our whims or subtleties that the divine splendour is manifested but by the criteria of grace and realism implicit in the splendour. The Jesus of history is crucial to the Christ of experience, on this understanding, because it is in the concreteness of Jesus' 'egoless' Christhood that personhood in each of us becomes the receptacle of the energy of grace there released for our transformation. In that experience of liberation from karmic bondage, from the *māyā*-illusion of egoism, our worship of God in Christ need not be preoccupied with the metaphysics of divine personality. The experience is articulate in the devotion, 'that God may be all in all'.

The sense, prominent through all the foregoing, that the singularity of Jesus as the Christ belongs in and with a historical realism, is vital to the struggle for social justice. The practical implications of the Christology we have been studying in two Indian exponents were developed in the pioneer work of Paul D. Devanandan and the journal *Religion and Society*.[27] For all the devotional ardour they may generate the *avatāras* which respond primarily to soul-wistfulness within a static social scene, as for example, in popular reading of the *Gita*, have no motive-relevance to the burdens of poverty, injustice, deprivation and oppression. It was Devanandan's conviction that the issues between faiths – in his case Hinduism and Christianity – could best be broached in positive commitment to the living present, not in the abstractions of formal comparison.

This emphasis aligned readily with many of the inner preoccupations of neo-Hinduism and with the pervasive pressures of secular assumptions upon all religious faith and *cultus*. Nationalism pointed in the same direction in that, while it made new demands on the religion which undergirded it, it further required that religion to abandon the quiescence, or the torpor, or the indifferentism which the old order had occasioned, and relate actively to a contemporary vocation. There can be no doubt that wherever realism is urgent Gethsemane comes into its own. The more surely one is immersed in humanity and its discontents as aspiration kindles them, the more those dimensions which make the singularity of Jesus' Christhood are seen to measure what response has to mean. Response is enabled by the working of that Christhood in the energy by which it is multiplied into discipleships which undertake its future in the confidence of its once-for-all incidence and its present truth.

But how far must these multiplied discipleships be articulately identified with the faith and the community that are custodian of the secret and the house and household of its story? To this question we now turn.

NOTES

1 Herbert Butterfield, *The Origins of History*, ed. Adam Watson (New York 1981), pp. 162–3. The word 'fit' has been substituted for the word 'click'. The brackets are in the original.

2 To borrow a term much loved of Buddhists as a possible English for *sunyata*, instead of 'emptiness'. See, e.g., Abe Masao, writing in F. Franck, ed., *The Buddha Eye* (New York 1982), pp. 203–7: 'One may awaken to "suchness" in which everything is realized in its uniqueness and particularity.' It is bewildering to be told that awareness of disparate identities is to awaken to the 'no-thing-ness' of all of them. But the intriguing term 'suchness' is used here simply as a synonym for 'identity' – here of Jesus as the who and how of Messiahship.

3 i.e. 'distinctively' or 'disconcertingly' as well as 'alone'.

4 Or else pseudo, like Sabbatai Sevi. See Chap. 5 note 16.

5 Robert Browning, *Easter Day*.

6 Arthur D. Nock, *Essays on Religion and the Ancient World*, ed. Zeph Stewart (Cambridge, Mass., 1972), 'Early Gentile Christianity and its Hellenistic Background', pp. 83–4.

7 See Chap. 7 note 46.

8 It is Paul, in 1 Corinthians 11.25f., who records a command to repeat the ordinance, and then Luke follows suit, 22.19.

9 An authentic Hindu being firmly exclusivist! In *Young India* (31 Dec., 1931), p. 418. See note 11.

10 See Margaret Chatterjee, *Gandhi's Religious Thought* (London 1983), pp. 21f.

11   *Young India* (11 August, 1927), p. 251.

12   D. A. Thangasamy, *The Theology of Chenchiah* (Bangalore 1966), pp. 1–5. See also Robin Boyd, *An Introduction to Indian Christian Theology* (Madras 1969), pp. 144–64.

13   In *Vatican 2, An Inter-Faith Appraisal* (Notre Dame 1966), p. 262. This would seem a very faithless comment on the abidingness of Jesus as the Christ. 'Fixed once and for all' hardly coincides with the reality of the ever present, never resting, Holy Spirit. Does 'for all' mean all times or also all peoples?

14   See note 12 above.

15   Herbert Butterfield, *Christianity and History* (London 1949), p. 146. His broadcast lectures on the BBC were deeply influential at the time. The difficulty with his dictum is that to 'hold to Christ' one must be *relatively* committed to much else, without which there would be no 'holding to' him. cf. Chenchiah, quoted by Boyd, op. cit., p. 147: 'Let it be understood that we accept nothing as obligatory save Christ. Church doctrine and dogma, whether from the West or from the past, whether from Apostles or from modern critics, are to be tested before they are accepted.' Tested whereby?

16   *Rethinking Christianity In India* (Madras 1939), p. 164. Chenchiah adds: 'or the political ideology of the State of Rome'. The charge needs more careful expression but the point of immediate relevance is the sense of an improper cultural dominance in the interpretation of Christian faith and experience.

17   Quoted in Thangasamy, op. cit., p. 19, from *Miller Endowment Lectures*, p. 56.

18   The same point was forcibly made by James Denney in *Letters of Principal James Denney to W. Robertson Nicholl*, 1893–1917, pp. 120–6. See Kenneth Cragg, *The Call of the Minaret* (New York 1956), pp. 315–16.

19   P. T. Thomas, *The Theology of Chakkarai with Selections from his Writings* (Madras 1968), p. 46. cf. also p. 51: 'Jesus is the predicate of God.' There is, however, a looseness in Chakkarai's thought when he adds here, in strangely dubious phrasing: 'or if you prefer it for the sake of a nominal adherence to the demands of monotheism, God is the predicate of Jesus. But our preference is to define the unknown God by the somewhat-known Jesus.' If he really means his adjectives here his 'preference' is totally untenable. Nor should the demands of monotheism be 'nominalized'.

20   C. F. Evans, *Explorations in Theology 2* (London 1977), p. 120. Evans writes further in this context: 'That the Messiah is an historical figure is of immense importance, because he is thereby established as truly human, and attention is fixed upon what men do and are.'

21   Both works were published in Madras in 1932.

22   *Jesus the Avatar*, pp. 172–3.

23   ibid., p. 220.

24   'Hinduizing' is no doubt a crude phrasing but may be allowed despite its looseness to characterize Chakkarai's thoroughly biblical sense of how the gospel history marries with his Indian account of its impact in the soul.

25 In P. T. Thomas, *Selections*, op. cit., p. 92.

26 ibid., p. 87.

27 Paul D. Devanandan (1901–62) wrote *The Concept of Maya* (London 1950), and a rich flow of articles to the *Journal* of the Christian Institute for the Study of Religion and Society, at Bangalore, of which he was the mainspring and first Director. His conviction was that the bearing of Christian faith, and of Christology within it, could best find register in Hindu consciousness in the context of the immediate, contemporary issues in society, in state and education. In that pursuit he was passionately convinced of the reality of conversion into the faith which had Christ and Christology in trust. But that custodianship must participate in all the situations of the Indian nation, read by other lights and dominated by another ethos.

10
Souls and His Name

'Messiah isn't only Jesus: he is all of us and that is why he's called "Emmanuel"',[1] wrote Ernesto Cardenal, Nicaraguan priest and poet. How far can 'all of us' extend where Jesus is the common theme, or action could be said to be in some sense 'messianic'? There has been wide currency in the last quarter century of the notion of anonymous Christians and, by and large, it has failed to make its case.[2] For it is rightly thought to be condescending or gratuitous. The alleged anonymity could readily be reciprocal and, either way, putative. But would the thought of associate Christians be more feasible, if the will to such was genuine both outside and within the churches? At least the anonymity would be gone, if it was ever there, but a forbidding otherness, enforced or assumed, would be overcome. Through all the foregoing chapters we have been aware, in varying degrees, of a will for Jesus but in dissociation from institutions, doctrinal and historical, which traditionally belong with him.

Yet that tradition has firmly at its heart the call to belong, the incorporate nature of fellowship and the sacrament of baptism. Its hospitality as – so it believes – proxy for God's is not indifferent; it is ardent and genuine.[3] It does not invite to ideas for discussion but to grace and discipleship. Its gospel is about a love that embraces and does not patronize. Its understanding of human need calls not for associates but for penitents. It wants people in and with the text, not in the margins. It is inherently conversionist. To preach is to reach each, in hope if not in fact.

So to insist is loyal Christianity. But if we must face – from the previous chapters – plural Christologies must we not allow plural discipleships? If happenedness in the world of the Christ-principle can be diverse, must not happenedness in the soul be also diverse? Will it need to be related exclusively to one institutional religion? May what, by a messianic test, we must see as the work of grace in mind and character be authentic outside formal Christianity? The question whether conversion is necessary seems to be a corollary of pluralism. It is widely answered in the negative. It would be sounder to ask, in the light of plural faiths, what is the conversion which is always necessary and what are its auspices. *Auspice Christi* may well be the universal factor in the righting of selves, in the love that knows itself redeemed and must in turn become redeeming, forgiven and forgiving. But is this always and only *auspice ecclesiae*?[4] If so, we are back with the insoluble puzzle of plural faiths, and without a policy in interminable debate. But, if not, what then of the continuing and urgent role of *auspex ecclesiae*?

> John, answering him said: 'Master, we saw one casting out devils in thy name and he followeth not us, and we forbad him because he followeth not us.' But Jesus said: 'Forbid him not.'

How should we read this incident (Mark 9.38–9 and Luke 9.49–50) in contemporary terms? John here is echoing the phrase 'in my name' which Jesus, according to the context in either Gospel, had used in the immediately preceding exchange about 'receiving a child' as, in fact, 'receiving' Jesus. What, precisely, in context, could the 'name' of Jesus signify invoked by someone not a disciple? Had this 'outsider' kindled to the emulation of Jesus' ardour about the misery of human bedevilment? yearned to ally with a liberating hope? sensed an unspoken invitation to enlist in the good news? Had he moved merely from some exciting hearsay in lack, as yet, of any personal encounter with Jesus? Was he, so to speak, an early associate Christian before the word was invented by which the articulate secret would be identified?

It is impossible to say. We defer some reckoning with the imperative name – imperative to compassion even for the frailest, imperative to the mastering of evil – for study in the crucial passage in Acts 4.12. But we carry forward to it the gentle prohibition of monopoly of 'the name'. Yet, we must heed the name if we would know who it is for whom we must concede discipleships other than our own. For there is no ending of monopoly in the absence of identity. There is merely plurality.

II

Before coming squarely into this searching issue, it will be well to reflect, in preface, on how like the disciples in that episode all religions are. Their salient characteristic – and one which tangles and embitters the whole question of converting and being converted – is a tenacious, institutional concern for their continuity and thus the rigorous retention of their dogmas, their rites and their adherents, the last most of all. Faiths do not readily 'let their people go'. It is this which so sadly impedes the inflow of new meaning from outside and creates a situation almost impervious to truth not already possessed and sanctioned. It is obvious that evangelism often plays into the hands of this instinct to resist – a fact which has long been the anguish of mission, especially among Asian faiths and cultures.

Religions, in this institutionalized cast of mind, suffer enormous stagnation and exhibit a stolid unloveliness. The will of the few to relate meets the solid impasse of the many. Mission assumes the guise of the predator. Dogmas, rites and symbols cease this way to be essentially signs and servants of the transcendent and become themselves the sanction of deep and sometimes dark vested interests. God or *nirvāna* become the guarded of the guardians who find their authority, their impenetrability of mind, from the championship of much else besides religion, whether culture, office, prestige, tradition, even xenophobia, enmity and malice. Religion is never unlovelier than when it is self-consciously defensive. This tends to be its frequent posture, not least when aware of pluralism or the threat of otherness, secular or spiritual.

This situation, so long evident, so far formidable, makes it urgent to ask whether there is not some way of turning the flank, of by-passing the obstacles, of avoiding, as much as in us lies, to incur this impasse. Could there be a way to 'associate' truths across frontiers with us Christians possessing from Judaism or Islam, or Buddhism, or Hinduism, whatever we truly can, ignoring – to that extent – that it belongs elsewhere among those 'who follow not us'? Then could 'those who follow not us' in the faith of 'God in Christ', of 'Christ crucified' associate even so with the meaning of the love that suffers, there identified, as the one power by which, in the end and in the whole, evil is alone redeemed? Will they be 'associate Christians' if, in that love's name, they master the demons of self and sin? May an authentic practice of the Christ-principle link them in some sense with the custodial faith of the Christ-Event? This will not make them 'anonymous'. For the presence of the principle will be evident. Hypothetical 'anonymity' anyway was only a dubious way of conceding, not surmounting, the very fact of establishment antipathy we are deploring. It is not in anonymity that the Christian can know and confess what it is to be 'associate' Jew, or *muslim*,[5] or *bhakti* disciple, or *vidya*-seeker.

This aspiration, either way, will still leave us with sharp problems both of mind and spirit. It may make only scant headway into the mutual hardening of heart to which institutional religions are so prone when made seriously aware of each other. But it may serve to focus on what, essentially, conversion ought to mean in the world as it is. It counters the sense in which seeking it, in formal terms, somehow inferiorizes the other faith. We have to ask what, in fact, if not in intention, in effect if not as cause, evangelism implies about the beliefs it addresses. For if the implications are not honestly faced in the seeking of recruits, they will come home to roost in the subsequent discipleship. If not at the first encounter, certainly in the resulting nurture of adopted faith, the old will demand reckoning in the psyche if not in the confession.

And the old will entrench itself in self-assertion. Its instinct to behave as self-sufficient will take confirmation from the implied inferiorization. Disciples may have migrated but the systems stay suspicious or immune. The question remains pressing, beyond the success of failure of such migration – in any direction – what to do about their otherness and its closing of the doors. How will self-sufficiency give way to a posture of mutual attention without which truths are embargoed?

The exclusive principle has long been assumed on all hands. Even Hinduism which with some justice prides itself on a hospitable stance is, from that angle, just as rejectionist of Semitic instincts as it sees them to be. An undiscriminating tolerance repudiates intolerance and, so doing, rejects intolerantly faiths whose loyalty requires them to discriminate. It is hard to say which is the more lethal to the other. Hinduism, too, has often showed its resistance to criticism of the caste system and by its very reverence for all reverence can be very irreverent about the will to convert out of it. It is no less susceptible to nationalist fervour than other faiths which have rigorous dogmatic systems.

The so-called Athanasian Creed is a ready example from within Christian tradition, with its anathemas about salvation joined to highly complex doctrinal definition. *Extra ecclesiam nulla salus* has long been a hard, uncompromising dictum. The other Semitic faiths have their versions of the same rigorism. Chief Rabbi I. Jakobovits wrote:

> As a professing Jew I obviously consider Judaism the only true religion. The recognition of other faiths as 'equally true' is branded an apostasy in Jewish law (*Sanhedrin* 63a, based on Exod. 22.20). Judaism, to be true to itself, is bound to reject, for instance, the divinity of Jesus or the prophecy of Muhammad as false claims, otherwise its own claims, such as the supremacy of Moses' prophecy and the finality of the Moasic law . . . could not be true.[6]

All non-Jewish religious worship is *avodah zarah*, 'strange worship'. There is an operative sense in which the Jew is the only authentic monotheist.

The Rabbi's mention of 'apostasy' takes the mind at once to Islam. On the one hand there is 'no compulsion in religion' (Surah 2.256). Yet any formal Muslim withdrawal from Islam is an act of treason, almost literally, since adherence, unless exempt by birth outside the Islamic faith, is compulsory. Islamic religious identity is politically constituted by classical Islamic doctrine as stated, for example, by Ismail al-Faruqi, for whom a Muslim's contracting out of Islam is political treason. On this score there could be no genuine register of religious meaning that would not be treachery. Every would-be 'convert' is a quisling, a spy, or a miscreant. Faruqi writes:

> A person may move from a non-Muslim *Ummah* (i.e. tolerated religious community politically under Islam) into the Muslim *Ummah*, for such movement does not imply abandonment of the ideology of the Islamic state or the forsaking of loyalty to it. Movement from the Muslim *Ummah* to another . . . necessarily implies the repudiation of the Islamic state . . . To convert out of Islam means clearly to abandon its world order which is the Islamic state. That is why Islamic law has treated people who have converted out of Islam as political traitors . . . It must deal with the traitors, when convicted after due process of law, either with banishment, life-imprisonment or capital punishment . . . But Islamic political theory does allow converts from Islam to emigrate . . . provided they do so before proclaiming their conversion . . . But once their conversion is proclaimed they must be dealt with as traitors to the state.[7]

How, then, can free inquiry exist, if the penalty for a truth-discovery not approved by Islam is exile or death? How would 'due process of law' take cognizance of weighing the mystery of the cross or the appeal of Buddhist *dukkha*? Or how would a slow, perhaps hardly perceptible, loss of faith within the Muslim citizen be detected in the course of a continuing and, therefore, unexceptionable, citizenship? The danger of non-faith *inside* political status is implicit in such a passage as Surah 49. 14–18.

Such rigorous equation between faith and political allegiance, leaving no viable loyal options to the former among born Muslims, measures the legalized finality of Islam according to its *Sharīʿah*, or sacred law. It symbolizes graphically and tragically the tenacious instincts of formal religion which, on many hands, inhibit the register of mutual relevance between faiths and rule out those attitudes of attention which might carry meaning across. It is as if the very notion of 'conversion' conspires to disqualify whatever might, or might not, prove its antecedents, namely, humility, honesty, openness, friendship, soul-quest, and mental liberty. It is almost as if religions have annexed God to their own custody, made themselves sole agents, proprietors, of the transcendent. They suffer the consequences of their pride in the nemesis that condemns them, short of self-questioning, to become yet more proudful.

If, then, our Christian concern is with the trust of the Christ-Event how do we best obviate the enormous barrier of this religious self-sufficiency? Is there a way of disciples finding themselves such the more readily for being *not* of our 'making'? How should we remain hospitable without prosecuting hospitality'.[8] Or what should we say of those who suggest that our baptism is simply our brand of circumcision – the badge of the acceptable? What, given this formidable inter-religious corporate otherness of mood and identity, is the wisdom of the gospel? How should we think of 'the name of Jesus the Christ' and these possessive camps – for such they be – of mankind?

III

This leads us to study the crucial passage of Peter's sermon, according to Acts 4.12, in which he affirms that 'there is no other name given under heaven among men, whereby we must be saved'. What does he mean by 'the given name'? His context, like his audience, is wholly Jewish and he presupposes all the rich Hebraic associations of 'the name of the Lord', the revealed nature of God as given into human trust for address and reliance, for invocation responsive to divine grace. He proceeds, with all his listeners, on the messianic hope, on 'he that was to come', as we have seen in Chapter 5. His bold theme is that this divine name and this messianic hope are now realized in Jesus who was crucified. His hearers know well that the messianic yearning is their singular anticipation, the shape of everything for which they wait as Jews. This, he declares, is now disclosed, fulfilled, made good and actual in Jesus through the cross. That which held all our hopes now claims our whole faith. God's fulfilment demands our total response.

'The name', then, is no mere label, a formula, a password, a magic external to the need. On the contrary it is that which alone suffices for the human crisis 'under heaven'. It is the down-to-earth action of divine grace, the *datum* of God. The cross of Jesus as the action-pattern of Messiah identifies what it takes to redeem mankind and, doing so, redeems. This is the meaning, this the efficacy, of 'the name'.

Would it, then, be legitimate to paraphrase Peter's words as they might be heard by Hindus, Buddhists, Muslims, animists, to whom he was not speaking? Might such a paraphrase run as follows: 'There is no saving evil situations except through the love that takes and saves them at its own cost. There is no other way in this whole wide world whereby redemption happens than the action-pattern of the Jesus who fulfilled the messianic hope, the hope which was the Hebraic form of the human yearning for the decisive answer to the wrongness of us all'. Peter, of course, was entirely innocent of all knowledge of the *Gita*, or of the Buddha. Islam had not then come to be. One cannot intelligently take him as in mind of the *Upanishads* or the Qur'ān. Translated into the idiom of their custodians we must understand, first, the projection into those worlds of the messianic yearning duly rendered and related, and secondly the Christian conviction of its realization in the singular terms of Jesus and his cross and resurrection. Only so shall we be loyal to the sense of that which Peter's speech identifies, in the hearing now of those who were within neither his audience nor his perspective.

This leaves us asking whether the action-pattern can be found elsewhere. That question can only be faced within the meaning of Peter's claim about the one 'given name' – 'given under heaven', i.e. of and from God in human actuality. Peter is linking the singularity of Christ's redemption with the unity of God. His sermon states the role of Jesus as singularly the Christ later formulated in the creeds in the words: 'the only begotten Son . . . one in being with the Father'. This confession is vital. But it must be read aright. The theme of redemption is necessarily linked to the conception of divine unity.[9] It *is* readily possible to think of sacrificial or propitiatory acts in a polytheistic world. Indeed such 'saviours' proliferate in Hinduism itself and animism is replete with rites of offering intended to retrieve or restore broken situations. By contrast, however, to affirm the unity of God, to bring all 'under heaven' within the authority of a single sovereignty, a sovereignty in grace, is by the same token to bring all such shadowy, multiple or desultory feeling after 'redemption' into the sufficient and inclusive aegis of the divine Lordship, both in initiative and fulfilment. This is what we mean in confessing Jesus as 'the *one* Christ'.[10] The God, of whom we say that Jesus is the Son, unifies by his own unity the mystery of atonement. The expression of his own nature as love, in the context of the human wrongness, is not diversified or ambiguous or equivocal. It is singular and inclusive in the singularity of the cross of Jesus. To speak of 'the only begotten' is to confess 'the unreservedly given'. God is not partialized in the meaning of Jesus as the Christ.

But – equally important for our theology – he is not 'individualized' as if forfeiting or forgoing his divine nature. That the Christ-Event is *this* and not something else does not imply alternatives within diversity, so that the cross is incidental, not integral, to divine Being. Its particularity is not of that sort, as the particular might be with us, an option or a whim. 'With him is no variableness'. 'In Christ all fullness dwells' incarnationally. The inclusiveness of the cross belongs with the unity of God.

It is this conviction which allows, indeed requires, us to anticipate its capacity for incidence as the principle of human lives even outside the church-community which is the historical and the vital custodian of its reality and meaning. When Rabindranath Tagore observed that 'God was generous in his distribution of love', he added that it was false to think it had been 'restricted to a blind lane abruptly stopping at one narrow point of history'.[11] False indeed. But faith in the cross is not that way. To see it as a single, comprehensive atonement is not to imagine that the claims of penitence are not continuous. To believe in the forgiveness of sins as that which we freely receive in the one inclusive redemption through Christ is not to say that we do not believe in the forgiveness of sins as the constant practice of our own relationships. To know 'the only begotten Son' and 'Saviour of the world' is not to exclude salvific acts of our own within society. Rather it is to be the more minded and enabled for them. But such salvific acts are not, as some in Hinduism demand, a merit-quest, a *swadharma*, a be-your-own-saviour stance. They are the reproduction, as far as in us lies, of the Christ-principle in meritless gratitude for the Christ-Event.

IV

To draw this Christ-principle from the Christ-Event and to hold that the former might live in souls without adequate acknow-ledgement of the latter, is to raise the whole issue of the Church. Indians may be conspicuous, but not alone, in querying the incorporation of truth-possession on which the Christian Church proceeds. It looks to them like an exclusion of the rest of the world from participation in its inner life. It matches exclu-sive truth by exclusifying community. It seems thereby to pre-clude or discourage interest in Jesus except on its own terms. Given all the long conditioning of its Greek, Latin, western vicissitudes, it is seen opposing those terms, even if unwit-tingly, to all the local, national aspirations of 'outsiders'. It pro-vokes emotive issues around conversion which obscure the essential significance of inward *metanoia*. What has to happen, savingly, within the personal life is linked, often to its own impediment, with the interests of an alien institution. Those who do not belong – often for reasons which, to them, seem authentic and perhaps even 'Christian', feel as if to say: 'We are forbidden because we follow not with them.' What should our church-loyalty think in becoming aware of this feasible par-allel to such 'associates' in the gospel incident earlier quoted? Or, if we are not aware, what does it say of our sensitivity? Can there, then, be authentic meaning to 'conversion' other than transition or migration into the ecclesiastical institution in whatever shape?

Here we face a profound paradox. On the one hand the his-

torical Christian 'institution' is where the reality, variously
defined as Christology, was decisively and corporately confessed. Between Jesus' death and the superb hymn to Christ
in Philippians 2.1–11, just twenty or so years elapsed and more
happened in those two decades than in a succession of centuries. But what there we might call reality-in-realization, christological coming-to-be, passed down into church history with
the developments that are inseparable from the sequence of
time. No faith lays more emphasis than Christianity on the
history of its origin. But that emphasis moves in and with a
living tradition and the continuity of experience. These have
diversified the trust of, and the witness to, that origin. The
basic appeal to history can finalize itself, as Christianity does,
in the Christ-Event but, being historical, it cannot finalize, or
make static, how that reality abides in the trust of the generations. What is in time has the necessity of abiding only in
terms of the particularity of every given point in what can only
be successive.

To the time-factor we must also add the place-factor. The
New Testament has its own and to that very Hebraic framework
we owe the Messiah-Christ theme *via* the Greek idiom which
has so large a part in Scripture's Christology. Each moving
place-factor means that other cultural idioms must find their
way into the confession of Christ *and* the consciousness of the
Church that confesses him. If Athanasius could boldly assert
that in the theophanies of the Old Testament and the visions
of God told of the patriarchs 'the *Logos* was learning to become
incarnate',[12] will it be fair to ask whether the same prospective
quality may not belong with some of the poetic visions of Hindu
seers? The concept of a 'learning *Logos*' is startling but, if it
holds, is surely transferable.

Hebrews 12.2, describing Jesus as the *archēgos* and the *teleiōtēs*
of faith, may be read in this sense. He who inaugurates and
pioneers, is he who brings to consummation. The immediate
reference is undoubtedly to the quality and nature of the Christ-
Event, and 'obedience to death, even the death of the cross'.
But may it not also define how that 'reality-in-realization' (as
we called it) gathers to its fullness all that can be seen as 'minded
towards it' (as Hebraic theophanies are believed to be) wherever
they are found? By what, otherwise, shall we identify those
of whom it is said: 'He is not ashamed to call them brethren'
(Heb. 2.11)?

The early Church assumed and taught its non-Jewish converts that the Hebraic patriarchs were their patriarchs, the Judaic history their history. They were thus put in possession of a past which was not their own. Must not the Church, in its wholeness, be possessed of the past behind any access to it? Otherwise how is it universal? To be sure, that Hebraic past has its peculiar relevance to the Christ-future. But if he is 'the Word made flesh' can it be the only relevance? If there is a past that is present in every reckoning with Christ whatever the culture, will *that* past not determine the antecedents wherever, on their part, 'the *Logos* is learned'? If so, and inasmuch as the historic Church has not been equijacent to all cultures as by vocation it must be, can there be discipleships presently outside it which are none the less responsive to Jesus in his messianic quality? May there be, in that sense, souls who think and live 'in his name', to whom we might apply the words of Jesus: 'He that is not against us is on our part'?

That Jesus had there a tolerance that possibly dismayed or displeased the disciples may be taken to hint that the Church too, for reasons deep in its allegiance, may be more rigorous about credentials than the Lord himself. 'He that is not against us . . .'; what of that before we can wisely say: 'He is on our part'? Must we not heed both parts of the dictum? Further, will not too sanguine a sense of associates with us, in 'Messiah', blunt the urgent criticism Christian faith must surely bring in respect of the systems and the traditions out of which they come? What of the apparently counter saying: 'He that is not with me is against me'?[13] Indeed. But may the urgent criticism not better, and more surely, come from those within the traditions that need it in the context of such identity with Jesus as they are ready to bring? May not a certain identity with him in action precede awareness of doctrine and be perhaps altogether cut off if we make the latter a prior demand? In 'bringing forth crisis unto truth', the gentle servant does not 'quench the smoking flax or break the bruised reed'.

V

It is time to ask, in general but not exclusive reference to India, what 'souls in Christ's name' might mean, having in mind that Christology of action – Gethsemane before Chalcedon – we have studied in Chapter 5 and noted in Indian theology. This joins together, inseparably, atoning love and incarnate Lordship. In the human, and the Indian, scene, taking part in such a Christology must mean a compelling sense of human solidarity, an awareness of the weight of evil, the will to a personal and corporate penitence in face of evil, the need to atone and become mediators of forgiveness, and, through all these and on account of them, a quality of vicarious love. That these are the truly Christic dimensions none can doubt. It is for the sake of these and their sure ground in the nature of God, the God of whom we say that Jesus is the Son, that conceptual Christologies were duly enunciated and made *de fide*. But as those mental determinations of the Christian faith were *ex eventu*, long subsequent to and derived from the Christ-Event, so they may be still in the comprehension of those, as in India, remote from their vocabulary and their concern. We will return, in Chapter 14, to the role and the necessity of the custodial community and the custodial creed, of the Church teaching a doctrine. Our study now is how the practice, however frail, of that by which Jesus was the Christ and 'Christ is God's', may be in the Indian context the way he would have us recognize what is 'on his part'.

It would be natural to expect that such participation in the significance of Christ in the Indian context would involve the ruling Hindu concept of *karma*, the entailing of evil out of a past into a future. Duly pondered it may be said that this entailing was part of the New Testament meaning of 'the wrath of God' – the inward nemesis of wrong-doing in which evil brings its own frustration and retribution.[14] Evil only does so, however, in the absence of repentance, penitence being precisely that which inwardly arrests and halts the evil sequence. But because evil incorporates others in its consequences and is never merely inward and private (where the guilt is), forgiveness waits upon the reaction of those who, caught in its issue, suffer from its results. The karmic law, so deep in Indian reckoning, captures the truth of this inter-relatedness and the inexorable quality of the consequences of deeds. What it does not and cannot allow, on its own premises, is that past-momentum is reversible by the quality of the responsive suffering vicariously borne. For this would mean that what is future to the evil deed (namely the act of forgiveness) can undo its committedness. It also means that the evildoer can be, and has to be, in a position of receiving, freely, from outside himself that on which his whole wellbeing turns. Any such acceptance to be forgiven flouts the karmic law by which the entail of one's deeds is wholly one's own and no extraneous 'merit' avails for a 'salvation' ahead, the quest of which is essentially one's own.

It is just here that the grace of the gospel is so deeply paradoxical. *Karma* says that an event originates out of the past as its necessary, or inexorable, condition. How could it be said to originate out of what is yet future? That (as yet) indeterminate future can only come out of the determinant past. This, however, is to ignore the fact that the forgiving response on the part of the wronged – if forgiving – party is already within the waiting future from the quality of heart. The good Samaritan in the story does not become such a man: he is such in the present actuality of what he *will* do. The event, when it occurs, merely elicits itself from how he is. Charles Hartshorne oddly remarks: 'No truth obtains until the thing it is true of exists', and makes it a ground for non-futurity in the karmic sense.[15] But this is to miss how some 'existents' have potentiality, so that 'truth obtains' before the practice of what it involves exists. Event brings it into play but does not bring it into being. Given the reality of grace, God's or ours, we need not read time always in karmic terms.[16] Grace can anticipate and be anticipated. And such grace is inherently one of external relationships belonging between people and can never be understood in the wholly internal workings of karmic merit or demerit. The heart of the gospel is that the grace of God which awaits our penitence already dependably exists in the measure of the wounds of Jesus.

If and when such acts of costly forgiveness occur within Hindu tradition may they not amount to a mastery of the demonic in Christ's name? Albeit defying the karmic law which does not admit of such reversal of entail, will they not in measure be redeeming it by fulfilling, in a contrasted way, its own emphasis on shouldering what is one's duty and calling? That duty is not, now, the role of a caste status to be borne without demur, but instead the role of a forgiving fellow-human acknowledging what has been learned in Christ, namely a taking up, an undertaking, of whatever comes to us of wrong *via* our human nexus with wrongdoers, and by such taking, accomplish redemption? May such learning in his name be analogous to Paul's claim about the very different 'law' of Torah, namely that it could be our pedagogue to lead us to Christ'?[17]

But do such approximations to the Christ-principle happen

in souls outside the Christian institution? In his *With and Without Christ*, Sadhu Sundar Singh (1889–1924?) has a chapter on 'Non-Christians with Christ', in which he wrote:

> I know quite a number of non-Christian leaders in India who are much influenced by the spirit of Christ but do not realise how greatly He has conquered them.

He continued with a narrative:

> One day I went to preach to the pilgrims at a town on the river Ganges. Just as I took my stand a pundit came and sat by me and asked: 'Have you also come here to bathe like other pilgrims?' I said: 'No, I have already bathed by faith in the blood of Christ . . . and have no need for ceremonial bathing in the Ganges.' When the pundit heard this he was amazed, but my own amazement was no less when, with beaming face, he said: 'That is splendid swami, I too have come for the same purpose', and with great love he embraced me . . . We both preached the Gospel to them and they listened attentively.
>
> Then one of the pilgrims asked: 'By Christ, do you mean Krishna, or some other incarnation?' Then the pundit repeated a few Sanskrit verses and said: 'We are preaching not about Krishna but about Christ, the sinless incarnation promised in the *Shastras*. For Krishna did not come to save sinners but to destroy them (*Gita* iv. 8).
>
> The pundit . . . told me his story. 'I had often heard about Christ, but owing to my prejudices I used to keep as far away from missionaries and Christians and their Christ as I could. But it once happened at Allahabad that I met two learned men belonging to the Secret Society of Christians. They were Sanskrit scholars and at first I thought them to be Hindus, but little by little they proved with great clearness that Christ alone is the Saviour. In a few days all my abhorrence and misunderstanding of Christianity disappeared. Then these two Sannyasis baptised me in the Jumna river . . .[18]

Sadhu Sundar Singh himself was the finest example this century of a Christian discipleship in Indian idiom. Openly baptized and undergoing bitter persecution and privation in the name of Christ, there was nothing 'associative' about his faith in Jesus' name. Yet, with his saffron robe, his Sikh turban and his sadhu pattern of life accepting both sustenance and obloquy with equal serenity on his wandering pilgrimages of witness over Asia, he expressed the name of Jesus Indian-wise. In his constant accent on prayer and meditation he held loosely to

structures ecclesiastical. He declined to be ordained. Christology he saw as Christlikeness in souls. His own faith was in
no way syncretistic. Nor did his disillusionment with much
western Christianity during his visits to Europe shake his own
allegiance. Yet he counted his Sikh/Hindu mother's nurture
his surest, truest school of theology.[19] There is little clear evidence of the identity, growth or significance of those secret
sannyasis in Christ of whom it so thrilled him to speak. Unlike
Francis of Assisi whom he so much resembled, he founded
no brotherhood, while Paul's 'care of all the churches' was
never his burden. In his intensely Christian spirituality, he
believed that 'the sphere of revelation of the divine *Logos* –
the Christ – includes far more than the New Testament story
of redemption with its Old Testament prologue'.[20]

As with C. F. Andrews, so with Sundar Singh, the intellectual
obligations of this conviction of the universal *Logos* present in
the faiths of India, were not worked through into formal shape,
as perhaps they never can be. Sure personal experience suf-
ficed. Divine revelation is consummated in the historical Jesus
and his cross but is everywhere refracted in the human search.

VI

Despite his distinction between 'Christians without Christ' and
'non-Christians with Christ', his trenchant criticism of academic
theologians in the West to whom one would not go in distress
or heed in ecstasy, and his equally firm criticism of Hinduism
and Buddhism,[21] Sundar Singh symbolized superbly a Christian, not a Hindu, relation between the Indian soul and the
Jesus-name. To understand how differently they may be related
there is no more inclusive figure than that of Mohandas Gandhi.
He exemplified in sustained encounters with evil that corporate
penitence, acceptance to suffer, and the vicarious principle
which, above in this chapter, we said might be drawn from
aspects of the idea of *karma*. Gandhi invoked them to resist
and undo the worst manifestation of the karmic principle,
namely 'untouchability'. This he identified as a dark and selfish
distortion of *karma* viciously made in evil self-interest and perpetuated by apathy and acquiescence and wilful social exploitation. It will bring out the cross-reference which is our concern
here if we ask whether there is any sense in which Gandhi's
costly struggle over the caste system can be fitted within the
import of Acts 4.12. Was there in his thoroughly Hindu effort

any implementing of 'the name', the energy of an active, burden-taking redemption, without which there is no 'salvation', in his strenuous summons to soul-force? This involves a further fascinating query how far the Christ-model in Jesus may find fulfilment, all official conversion apart, within an existing other faith, which is thereby taken into the cross-dimension, inside and not against its own religious reading of humankind.

Gandhi approached the scriptures of the Hindu tradition, the *Dharma Shàstras*, with a possessive independence of mind. He required that they be interpreted in terms consonant with his own conscience. This, in itself, was significant and owed something to that characteristic of Hinduism which makes it differ from Semitic-style or absolutist revelation. But by the same token he knew he confronted massive, popular assumptions, absolute in practice in their tenacious hold on credulity and on Brahmanic self-serving. Against these he insisted that the authentic caste pattern of Hinduism taught contentment with the duties of one's birth station and the discharge of such duties on behalf of the common good in community. In this respect one could detect a certain resemblance to Plato's doctrine of due fulfilment of one's role within a social whole.

It followed, Gandhi emphasized, that however menial such duty might be, no one should be despised in doing it. Hence the urgent, ardent campaign for the abolition of 'untouchability' duly achieved juridically after India's independence. Its actual eradication has been much harder to make good against the grain of hardened prejudice and religious advantage and sheer popular inertia. It was in the periodical *Harijan* (Children of God) that Gandhi pressed home the theme of redeeming evil by a resistance of the spirit which bears it away by undertaking to be creatively under it as a burden solely with the resources of a will that is good. Could we, or should we, fit this into the meaning of Peter's 'only Name'?

The comparable principle of non-injury as the 'weapon' of soul-action, aimed at *metanoia* in the ruling power, informed Gandhi's whole strategy both within and on behalf of the Congress Party in the quest for independence and the end of the British Raj. He wrote in *Young India*:

I have ventured to place before India the ancient law of self-sacrifice. For *Satyagraha* and its offshoots, non-co-operation and civil resistance are nothing but new names for the law of suffering . . . Non-violence means conscious suffering. It does not mean meek submission ... but it means pitting of one's whole soul against the will of the tyrant.[22]

He spoke of *Satyagraha*, soul-force, as the natural law of the human species and a quality of complete innocence. In those senses he ignored the more radical Christian insight into the tortuousness of the human heart. Gandhi, indeed, had to struggle hard against manifestations of hatred with more obvious claim to be 'the law of the human species'. But the vision – which he had largely from Jesus *via* Tolstoy and which was gospel to Martin Luther King – surely lay close to 'the Name' named at the cross. That it was invoked within a political struggle, and that its success owed something to the 'touchability' (as opposed to implacability) of the ruling power, does not diminish its relationship to Christ. For all the congenial inclusiveness of Hinduism here was a radical exclusiveness, an affirmation of a *nisi Dominus frustra*, an *only* way.

Disclaiming any rational, intellectual solution to the mysteries of life and of God, Gandhi was intuitively sure that 'God is Life, Truth, Light, He is Love'.[23] He went on:

> I call God long-suffering and patient precisely because He permits evil in the world. I know that He has no evil. He is the author of it and yet untouched by it.[24]

There are ambiguities here to require a Christian discrimination. 'Untouched', indeed, in the sense of 'uncontaminated', but not in the sense of 'indifferent'. While sharing Gandhi's instinct that a 'policy' on our part towards evil is more important than a philosophy about its meaning (assuming the latter were possible), Christian faith understands a divine *kenosis* of love in the given creaturehood of man, as the setting of a divine fellowship, in freedom, through grace. God is only 'the author of evil' in that context of his intention in man.

Hinduism hardly shares those convictions explicitly. The hampering ambiguity the gospel would wish to resolve. But that necessity should not obscure the precious truth within *Satyagraha* of bearing wrong without retaliation and so disowning and defeating evil without entailing evil further – as all else does except the love that suffers. Could this be embraced in the comment of Jesus to his 'official' disciples about one who, unofficially was, nevertheless, 'on their part'? Is there not something Christic here? Does it not raise the question of Christian implications for continuing – other – religions? Certainly Gandhi's disowning of 'untouchability' was far more efficacious than efforts of the churches or the incidence of accessions to them. What is the missionary motive to conclude from its arguable fruits within, as distinct from its recruitments out of, other faith-systems? Will it be merely romantic, or sadly incongruous, to discern in 'the name above every name' a relevance for faiths which, nevertheless, do not confess it such credally, still less adhere to it formally?

VII

It is perhaps in order to pause here and consider how 'the Name given', in Peter's sense, came to be known as such historically within the messianic hope in which he firmly housed it. For we might then wonder whether there should be recognized in Gandhi something analogous to that in the Hebraic tradition within which 'the Name' was first identified as the one saving Name. If so, may those first implications towards 'the Christ' in the biblical history yield a clue by which to understand something implicitly akin long after the Christians' Christ and in another idiom?

Such surmise takes us to Hebrew prophecy. It has often been remarked that Hinduism lacks the prophetic element, perhaps because its concepts of God have never been firmly moralized. Yet Gandhi's insistent witness *against* Hinduism from Hinduism and his moral indignation about the monstrous falsehood of 'untouchability' had something of that Hebraic passion. He felt that meaning and privilege had been suborned to selfish advantage and that institutions had to be defied for their ethical falsehood however buttressed by passivity or hypocrisy. If we can see Gandhi, in such sense, as in any way 'among the prophets', then we are ready for a study of how such prophethood, in the Hebraic story, ripened towards what Christians realize as the Name of the incarnate Lord, the Christ.

The more Hebrew prophecy, supremely in Hosea and Jeremiah, became a travail in the context of evil, the more it ceased to be just a word spoken, a protest made, a message sent; the more such 'office' as spokesman deepened into a person making significance concrete. Prophecy became biography, as we have noted in Chapters 3 and 5. Being, as it were, proxy for God (who sent them) these prophets became proxy for God in bearing the enmity their witness incurred, an enmity meant for God and against them. Their personalities to a degree incarnated the issue between God and the world and did so in the form of a suffering of the burden. Jesus deepened and ripened this clue into the ultimacy of '*the* Word made flesh', by taking and undertaking redemption as the very will and nature of the Father whom his obedience expressed.[25] Thus was known 'the Name above every name', warranted and then invoked, invoked because warranted in that mutuality of heart we have earlier studied between the Jesus of the story and the Church of his recognition. His name was no arbitrary bestowal but the disclosure of the saving grace of God.

That movement of prophetic experience towards and into the Incarnation is, for Christians, a fulfilled history, given now and for ever into our history, written into spiritual finality and not to be superseded or overtaken in its abiding futurity. But does that conviction discourage us, or disallow us, from seeing anything analogous to its human antecedence in burden-bearing prophethoods in history elsewhere? It would seem not. Does Gandhi represent within Hinduism a comparable accusation of wrong on behalf of God and a like readiness to undertake what embroilment in the struggle for love entails, and being wholly taken up to one's own cost in such undertaking? There is surely no figure in India or elsewhere in modern times who poses more squarely, more probingly, than Gandhi the question about 'associates' of the Name. The Name proclaimed by Peter's sermon is not claimed by him arbitrarily or arbitrarily enforced. It is first bestowed by God[26] and that bestowal only registers and seals the centrality to God himself of the love that suffers. The Name, then, has to be seen, heard and loved, as the index to a meaning for ever accessible to wondering recognition and so to patient invocation. Such calling on the Name celebrates and receives a once-for-all redemption and owns a pattern that demands to be followed. Are there discipleships of the pattern not yet of the celebration?

These reflections might have been set in the context of that *bhakti* devotion which is no less central to the soul of Hinduism than the theme of *karma*. It is much saluted by Christian 'dialogue' with the multi-faceted faith of Hindus. *Bhaktas* might then be associated with the Christ-love of a Christian idiom. But there are large questions here and we content ourselves, in a daunting proliferating throng of Hindu concepts and rites,

with the two seminal figures, Sundar Singh and Gandhi, inside
and outside the church-faith, as focal studies of an Indian relation of soul and name. We remit to Chapter 14 the urgent questions arising from Christology in diversity, namely why many
who have recognized and loved *a* Christ or *the* Christ in Jesus
nonetheless withhold themselves in varying degrees from the
Church. How should we understand this attraction of the Lord
and deterrence from his Church? What is implied for a custodial
theology?

But is the whole confidence in the human *persona* which
throughout we have been assuming, whether under Islam, or
Judaism, or Hinduism, essentially misplaced? That is the bleak,
perplexing, yet strangely stirring question with which Buddhism confronts us all. To take account of it is the task of the
three following chapters.

Albert Schweitzer, musician, theologian and medical missionary in the heart of Africa, the sage of Lambarene, felt in
1906 that

> In the very moment when we were coming nearer to the historical
> Jesus than men had ever come before, and were already stretching
> out our hands to draw Him into our own time, we have been obliged
> to give up the attempt and acknowledge our failure ... We must
> be prepared to find that the historical knowledge of the personality
> and life of Jesus will not be a help but perhaps an offence to religion.

He continued:

> The truth is, it is not Jesus as historically known but Jesus as spiri-
> tually arisen within men, who is significant for our time and can
> help it. Not the historical Jesus, but the spirit which goes forth from
> Him and in the spirits of men strives ...

It will be clear from all the foregoing in Chapters 5, 6, and
7, that this sceptical reading is by no means as 'obligatory' as
Schweitzer assumed and argued. There is a surer, decisive picture, warranting what it is warranted by, namely the conviction
of victorious, suffering Messiahship by which the Church lived,
and lives.

Insisting that 'Jesus as a concrete historical personality
remains a stranger to our time', Schweitzer nevertheless concluded with words that have become famous.

> He comes to us as one unknown, without a name, as of old, by
> the lakeside, He came to those men who knew Him not. He speaks

to us the same word: 'Follow thou me!' and sets us to the tasks
which He has to fulfil for our time. He commands. And to those
who obey Him, whether they be wise or simple, He will reveal
himself in the toils, the conflicts, the sufferings which they shall
pass through in His fellowship, and, as an ineffable mystery, they
shall learn in their own experience Who He is.[27]

'As one unknown': that was Schweitzer's verdict on the story
of the first 'call to follow'. Jesus may indeed be known in a
'following' which is not a 'confessing'. So it has been in some
of India's Christologies. Yet it is strange indeed to hold in such
scepticism the verdict of those 'by the lakeside' who following
in 'toils, conflicts and sufferings . . . in His fellowship' yielded
for all time the New Testament itself. The promise Schweitzer
discerned in the spiritual Jesus of an identity to be 'learned'
only in experience, is made good continually wherever there
is heed. Is there less reason why we should rely upon it in
the case of those first learners and their experience of who
he was? Is the distinction between the historical and the spiritual necessary in truth, however apposite in the breadth of
the world? 'If Messiah isn't only Jesus but all of us', since he
is called Emmanuel, can this be so unless the faith of some
of us is tethered to the Messiah he really was? Christologies
can well be multiplied, given the singular Christology.

NOTES

1 Ernesto Cardenal, *Love in Practice, The Gospel in Solentiname*, trans. D. D.
   Walsh (London 1977), p. 35.

2 Its main advocate is Karl Rahner; see *Schriften zur Theologie* (Zurich 1957),
   where, after Prop. 2 on evidences of divine grace in other faiths, Prop.
   3 says: 'Christianity meets a member of an extra-Christian religion not
   as a non-Christian but rather as a person who, in certain respects can
   and must be considered as an anonymous Christian.'

3 Sadly, this statement of the open vocation of the Church, 'that you also
   may have fellowship with us . . .', has to be qualified by the actual
   *in*hospitality evident in many forms and on many counts in various contexts, where suspicion, prejudice, racial factors, language and tradition
   engender rejection or lukewarmness.

4 *Auspice Christi* is a term this writer has long cherished after receiving it
   from the late W. R. Moore, of Charlbury Road, Oxford, a generous dis-
   penser of hospitality to students, combined with New Testament readings.

The *auspex* was one who 'divined' from the flight of birds, or officiated at weddings. Hence the sense here of the 'auspices' under which one lives and belongs.

5 The small 'm' is significant. Arabic never capitalizes letters anyway. But the sense of 'Muslim' would be the official, established faith-community member which a Christian could not intelligently claim to be. However, he/she might reasonably consider that there were authentic dimensions of 'Islam' in Christian belief in divine unity, creation, the status of man, the sacramental meaning of the natural order, prophets and patriarchs, and much else.

6 Immanuel Jakobvits; *The Condition of Jewish Belief* (New York 1966), pp. 112–13. See also Louis Jacobs, *A Jewish Theology* (London 1973), pp. 285–6. According to S. D. Goitein Maimonides also regarded Judaism as the only true religion.

7 Ismail Ragi al-Faruqi, *Islam* (Illinois 1979), p. 68.

8 It is intriguing that in Romans 12.13 Paul uses the same Greek verb which occurs in Acts 26.14f., of his persecuting zeal (*diōkō*). He urges the Roman Christians to be addicted to the welcome of strangers.

9 In *The Transcendent Unity of Religions*, trans. P. Townsend (New York 1953), F. Schuon writes in the contrary sense. He notes, correctly, that 'the idea of redemption might be associated with a polytheistic doctrine', and on the basis of that possibility misses the integral place of the Christian understanding of atonement within the nature of God. To see that 'the idea of redemption is not necessarily linked to the concept of divine unity' is proper, but it cannot be a comment on Christianity.

10 We do not have in mind here the ontological questions which, for example, preoccupied Frank Weston in his exposition of *The One Christ*, London 1907. He sought to elucidate, within the exchanges of that decade, 'the exact content of the Subject, or Ego, of the manhood of our Lord'. Our concern here is with 'God and man in one Christ' as the cross expresses the divine love in the measure of human need. A Christology of action, rather than of essence, confesses the unity of God in acknowledging the centrality of the cross.

11 At the Parliament of Religions in Calcutta, quoted by Gandhi in *Harijan* (13 March, 1937), p. 39.

12 As cited by Clement C. J. Webb in 'Christianity as the Climax of Religious Development', a pamphlet, 1908.

13 Matt. 12.30 and Luke 11. 23. In these passages Jesus is laying down the conditions of personal discipleship which must be decisive and unequivocal. In the contrasted saying he is commenting on the disciples' report about the outsider. The explanation would seem to be that we must be resolute about our own discipleship but tolerant and hopeful, non-judgemental, about the posture of others.

14 B. H. Streeter and A. J. Appasamy, *The Message of Sadhu Sundar Singh* (New York 1927), pp. 124f.

15 Kenneth K. Inada and Nolan P. Jacobson, ed., *Buddhism and American Thinkers* (Albany 1984), p. 10.

16 One might venture the inappropriate analogy of the light we have in seeing the stars. Within our experience it is 'future' light. We presently have what was the future's: time – in this case aeons of it – possesses us of it out of the futurity in which it was coming to us. Likewise, in grace we become aware of what was 'minded towards us' from afar – in God eternally and in the cross historically.

17 The *paidagōgos* in Galatians 3.24 was the Greek slave who saw that the otherwise wayward pupil got to school.

18 Sadhu Sundar Singh, *With and Without Christ* (New York 1929), the chapter pp. 26–53, the story pp. 37–40. He also has a chapter on 'Christians without Christ'.

19 Streeter and Appasamy, op. cit. p. 5.

20 F. Heiler, *The Gospel of Sadhu Sundar Singh*, abridged trans. Olive Wyon (New York 1927), pp. 218–19. Heiler points out that Sundar Singh was converted to Christ as a youth of only sixteen through a vision of Jesus as 'the light of life'. Though he knew the *Gita* by heart and was familiar with the Qur'ān he was too young to have absorbed a full knowledge of Indian religion and philosophy. Nor were his gifts those of formal study (pp. 247f.).

21 For example, 'Hinduism and Buddhism have dug canals but they have no living water to fill them'. 'When the sun rises the stars lose their radiance. When the Wise Men reached Bethlehem they no longer needed the star, for they had found the Christ.' Heiler, op. cit., p. 220.

22 In *Young India*, 8 August, 1920.

23 ibid., 11 October, 1928.

24 ibid.

25 On this theme of prophethood pointing forward to the Incarnation by the logic of 'truth through personality', and the word brought merging into the life lived, see Terence E. Fretheim, *The Suffering of God* (Philadelphia 1984), pp. 149–66, and Chap. 3 above.

26 Writing in Inada and Jacobson, op. cit., p. 141, R. C. Neville observes: 'Names are bestowed and not claimed.' His context has to do with the name 'God' and whether 'God' is 'a determinate entity', or 'must be construed as determinate only in the world and . . . indeterminate apart from the world'. Thus to have 'God' so named is 'bestowed' by man, not 'claimed' by God. Such discussion apart, one could apply the same rubric to 'Christ'. Is the name/identity, as it were, 'bestowed' on Jesus by believers? Or is it affirmed by him and by God of him, so that Peter (and any other apostle) proclaims it for responsive recognition? The New Testament clearly believes the latter. The point is vital in any christological discussion. Has the name of Christ authority *per se* as the *datum* of God (Acts 4.12), or is it used in subjective human address which bestows it on Jesus? In other words does the faith invent the name or the name invite the faith?

27 Albert Schweitzer, *The Quest of the Historical Jesus,* trans. W. Montgomery (1910), pp. 399–401.

The Buddha and the Self

11
'A Will for which "I"'

I

'To obey a will for which "I" is in no respect a goal',[1] was the steady set of soul of Dag Hammarskjöld, as confessed in his spiritual diary, *Markings*, a journal of the self filled with partially Buddhist thoughts yet belonging unmistakably with Christian discipleship. The phrase isolated in the chapter heading captures essentially, in its ambiguity, all that is radically at stake between things Christian and things Buddhist. Whether, as we must see, the rubric is either: 'Desire not to desire', or 'desire a right desiring', a matter of will, however paradoxical, is involved. In the familiar Buddhist metaphor, forbearing to fuel the fire of desire so that it simply goes out, means a decision, if not in the fire certainly in the fuel-handling.[2] So will is present even if only in opting for the abatement of will. The will to extinguish is itself a using of the will.

Either way the self is involved with itself. Hence the aptness of 'which "I"', the phrase turning into a question as a theme of interrogation. It might be thought that to write of an 'I' which is 'in no respect a goal' was to state the Buddhist *anatta*, the actual 'goallessness' of the ego, its being an illusory individuation which has to be first confessed to be such and then disavowed. There is no abiding significance to personhood. Self-consciousness has to be seen through as vacuous.

Hammarskjöld, however, is writing about a completely different awareness of the ego. He distinguishes altogether between selfhood and selfishness. The one may certainly be the harbour of the other, the other the ruin of the one. But, for him, there is no inevitable or irretrievable selfishness about the ego, as there is for the Buddhist. On the contrary, he is resolved 'to obey a will for which "I" is in no respect a goal'. To do so, he assumes the will of an 'I' which can place itself wholly under an authority not its own, truly 'goalless' by an abnegation which leaves him free to serve the goals he acknowledges as Christ's. This is the sort of 'disinterest' in self-seeking impossible on the Theravāda Buddhist reading of mankind, where 'seeking-for-the-self' is synonymous with 'becoming-in-a-self'. Hammarskjöld yearns to participate in the world in a Christian detachment, deliberate and sustained, *from* the self-centredness which is selfishness, not *by* a Buddhist attrition of the self-centredness which is our selfhood. For the latter, at least by its theory, abnegates the very personhood within which the 'I' can will unselfishness. Hammarksjöld is like an instrumentalist who brings everything he has to render a musical score which is not his own. He does so, not by unfuelling the ardour of his dedication, but by kindling it steadily, for the music's sake, from his own being. Far from 'desiring not to desire', he 'desires' intensely from an ego-centre which is at once transcended and fulfilled, fully trusted and yet also curbed, authentic by a positive negation.

It is the task of this chapter to study and sift the Buddhist/Christian theses about selfhood thus summarily stated in preface to more adequate formulation. This involves, firstly, a careful reading of Buddhist 'emptiness' lest its radical criticism of Christian personhood should be blunted by the sort of non-comprehension of which Buddhists so often complain from western expositors and – it may be added – admirers. We will concentrate here on 'the will for the "I"', its atrophy – how conceived in theory, how sought in practice, or, by contrast, its nature as decision and crisis, spelling frustration or fulfilment, tragedy or benediction. We will leave to Chapter 13 the discipline of the Eightfold Path, with the happy suspicion that Buddhism may proceed more blessedly than the bleakness of its philosophy, at least in the Theravada form, might suggest. The intervening Chapter 12, pausing over 'negative capability', provides occasion to query some aspects of the Buddhist point of departure in the fourfold truths it sees in the *Tilakhana*, the analyses of *anicca, anatta* and *dukkha*. For it must be a vital part of any Christian cross-reference into Buddhism, before we come to the techniques, as it were, of its 'way of salvation', to question the clues from which it begins in transience, illusoriness and burdenedness, as being either adequate or exclusive clues to the human situation.

II

Buddhist awareness is most characteristically symbolized where imaginatively it begins, namely in Sakyamuni's foray from the palace in order to know and meet the world. There he encountered in the traditional story, a sick man, an old man and, finally, a corpse. The truth of the world confronted him in disease, decrepitude and mortality. The impulse to leave behind immunity, luxury and privilege, to know in youth as Lear learned in age, the truth of 'unaccommodated man' was wholly sound. The Buddha to be, however, left behind not only advantage and consolatory things, but also power and rulership and, significantly also, wife and child and all that belonged with the sphere of reassurance, of delight and promise, of hope and achievement, political, marital, domestic and social. If, as some narratives conclude, he met also after the spectres of decay, a joyous one in state of bliss, he did so only on the further side of the human positives his transit had forsaken.

Through all the rich diversity of Buddhism in its long and wide dispersion – to which we can do no justice here – two implications of that 'genesis-story' of the faith have determined its whole ethos. Cross-reference will be occupied with them throughout. They are the highly individuated order of awareness and time in its incidence as chronology. Illness, senectitude and demise belong with the private self, in terms of Sakyamuna's pity, and they belong with a temporal sequence in which 'the sense of an ending' dominates, if it does not forfeit, the sense of a content. To use a Greek distinction, what happens happens in *chronos*, not as *kairos*. That the sick had been whole and achieved, the old had been young and delighted, the dead had truly lived: these qualities of their existence are submerged for assessment in the temporal preoccupation with their submergence in pastness. The sequence of the sick, the old and the dead, argued, as it were, a renunciation of existence, whereas it would have been possible to emerge from the palace and find existence an annunciation.

That time's lapsing cancels time's meaning parallels the other quality of the story, its focus on the lonely, physical experiences of frailty, decay and death. Sakyamuni took stock of human privacy and mortal flesh, of generic man in natural contingency and flux. Moses' venture from inside the Pharaonic palace confronted him with Hebraic man. He was caught in a tension not only between plenty and penury, pride and poverty, but between his birth and his adoption. He was wrestling with ethnic identity and social injustice. He encountered humanity, not in the raw of mortal fate, but in the raw of slavery, oppression and political despair. He was not the spectator of death but its violent agent. The corpse was of his own making in the name of liberation. His next discovery was of Hebrews in a strife of brothers, an embryonic civil war of the desolate unable to wage a revolutionary one. The definitive Exodus out of Egypt under Moses occupied the Judaic faith in much more than personal, physical change and decay. It rooted them in kin and land and memory, gave them a purchase on the future as 'people to God', for whom the one-time sick and old and dead became 'all our fathers under the cloud and passing through the sea'. It would be fair to say that everything distinguishing Judaism from Buddhism is implicit in that primary contrast in the founding history-legend.

Muhammad's issue into history is different again. His departure is not from simple human misery, nor yet from foreign bondage and tribal liberation. His people are already in their territory. But they are divided by feud and blood revenge. Their chronic disunity tallies with the plural worships. His sense of vocation comes in anathema against *shirk*, in the sense of the precedent of prophethood and the assertion of divine unity. The ruins he sees in his mercantile travels are those of Mada'in Salih,[3] of whole peoples and their buildings overwhelmed in disaster because of their idolatry. What besets him is the mystery of history at large, in which this corpse or that has no private pondering. It is the living Quraish he sees, and challenges as usurers, exploiters, hoarders, the unworthy 'establishment' of a Mecca perverted, as their emporium, from its Abrahamic, pristine purity. As elsewhere, so in Islam, the founding story becomes definitive of all else, both in theology and corporate mystique.

The point of these other 'origins' is simply, in this context, to underline the focus of Sakyamuni's awakening awareness on sheer human, personal finitude, all politics, society, culture and history apart. Religion, some have thought, is what we do with our own solitariness.[4] Buddhism would seem to approve the definition. It is our response to contingency, frailty and transience understood as distress. Is it because the Buddhist point of departure concentrates so sharply upon the personal, private experience that it sees the predicament so darkly? If larger dimensions of human discovery, in nature, time, society, in art and music, in personhoods around the person, were in place – not fondly to exclude the bracing shadow of mortality but to let it glow with mystery – then would not the diagnosis itself be the more coherent? If so, there is this strange paradox about the Buddhist thesis of the self, namely that the loss of the self is almost self-fulfilling. It argues from a logic of its own which it has first restricted in order that its case may stand. Its necessity to have a doctrine of escape stems from its confinement of the range of relevance.

There are other paradoxes in Buddhism to which we must come later. The fact of paradox does not, of course, disqualify the faith that clings to them. There is no religion exempt from paradoxiality. Christians should be least minded of all to urge against it. Nevertheless the question must persist whether there is not, somehow, a self-desolating quality about the Buddhist account of personhood, whether its vision does not have to be invited, not into dispute, but into enlargement or – if need be – into dispute about enlargement. If it allowed a more comprehensive analysis, it would analyse a more comprehensive selfhood.

Yet here it is the captive of its own distrusts. Its philosophy inhibits it from what might be its liberation. It disallows the larger relevance of human experience by first deciding on an interpretation from which it must be excluded. It is minded to do so by its own demand to be undeceived. Those who see things differently are *ex hypothesi* not to be heeded because, by that very token, they have not, in Buddhist eyes, begun to take the point of Buddhism. Since they speak from within illusions they should first renounce, they deserve no credence from those for whom such renunciation is the primary thing. Perhaps more than any other faith Buddhism requires to be met only on its own ground. Its case is that so often others fail to do so, or are quite unable. It therefore becomes our vital task to attempt the radical understanding Buddhism asks of us. One way to seek to do so – which has other potential benefits in study – will be to align much partial Buddhist-style sentiment elsewhere and see how it is different from a Buddhist reckoning with selfhood that is not partial.

III

Matthew Arnold's celebrated poem, *Rugby Chapel*, captures as well as any the sombre mood of human finitude so characteristic of the Buddhist faith and does so, no doubt all unconsciously, with the familiar Buddhist metaphor of the lapsing wave on the face of the sea – momentary, pointless and gone.

> What is the course of this life,
> Of mortal man on the earth?
> Most men eddy about
> Here and there – eat and drink,
> Chatter and love and hate,
> Gather and squander, are raised
> Aloft, all hurled in the dust,
> Striving blindly, achieving
> Nothing: and then they die,
> Perish – and no one asks
> Who or what they have been,
> More than he asks what waves
> In the moonlit solitudes mild
> Of the midmost ocean have swelled,
> Foam'd for a moment and gone.

'Hail nothing, full of nothing, nothing is with thee', as the cynic said, in a brash attempt at blasphemy. Arnold, to be sure, in the same poem, wills to exempt his great father, Thomas, and, perhaps, with him something of what the Chapel symbolizes because of him.

> That force
> Surely has not been left vain!
> Somewhere, surely, afar,
> In the sounding labour-house vast
> Of being, is practised that strength,
> Zealous, beneficent, firm.[5]

But the very repetition of the 'surely' tells a dubiety which, on Buddhist terms, had better renounce its hope of consolation and let that supposed 'labour-house vast of being' be the sha-dow-play of becoming which is all it is. Matthew Arnold, in the more impersonal *Dover Beach* poem, away from the spell of his father, is more fully aware that any honest religion will be non-consolatory.[6] Did not even Wordsworth write of 'melan-choly fear subdued by faith'?[7] A right faith will not go on doing so, given the futility of transience, and suffering. Humanity had better forgo its great expectations and face 'bleak house' for what it is.

Nor will the perceptive find exemptions after the manner of Nietzsche who echoed the Buddhist story of Sakyamuni and read into it only a selective doctrine meant for those to whom 'desistence from life must be preached', those who 'long for doctrines of lassitude and renunciation'.

> They meet an invalid, an old man, or a corpse – and immediately they say: 'Life is refuted'. But they are only refuted and their eye, which seeth only one aspect of existence. 'See to it that the life ceaseth which is only suffering.' Are ye not very ripe for the sermon of death? Everywhere soundeth the voice of those who preach death, and the earth is full of those to whom death hath to be preached.[8]

But that distinction between the superhuman virile ones and the death-wishing masses has no place in the compassion of Buddhism. Nietzsche's own story is the best refutation of his 'gospel'. What the Buddha meant by *anicca*, *anatta* and *dukkha* admits of no aristocracy of exemption.

Yet it is always being partially approached by poets, novelists, dramatists in the world outside Buddhism. 'Sick with desire, and fastened to a dying animal', W. B. Yeats wrote of himself.[9] Life is readily seen as a reprieve from death for 'the time being'. Or, suddenly, the sense of sheer individuation takes possession of us and we wonder apprehensively about what it is that makes 'me' 'me', and what it might be like to be self-divested. Even Alice in her Wonderland has oddly Buddhist thoughts in asking: 'Who in the world am I?'

> Ah! that's a great puzzle. I'm sure I'm not Ada. It might lead you know to my going out altogether, like a candle. I wonder what I should be like then.

And Alice, fearing for herself, 'tried to fancy what the flame of the candle is like after it is blown out'.[10]

Or, such realist fantasy apart, there is the nausea of sated souls, that seeks release in misogyny and bitter rejection of others as in themselves the bane of life. Thus, *Timon of Athens*: 'My long sickness of health and living, now begins to mend, and nothing brings me all things'.[11] Or, again, there is the familiar Stoic device of giving no hostages to fortune, keeping all one's options within one's own power, abstaining from love and so avoiding the risk of hurt, interpreting life as an exercise in willed immunity from its ravages by willed exemption from its expectations.

All these, however, and other forms of the loss of the self, willed or wistful, in literature and life are only partial in their feel for the Buddhist case or their adoption of the Buddhist metaphors. They may share a kinship but they do not make a religion. As formulated in Theravāda Buddhism, *sunyata*, or 'emptiness' is much more than pessimism, or weariness. It is not a negation which assumes some entity capable of being first characterized and then denied. It is, rather, a silence to halt improper questions. It is not 'Nothingness', but rather 'no-thing-ness', with a necessary hyphen to denote that 'thingness' itself, on any plane, divine or human, eternal or temporal, this or that, is being negated. *Sunyata* is not denying what was ever there but denying its 'ever-there-ness'.

It is this absence of any ultimate ground of existence, any self-sufficient reality, which underlies the Buddhist view of transience and illusoriness as defining the human condition. It is sounder to face it in totality before reckoning with its implications for the person. It certainly entails a cognizance of daily life in its terms: by dint of the familiar counsel of non-attachment, without explaining why 'attachment' should be so significant as to need renunciation, if all things are bound into a relativity so entire and dense that no particularities can mean or matter. All 'being-ness', so to speak, both eludes and deceives us: there is only 'becoming-ness'. Even this is no more than an emptiness, a structure of seeming, within which there is neither ultimacy nor absolute. The Buddhist path is then designed to develop within us an alignment, on our part, with this ultimate 'indifference'.

The Christian theologian may perhaps find a feasible parable of this 'non-entity' theme, in the Judaic, Christian and Islamic denial of idols. As in the Qurʾān and in Paul's writing to Corinthians, the *mushrikūn*, the 'idol-creditors', are not being disabused of anything that was ever there. Idols are non-existent, essentially. But they very much 'exist' in the imagination, and the ritual strategy, of their worshippers. It is this pseudo-reality from which idolaters must be delivered, so that it no longer holds them in credulity. Such deliverance, however, does not deprive them of what they ever truly had; it only ends an illusoriness to which 'reality' was given only by their self-deception.

What idols 'are' to the *mushrikūn*, absolutes, priorities, ultimacies, are to the theists, the believers, the non-Buddhists, namely the illusions of their minds or wills, stubborn indeed (as idolatries are), but equally to be renounced in a renunciation which does not 'negate' anything that was there to be negated except fictionally.

The weakness of this analogy, plainly, is that idolatry *is* a negation of what – if we take this 'option' (for 'option' either position is) – is truly 'there'. The point of the non-entity of idols is that they suborn what they misconstrue. Their worship is falsified, not on behalf of an all-inclusive vacuity (in which their falsity need not be detected, still less arraigned), but in the name of a right worship. In this sense we cannot rightly compare non-entity identified within a structure of meaning with the non-entity-ing of structure and meaning altogether. The parallel perhaps helps our Christian theology to take the point of what is being said in *sunyata*: it does not make the point persuasive. To be intelligible is one thing, intelligent another.

However, it is important for us to appreciate inclusive non-entity for what it is and how it seems in Buddhism. For 'seem' it does, just like everything else illusory from which it alone purports to be exempt. It, therefore, will not be fair to say, as B. H. Streeter did:

> Salvation dawns when we begin to find ourselves out (most of us are deceivers). That is the difference between the Christian and the Buddhist; each has seen through a fraud, but to the Buddhist the fraud is the universe, to the Christian it is himself.[12]

Though being 'frauds' in and to ourselves is a valid theme to which we will return in pondering 'desire', it is false to Buddhism to make the universe a fraud. To do so misses the point. It attributes intentionality to the universe as ever purporting to be anything, moral or immoral, that might deceive and snare us into trusting it and then play false. The 'ensnaring', which is very real, is our own misreading. To think it an objective fraudulence practised on us is to stay within the illusion that it should not be so, whereas it merely 'seems'.

IV

It would be right to let this be the bleakness (from our angle) that it is, and not attempt to retrieve some kind of vague theism from the stance, as some Christian thinkers try to do.[13] All religious devotion, certainly in 'God' terms, has to be seen as 'empty' both of content and claim. Just as Malebranche exclaimed on first using 'scopes' (tele- or micro-): 'This is the end of size', so we have now to say: 'This is the end of worship.' Desire for any significant 'beyond' is dissipated. To believe in 'God' would be to 'hierarchize' experience, to construct related-ness (which is all there is) into sovereignty, to cling to some universal form of authority over all, just as we cling to the particular autonomy which we assume to be our 'selves'. Indeed the two constructs are often taken to be mutually con-firming, as when we say: 'O God, thou art my God, early will I seek thee', where 'art' and 'seek' illusorily sustain each other.

Some exponents of Buddhism, Christian or other, claim to rescue some 'religiousness' from this situation, despite the exclusion of worship, on the ground that the intention within it has to do with 'salvation'.[14] Agreed let it be that things Budd-hist are never merely 'theory'; the 'Way' is all-important, as we must see in Chapter 13. But to claim a soteriological purpose in the acknowledging of 'emptiness' is to call in radical question what 'salvation' means, even begs the question of it altogether. On any other count, it would be, so to speak, a salvation in spite of itself. A conceding of the effective disintegration of the self as extrinsic to total relativity may strangely coincide with everyday living. But on Christian understanding of 'salva-tion' it has not begun to measure either the reach of self-cent-ring evil, or the crisis of real 'happenedness' within the soul of saving. It is probably futile to debate whether Buddhism, in its radical Theravāda form is, more than a philosophy, a religion. Thinking makes things so, either way. But it must be seen that its *Dharma* does something radical to what religion otherwise has signified. There is a drastic sense in which Budd-hism altogether militates against 'religious' springs within us, of wonder, praise, mystery and joy, by its strict abatement of 'desire' for 'the absolute', its concern to teach, promote and 'service' an ultimate indifference. That it does so as its solution to practical experiences of sorrow, flux, pain and death, may evidence its compassion, but hardly suffices to interpret them. Is freedom from the flux of experience, even supposing we attain it, any saving freedom from the self? To the emptiness within, because of the emptiness beyond, we must now come, asking: 'A will for which "I"'?

V

It is clear that Christian faith has a radical quarrel with the Buddhist equation between selfhood and selfishness, between the 'I' of egocentric physique and the 'I' of egocentric aggression, avarice and pride. Is it, we must ask, proper to identify being-in-a-self with being-for-a-self? Or, more precisely phrased, is the being-for-a-self (entailed as it necessarily is by being *in* one) also and always 'selfish', competitive, acquisitive and reprehensible? Can we not legitimate 'desire' provided we do so with radical honesty and due perception of its always crucial 'crisis'? Does the fact that we look out from behind two eyes mean that our looking must always be wrongly 'desirous', or the fact that our digestion (like our toothache, if we have it) is our own requires that our intake is for ever gluttonous? Must it not be said that the decision for which 'I' life-wise is implicit in being a self at all, that the self is truly a responsibility with itself? Does not self-consciousness *per se* involve, not simply the sense of being *subject* to sequential phenomena but of being also *object* to oneself, an entrustment, almost, of 'self' to 'self'? May not the Buddhist quest for 'right understanding, mindfulness' and the rest of the Eightfold Path, mean such awareness and in fact do so better without the philosophy of the 'emptiness' within which and because of which they allegedly are pursued? Are the achievements of self-transcendence, studied in Chapter 10, not happenings within authentic selfhood and in no way self-dissolving?

The assurance of these questions in their phrasing had better first keep faith with Theravāda teaching, lest we answer them with a confidence the Buddhist will say only proves how impervious we have become to the reality of illusion. If so, this is not the only philosophy to read non-persuasion as indicating only an inability to understand, not any serious question about the case made.

Anicca, anatta and *dukkha* make a formidable trio. Life is fleeting, flux un-'real'-izes the self and the nature of experience is, therefore, essentially anxious and distressful. *Tanhā*, or drive to be and to possess, however, keeps us bound to illusory 'being'. Only in abating such will-to-be by a deliberate discipline to let the illusion no longer illude can we be emancipated into a liberating non-attachment.

Aspects of adversity, from womb to tomb, the rough incidence of human finitude, let us defer to Chapter 12, where a possible different reading of life as vicissitude can be appraised. If transience as the only clue is there to be challenged, we can stay in present context with the *anatta* theme of the self as no more, no other, than a sequence of sense-states, just as external events registered by the senses are no more than a flux of phenomena. This angle of Buddhist thinking is familiar enough in western philosophy. Schopenhauer and David Hume echoed it in their own idiom. If one starts from a restriction of our relatedness merely to sense experience, ignoring other dimensions of personhood, one can easily arrive at a conclusion that sense-experience is all and that, quite evidently, it is always flowing and fleeting. It is true that there is nothing in the mind which is not first in the senses, as all the empiricists insist. But it is true only in terms of presentation to us and not in terms either of feasibility or of relevance. In this area, we could surely leave to Immanuel Kant the rejection of *anatta* (in European guise) argued from the senses alone, with his rewriting which runs: 'There is nothing in the mind which is not first in the sense except the mind itself.' Nor did the empiricists really *live* their philosophy – a point to which we will return in the Buddhist scene. Certainly David Hume assumed he had a *persona*, enjoyed it enormously and presumed on its social recognition. It is hardly wise to profess a philosophy which one necessarily abandons in actuality. To plead intellectual honesty for it is to delimit, perhaps only as an academic exercise, what one has to be honest about. It is odd that a *tabula rasa* theory of the mind (on which sense-experience then inscribes 'knowledge') should partner, across continents of culture, the Buddhist philosophy which has a *tabula rasa* as its goal.

The organization of experience, derived from the lowly senses, surely requires us to engage with the world it presents, to gather it in memory, to anticipate it in prospect, to interpret it for meaning, and to transact it in its requiring of society, economy, response and interpretation. If we invoke Marx's phrasing, we have to be 'at' the world if we are 'in' it. It is hard to see how we can, or should, neutralize it, when it does not admit of neutrality. Are we to say, with the student wit on the campus notice-board: 'Tomorrow has been cancelled for lack of interest'? Were we to do so, we would still be in decision and, therefore, in selfhood. When tomorrow had

become today, the lack of interest would be proved impractic-
able in its cancelling and incongruous in itself.

The Buddhist case here really resolves itself into whether
'relatedness', undeniable as it is, argues no-thing-ness. Agreed:
the chariot, as 'entity', has wheels but they are not it. Wheels
have hubs but are other than they. There is a chassis which
is not the chariot, shafts which are not the chassis. Yet the
chariot is there, in the relatedness which is used to argue its
un-reality. True, a circle is not the centre, nor the circumference,
nor the radii, nor even the relationship between these. To concede that they are all mutual and interdependent and having
reality only in that relatedness is surely not to say that there
is no circle? Or, moving the analogy into personhood, are we
to say that an ego must, or can, be dissipated merely by allowing
that it is a manifold? Life is not a sheer sequence of impressions,
a succession of states: it is where these concern actions, attitudes, choices, and relatednesses which do not merely happen
but obligate and compete and struggle and falter and attain.
The very choice by which we will – if so it be – to promote
ultimate indifference, to exchange illusion for imperturbability,
will mean there is an ego choosing. Self-transcendence can only
be understood within a self which is not elided in its meaning.
We are back to Hammarskjöld's theme of 'a will for which "I"'.

VI

This does not conclude the business we have with the notion
of *anatta*. But perhaps we can take it further by asking, as Max
Müller did, how it comes about that such vast numbers of
Asians, of many nations and through long centuries, have
espoused and held impressively to convictions seemingly so
bleak and grim. How should a way seemingly so negative about
the annunciation of existence, so resistant to the invitation into
being, into the arts, into the risk and thrill of living, so distrust-
ful of the arguable friendliness of the good earth and the mystery of birth, have had so firm a purchase on the wills and
minds of humanity in Asia?

Answer takes us into three areas which we must ponder
before coming to the positive welcome to 'desire' which, on
Christian ground, can not only admit of authentic selfhood
but essentially shapes and fulfils it. The first is the deep distinction between monkhood and the 'laity' whereby vast masses

of the population in Theravāda territories participate, as it were, by proxy in the austerity of the monks whom their offerings support. The second is the perennial presence of animist faith and practice meeting the need of popular, viable, consolatory religion in the daily world. The third is the fact of Mahāyāna Buddhism with its dimensions of grace and colour and human sympathy, its gentler reading – and meeting – of the human condition. Each of these mitigating, or at least modifying, factors implies a commentary on the Theravāda scene which it is important to assess.

One implication of the first would be to suggest we see Theravāda Buddhism as a verdict, at least in practice, not against matter but against Mammon, not against acquisition but the love of it, not against participatory 'desire' but against the pride and menace of it. In that case the pattern might be loosely aligned with the monastic tradition in the Christian scene. Some are dedicated to the renunciation of wealth as a salutary reminder to those engaged in the wealth-seeking by which the bearers of the counter-example are sustained. That some such paradox is inescapable still leaves us with the question whether what is, on this score, essentially exemplary, needs to be sustained by a doctrine so radically and inclusively hostile to the necessary operations of the world: birth, family, nurture, education, trade and culture.

In any event, monks are recruited from sources and 'desires' their status forbids. Life only persists in terms and by means which monkhood excludes and disowns. The begging-bowl is doubtless a valid reminder of the deceitfulness and transitoriness of the material world. But may its adoption as a way of life, for all its exacting humility and its discipline of privation, not also abnegate religious guidance of society in its manifold collective occasions of profligate pride and the indiscipline of possession? Does the élitism of the Theravāda oversimplify the ethical task of religion? Or privatize its whole duty in addressing the 'desire' issue in persons within the *Sangha*, while the political, economic, institutional forms – or ravages – of 'desire' are pursued in a 'lay' world?

In practice, no doubt, the *Sangha* does participate in the collective or 'lay' domain. Monasteries have even been nurseries of political and nationalist assertiveness. They have sometimes been turned into armed camps for better achievement of such ends in the state. Institutional poverty, as the Franciscans found, has a way of finding wealth accruing and possessions dispossessing it of its ideal. Non-attachment may justify as well as renounce its opposite. These situations are well known and in no way confined to the Buddhist scene. Nevertheless, it is right to take the implications into the generating philosophy which, though it may concede these practicalities, does not take their relevance into its theory.

Moreover, the status of the monks tends to legitimate wealth for those who can then seek it on behalf of them. Further, the doctrine of the wheel of life and reincarnation admits, for those so minded, of escape from austerity by the plea of deferment. For the present one may 'desire' and acquire and achieve, postponing indefinitely the renunciation one acknowledges to be proper.[15] Such possibility in no way impugns the sincerity of the genuine: its presence only underlines how devious situations can be.

Not only devious, but wistful and precarious. Hence the second main element conditioning Theravāda religion, namely the sense of cosmic forces in nature, of ritual encounters with mystery and menace, which is animism. Aloysius Pieres wisely cautions the student:

> Learn first the folk language: assist at their rites and rituals: hear their songs: vibrate with their rhythms: keep step with their dance: taste their poems: grasp their myths: reach them through their legends.[16]

It would not be wise, as some have done, to characterize Buddhism as in fact a philosophy striving to be also a religion. Such a verdict, however arguable, is too trite. What is true is that all faiths 'humanize' their conceptual aspects *via* popular devotion. Religion in ordinary life is often quite other than its formal intellectualists or custodians wish or conceive it to be. Day-to-day Buddhists even in the northern Theravāda realms give to the teachings of their 'Elders' an idiom of their own in which animism permeates *Dharma* and celebrates the Buddha.

The rise of the Mahāyāna forms of Buddhism, often described as 'Southern Buddhism', reflects this adoption and to a degree canonizes it. With its dimension of grace and its innumerable compassionate *bodhisattvas*, the Mahāyāna stream of Buddhism softens the rigours of the founding tradition. It allays the severe loneliness of the individual path of the Theravāda version of the 'Way'. The goal of *Nirvāna* becomes more gently accessible thanks to the concessions made to symbol and imagination, and the means of grace which it approves and dispenses in rite and festival, in poem and legend, in pledge and succour. It is fair to say that the rise of the Mahāyāna *per se* and of the several innovations within it, are a significant commentary on the conceptual severity and practical rigour of the Theravāda – a significance not to be discounted by the fact that, in some of its aspects, Zen Buddhism represents a return to Theravāda ideals. These will fall more properly for review in Chapter 13. Where religion is resolutely non-consolatory in its essence, relief necessarily comes breaking in and need, if not discipline, will have its way.

VII

To ask why an honest faith has to be non-consolatory in this human world is to come back to our initial question about 'a will for which "I"'. If even Buddhism, as we have now seen, is in tension with itself about its dark thesis, so that its own multitudes and its inner evolution revise it more hopefully, perhaps a Christian cross-reference may venture the thought that the thesis is captive to its own fear of being captive? Or is there something in the Asian mind or psyche which prompts a trust in fundamental distrust? It cannot be the Asian landscape which is as lush, as humid, as arid, as benign and harsh, as any other continent's. Or is it that India, through Sakyamuni the Buddha, resolved to afford the world at large a version and a measure of itself which would deter all shallow thoughts and desolate all glib surmises?

Human birth issues into a will to survive, indeed is synonymous with entry into being. We may 'cry', as Lear had it, 'that we are come to this poor stage of fools'. But we do not in coming so identify it. On the contrary, we announce our presence with determined assertion and so it continues through all the fascinating, if precarious, discoveries of environment and its amenability to ourselves. Nurture, education, relationship, growth, awareness, in their progressiveness, all assume intention and significance. Illusoriness, or disillusionment – if such it be – only supervenes later in retro-reflection. Why do we only have the secret of our deception by an initiation which never suspects it and would persist if it did? Life certainly proceeds as an intention which takes an outward intendedness

in its stride, finds a world awaiting discovery, comprehension
and acceptance. We only turn this quality of experience into
abstract conjecture if we ask why, on Buddhist premise, we
should have been immersed into being at all, why all that is
human was ever ensnared into the task of getting un-snared.

The question, no doubt, is pointless if we look for an answer.
It is not, however, pointless if it prompts suspicion of the
premise within which alone it arises. Interpretation of existence
anyway involves an option. A fundamental posture of distrust
may be warranted. But so *may* a will to negate negation and
opt for the positive. We may well incur more burdens that
way – a fact which will occupy Chapter 12. But that may well
be taken as its commendation. Renunciatory as unfuelling the
fire may be, and in some directions admirable, there are finer
and sterner tests in fuelling it rightly. Earnestly to incur the
world, its arts and skills, its tasks and tests, its morrows and
sorrows, may be reading selfhood as it was meant to be read.
Pregnancy is not cancelled by still-birth: it is defrauded. Is there
not something about the very nature of life and being which
is similarly cheated when read exclusively in terms of *anatta*
and *dukkha*? Either way, we start with a will to be, whether
for relinquishment as a flux to be detected as illusory, or for
acceptance as a potentiality to be discerned as real and having
within it, thereby, a veritable crisis of decision.

VIII

The sense of personal being as an annunciation, an invitation
into selfhood to which zest, ardour, energy, and gratitude are
the response found lively celebration in the poems of Thomas
Traherne. In 'The Salutation' he wonders about his emergence
out of unwombed 'nothingness' into the sheer fascination of
being.

> I that so long
>   Was nothing from eternitie,
> Did little think such joys as ear or tongue,
>   To celebrate or see:
> Such sounds to hear, such hands to feel, such feet,
> Beneath the skies, on such a ground to meet.
>
>   From dust I rise
>   And out of nothing now awake,

These brighter regions which salute mine eyes
    A gift from God I take
The earth, the seas, the light, the day, the skies,
The sun and stars are mine, if these I prize.

    A stranger here
  Strange things doth meet, strange glories see:
Strange treasures lodged in this fair world appear,
    Strange all and new to me.
But that they should be mine who nothing was,
That strangest is of all, yet brought to pass.

It is from within such sentiments of grateful wonder that the
Christian instinct would question the contrary Buddhist instinct
to disavow them. Far from suppressing or disfranchising
'desire', Traherne's poems dwell in the word and the idea.
One of them uses it as a title and rehearses its many themes
before concluding in a climax of thanksgiving:

    For giving me desire,
    An eager thirst, a burning ardent fire,
    A virgin infant flame,
    A love with which into the world I came,
    An inward hidden heavenly love,
    Which in my soul did work and move
    And ever ever me enflame
    With restless longing heavenly avarice,
    That never could be satisfied,
    That did incessantly a paradise
    Unknown suggest, and something undescried
    Discern, and bear me to it: be
    Thy Name forever praised by me.

Pondering his own inner soul in joyful acquisition of the myster-
iously presenting world around, he

    ... sought
    For all that could beyond all worlds be thought.
    It did not go or move, but in me stood,
    And by dilating of itself, all good
    It tried to reach: I found it present there,
    Ev'n while it did remain conversing here,
    And more suggested than I could discern,
    Or ever since by any means could learn.

Vast, unaffected, wonderful, desires,
Like native, ardent, inward, hidden fires,
Sprange up with expectations very strange
Which into stronger hopes did quickly change.

It is odd how the Buddhist vocabulary, all unbeknown, recurs, but in the contrary sense: fire, flame, discernment, even 'avarice' boldly turned upon itself into good. 'The empty' is there too, but 'like to large and vacant room, for fancy to enlarge in, and presume a space for more ... in the fair fabric of the King of kings'.[17] A Theravādin would doubtless fasten on the words 'for fancy to enlarge in', and dub the sentiment fanciful. There will, however, remain the question who it is who must be undeceived? And option that will always be. Existence leaves to us whether to read it as annunciation or renunciation. There is no doubt that Thomas Traherne sweetly celebrates what is the Christian verdict. We shall always need the warning of Arthur Hugh Clough's lines:

> But play no tricks upon thy soul O man:
> Let fact be fact and life the thing it can.[18]

Yet fact being fact is precisely what the mind of faith decides. Here it is futile to try to reconcile the utterly diverse readings, in Buddhism and Christianity, of what 'the fact' is, in the manner that some have tried to do. John Cobb, for example, writes:

> Christians can retain but transcend personal selfhood in a way that corresponds with the Buddhist dissolution of the personal self.[19]

The practice of discipline may 'correspond', but never the thesis about selfhood on which it is postulated and on which it turns. To 'retain' and to 'dissolve' are quite contrasted. The only way to state a compatibility would be to say:

> Christians will to transcend self-seeking in the accepted trust of the personal self: Buddhists will to transcend self-seeking in the required dissolution of the personal self.

One cannot equate the locus and theme of decision which, in the one case is a selfhood to be received in its meaning, and in the other case is a selfhood to be let go as illusion.

It is part of the merit of western existentialism, which in certain senses shares a Buddhist mind, to have recognized and stressed this crisis of decision in its concern with commitment and the abyss of nothingness. It must be said, however, that its compulsive sense of human crisis takes its cue from aspects which are themselves options, not sole determinants, of the human scene. It may be human pride, as in Nietzsche, unable to come to terms with human finitude: or the futility, boredom and vacuity of sensual living, as with Sartre: or the complacent hypocrisies of religion, as with Kierkegaard: or, as with Camus, an oppressive sense of absurdity demanding that man defiantly affirm his own will to be, helped – if only absurdly – by sun and sea and sex and all else sensuous. In a different idiom, it may be the social estrangements of an exploitative economic order, as in Marx. None of these, as we saw, figured in the story of Sākyamuni's venture into human meaning. But all of them *can* be read as 'the wound of absence' and *can*, therefore, be held to argue against themselves the significance of 'absence' as 'a wound'. These 'cross bearers without faith', as they might be called – for they all, indeed, 'suffer' – may be seen as reluctant witnesses for the other option taken by the Trahernes of this world.

J. R. Seeley's *Ecce Homo* burst upon Victorian, English Christianity as something of a bombshell. Critics thought he was deliberately, and for some culpably, evading the issues of Christology – emotive then as now – by his focus on the teaching of Jesus and his moral authority. It is true that Seeley paid little attention to the tragic context in which the words *Ecce Homo* were first used. But, with arresting lucidity and verve, he presented what he called 'the enthusiasm of humanity' as the ever expectant, ever desirous quality of Jesus of Nazareth. Indicting what he called the 'paralysis of the heart', Seeley heard in the accents of the Gospels the affirmation of love within the annunciation of personhood and the adventure of community. 'No heart is pure', he wrote, 'that is not passionate: no virtue is safe that is not enthusiastic'.[20] This he believed he had from Jesus, who by his love shed an eternal glory on the human race, who both demanded and inspired a hope in self and a self in hope. Only so can we reverse that negative incapability which, whether from fear, or sloth, or doubt, or cynicism, or despair, immobilizes or destroys a right desiring.

That we can be rightly desirous is, then, the affirmation and the enterprise of the Christian gospel. That it needs to be taken into deeper, darker realms than Seeley took it in that single study, is clear if it is to be complete as gospel. Those realms are the preoccupation of the chapter to follow. This one we leave with a conclusion identifying 'desire', not as the arch-villain, the lurking deceiver, the sure falsifier, of the self, but as the quality which authenticates and fulfils it. In so identifying 'desire' we must be clear about the 'desire' we identify. It must be 'a will for which "I" is in no respect a goal', in order that the 'I' may be in every respect a servant, possessed in dispossession. The happenedness which we explored in Chapter 10 is no surmise or fantasy. It need not yield its meaning to Theravāda philosophy. How its meaning might align with Theravāda or, perhaps more readily, with Mahāyāna practice we have still to see. Meanwhile we have to explore inclusively what Pilate's cry, *Ecce Homo*, compels us to heed and understand if our Christian faith in 'right desiring' – its possibility and its attaining – is not to sound altogether sanguine in Buddhist ears and hollow to their discipline. For this we may find a framework in the poet Keats' words about 'negative capability'.

NOTES

1   Dag Hammarskjöld, *Markings*, trans. L. Sjöberg and W. H. Auden (New York 1964), p. 98.

2   There is an intriguing 'astigmatism' in this familiar metaphor of not fuelling the fire, in that the fire, which represents the self does not, in real life, feed itself (unless the fuel be in its path). The fuel, i.e. desire, is somehow supplied by a third party, i.e. the will to do the fuelling. In personal experience the will and the fire are one. This, in turn, might indicate that 'fuelling' is not about whether, but about which fuel. In the other metaphor of waves on the ocean's bosom no will (either to rise or subside) would seem to be involved but only the ocean's swell.

3   Charles Doughty's *Arabia Deserta* (London 1888) describes these awesome ruins which the Qurʾān appears to have in mind in its reminder of the transience of all the works of men and the nemesis with which history under God visits unbelief.

4   A dictum of the American philosopher, Alfred North Whitehead. *Religion in the Making* (New York 1926), p. 16.

5   Matthew Arnold, *Lyric and Elegiac Poems* (London 1895), 'Rugby Chapel', p. 191.

6   'Dover Beach' mourns what Arnold took to be the ebbing tide of faith; ibid., pp. 63–4.

7   William Wordsworth, *The Recluse*, I, 1.768.

8   F. Nietzsche, *Thus Spake Zarathustra*, Pt. 1, Chap. 9, 'The Preacher of Death'.

9   *Collected Poems of W. B. Yeats* (New York 1956), p. 191, 'Sailing to Byzantium', St. iii.

10 Lewis Carroll, *The Complete Works* (London 1939), 'Alice's Adventures in Wonderland', pp. 21, 24 and 25.

11 William Shakespeare, *Timon of Athens*, Act 5, Sc. 1, line 190.

12 B. H. Streeter, *The Buddha and the Christ* (London 1932), p. 164.

13 Among them, for example, Lynn De Silva, 'Christian Reflection in a Buddhist Context', in V. Fabella, *Asia's Struggle for Full Humanity* (Sri Lanka 1979), pp. 96–107; and the same author's, *The Problem of the Self in Buddhism and Christianity*, London 1979.

14 Fred Streng, *Emptiness: A Study in Religious Meaning* (Nashville 1967), explores *sunyata* with care and perception but insists: 'Emptiness does not destroy everyday life but simply perceives its nature as being empty' p. 168. The 'soteriological intention' of the doctrine suffices, in his view, to make it 'religious'. This would appear to beg the question of 'salvation'.

15 N. Ray, *An Introduction to the Study of Theravada Buddhism in Burma* (Calcutta 1946), p. 165, cites a Burmese merchant: 'Before I reach Nirvana, may I prosper as a man and be more royally happy than all other men . . . More especially I would have a long life, freedom from disease, a lovely complexion, a pleasant voice and a beautiful figure . . . Gold, silver, rubies, corals, pearls and other lifeless treasure, elephants, horses and other living treasure – may I have lots of them. By virtue of my power and glory I would be triumphant with pomp and retinue, with fame and splendour.'

16 Aloysius Pieres in V. Fabella, op. cit., p. 77.

17 Thomas Traherne, *Centuries, Poems and Thanksgivings*, ed. H. M. Margoliouth (Oxford 1958), vol. ii, 'The Salutation', St. 3, 5 and 7, pp. 4–6; 'Desire', St. 1, p. 177.

18 Arthur Hugh Clough, *Poems*, ed. F. L. Mulhauser (2nd edn Oxford 1974), 'Dipsychus', Scene V, 11. 100–1. p. 240.

19 John R. Cobb, *Beyond Dialogue: Towards a Mutual Transformation of Buddhism and Christianity* (Philadelphia 1982), p. 114.

20 J. R. Seeley, *Ecce Homo: A Survey of the Life and Work of Jesus Christ* (London 1865), p. 8. This work was originally published anonymously. The book made a profound impression with its ability to capture and communicate the sheer thrill of gospel ethics, the energy, zeal and hopefulness evident in the ministry and impact of Jesus. But some critics were dismayed at its silence about formal Christology (which the author did not discount but simply did not include) and suspected the silence as perhaps a subtle form of unorthodoxy or a hidden sympathy with Strauss and Renan, the reductionists. The whole spirit of *Ecce Homo* is caught in the sentence quoted.

12
'Negative Capability'

John Keats was never old and therefore could never have filled that term in the Buddha's discovery of human life in the raw. But sickness of a mortal sort dogged him through his few poetic years and he was steadily aware of his corpse-bound progress through them which his amazing fertility of mind only made the more heavy with pathos. He wrote to his reader:

> This living hand, now warm and capable
> Of earnest grasping would, if it were cold
> And in the icy silence of the tomb,
> So haunt thy days and chill thy dreaming nights . . .
> . . . see, here it is,
> I hold it toward you.[1]

Fears he had that he 'might cease to be', before his pen had 'gleaned the teeming brain', were his constant, youthful pain. He therefore gives to Buddhist *dukkha* a telling biography. 'Fastened to a dying animal', his spirit splendidly reversed Yeats's lines earlier quoted:[2] not 'sick with desire', but 'rich with desire'. 'I am certain of nothing', he wrote, 'but of the holiness of the heart's affections and the truth of Imagination'.[3] Where is happiness but

> . . . in that which becks
> Our ready minds to fellowship divine,
> A fellowship with essence?[4]

It was out of this alert, expectant, perceptive desirousness that he penned the often quoted words to his brothers about

> the quality Shakespeare possessed so enormously – I mean Negative Capability, that is, when a man is capable of being in uncertainties, mysteries, doubts without any irritable reaching after fact and reason.[5]

Negative Capability is a very positive thing. The primary word is 'capable'. It denotes an ability only 'negatively' linked because it consists in the capacity *not* to be thwarted by just those considerations which, as *anicca*, *anatta* and *dukkha*, persist in interrogating the human condition. It is a capacity to allow them as questions, but *not* to concede them as verdicts, nor as dissuasives from the acceptance of meaning and the summons of desire. It is far from supposing an unambiguous world but it refuses to resolve the ambiguity by yielding to its negative implications. Rather, it embraces the great, mysterious positives and allows these to contain all the unanswered issues which, if spelled out by the negating option (and it *is* option, *not* certainty), would stifle the imagination and predispose the will to distrust all desire. Hence its ability to 'be in uncertainties' with a heart-certainty despite them. Hence, too, a grace to surmount the 'irritability' of mere logic.

The aim of this chapter, by this route, is to study the Christian meaning of 'negative capability', the affirmation of things which has to be made in, through and beyond negation. The central point of Christian baptism is here, the recognition of the self we must negate on behalf of the self we must become. That which we have to be ready 'to let not be' as the secret of right desiring, is also at the heart of the Christian incidence of death, in the will to a forfeiture (albeit also inescapable) of that mortal order of the physical in which alone, as yet, we know and have ourselves. In these terms we may hope to be in honest cross-reference with the urgent themes of Buddhism.

Beginning – and for these paragraphs continuing – with John Keats is not to yield to the easy temptation to claim either Keats or his beloved Shakespeare as articulating Christian faith explicitly. Keats once wrote, ambiguously, to his Fanny Brawne, in the passion of his love: 'I appeal to you by the blood of that Christ you believe in.'[6] Perhaps he was exempting or including himself. We cannot tell. Here it matters not. He certainly was of the spiritual kin of Thomas Traherne, who would have understood, when, for example, Keats wrote: 'Probably every mental pursuit takes its reality and worth from the ardour of the pursuer, being in itself a Nothing ... things semi-real require a greeting of the spirit to make them wholly exist and nothings ... are made great and dignified by an ardent pursuit.'[7] He had 'a greeting of the spirit' even for the sparrow that hopped on to the window-sill and shared the urgency of its furtive pecking.[8]

The 'capability', then, to be 'in doubts' stood in the warm positive of willed participation in the world of sense and society, which Keats saw – in the famous phrase – as 'a vale of soul-making'. 'How are souls to be made?' he asked. 'How but by the medium of a world like this?'[9] Through mind and heart and will – what might, less poetically, be called the art of attention through a principle of interest – personhood was fulfilled, and people became souls with identity. It was by true contact with the things of, and beyond, sense that the self became real to itself and found vocation. In John Keats's soul it was the vocation to poetry as the celebration for love's sake, of the sanctity of all experience. This was his conviction matured to its climax against the grain of a wasting tuberculosis which writ large its threat in his brother Tom's death and his own stricken lungs. The mind had to be 'a thoroughfare for all thoughts', responsive intuitively to scenes, and situations and people, learning in them 'to buffet with circumstance'.[10]

II

Is it a fair reckoning to set Buddhist renunciation of being against this pattern of thought and commitment? Some aspects of the Eightfold Path, yet to be studied, may approach it but only in spite of, rather than thanks to, the philosophy of *anatta* and *dukkha*. The capability to take negation and resultant soul-making *via* all experience, both glad and grim, strenuously refuses the notion that because things pass they have not really been. For, precisely in passing and requiring a posture which takes from them what, in character, abides into a future, they are not lost in transience. Fleetingness, therefore, ceases to be the only or the final factor from which to reckon. The Buddhist assumption that transience spells vacuity is disproved. The point about what passes is not *that* it does (sheer *chronos*) but *how* it does – the 'how' determined by the will to engagement. If the significance of experience is not what happens but how we relate and respond to what happens, then the fact that experience is always in sequence does not mean that its transitoriness cheats us, as the *anatta* concept alleges. On the contrary, it shapes and forms us within an always critical self-determination. To adopt a Hume-style thesis that the self can only be identified as a serial of impressions could be likened to insisting that minute stills on a film tape can yield no moving, living image. The flux which is said to isolate them is the occasion for a unity.

Doubtless, this sense of an authentic selfhood in time has to face – as we will later in this chapter – the seeming veto

of death and personal demise. The more we understand personhood as maturing, ripening, degenerating, corrupting – whichever it be – in the register of experience, the more we accentuate
the significance of personal mortality. That fact is, perhaps,
the strongest consideration for doing so, since we hardly make
sense of life without a realism about death. The immediate
point, however, is the radically different view of time which
'soul-making' entails as contrasted with that of Buddhism. If
we state it in explicitly Christian terms it means that temporal
flux conditioning us and all is not to be thought of as a sword
of Damocles, the menace of impermanence. Rather we may
see it as the cup of Christ, 'a baptism we are being baptized
with', in a significant economy of grace.

That this has been so with countless souls, through Christ,
is not in doubt. When John Bunyan rhymed his *Prison Meditations*, through twelve years of incarceration for conscience's
sake, he sang:

> When they do talk of banishment,
> Of death and such like things,
> Then to me God sends heart's content
> That like a fountain springs.
>
> The truth and I were both here cast
> Together, and we two
> Lie arm in arm, and so hold fast
> Each other: this is true.
>
> This gaol to us is as a hill
> From whence we plainly see
> Beyond this world and take our fill
> Of things that lasting be.[11]

One of the famous contemporaries of John Keats, and long-
lived, was William Carey. His great enterprise of inter-faith
translation suffered a grievous blow in March 1812, when a
disastrous fire at Serampore destroyed numerous translations,
including the *Rāmāyana*, fourteen founts of oriental types,
precious MSS of his polyglot dictionary from Sanskrit, various
grammars and papers. The great printing shop was completely
wrecked. In one night the work of decades was destroyed.
Carey, already stricken with a private grief, stood in the ruin.
A colleague recalled his words:

> I had lately brought some things to the utmost perfection of which
> they seemed capable . . . with perhaps too much self-congratulation.
> The Lord has laid me low that I may look more simply to Him.

With so much irreplaceably gone in molten waste and charred
embers, Carey's companion wrote:

> Return now to thy books: regard God in all thou doest. Learn Arabic
> with humility. Let God be exalted in all thy plans, purposes and
> labours. He can do without thee.[12]

The quality is in the last sentence: 'He can do without thee',
in no way said as a gesture of defiance or a spasm of sullenness.
For then it would have read: 'Let him do without me!' The
bitter blow releases a sharper perspective. It is part of humility,
not to say of death, to accept our dispensability. The fact that
time will in the end dispense with us, require us to forfeit our
mortal selves, is not read here as warranting umbrage (which
would be futile), nor distress, nor some idea that we can feign
to desist meanwhile, supposing thereby to forestall the pain.
It is read as the secret of our discipline through Christ, namely:
'You are not your own.' Such negating tragedies as Carey suffered educate and liberate us into capability and give us back
our personhood more fully made.

Transience, then, is not, for the Christian, that in which
personhood is made unreal and so discounted: personality is
around flux comprising and transacting it. The cirumstantial
is never merely such: it is existential, cumulative, critical. Are
we to say that at birth we become, as it were, the yet undead?
In Christ we are far from 'that nothingness which', as Schopenhauer had it, 'we shall be obliged to recognize in the striving
of will in all its phenomena'.[13] We are subjects of experience,
to be sure, but not merely subjected. It may be odd to ask
with one of D. H. Lawrence's characters: 'How could he say
"I" when he was something new and unknown?'[14] For none
of us are wholly new or unformed, and cannot be born when
we are old. But that the 'I' is ever forming is the nature of
life. The more alive our consciousness the more it possesses
both itself *and* its context. Atrophy of the self is not naturally
willed. Need, interaction, language, speech all relate us; we
belong and become within the relating. Will not the self, at
least in mortal terms, persist under and through all intention

to let it *not* engage? Desire will be consciously present in the
'undesiring', perhaps the more so for the paradox of being
ostensibly renounced. Self-denial, understood in Christian
terms, cannot obtain in that which persists in spite of it. It
can only happen spiritually within a reverent, gentle self-
acceptance. Or so the gospel holds. Negative capability can
only belong in souls being made, not in selves unmaking.

III

These thoughts about transience, which we are still taking
in purely individual terms (deferring history writ large), bring
us back to the sense of personhood as being in crisis through
the tensions and ambiguities of desire. Literature is full of this
theme. Russia gives us both Rashkalnikov and Anna Kare-
nina, the one tempered and fulfilled in the acceptance of
penitence and love, the other trapped, enslaved and broken.
Dickens portrayed with great verve and insight the subtleties
of evil in his Chuzzlewits, his Miss Haversham, his Murd-
stones. With equal conviction he traced the regeneration of
Dombey, of Magwitch and Gradgrind. Scrooge may be all too
melodramatic a convert. But there is no mistaking Dickens's
mind for the mysteries of human transformation in the soul-
options of life. Nor, for all his sitting loosely to establishment
religion, was there any doubt of the sources of his vision of
humanity, and his portrayal of the depths of evil and the reach
of love.

> All my strongest illustrations are derived from the New Testament;
> all my social abuses shown as departures from its spirit: all my
> good people are humble, charitable, faithful and forgiving. Over
> and over again, I claim them in express words as disciples of the
> Founder of our religion: but I must admit that to a man (or a woman)
> they all arise and wash their faces, and do not appear unto men
> to fast.[15]

Dickens, of course, was a great exponent of what might be
called the ministry of obstacles. He loaded the odds against
many of his characters so that, by criteria of much more recent
psychology, they would be hopeless victims of neurosis and
pathologically written off. Yet he saw them emerging precisely
because he reckoned vitally with the realities of hope. His social

conscience, it could be said, was quickened by negative capability, by the will to engage in a way that any premise of 'emptiness' never could.

Wherever we draw instance from literature in this sense, we must recognize, in all sources, the fact that this theme of time significant for character does not obtain without will. It has to be admitted that there is everywhere a steady circumscribing of potentialities because of temporal flux. People, whether in literature or in life, may grow more or less desireless because of time. Years anyway limit the options we may still take by dint of those already taken. There is a forfeiture of alternatives. Nor is circumstance to be discounted. It is not wise to exaggerate the autonomy of private persons.[16] Negative capability may hardly ever emerge, still less win through. Yet this acquiescent personhood is not *sunyata*. If it is an emptiness, it is so by default and could always be kindled anew. If in some it develops into a deliberate renunciation, or a resentment which nurses itself by brooding into one, this will in no way either emulate or fulfil the Buddhist pattern. The latter is no mere reaction to disappointment: it is a philosophy to obviate the risk of it.

Nevertheless, to remember the limitations of the human lot, to be on behalf of the oppressed in the manner of theologies of liberation, is to be called all the more to engagement with the world. There are constant occasions for vicarious desire, for the will that wills for others who, by whatever cause, cannot yet, or ever, will for themselves. The risk of suffering which, in private terms, the Theravādin is set to counter by renunciation, is already there within society, in the fabric of the social order, or disorder. Nor can it be countered in community merely by alerting others to its pain. Rather it becomes a wider, sharper call to that readiness for identity with others which 'enthusiasm for humanity' arouses.

In one of his many poems haunted by what he sees as the privations of his native Wales, R. S. Thomas captures this quality of 'waiting for redemption' which situations around present to open conscience.

> Always the same hills crowd the horizon,
> Remote witnesses of the still scene.
> And in the foreground the tall Cross,

> Sombre, untenanted, aches for the body
> That is back in the cradle of a maid's arms.[17]

It is perhaps here in awareness of the deep pain of the world
that there is a mutual sympathy between the Buddha's readiness to encounter reality outside the palace and the Christian
centrality of the cross. At least they are akin in the sense of
Keats's words

> . . . those to whom the miseries of the world
> Are misery and will not let them rest . . .

contrasted with

> All else who find a haven in the world
> Where they may thoughtless sleep away their days.[18]

The contrast is one which both gospel and Dhammapada share.
Where they differ is in the reach and range of misery and the
terms in which it forbids them rest.

IV

It is here we need to consider the Buddhist clue of transience
by relating it to the Christian sense of history on the world
plane, time in the centuries of the human drama rather than
in the span of private years. Patience, and its correlate, compassion, are crucial words in New Testament vocabulary and are
applied to God himself. Patience and transience do not consort
well together. There is no place for hope in mere flux. Biblical
patience is capable of sustaining negations because it understands *within* history that by which history is to be interpreted
and lived. In the theme of 'happenedness' in Chapter 9 that
understanding was explored. That Christ-Event affords the
principle of response in which all that eventuates is to be undertaken, whether in the biography of the self or in what perhaps
we may call the biography of the world.

The Buddhist would deny that it has one. *Dukkha* means
more than seeing history as cyclic. Cycles are so inconceivably
vast that the very idea of history dissolves, eluding any register
of relevance. On the sort of time scale consonant with human
criteria of memory and imagination, there would certainly seem
to be a biography of things. To this content of history, as distinct
from its mere passage, it is surely necessary and intelligent
to relate. For it clearly has an evident momentum, if no logic.

It will not allow us to be neutral, since it is continually acting upon us in change and challenge, requiring constant decisions about the very meaning of our human-ness. To characterize it as mere transience may arguably justify a partial withdrawal of some from its thrust, as a gesture for the rest in their assessments. Most religions have such monastic devices that are salutary for society. But the realities both of society and history forbid that they can be more than gestures. There is something inexorable about the course of human time which disallows a neutralism and demands a concern about ends, about a *telos* in the whole.

In respect of historical *telos*, it may be that we can only conclude a lively agnosticism. But it cannot be an agnosticism that exempts us from participation. It is here that New Testament patience has so large a role or, in other words, that negative capability is so crucial. Eschatology has always been difficult of formulation because of the ambiguity of the word 'end'. The 'end' of time in the serial sense is as hard to visualize as its beginning, though our time category of thought has us always trying. If we read 'end' as goal and purpose – as we must if we are to have meaning in time here and now – then history, however we interpret it, is not mere transience.

Contemporary time confronts us with this fact more crucially than any earlier day. We are faced on every hand with accelerating change, some of which threatens, or promises – as the case may be – to revise our version of ourselves. Easy notions of 'progress' or artless ideas of mechanical 'process' have had their day. But is *homo* to be held no longer *religiosus*? Has technological autonomy outrun the sense of sanctuaries? Given that the future is no longer what it used to be, what shall futurology make of it? Or what is the point of the fact that we are preoccupied, nervously and uncertainly, with futurology at all? Is that the current form of eschatology – a 'further' that is never attained?

The past yields so many legacies but withdraws many of its precedents when we look to know how to inherit the first and replace the second. We cannot fool ourselves that nuclear power is not a different weapon from the cannon, as the cannon was from the bow and arrow, or pretend that environment is any longer secure in nature's ecology and the former lowliness of man. Our national tribalisms are outmoded by our ubiquitous technology but we find them politically and emotionally insistent. Some of our inventions, dispensing both with manual dexterity and mental engagement, bringing technical ingenuities into the most personal realms of meaning and community, re-orient or disorient our very comprehension of ourselves. The sciences of psychology and sociology, taking their cue – not always soundly – from the more viable physical sciences, often succeed more in analysing our experience than resolving it. At least they give us to know, from angles earlier unsuspected, what uncertainties, mysteries and doubts we are in.

It is just the fact of *being in* what time now contains, and spiritually 'containing' what being in it means, which is here in point rather than any catalogue of change. It is to say that transience is no adequate category by which to see history. Indeed the very 'pain' which Buddhism locates in *dukkha* as 'impermanence' only afflicts participation. What merely flows, we may say, flows over. Even the popular notion that time heals avails only by letting time pass. It is when we refuse to concede that it merely lapses, when we incur how it torments, afflicts, daunts or tests us, with its irreversible losses, its enigmas and its distresses, that *dukkha* comes fully into us. If we could be saved by conceding transience, transience would save us of itself. That we do not let it do so is precisely because we take time as significant and ourselves as liable. The Buddha was right in coming back to humanity with his saving compassion: only wrong in the illusion that their saving within time could be *from* time.

V

On every count, then, of private personhood and open history at large, a Christian faith must hold with the significance, not the illusoriness, of events and experience. It interprets all by the paradigm of that sacred history which we pondered in Chapter 9. What that sacred history yields us is not always an explanation and sometimes only a hint. But what it always yields us is a pattern, a policy we might almost say, a theme of patience and action. And it is bold to say that the pattern it avails us is rooted in the being and nature of God. This is the meaning of divine patience. The creation as entrusted to man for historical custody, within the parameters of its own order and science-affording quality, means a divine intention for the human means to divine ends. The biblical sacred history, in its New Testament form, both illuminates and enshrines the pattern of bearing what is contrary as the secret of its salvation. It sees the love that suffers as the very meaning of divine Lordship. We see God, in Christ, in a capability for all the negations, the perversities, of which mankind is culpable in what we have called 'the biography of the world', his world. It is the capability, not merely of the creaturely mandate of freedom in which they transpire, nor merely of the law of righteousness by which they are accused, but – because of these and beyond them – the competence to outlast them and outlove them in 'the kingdom and patience of Jesus Christ'.

Whereas on Buddhist ground it is the tragic in our condition as human[19] which quite precludes any notion of ultimate significance, let alone of 'creation', on Christian ground it is the perception of the tragic which informs our understanding of the Creator. What makes it so is the intention, discernible in man, and belonging in God. *Dukkha* is not, then, a lostness, a despair legitimated by meaninglessness. It is the burden of our wilful enmity to the divine intention – an enmity which, in their self-consistency, the resources of divine compassion are ready to sustain, and so repair. Christ and the cross are the point and sign of this divine grace and the pattern of its resourcefulness.

It is the grace of being vicarious which Christian faith attributes to God. It means a divine being-on-behalf-of *vis-à-vis* our humanity and our human situation. It is a shape of truth which can only be understood as freely self-limiting in God. Only so could divine ultimacy, divine greatness and sovereignty be authentically preserved, but only so, also, could they be credibly acknowledged. This indeed is, one might say, the Christian temerity, to see God as self-giving, were it not warranted by what we recognize in Christ. Given such warrant – which only faith discerns – the temerity would consist in doubting it.

So we believe and wonder in this conviction of divine patience and compassion. We find it there in the meaning of a creation, as a divine liability incurred by the heavenly enterprise of mankind. Creation, in that sense, is already *kenosis*, a divine acceptance to be liable for man, with man made liable for what is also God's in the trust of creaturehood. There is *kenosis* too in the steady attendance of the Holy Spirit on the vagaries, the lethargies, the frailties, of men, dull of mind, and slow of will, and cold of heart.[20]

And, centrally, in the ministry and passion of Jesus the

Christ, in the eventfulness we studied in Chapter 9, stands the same pattern of divine vicariousness. Seeing the cross within its antecedents in Jesus' teaching, we perceive also the self-disclosure of the divine nature, the paradigm of how we should identify what is ultimate and sovereign. Here is 'God's regenerative argument', as Horace Bushnell has it,[21] 'the Name whereby we must be saved'. 'The Name' is not some abstract formula, devised to satisfy a scheme or supply a password. It is the reality of what love means and how it saves and to what it calls in a world we can intelligibly call God's and recognize with honest shame as ours.

VI

If we measure the capacity of God to undertake man in this costly way, the fact of being-on-behalf-of becomes the clue to understanding of our personal self. To this Christian form of what Buddhism calls 'non-attachment' we must now come, but only against the background of the faith in the patience and compassion of God. It does not propose to surmount selfishness by disavowing selfhood. On the contrary, it requires and recruits the self in order to 'un-self' it in the sense in which 'un-selfing' has to be, namely, not by an impossible 'un-desiring', but by a desiring rightly. This is the resolution of the issue we remitted from the previous chapter in order, first, to explore the question of transience. Oriented by the foregoing, we are back with Hammarskjöld's yearning 'to obey a will for which "I" is in no respect a goal'.

The clue to themselves which the disciples of Jesus found in his cross and resurrection came in their discovery of the costly reality of divine grace evident in those events. It was a self-awareness out of a dark trauma of despair and dereliction. It reversed the shattering experience of defeat and betrayal which was their side of the Gethsemane climax. Only by being brought, there, to the end of themselves and of their self-assessments, thus far untouched by tragedy, could they come through into a right self-possession. It was as if they had to be found capable of the supreme negation of the cross to everything sanguine and selfish in them, before they could find themselves in truth. What lay at the heart of their defining, refining experience was not, as with Sākyamuni, the fleetingness of time *per se*, but the agony of an immediate point in time, a climax in their personhood. They found salvation in a crucible, not out of a flow, through a desolating event, not contemplative absorption.

The contrast here, stark as it is, determines the difference between Christianity and Buddhism, between the New Testament and the Dhammapada. 'Enlightenment' might arguably describe both occasions in their definitive character but only in radical distinction about the nature of the light. The other common element was the obligation to mission. Sākyamuni, at length attaining the insight and bliss of the Great Enlightenment by prolonged meditation under the Bodhi tree near Varanasi, became thereby the Buddha and knew his destiny to emancipate humanity by the preaching of the Four Noble Truths and the Eightfold Path. The mission of the first Christian apostles stood in the conviction that their own biography had passed through a crisis of discovery in which, through anguish, they had in Jesus the suffering credentials of God's love. They realized that it authorized them to 'go into all the world'.

It was then that the 'enthusiasm for humanity' which characterized – as we saw – the expectancy and liberating quality of Jesus' teaching came into its own in a community of its reproduction. For all their doggedness and simple fidelity, Jesus had little effective success with his disciples prior to his passion. The gospels are very frank about their incomprehension and thoroughly human frailties – a frankness which many guess is the more credible for being recalled when they had become apostles. But what transformed them from disciples into apostles – the terms are very significant – happened only out of the experience of the death of their naive identity, the end of the selves they had hitherto been, and their becoming possessors of 'newness of life'. Jesus 'was known by them', says the Gospel (Luke 24.35), 'in the breaking of the bread'. It could also be said that 'he was known of them in the breaking of the heart', on the further side of the brokenness they went through in the crisis of Gethsemane, when 'all forsook him'.

Here in the history of the personalities in whom the Christian Church began we have the epitome of the Christian crisis of the self, the actual bio-graphing of what must be *let die* and what may, thus, be *let be* in the Christian experience of grace. Peter and James and John and the rest lived through the death of all their 'desire' in Jesus, their self-estimates belonging with it. These went in the emptiness that ensued on their bitterness and confusion. It was what came on the further side of these which gave them to be selves again, with a new being. Such is resurrection.

VII

It would be straining John Keats's meaning in his context to see Christian personhood in these terms as the capability for 'negation' within the self which is, thereby, a positive selfhood. He meant a tolerance of adversity and perplexity, sustained by a loving will to be and to relate which refuses to be deterred by logic or the lack of it. He meant a *nil desperandum* of insistent equanimity, in the poetic soul. Nevertheless, it is fair to borrow his language for Christian statement and it allows us lively cross-reference into Buddhist meanings.

In his expository theology Paul develops the unselfing into selfhood we have just studied and centres it likewise around the Christ-Event. He requires his readers to sustain a strong negation: 'You are *not* your own.' They have to be capable of being dispossessed. 'Reckon yourselves to be dead', he tells the Roman Christians, 'but alive to God through Jesus Christ.' He sets this in the framework of the Hebrew Passover with its 'no longer' and its 'henceforth', its celebration of a past left behind and a present attained, the 'No' said to Egypt and Pharaoh, the 'Yes' said to the promise of liberty and land. 'Christ *our* Passover is sacrificed for us: therefore let us celebrate.' He teaches that the cross and resurrection of Jesus are the historical place of a moral significance. 'Be risen with Christ', he writes. He calls for a 'conformity' to Christ's death (what is this but a capability?) in the inward man. By this he means 'a death to sin and a new life to righteousness'. His words about being 'crucified with Christ' might seem extravagant sentiment if we had not understood his mind.

As he reads it, Christ undergoes a drama of rejection unto death, a rejection which expresses and enacts 'the sin of the world'. What thus is done to Jesus he identifies as the qualitative sinfulness of human selves, of his – Paul's – own self. What, then, in him and in us all, rejects Jesus has itself to be rejected, disowned, put to death. Only so can such selves, acknowledging their cross-displayed identity, be brought, raised, lifted – as Jesus was whom they victimized – to newness of life, to another selfhood out of the crucifying one. The transposition within the analogy is stark and arresting. Jesus the crucified becomes the analogue of the sin that made him so, the innocent of the guilty, the immolation of the immolators. His risen power over the evil in their doing translates into the grace which frees them from it. Because they are actually mirrored in the deed, they can be morally transformed by its issue, on condition of their accepting its verdict against themselves *and* its authority for the selves they are to be. 'Christ in you the hope of glory.'

It is thus that Christian faith and sacrament relate most vitally to the Buddhist reckoning with the self-question. It may be that the Eightfold Path, awaiting thought in Chapter 13, shares, by its own idiom, in some aspects of the Christian pattern. For those precepts about 'rightness' serve, as it were, to organize and discipline the attainment. Baptism, in Christian tradition, has always been understood as the shape of discipleship. Its imagery belongs with the themes we have just reviewed in Paul. 'Signing with the sign of the cross', in a context of personal repentance and personal faith, means this readiness for a self to negate and a self to fulfil. What we will to renounce is for the sake of what we are set to obey. There *are* desires, ambitions, impulses, imaginings of ourselves, which we disown, so enabling the desires, aspirations, fulfilments which we cherish and undertake. Such is the constant crisis of the self, never finally or securely passed in life, always present yet also always policy-ed (if we may so speak) in the meaning of baptismal confession and grace. Desire is, thus, the theme of perpetual discrimination that it may be rightly discerned; not inclusively negated so as to destroy its authentic occasion, nor loosed into inauthentic choice and act. Desire is thus its own monitor. 'Love loves to love love', it is said,[22] but a right love only worthily. Such feasible self-monitoring would seem to be impossible on Theravāda premises, though impressively achieved by Buddhist practice.

That grace enables such a personhood, entrusted with desire about desires, is the theme of baptism, as derived from the New Testament. Water takes us back to the Exodus imagery, to the gone and the come of transit through Red Sea and Jordan, the negation of the old, the affirmation of the new. Such waters of symbolic history may, of course, be linked more naturally with the age-old symbolism of washing whereby fabrics are transformed from old stain to new clean. Both these images are joined to the cross and resurrection of Jesus – the cleansing and the crossing – as figures of discipleship *via* what is

repudiated and what is embraced, the abating, as a Buddhist
might phrase it, or, better, the ousting of false desire, for the
framing and furthering of the right one. Being innocent of
desire, or guilty and frustrated in all desire, is no part of the
Christian case. It is within the meaning of the sacrament that
the symbol of a single act, the baptismal event, expects a continuity. But what has to be perpetual is enabled by the fact of
having been once for all transacted. That 'he/she may continue
thine for ever', is the traditional language. It is a matter of
being what we are. The ordinance binds us over to the fulfilment: the fulfilment is vested in the status. 'You are Christ's',
self-dispossessed, self-repossessed.

VIII

It may be asked whether all this is not as ingenuously preoccupied with individuation as Buddhism is suspected or
accused of being. We complained earlier that Sākyamuni,
unlike Moses, took his inquiring way only into the private burdens of age, sickness and mortality. Does not all the foregoing
about baptism and desire similarly confine itself to the personal
equation? Is such right desiring any more realist about the outer
world of politics and social structures than undesiring? Have
we not both alike supposed that desiring and undesiring are
viable in the open world? Are not the most of mankind caught
in webs of power where they are victims, not agents, their
choices already filched from them by the inexorable facts of
poverty, ignorance, castes, injustices, oppression, superstition,
fear and strife? Have we sadly assumed an autonomy, whether
to opt *out* into *sunyata* or to opt *for* by grace, which man hardly
possesses? Can either really cope with the pressures of secularization or with the law-unto-itself situation which belongs with
current technology?

Collectives breed and drive collective desires or are driven
by them. The appetites and passions of politics and money
and party and state are rarely amenable to renunciation and
cannot be curbed by counsels meant for private selves. Yet
they so far dominate and dictate the systems and spheres within
which private selves exist. Are not all religious prescripts, in
that sense, threatened with irrelevance or futility? Can we
resolve the pain of the impermanent by the cult of the imper-
turbable? Is the impermanence the real tragedy, the actual

dukkha? Or should we locate it in the travesties of human dignity rather than the flux of human time? In any event, how do we reach or maintain the faith-solutions, either Buddhist or Christian, to which we are commended, within the actualities of the public world?

It is here that there is point, as well as pathos, in the Christian form of 'negative capability', the ability to be in and yet against, to sustain a 'No' even where it does not yet, or ever, avail, just as Wilfred Owen in his war letters described himself as 'a conscientious objector with a very seared conscience'.[23] The Christian, to be sure, can 'desire' for society, hold and serve attitudes, criteria and priorities, which *via* persons – given enough of them – might also characterize peoples, institutions and public interests. Multiplying such persons will always be the concern of the gospel. There *are* degrees to which public conscience may be shaped by private aspiration. It is urgent to resist the temptation to concede irrelevance which, otherwise, might be self-fulfilling. Social history is frequent in its register of creative minorities.

Nevertheless the spiritual capability which does not avail in positive ways must continue to negate what it cannot regenerate. This will to resistance is deep in the baptismal formula. 'Do you renounce evil?' belongs with: 'Do you turn to Christ?' It may well be that it is not so much impermanence that dismays us but persistence – the persistence of wrongs and treasons to good and to hope, which possess such staying power among us in the shape of enmities, suspicions, exploitations, vested interests. There is, in Christian perspective, a place for corporate penitence, a call to vicarious humility on behalf of the proud and hallowing in proxy for the godless. 'Where there is blasphemy let us cry: Glory!, where there are markets merely, let us speak sanctuaries.' Without this instinct to apologize to God how will worship be authentic or society be saved from itself? The Christian call to a right desiring is not only for inward heeding but for outward hearing.

Political institutions, economic structures and social patterns vary widely in the degree to which they are, or can be made to be, responsive to private conscience. To maximize their responsiveness will always be the duty of a Christian citizen. But within them, however they may be, the self is not for purchase. It is vital to retain the will to will rightly, to be in uncertainties and doubts without any easy reaching after solace and neglect, or to resign one's judgement in weariness or capitulation. There is point in the old tradition of Muhammad: 'If any among you see evil things, he should change them with his hand: if he cannot do that he should change them with his tongue: and if he cannot do that he should change them with his heart.' [24] Action on one's own part, if feasible; protest and persuasion alerting a wider concern; and otherwise – if this be the meaning of the heart – holding out inwardly against evil while it persists, stoutly retaining a love that would undo it, an emotion that refuses to concede. Thus, to 'desire a right desiring' is a vocation *of* the person but thereby also *for* society, an antiseptic, healing, saving quality by which the self is inwardly righted in being on behalf of beyond-self.

IX

The final dimension of experience in the Buddhist, as indeed in every analysis, is death. Sākyamuni encountered lastly a corpse. There is indeed something awesome about the sight of the dead and, as Whitman's poem has it, 'the living looking upon it'. [25] What is, what means, this coldness once so warm, this numbness once so alive, this stillness once so vigorous? How are we to understand the whence and whither of mortality? Does it warrant the Buddhist perception of a living unreality? What does the evident cessation of the spirit/body partnership as we know it require us to believe about either? If we think of something in continuity, if only for the long stages en route to *nirvana*, in what does it have identity? If we think of its single tenancy, its once life-span, what lies beyond that term and by what version of the partnership that once housed it?

A cross-reference theology with Buddhism has many tasks at this point. A Christian instinct in shouldering them would be to commend an attitude to death which, in the main, may be a surer and more interpretative way than a theory concerning it. Here the theme of baptism is again our clue. Death, as we have seen, in analogical terms is a constant figure of baptism in the New Testament. In literal terms, in the physical order, it is the terminal forfeiture of our selfhood in the form in which we have known it. 'We owe God a death.' [26] It is the ineluctable event, which requires of us a ceasing to be. In anticipation it is the No awaiting us to all we are and all we treasure: in incidence the No said to our mortal selves transpires. In that sense 'negative capability' is none other than a synonym for mortality. We have to tolerate, to concede, to undergo an entire self-negation. The sense that it is so accompanies, in greater or less degree, all our living days. We are, mortally, fires destined to go out. Nature, or accident, will see to the unfuelling. In that sense Buddhist discipline does within time what time anyway will do.

Therein lies a clue which Christian faith retrieves and enlarges. We may will our consent to what – albeit inevitable – asks of us a self-surrender, a letting go of all we are, an acknowledgement that 'we are not our own'. We are leaseholders, not owners. Is not such surrender finally and physically what spiritually and steadily baptism in Christ has been asking of us all the time. Death is the great 'un-desiring' in its very incidence, the disengaging from all we see as ours and us. To coincide volitionally with that self-forfeiture is our destiny and our decision – the one with the other. That circumstances, of lingering or suddenness, may not permit volition then, need not preclude it earlier, when mind and will are free.

Are we not then within a parable all the time of what Christian discipleship means? Are we not invited to be counting ourselves not our own by virtue of our commitment to Christ? Must we not let die the false ambition, the wrong motive, the base desire, being capable of the negative of the 'me' that is self-enamoured, for the sake of the 'me' that Christ indwells? This is no 'die-before-we-die' philosophy, no morbid masochism, or self-hatred. On the contrary it is the negating power of a positive grace which needs and recruits me. It is the sacrament of a selfhood for which unselfishness is a capability through love, but only on the principle of the dying out of what otherwise would fuel the evil *tanha* every Theravādin flees.

By thus discerning between selfhood and selfishness a Christian openness to grace and the ready will it must take in train both confirms and disavows Buddhist un-desiring. There *are* fires to be let die out within us. There *are* fires rightly fed by the fuel, not of our appetites but of ourselves, our outgoing in love and in sacrifice and so in fulfilment. We are restored authentically to ourselves by a discipline of self-offering enabled and fashioned by the self-giving of Jesus as the Christ. 'Let this mind be in you which was also in Christ Jesus' is the apostolic bidding into this pattern of self-awareness grounded in the Christian vision of the patience and compassion of God. 'Bidding' is the right word. For it is no static thing, but only a steady 'reason of the heart' answering to grace.

On this reading of the self, transience need not spell dismay. It is rather the incidence of vocation, the span of significance. The span, to be sure, is mortal and brief. But if faith reads baptism by the analogy of death, as we have seen, then the analogues may be reversed and death in its physical incidence be read as a baptism into life. In either case there is the same principle of a yielding up whereby we acknowledge ourselves 'not our own' – in the one case spiritually, in the other terminally, in both into 'newness of life', the one 'newness' here and now in the self, the other eternal. Where that faith obtains and holds, death itself need not be seen as the third proof of 'emptiness' but the final proof of grace.

X

We come back then to 'the vale of soul-making' from which the chapter began, to the conscious self as deliberately shouldering its own meaning and taking existence with an acceptance, which is more than tolerance, that accepts to belong, to desire, to engage, to venture and to celebrate and penetrate all experience, as much as in us lies. Such acceptance is not an effort to domesticate experience or to rescue some personal area of meaning out of meaninglessness. It is not a defensive stance keeping chaos at bay at all costs.[27] It is a zest within finitude into the open possibilities of a context which invites us into engagement *via* nature and community, given and received. Desire, in a realm of ends continual creates desiring in a steady expending and receiving of our selfhood.

This must mean an appreciative self, whereby, in Hammarskjöld's words, 'I am out of myself as a stumbling-block, into myself as fulfilment.'[28] But it must also mean an appreciating self, in the fine sense of the word,[29] a self set to resist and reverse what trivializes and marginalizes others and thus to serve their larger worth. It is perhaps ironical that Buddhist philosophy cares deeply about bringing to nought the individual self, when society is so often doing it anyway to others by injustice, consumerism, human dispossession. All that crudely or subtly depersonalizes and alienates human experience summons us to counter it by a steady affirmation of meaning, dignity and personal claim. Can this well be unless there is an active sense of relevance, and so of significance, within ourselves? It might also be said that we need to be actively affirmative selves, if selves anywhere, and against all odds and conspiracies, are to be affirmed.

Active consciences are no doubt a temptation to self-esteem, furtively seeking reputation, or influence, or satisfaction. But these evils have to be countered in the context where they lurk, not in its neglect. Enfranchise, not disfranchise, is surely the word which should obtain in our relation to the human manifold. To 'undesire' the exchanges of life and society, entailed in 'undesiring' our selves, yields the situation to the false collective fuels always ready for kindling. The internal and external relations of all desire define each other. We cannot belong in the world in abeyance of our own being. Thus the becoming of others is bound up with our own, and this is true for good and ill. To conclude that we, and they, have been shot by some poisoned arrow, so that the one significant thing is to pull it out, is indeed to make ourselves its target.

> Love's possibilities of realization
> Require an otherness that can say 'I'.[30]

So we return, fortified, to the Christian dimensions of desire and comprehend the 'Otherness saying: "I"' as God himself, with both nature and grace the spheres of our hearing and replying.

> My eyes for beauty pine, my soul for Goddes grace:
> No other care or hope is mine; to heaven I turn my face.
> One splendour there is shed, from all the stars above:
> 'Tis named when Goddes name is said, 'tis love, 'tis heavenly love.
> And every gentle heart that burns with true desire,
> Is lit from eyes that mirror part of that celestial fire.[31]

There is an intriguing passage in Herman Melville's *Moby Dick* in which he captures the Buddhist theme of absorption out of self and does so, appropriately, in 'oceanic' ways, then abruptly brings the self starkly back to liability for its precarious actuality. The sailor is up in the rigging.

> Lulled into such an opium-like listlessness of vacant, unconscious reverie is this absent-minded youth by the blending cadence of waves with thoughts, that at last he loses his identity: takes the

mystic ocean at his feet for the visible image of that deep, blue, bottomless soul, pervading mankind and nature ... In this enchanted mood, thy spirit ebbs away to whence it came: becomes suffused through time and space ... There is no life in thee now, except that rocking life imparted by a gentle, rolling ship; by her borrowed from the sea; by the sea from the inscrutable tides of God. But while this sleep, this dream is on ye, move your foot or hand an inch; slip your hold at all; and your identity comes back in horror ... with one half-throttled shriek you drop through that transparent air into the summer sea, no more to rise for ever. Heed it well ...[32]

Whom, indeed, we are to heed in this graphic sequence is the whole, perhaps the irresolvable, issue.

There are significant senses in which Buddhism, through its wide diversity, is better than its rigorous Theravādin theory, which, nevertheless, it has been vital to examine since, however alleviated in practice, it colours all else. To explore this practice as 'the middle Way' belongs to the next chapter. It may perhaps be anticipated by a different metaphor from Melville's. The resonance of the familiar gong which rings around the pagoda or shrine – does it speak the merit of the devotion the monk offers and thus a lingering attachment, *via* merit, to a self retained in the very will to forsake it? Does it reverberate the summons to all, from the asceticism of the *Sangha*, to guard against the snares of selfishness? Or is it the consecration of all sound as a reminder that in nature, art and grace there is the sacramental principle which, duly perceived and welcomed, will hallow all the being of the self, fade as its doings may in this transitory life?

NOTES

1   John Keats, *Poetical Works*, ed. H. W. Garrod (2nd edn, Oxford 1958), p. 553.

2   See Chap. 11 note 9.

3   *Letters of John Keats, 1814–1821*, ed. H. E. Rollins, 2 vols (Cambridge, Mass., 1958), vol. i, No. 43, Letters of 22 Nov., 1817 to Bailey, p. 184.

4   *Poetical Works*, op. cit., 'Endymion', p. 88, 11.777–9.

5   *Letters*, vol. i, No. 45, Letter of 28 Dec., 1817, to George and Tom Keats, p. 193.

6 ibid., vol. ii, No. 271, Letter of 5 July, 1820, to Fanny Brawne, p. 304. On Keats's attitude to religion see, e.g., *Collected Poems*, p. 532, 'A Sonnet written in disgust of vulgar superstition'. For strictures on the clergy see *Letters*, vol. ii, No. 199 (21 Sept., 1819), to the George Keatses, re the Bishop of Winchester.

7 ibid., vol. i, No. 67, Letter of 13 March, 1818, to Bailey, p. 243.

8 ibid., vol. i, No. 43, Letter of 22 November, 1817, to Bailey, p. 186.

9 ibid., vol. ii, No. 159, Letter of 21 April, 1819, to the George Keatses, p. 102.

10 ibid., vol. ii, No. 199, Letter of 24 Sept., 1819 to the George Keatses, p. 199, and vol. i, No. 55, Letter of 23 Jan., 1818, to Bailey, p. 210.

11 John Bunyan: *Miscellaneous Works*, ed. R. Sharrock (Oxford 1980), vol. iv, *The Poems*, pp. 45–7, Stanzas 20, 33 and 34.

12 George Smith, *The Life of William Carey* (1922 edn London), pp. 197–8.

13 F. Schopenhauer, *The World as Will and as Idea*, vol. i, pp. 192–5.

14 D. H. Lawrence, *Women in Love* (New York 1920), p. 417.

15 Donald Macrae, *Amongst the Darkies and Other Papers* (Glasgow 1876), p. 127, quoting a letter of Dickens to Macrae. See Dennis Walder, *Dickens and Religion* (London 1981), p. 1.

16 As in the conspicuous case, for example, of the writer, Don Cupitt, in *Taking Leave of God* (London 1980), and other works where it might appear that all mortals could cope with the abstractions of the conversations in Cambridge Combination rooms.

17 R. S. Thomas, *Selected Poems*, 1946–68 (London 1973), 'Pieta', p. 93.

18 John Keats, *Poetical Works*, ed. H. W. Garrod (2nd edn Oxford 1958), 'The Fall of Hyperion', p. 513, 11.148–151.

19 It is, of course, false, in strict terms, to call it 'tragic', since that word presupposes something significant and liable.

20 cf. the comment of Horace Bushnell, *Vicarious Sacrifice: Grounded in Principles of Universal Obligation* (New York 1866), p. 85: 'If the sacrifices of the much enduring, agonizing Spirit were enacted before the senses, in the manner of the Incarnate life of Jesus, he would seem to make the world itself a kind of Calvary from age to age.'

21 ibid., p. 161.

22 James Joyce, *Ulysses, A Short History* (Penguin edn 1971), p. 331.

23 Wilfred Owen, *Collected Letters*, ed. Harold Owen and John Bell (London 1967), Letter 512 to Susan Owen, p. 461.

24 A tradition of Muhammad in very frequent currency. See, for example, *Al-Muqaddimah* of Ibn Khaldun, trans. F. Rosenthal (London 1958), vol. i, chap. 3, sect. 6.

25 Walt Whitman, *Leaves of Grass* (London 1907), 'To Think of Time', p. 386.

26 William Shakespeare, *King Henry IV*, Part 2, Act 3, Sc. 2, line 251.

27   cf. W. H. Auden in 'For the Time Being', *Collected Poetry* (New York 1945), pp. 410–11:

   Person has become a fiction: our true existence
Is decided by no one and has no importance to love.
          . . . no nightmare
Of hostile objects could be as terrible as this Void.

28   *Markings*, op. cit., p. 130.

29   i.e. not 'appreciating' as one who sheds a benevolent approval, but one who evaluates and recognizes worth discerningly.

30   W. H. Auden, op. cit., p. 447.

31   Robert Bridges, *Poetical Works* (Oxford 1953), 'April, 1885', p. 286.

32   Herman Melville, *Moby Dick*, Chap. 35.

13

The Will Desiring the Way

I

It is a familiar truism that faiths are often better in their concepts than in their practice. For they are all capable sadly of falling short of their obligations within their definition of truth. The reverse situation, though less often noticed, is no less noteworthy, in which faiths in their lived expression are better than their avowed teachings – or, at least, than those teachings, by their own mandate, are popularly assumed to be.

This is certainly the case with Theravāda Buddhism. The student of its psychology and its focal concepts of *dukkha, anicca* and *anatta* might well be puzzled to know how it could ever constitute a liveable religion. The desolating dogma that to know experience is 'to burn with thirst',[1] seems to preclude any delectable wonder from the senses, any legitimate exercise of will, any authentic desiring or anything genuinely desirous in life. Where personhood is so wholly evaporated in mere flux, where transience is allowed to negate all significance, and where 'negative capability' is excluded as an answer to the mortal condition, we would seem to be in a bleak house indeed. Even when one concedes that only some are within the vocation of monks of the *sangha*, their example is nevertheless the wise moral for the rest. Would it be merely a crude misunderstanding to surmise that, somehow, Buddhist humanity must be different from its stark philosophy, must necessarily transcend, edit or amend its theory in its practice, its meanings in its living?

So, indeed, it proves. Buddhism is one with other faiths in the ability to live itself in terms that modify itself and so to prompt the wise observer to know it accordingly. It is to the practice of Buddhism we must now turn. This means the study of the Eightfold Path and, in it, the will desiring the way.

For will, clearly, is here involved. Even 'undesiring' has to be desired. Though the self may be in theory an illusion it belongs, in some sense, with the enterprise that aims at its surcease. However transitory the scene, the Eightfold Path proceeds within a psycho-physical situation. Theory may demand that this be called 'the conventional self' to safeguard the doc-

trine that it is not ultimate. But, conventional or not, it is in
some sense a self exercising a will about itself. Though 'craving'
– in normal usage a reprehensible word – is generally used
to translate *tanhā*,[2] thereby tending to exclusify unworthy elements in 'desire',[2] the reiterated denominator of the 'right' version, in each of the items of the Eightfold Path, must mean
that 'right' and 'wrong', 'skilled' and 'unskilled', exist as distinctions within desire. One may thus speak, intelligibly, of 'unsel-
fish craving'. If the Buddha said, as recorded in *Angutara Nikaya*
1.58; 'Put aside what is unwholesome', then the wholesomeness of some desire must be allowed. The will could hardly
be disciplined into a right intention if its only experience was
'to burn with thirst'. Nor could there be point in its discipline
if transitoriness vetoed all significant striving. Nor could the
claim be made that there is a way of salvation in the harnessing
of craving unless desire – as in Christianity – has a legitimate
place and role in the destiny of the self. Could any long-term
worthlessness of desire – as in Buddhist theory – conceivably
ride with short-term assessment and pursuit of its worth? Is
the sought goal of the Eightfold Path not put into radical question by the very logic of the going in it?

These considerations, in the light of the well-nigh universal
tension in religion between dogma and doing, need in no way
detract from the positive appreciation of Buddhist practice. It
must be our task here to seek and find such appreciation, relate
it to Christian criteria of right desiring and to see how far,
in Christian terms, the Buddhist *way*, despite Buddhist theory,
might corroborate the Christian's reading of the self and salvation.

II

It would seem wise, and conducive to authentic religious relationship, if those outside Buddhism who study its prescripts
for freedom from desire and the element of discrimination these
must involve between sorts of desire, should give every possible weight to the positive implications such prescripts involve.
There is no service either to honesty or hope in neglecting features which can be identified within a system which, broadly,
is assumed to lack them. For such neglect invites the charge
that the picture has in fact been misunderstood. There are exponents of the Eightfold Path in both East and West who plead

that outsiders have too often failed to reckon with a discernible Buddhist psychology of the will and of the senses which has room for worthy and even delightsome desire. Sheer pessimism, though often alleged about Buddhist abnegation and non-attachment, may be too crude or crass a verdict. It would certainly be a Christian's duty to maximize whatever in Buddhism would allow one to speak of 'selfless persons'[3] in whom personhood was real and the selflessness was that of character, not of extinction.

Part of the difficulty here is that of the vocabulary of the Pali Canon. It is fair to ask whether there is a Pali word which consistently and unequivocally denotes desire as good? Bruce Matthews, for example, exploring vocabulary in *Craving and Salvation* finds rare occasions when even *tanhā* ('craving') may be somewhat retrieved for a good sense. But *chanda* he translates as 'lust' as well as 'love'. The analysis, however, is more hopeful than convincing and though adjectives applied to words denoting will and desire may serve to distinctions these are likelier to relate to 'skill' and 'profit' within the Theravāda discipline than to moral quality *per se*.[4] That fact suggests only the consistency of the scheme within itself. Desire and volition are assessed, and assessable, essentially in terms of how they align with the demands of the Eightfold Path.

Even so, that Path, requiring, as it does, a discriminatory posture within self-consciousness, also requires evaluation of will and desire and, therefore, a certain hierarchy or structure of value. Such decision about relative worth is not allowed – within Buddhism – as it must be in Christianity, to argue, still less to undergird, any cognate value in selfhood *per se* or in the ultimate significance of life-experience.

This is so because consciousness, in the Eightfold Path, is being trained to extinguish consciousness. The conceptual and cognitive functions within it are learning to abnegate their role so that the craving they feed may cease to turn the wheel of existence by passing on, into rebirth, that force or energy which wills to go on being, in the karmic sequence. That sequence abnegation is set to terminate. 'Desire', even when adjudged more apt or judicious, on Buddhist terms, and thus more 'worthy', is still not authentic as belonging to a personal soul existentially ripening or coarsening by moral obligations accepted or denied. For no such soul exists. Buddhism reads the psycho-physical situation only in empirical terms and causes, not in metaphysical or final meanings, and it does not concentrate such existence within a single mortal span. Death, therefore, does not 'concentrate the mind', in the other sense of the verb. It is, rather, only an episode in the thrust of rebirth which abnegation strives to halt and finally escape. It is thus that evaluations of will, intention, and desire, on the Eightfold Path are occupied, not with character and personhood as the ultimately significant dimension, but with empirical utility on Buddhist terms and within what these interpret as a series of dependencies mistakenly assumed elsewhere to belong to personal soul or substance.

Any belief in such soul or substance is seen in Buddhism as a form of the grasping which abnegation must deny. What volition has to do, therefore – and this is its sole function – is to counter the illusion of selfhood, the craving after 'me' and 'mine' which alone sustains personality. It is we who attach egocentric values and meanings to our perception of the material world. Sense information is pertinent only to this illusory ego. Though its delights, on some Buddhist showing, may be noted, perhaps even prized, sense experience has to be resolutely disarmed, demobilized, as it were, so that it no longer conspires to instigate our grasping and our striving. On this view, the egocentric perspective that leads to *tanhā* entirely monopolizes the egocentricity in which the psycho-physical situation consists. In other words egocentricity, in its moral and reprehensible sense, necessarily characterizes the egocentricity which is our physical condition.

Even so, within interpretation thus sharply at issue with the Christian reading of the human meaning, it is possible to register deep Christian relevance in the elements of the Eightfold Path. The Buddhist may well disallow that these can obtain the entire philosophy apart. A Christian conviction will be that they do well to be retrieved from it. But leaving that crucial conflict aside, the 'right' dimensions on the Path, interpreted diversely because of it, have, nevertheless, a promise of significant kinship. Right understanding, right thought, right speech, right action, right livelihood, right effort, right mindfulness and right concentration are surely a commendable list. Ignorance of their Buddhist context could easily transpose them into a scheme of theological ethics. We must renounce such ignorance here. Yet, in their due, and often subtle, context in the Pali Canon, they can yield much congruence with a Christian sense of the crisis in and around all human personality.

They go to the heart of conative psychology. They deal with the springs of action within *citta*, or mental temperament. They discriminate between impulses and scrutinize the stimuli to which these respond. Desire may be affirmatively used in the unseating of lower, less worthy desire. The self may rise above the sequences of dependencies by which it is enthralled. This is no training in holiness by Buddhist lights. But has it not analogy with that Christian concept? To a degree here the bases of motivation may be deliberately changed within the self.

In some interpretations of the Eightfold Path even the senses may be partially validated, if not enjoyed, within such deliberation of desire. For there must be a close link between the quality of will and the ordering of the senses. To liberate the one from what is coarse and vulgar must require the winnowing of the other, a sensuous discretion of the sensuous. What degrades or refines in the *citta* and the thinking has already done so, either way, in the senses and the registering. The senses must be redirected by the will, if the will is to be differently minded. Whether there is room here for any veritable celebration of the senses such as the sacramental principle in the Semitic faiths enjoins must be doubted.[5] The senses being recruited and employed in divine praise means a different perspective from their being well guarded at the doors of perception. Nevertheless, their relevance to the wholesomeness, or otherwise, of the self is a kindred theme of Buddhist and theist alike. This may seem a modest mutuality in the light of the steady Buddhist emphasis on transience as neutralizing all satisfactions and on the senses as only instigators of self-interest. But the will to cross-reference must realistically greet all it can in order the better to grapple with what remains at odds.

III

The eight elements in the Eightfold Path are often divided into a threefold scheme: insight, morality and meditation. Right speech, action and livelihood in the centre relate to qualities which, in any context, would be factors in salvation. To refrain from slander, deceit, frivolity, harshness, and malice, of the lips and tongue, would tally well, for example, with the counsel of James in his New Testament Epistle on the same theme. Right action, in the same context, is taken to refer to several of the items of the Ten Commandments (six to ten), namely the repudiation of killing, sexual licence, greed, extortion, duplicity and envy. Right livelihood means the positive reversal of the foregoing so that one's means of subsistence do not turn on servicing false appetites in others as brewers, publicans, pimps, prostitutes, butchers, slave-traders do.

Such factors in a good society have kinship with Hebraic tradition and Platonic wisdom and Christian ethics. The underlying Buddhist philosophy gives them a distinctive rationale but sustains a comparable social benediction. It is the first two and the last three of the eightfold principles – those usually listed as insight and meditation respectively – which, by Christian criteria are suspect. For they ground their moral, mental discipline in readings of selfhood that seek liberation in what must be seen as impoverishment. Buddhist meditational psychology has profound insights into the deviousness and deception of the human ego, its capacity for illusion and frustration, its built-in menace to itself. But 'skill' with mental states, hard won as it must be by strict devotion to the *dharma* and rigorous obedience to the mentor, comes only at the cost of forfeiting the adventurousness, the spontaneity, the enthusiasm, of life which, for all their risks – indeed by dint of these – can and should belong with grateful acceptance of being and its wonder. The very currency of terms like 'skilled' and 'unskilled' suggests that technique is the clue to selfhood, rather than art and grace. Perpetual self-invigilation may be salutary and, indeed, heroic. But must it be perpetual to the exclusion at least of moments of disarmed delight in 'the God who lets us be'? It must always be a question whether we can effectively separate the admirable discipline of Buddhist meditation from the preoccupations on which it rests with the senses as snares, occasions as flux and relationships as transient.

Even so, the quality of character that can transpire is commendation enough. In the *Majjhima Nikaya* 1.129 there is a passage on meditating loving-kindness under suffering and provocation.

Whoever sets his mind at enmity is for this reason not a doer of my teaching. You must train yourselves thus: 'Neither will my mind become perverted, nor will I utter an evil speech, but kindly and compassionate will I abide, with a mind of friendliness, void of hatred ... I will abide suffusing the whole wide world with a mind

of friendliness that is far-reaching, widespread, immeasurable, without enmity, without malevolence.'

It is plain that no Christian conscience, or theology, could ever
quarrel with that quality. But, counter-wise, need a Buddhist
mind discount, exclude or disavow the living Incarnation of
such quality in an event of history, the cross of Jesus, received,
confessed and sacramentalized as the clue to a *kerugma* of grace
and the final warrant of a theology?

At all events we must all continue subduing 'unskilfulness'
– if such we see it – of our way with our bodies, our control
of our thoughts, our procedures with our economy, our transactions with time. Training of mental postures, attitudes, and
aptitudes, in the interests of character and the peace of society
and the safeguarding of others, will always be crucial. The
Buddhist is inhibited from seeing the bearing of Christian
redemption on all this by the sort of device which, in his own
context, Freud employs. By this all reluctance to accept the
premises on which the case rests only serves to demonstrate
the degree to which the other party is enslaved to his delusion.
Thus the critic can never win. Either he wisely capitulates, or
his unwillingness to do so is proof only of obduracy. To query
the philosophy of impermanence, of *anicca* and *anatta*, to sustain
conviction of a real self and a veritable personhood, is only
to attest how far illusion has gone. All the Christian can do
in his Buddhist relationship here is to invite his partner to sus-
pend his own conviction, albeit briefly, to ponder that his very
fixity with it deserves his suspicion, or at least his interrogation.
If he were to abandon his thesis as to the long-term worthlessness of desire he might have different thoughts about his short-
term meditational strategy in its discipline.

These serious issues between us, however, need not estrange
us in respect of the quest of character in a society of the would-
be 'skilful' in self-control. But there is one curious paradox about
meditation in respect of mortality. There is nothing so eloquent
of impermanence as the certainty of death, 'the sergeant who
is strict in his arrest'.[6] 'This mortal coil' is somewhat blunted
in its impress if experience on the way to demise is read, not
as a single span of individual being, but as a phase in a trans-
mortal continuum. As we have seen earlier, popular Buddhism
takes solace in the sensual postponement of discipline and *nirvana*. If there is procrastination in life, there will certainly be

through rebirths. But the urgent point is that what impermanence so threatens, on the Buddhist score, is not our mortal brevity but the very thrust of desire into rebirth. Yet it is also impermanence which is said to make such desire futile. However such a continuum is seen in relation to the mortal span of personhood which is its present stage – and our only experience of it – it would seem more logical to concentrate the menace of impermanence within a single lifespan (where it most obtains) rather than posit what must be described as a perpetuated impermanence of successive dyings. This is the more so, inasmuch as it is only the force of craving which underlies the continuum. Were we to think of the self as the gift of soul, and not force of craving, death would be a sterner mediator of the significance of transience. Life might then be alerted to the blessed garnering of personality, a ripeness of the years, rather than disciplined to a diminuendo of identity. Can desire be at one and the same time the force that makes us resist the truth of *dukkha* and the factor which alone makes it a truth?

IV

Sati and *samadhi*, the two final categories on the Eightfold *Path*, usually termed in English right mindfulness and right concentration, have much in common with forms of mystical discipline in other faiths. The aim is the steady purification and transcendence of the senses and, thereby, of consciousness also. From deliberate occupation of the mind with some focal form, one may pass to formless absorption and thence to the abeyance of all perception and feeling. One can think only space, and unthink all entities occupying space, or imagine such entities diminishing into infinitesimal proportions until all substantiality or measure is lost to them. Then one unthinks the space they occupied to realize its non-necessity, its essential emptiness. There ensues a kind of neutrality of attention which may lead on to a quality of consciousness which is unbounded, entailing neither perception nor non-perception. This may spell utter tranquillity, serenity, a calm freedom from all emotion. One is then beyond the mere neutralization of craving and the awareness of impermanence, into entire dispassion and cessation.

One intellectual question which dogs this technique of concentration is whether it is, or is not, a conscious effort, and
so achievement, of mind? If it is right to see it as a strategy
leading, nevertheless, into the ineffable, must it not be seen
as, in some sense, an application to and by the psyche of the
same 'science' which, in its empirical manifestations in the
natural order and the sense-world, the Buddhist's premises
have first renounced or even decried? Have we really eluded
the organs of consciousness and mind? Or have we only
banished from their field the normal, substantial, common-
sense *materia* with which and amid which they regularly oper-
ate? Can the ultimate wisdom be comprehended as a technique?
May not the search to transcend what ethically deserves to
be transcended proceed and attain its goal if, instead of unthinking the circumambient world of sense and time and pain, we
integrate it sacramentally into the search? How will the 'salvation' attained – if such indeed it be – relate, in the familiar
question-begging phrase, to 'things as they are'? For can there
be appropriate salvation in that which obtains only by abstrac-
tion from the passions, legitimate as well as guilty, of the social
world and which proceeds only within a private tranquillity?

It is precisely here that the Christian sense of the sacramental
embodies both a radical sympathy with the Buddhist quest and
a rejection of its proceeding. The sacramental principle of the
senses and their context, of the self and its society, is neither
merely empirical nor solely contemplative. It is not set to
renounce but to hallow. Hallowing handles and engages with
the phenomenal order, alert to its pitfalls and its snares but
ardent and responsive in its mysteries and its occasions, or
– to use a Buddhist term – its dependencies. Sacramental hallowing, on a quite contrasted perusal of things from that of
Buddhism, is no less vigilant for rightness of endeavour and
of action than the meditators of the Eightfold Path. It is no
stranger to the art of contemplation. For it lives in the dimension
of poetry as well as of practical attention. To proceed upon
the senses and the sciences as a sacramental engagement with
things and with meaning is to be no less committed than the
would-be *arhant* in Buddhism to the discerning of the mind's
vagaries and the will's wilfulness. 'The cleansing of the
thoughts of hearts' is its constant corollary. But this cleansing
happens, not in the voidance of things phenomenal, nor avoidance of the will to them, but rather in their consecration. The

body, then, and its gates of awareness and functions in action, become 'the temple which we have of God' (1 Cor. 6.19).

This Christian sacramental reading of body and self, and of the natural order in which they move, can be seen to have clear affinity with the Buddhist *sati*, or mindfulness, the seventh of the eight categories. For it spells a vigilant attention to the possession of the body and the situations of stimulus and suggestion in which it centres the self. But instead of revolving that attention around

> considering how the body is something that comes to be, or again how the body is something that passes away: or again . . . considering that coming to be with that passing away . . . [7]

until a ripe *sati* grasps after nothing whatever in the world, the sacramental interpretation of experience revolves its perceptions and employments around the acknowledged holiness of these, and the duty to translate that sanctity from an intention implicit to an intention fulfilled. Such translation enshrines the very crisis of time's content and the self's being which so earnestly preoccupies Buddhist psychology, but does so in a completely different idiom.

There is room here for the same restraint, reverence, chastity, decorum, even fastidious reservation, which Buddhism exemplifies and which *sati* and *samadhi* cultivate. But these, in their due proportions, will not disengage the self from participation, management and human authority. It will be precisely in the manner of utilization, exploitation, control and fulfilment in the material order that hallowing must avail and be made good. Transience will certainly beset this task but it will not deter or inhibit it. A steady mindfulness will be paramount but it will be a mindfulness of privilege in benediction, of crisis in entrustment, not of flux merely, or of the entanglements only, rather than also of the celebration, of the senses and their world.

To read life and the self as sacramental means that the material and the spiritual, the psychic and the eternal, interpenetrate. Laboratory and sanctuary are seen as one but have to be made so. Man is both technician and priest, chemist and poet. As with the *āyāt* of the Islamic Qur'ān, the same signs which alert the scientist as clues properly quicken the soul to wonder and the will to gratitude. It is important to insist that they are the same signs. Just as nature awaits our investigation

before yielding her clues, so 'things as they are' await our cognizance, our moral, social and personal engagement with their
meaning and their actuality. Mindfulness must go beyond
them, as in Buddhism, but thus to be mindfully within them
and about them.

It has been noted that where rivers are fordable, temples
are often found on their banks. Foot travellers on long journeys,
as religious pilgrims are liable to be, came where passage could
be had and their crossing anyway frequently had a religious
import. One of the Buddha's titles was *Tinno*, or 'one who has
crossed the current'. There is, perhaps, a metaphor here. But
the ford must be seen and used in both directions. From the
sensuous we come to the spiritual, because of the spiritual we
are returned to the sensuous. The sacred is present where the
transactions are. It is the destiny of what we call the secular
just as the secular is the raw material of the sacred. Or, as
the Latins had it: *ut doceat, ut moveat, ut delectet*.

The Christian witnesses that this awareness of the sacramental in the ordinary detaches – or, better, redeems – the human
volition from the tyranny and perversity of possession in terms
which Buddhism by its deep intention might appreciate. But,
if so, the *arhant*, actual or potential, would need to re-enter
the field of deliberate, perceptive and forthright attachment
to self, to things and to society. Restraint, detachment and self-
discipline will then march with commitment, participation and
engagement. He will be no less mindful of the deceitfulness
of things and the hazards of selves but he will counter them
by positive sanctification of life, not by cessation of will.

Or, returning to where the Eightfold Path begins, this will
be his insight. Understanding will be 'right', not alone by the
admission of flux, or dependent origination, but by vocation
to hallowing and redemption. There will be realized room
within events and phenomena for a dependent origination
which turns on authentic human decision or orientation of will.[8]

Let us illustrate from an extra-Christian source which, for
that reason, may be the more telling. Ezra Pound's famous
Canto XLV gives eloquent expression, under the theme of *Usura*,
to that wretched entanglement with greed and gain so abhorred
by the Buddhist. *Tanhā*, the poet in effect is saying, corrupts,
depraves and deceives the self, generating bitter *dukkha*. Yet,
as poet, Ezra Pound sees the *tanhā/dukkha* sequence (if we may
stay with the Buddhist terms) not simply as futility but as the

forfeiture of beauty, value, design, and joy in being and in making. It calls, therefore, not for a will to cessation, but a passion for correction, not for opting out but opting in, not for rejection but retrieval. *Canto XLV* accuses only in order to restore: it protests in order to overcome.

> With *Usura* hath no man a house of good stone,
> Each block cut smooth and well fitting . . .
> With *Usura*
> No picture is made to endure nor to live with
> But it is made to sell and sell quickly . . .
> *Usura* . . . rusteth the chisel,
> It rusteth the craft and the craftsman:
> It gnaweth the thread in the loom.
> None learneth to weave gold in her pattern . . .
> *Usura* slayeth the child in the womb . . .
> Corpses are set to banquet
> At behest of *Usura*.[9]

We are close here to the 'cankers' so frequently noted in Buddhism as besetting the human condition.[10] But 'gold in her pattern': is there any such? any wealth legitimated in the quality of its handling, the worth of its presentation, the weal in its working? Ezra Pound in his youth had memories of his father testing coins. For Homer Pound was an assayer in the U.S. Mint at Philadelphia. Hence, perhaps, his insight into values disvalued, his preoccupation with *Usura*. Hence, too, the irony of his poems, especially *Hugh Selwyn Mauberley*, about the sordid in the flaunted, the deceit in the esteemed.[11] Phenomena, as Buddhism well says, do entangle and deceive. Value falsifies itself in our hands. We are daily in a crisis of potential or actual self-deceit. It is the self-presentation of ideas in time, and not merely their flux, which shapes our delusions and consigns us to *dukkha*.

It is here that the sacramental principle makes strongly – if we allow it – for the re-presentation of ideas. It reads and minds every situation as a secular-sacred experience, a phenomena-housed occasion in which we are spiritually obligated. As analysts we enumerate, discern, concert and employ: doing so, we possess, exchange, transact, organize and interrelate. The structures of being, and becoming, which result invite us to their consecration in, by and beyond ourselves. Such consecration issues into celebration. There is vibration in the violin and mathematics in Beethoven. The will desiring the way finds it passing through things as a sanctuary, through the sanctuary things are.

V

All this, as hinted earlier in Chapter 11, returns us to the theme of creation which Buddhism abjures. A sacramental order belongs only with the humility and perception on our part of creaturehood and a theology of divine intention. But it also brings us, for the same reason, to the relevance of rite and symbol which Theravāda Buddhism so firmly excludes. Such exclusion explains, along with lay pressure, many of the changes which came with Mahāyāna Buddhism. When in Theravāda flowers are carried into shrines it is as tokens of transience rather than emblems of gratitude saluting beauty. No faith, of course, however austere, is wholly free of the symbolic. But it is the sacramental principle which both warrants and demands the recruitment of the senses, visual, tactile, auditory, in its obedience. The discipline of these does not preclude their employment, nor suspicion of them dictate their elimination. Meditation properly requires the abatement of distracting or distracted senses. But may they not in fact be better tamed and focused by that which truly wants them and gives rein to their righted capacities? The Mahāyāna tradition, and its many ramifications – too complex and daunting to venture upon here – is witness to this theme.

We have, then, to ask how we might interpret to the Theravāda world the will that is desiring the way in the Christian sacrament of bread and wine. We have seen in Chapter 12 how the scriptural theology of baptism relates to the Buddhist quest for self-negation. What does the other central sacrament say to the themes and aspirations of the Eightfold Path?

The answer is that Holy Communion establishes a sacramental situation with intention to express and transact, under the imagery of hospitality, the celebratory consecration of the natural order, in intimate relation to the central drama of Christian history. We must say 'a sacramental situation', not a spectacle. For there is partaking, in token of community. There is a table and a festival. Bread and wine are seen and handled as symbolic of the whole created order as humanly related.

Neither merely happens. Both are the product of fertility but only under human hands. Processes of soil and chemistry and weather and growth are tended, studied, fostered and fructified by skill and toil. These totally depend upon the givens of nature and those givens also yield only into active mind and will. The harvest comes only by this mysterious alliance and when it comes it calls for celebration.

But it also speaks community. There must be the distributive as well as the developmental, the economic and social as well as the scientific and the productive. So the communicant partakes in unison, in a posture of thanksgiving and a confession of obligation. The company is at a meal, but not for appetite and bare sustenance, instead for symbol and sign. Here is a strange, yet simple, occasion of the words: 'Taste and see that the Lord is good' (Psalm 34.8). The senses learn restraint, not by inhibition, but by that which employs and validates them in a setting of transacted holiness, of reverence and peace. That the elements (as they are liturgically called) also carry the history of Christ's passion and the receiving of his redemption – dimensions so hard to convey to the Buddhist ethos – only deepens the creaturely context of a custodial creation we are here expounding.

In such hallowing all fruits, works, or techniques, of this nature/humanity partnership, whether by plough or by microchip, whether of farm, factory, or nuclear fusion, are symbolized as themes of wonder, surprise, gratefulness, crisis and obligation. The sacrament could fairly be described as a frame of mindfulness, a point of concentration. The bread and wine were called a *sacramentum* from the oath of loyalty by which the Roman soldier was bound within his order. They are a focus for the senses and by the senses of the soul. The acceptance of their status as holy things and, from them, of the inherent sanctity to be deliberately ascribed to all else so worthy, surely fulfils, in its Christian bearings, those states on the Eightfold Path which call for right words, right deeds, right mentalities, right dispositions, for the abatement of enmity and the promotion of peace. If we allow the kind of trans-metaphorical insight which Dylan Thomas, for example, indulged in his poetry, and say:

> The force that through the green fuse drives the flower
> Drives my green age . . .

The force that drives the water through the rocks
Drives my red blood.[12]

then the celebration of the bread and wine will be also the consecration of the entire taut, tense structure which is the human body. The 'path' of all those faculties, sinews, powers and functions, is to and from 'the altar of God'.

VI

'Mindfulness', to adapt the *Digha Nikaya*, 'there becomes established.' And it returns the communicants to the living world. The productive and the distributive themes within the sacrament are plainly transferable to the day-to-day world, where the economic and the social areas of life are in urgent case for the 'rightnesses' of the Eightfold Path. It oftens seems puzzling to outsiders that Buddhism appears preoccupied with individual attainment of serenity. Though in the Mahāyāna tradition the compassion and grace of the Buddha and of *bodhisattvas* are full of vicarious concern, they are still within the prescripts of Buddhist philosophy – a concern to warn and rescue, to counter the illusions in which unskilled humanity is caught. Such rescue will be from, rather than with, the social scene, the human arena. *Samsāra*, to be sure, tells us, in the words of Hebrews 13.14, that 'here we have no continuing city'. But the trouble with our cities is much more than their flux and change. Their slums and their corridors of power persist with a stubbornness which cannot well be comprehended as merely flowing. Cessation of desire, it may be said, would solve the problem. But what of desires, angry, ugly, wild, and collective, which refuse to cease?

It is here that the familiar image of the lotus blooming from the mud, for all its fascination, hardly takes in the living situation. The lotus may be pure and unaccountably benign. But the mud remains. Are there not dimensions of collective evil and mass craving where a man on a cross, and wood and nails, would more comprehensively signal the pattern of truth and cleansing? Techniques of meditation are necessarily personal, to reach a final disowning, within the impulses of body and mind from which *tanha* proceeds. What can be the effective disciplines when these are writ large in corporate selfishness or tribal motives or class interest? Buddhism, it is true, brought emancipation from the caste system of Hinduism in that its Eightfold Path was open to all without advantage or handicap of birth, demanding only the will to take it. Yet, in Theravāda terms there was an élitism, and a privacy, about it, by virtue of its claims. How far does the unthinking, required of the monks and exemplary to the 'laity', integral as it is to meditation, nevertheless divert the will, or even the attention, from those grim areas of the human scene which pure contemplation must transcend or only entertain as parables of what must be escaped? Can there be a 'suffering' which actually undertakes them? Or, in other words, has *dukkha* too introspective a *raison d'être*? What dimensions of the pain or travail of it might there be from the fact that those central qualities of the Eightfold Path about language, action and livelihood, have been so grievously denied and decried in society at large and in the entail of bitter history, the false speech of propaganda, the inequalities of exploitation, the callousness of violent deeds?

It is precisely here that there is a strange irony about the basic Buddhist concept, attained by the Buddha himself in ultimate illumination beneath the Bodhi tree, namely 'dependent origination'. 'Who sees dependent origination', says *Majjhima Nikaya* (1.190–1), 'sees *Dharma*: who sees *Dharma* sees dependent origination.' The 'dependence' here is that of perpetual samsaric flux, embracing all in the sequence of non-abiding and unrelieved conditionality. But if one reads this interlocking, inter-entailing situation in the moral terms of Christian, indeed of Semitic, conscience, one is moving within just those tangled, haunting realms of collective guilt, of institutional sin, of corporate greed, and so of vicarious tribulation, which redemption faces and love must undertake. 'The bundle of life' is then seen and endured as a web of complicity and tragedy, where exploitation here spells disaster there, where power betrays the powerless, where culpable blindness originates tragic evil, where a pseudo-innocence pleads a criminal exoneration. What, it must be fair to ask, will private contemplation achieve in such a world, except perhaps a congratulation of immunity? Without sustained, imaginative, practical and costly, acts of redemption, the sequences which persist in human structures and societies will breed after their manner. For evil is only 'borne away' (as the ambiguity of the Greek verb has it in John 1.29) when it is 'borne'.

What happens within our human interrelatedness, social, economic, communal, personal, in ethical 'dependent origination', must be either love and truth ventured, or wrong wrought and incurred. On these, for either party in every exchange, must turn what further ensues, whether resentment, compound enmity, apathetic despair, or creative reconciliation. A meditative discipline may well educate what reaction should be, provide perspective in which to reach it, and generate the soul-resources with which to respond. But it will not do so as long as such meditation occupies itself only with the inward self and not with the human complex, with the samsaric philosophy of non-autonomy, rather than with the deeds and distresses of the will to autonomy in all its capacity both for contradiction and vocation.

It is a Christian truism that what matters in personal life-experience is not what happens but how we respond to what happens. Meditation must determine, test and sustain the criteria by which response must be guided. It must also equip the spirit to relate duly to the making of it. Is not the 'long' of long-suffering the resilience which, despite deterrence 'dependably originating' from lethargy or despair or confusion, is resolutely set to redeem the evil and undertake the good? Such resilience does not concede that there are no counter 'originations' arising from within the heart to resist and reverse the entail of evil or to translate into events the spontaneous impulses of good. Nor could it proceed upon the meditative principle, however laudable, in contemplation merely for *samsara*'s sake, but only through the contemplation which kindles moral energy. Wilfred Owen had it eloquently in his war poetry:

> when much blood had clogged their chariot wheels,
> I would go up and wash them from sweet wells,
> Even with truths that lie too deep for taint.
> I would have poured my spirit without stint
> But not through wounds: not by the cess of war.
> Foreheads of men have bled where no wounds were.[13]

Here, surely, is the verdict of the Christ-principle upon the deep intentions of the Eightfold Path, a commentary which asks through what territory it is walking. For the territory of this transient world, though it be the same human mortality, varies for the wayfarer according to the clues by which he reads it, the signs from which he draws its meaning. Consciousness, in the different religions, has a strange capacity to determine its own content, even from the same evidences and the shared reality. The body, too, serving consciousness and mediating it, yields contrasted signals, according to whether it is indwelt as a vehicle of serene repose, or passionate appetite, or grateful celebration and deliberate consecration, whether the focus is its navel, or its sexual power, or its capacity to be a temple.

The doctrine of the Pali Canon conceives of a force, or consciousness, passing over at death from one body-link to birth within another, even though the persistent-self idea of the partnership is an illusion. This tenacity, if such it be, whereby the non-persistent nevertheless persists is not only conceptually puzzling, it is also suggestive in the present context. If consciousness has this – on Buddhist terms – deplorable capacity to pass over into new physical embodiment, may not consciousness, in such personal identity, be thought capable of passing over compassionately into other selves with their all too real 'self-ness' present and contemporary? To venture the question is, of course, to leave the Theravāda concern with egohood in interior psycho-physical dimension, and to assume what Theravāda abjures, namely the societal and ethical authenticity of persons in relationship. That decision is certainly within the options of an intelligent assessment of our human experience. For the inter-personal situation, as we all know it, is no less relevant a clue to our religious interpretation of life than the Theravāda preoccupation with the strictly private psycho-physical entity and its *tanhā* thrust. Indeed, much more relevant might be claimed, since the appetitive urge on which Buddhism rests its case only 'burns as thirst' amid a human context. It is precisely that context which, if only taken warmly and steadily as evocative of courage, devotion, celebration and love, has the power to allay the burning of thirst and to transform it into generous desire – desire to be and to belong, to possess and to participate. Is it not in this direction that the developments in Mahāyāna Buddhism clearly point? There is much surmise, but little unequivocal evidence, that Christian factors, at the time of the rise of Mahāyāna, may have been involved. Whatever the history here may be, the implications are certainly Christward in a broad sense. For they have to do with the possibility of grace, the end of solitariness, and the legitimation of communion and community in the making of the soul.

VII

These reflections lead us to the final feature of Theravāda Buddhism in which all that is at issue with the significance of Christ comes to a head, namely the absence of final worth and ultimate worship. Despite sympathetic efforts within Asian and other theology to read something of theism into the ineffable *nirvana*, it seems clear that there is no place within Buddhism for the intentionality behind all things which is the theme of creation, of human creaturehood and of divine personality. This seems evident from the very assurance with which western writers influenced by Theravāda, like Don Cupitt, so confidently – indeed magisterially – announce the demise of traditional theism. So doing, they disjoin what centuries of Christian, Judaic and Islamic worship have steadfastly confessed, namely that the human dignity obtains under divine transcendence and that the autonomy we experience *qua* artisans, scientists, artists and poets is a gift and trust acknowledged within an awareness of a hospitality, a having-been-let-be, deriving from creative will, from God as gracious. Such an understanding of our being, as divinely commissioned and given crucially into our hands with a view to the divine glory *via* the crisis of our decision, is quite reversed in Buddhist reckoning. It there becomes an autonomy of ultimate enigma – in that the wheel of existence is inexplicable – and an autonomy of necessary voidance in cessation, a requirement to desist from what experience presents but philosophy finds illusory.

Where there is any rescue of transcendent meaning, as in Cupitt, it is constituted wholly in the human sustaining of values by which we assert our being, without reference to the givenness that theism affirms. On that score we are simply here with totality in human aegis, in no way referable to transcendent intention or creating will, and interpreted by ultimate criteria only and as *we* affirm and shape them. On such a reading of the situation, no Christhood could enter or avail. For Christhood belongs only within theism. Messianic achievement is continuous with, and sequential from, a Creator's faithfulness, as the Prologue of the Fourth Gospel tells.

The sense, unique to theism, that we are here as guests within divine hospitality and that all things are by fiat of divine responsibility, Buddhism categorically disallows. The consequent absence of those attitudes of wonder, gratitude, dominion, liability and vocation which such conviction teaches and sustains is the measure of the loss of worship. It is the price of taking the option by which, in the search for meaning and truth, we begin and stay within the human psyche and not with the mysterious whole around us, with the senses and with phenomena in their capacity to suggest illusion, not with personhood and the astonishing world in their ability to sustain significance.

There have been numerous intellectual ventures from within Buddhism to debate and disprove the Judeo-Christian-Islamic apprehension of God, some of them careful and reverent, others crudely controversial. But these, whether analogous to western, Humean, Schopenhaueran, scepticism, or otherwise, have never been the vital factor. The fact is that Buddhism, or at least its Theravāda form, has never wanted to be theological. If we use Immanuel Kant's famous phrase about 'the starry heaven above and the moral law within', Buddhism has opted essentially for the second and read it, not integrally in the context of the other so that there might be 'categorical imperatives' in some way pertaining to categorical indicatives, but severely within the context of a human psychology intent on its interior workings, temptations, appetites, frustrations and deceits. It is part of the meaning of the Christ that these, with all their urgent 'burning thirst' can find their answer only in the larger, broader context of creation under God and of God, acknowledged by our creaturehood, in the disclosure, responsive to just such urgency, which we have in Christ.

It is this challenge of a total exclusion of theology which Buddhism brings to theologians everywhere in whatever tradition. It is the challenge of complete otherness to what makes Jew, Christian and Muslim who they are. The otherness is conceptually total and there is little point in trying to reduce it. Techniques of meditation can never be the sum of salvation for the Christian. For he can never reduce what salvation intends or means to a transaction in the psyche by the psyche from the psyche. Salvation, for him, is 'heart and mind in the knowledge and love of God', with God the great initiator and *consummator* in Christ.

Nevertheless the meditative disciplines of the Eightfold Path, insofar as they are separable from its prepossessions, may serve the theist well, in alerting the soul to the pitfalls and vagaries of worship itself. The will desiring the way is no less prone to deception and disorder when it moves in the positive awareness of the phenomenal world proper to acknowledged creaturehood than when it passes through studied disengagement and abnegation. The sense of what discipline demands and why will be radically contrasted, as we have seen, by virtue of the recognition of the sacramental dimension both of body-habitation and of nature-dominion. But that deep contrast need not exclude a certain kinship of will by which Buddhist and Christian confess their liability for the selfhood from which all verdicts and pathways must begin.

The Buddha forbearing to enter illuminative bliss in order to enlighten others by delaying his own *nirvana* is a familiar theme wherever he is named, as also are the *bodhisattvas* of the Mahāyāna tradition who emulate such compassionate grace, for the aiding of mortals in need. It is perhaps here that we can best take leave of cross-reference into Buddhism by our theology. For the heart of what is between us may be expressed in the Christian readiness to see compassion as the very clue to sovereignty. Here is the central meaning of worship – the confidence to believe about what is ultimate and transcendent what we find ultimate in the intimacy of our own human finitude, namely a love which cares and undertakes and suffers. Such is the logic between creaturehood and Creatorship at the heart of biblical faith. The Christian reads the mystery behind the stars in the clues of human capacities for love and finds both disclosed in Christhood according to Jesus. Buddhism, it might be fair to say, is patiently compassionate almost in spite of itself – though the tasks of such compassion are set by its diagnosis of what demands them. The invitation from Jesus and his Christhood is to release that compassion from the constraints which *dukkha*, *anicca* and *anatta* determine and impose, and allow it as a presence from an otherwise excluded vision, a dimension differently grounded and fulfilled in the faith that makes it central to the cosmos and perceives it as the sure index to God.

The Buddhist may find that conclusion merely proof of incorrigible Christian illusion. But perhaps not. As long as compassion awaits us as the duty in which, for the Buddha, the

Eightfold Path terminated and for which its consummation must be postponed, need it be illusory to ask whether compassion might not encounter us in the very outset, not only of our own private mortal journey but as the crux of all things? If compassion is the goal where discipline arrives, may it not be the initiative whence all things derive? If so, we may turn with courage from what was climax for the Buddha to what is beginning in the gospel. Both Buddhist and Christian will find compassion bound into the very bundle of life and will continue therein. The impulses are sadly unlike.

NOTES

1 *Ittivuttaka* 23.

2 See the discussion of vocabulary in this theme in Bruce Matthews, *Craving and Salvation: A Study in Buddhist Soteriology* (Ontario 1983), pp. 74–85.

3 The title of Stephen Collins' *Selfless Persons* (Cambridge 1982), being a study of Buddhism.

4 Bruce Matthews, loc. cit., where soteriology is claimed for Buddhism simply on the ground that it 'intends' salvation, though the content of the term radically departs from what is held salvific elsewhere.

5 There can, of course, be no complete atrophy of the senses in human experience. Physical pain or its absence will be felt. But this is very different from the positive and legitimate place of sense-experience. The *arhant* of necessity continues to receive the record of the senses but their stimulus and significance have no entry into one's spiritual equilibrium.

6 William Shakespeare, *Hamlet*, Act 5, Scene 2, lines 350–1.

7 *Digha Nikaya* 2.292.

8 'Dependent origination' is a basic term and theme of Buddhist *Dharma* and denotes the law of entire contingency whereby all that occurs to finite things is conditioned by some factor or cause. By the stopping of ignorance (i.e. illusion of autonomy), it is held that the causal sequence can be 'undone' backwards in ultimate escape from *samsāra*. The sentence to which this note refers uses the term in a quite different sense, i.e. to affirm genuine initiative in interpersonal relationships.

9 Ezra Pound, *The Cantos of Ezra Pound* (London 1964), Canto xlv, pp. 239–40.

10 The term 'cankers' (*asava*) in the counsels of Buddhism denotes the harmful dispositions within consciousness which it is the purpose of the discipline to overcome. A Pali-English dictionary gives the definition: 'That which intoxicates the mind so that it cannot rise to higher things' (115). Sensuality is, of course, a 'canker', but the term concerns also the mind's proneness to pretension, idle speculation and indulgence in ignorant illusion.

11 Ezra Pound, *Hugh Selwyn Mauberley* (London 1920), Stanza iii:
'Caliban casts out Ariel: we see *to kalon*/Decreed in the marketplace ...'
('Tokalon' being the trade name of cosmetics, i.e. beauty consists in face
creams and powders. Artificiality corrupts all.)

12 Dylan Thomas, *Collected Poems, 1934–1952* (London 1952), p. 8.

13 Wilfred Owen, *War Poems and Others*, ed. with Introd. and Notes by
Dominic Hibberd (London 1973), p. 103.

14
Bona Fiducia Christiana

I

In his *Grace Abounding* John Bunyan tells of desperate disquiets in the biography of his faith, his search for inward peace. With his rural setting and his lowly trade one would not expect him to be troubled by the plurality of religions. But when doubts multiplied and tormented, it came to him that his struggling faith might have no better credentials than those of alien believers and their other creeds. He was agitated by the idea he was tempted, much against his will, to entertain.

> The tempter also would much assault me with this: 'How can you tell but that the Turks has as good scriptures to prove their Mahomet the Saviour, as we have to prove our Jesus is? And, could I think so many ten thousands, in so many countries and kingdoms should be without the knowledge of the right way to heaven . . . and that we only, who live in a corner of the earth, should alone be blessed therewith? Every one doth think his own religion rightest, both Jews and Moors and Pagans: and how if all our faith, and Christ, and scriptures, should be but a think so too?'

Our precious convictions only a think so too? We as much in make-believe as they? The exclusive problem as a doubt-breeder? The anxieties are familiar enough. Bunyan reached, as all do, for some reassuring authority, some guarantor beyond distrusting. In context his choice was Paul.

> I have endeavoured to argue against these suggestions and to set some of the sentences of blessed Paul against them . . . Though we made so great a matter of Paul and his words, yet how could I tell but that in very deed . . . he might give himself up to deceive . . .?[1]

Perhaps even the most venerated were not to be trusted. It is just what, or whom, we invoke to allay doubt that has the more urgent necessity to be exempt from it and for that very reason comes under the more anxious question. Surmise will always be the more menacing for those who want to be impregnable in their believing. Other religions, even if only

superficially realized, have a way of arousing the surmise and
so troubling the security. For Bunyan the anxiety was no mere
mental puzzle: it belonged with his whole integrity, his wrestling with sinfulness, his simple honesty of will.

'Only a think so too' – the verdict readily proposing itself
to us about others – has to be allowed to those others about
ours. Faith is not 'good faith' if it is only negative and dismissive
about plural creeds and religions. Its credentials must allow
the inspection of coexistence. This was the *bona fide* with which
we began in Chapter 1. We have since traversed four great
areas of religious expressions of faith, attempting by cross-
reference to submit the Christian convictions to their interrogation and to respond accordingly. The effort has yielded a variety
of themes and issues which must become in turn a task of
Christian self-interrogation. To these, in conclusion, we must
now pass.

II

But to have ultimate convictions suspect, by others or ourselves,
as only 'a think so too' is to raise radical questions about religious allegiance. These obviously have to do with much more
than intellectual believing. They involve themes of identity,
continuity, loyalty to heritage, social relationships, institutional
sanctions of behaviour and community, and much else within
the psyche, both collective and personal. They also require that
we face the sharp issue of just how the personal and the corporate interrelate in matters of faith. There is clearly no 'faith' without 'the faithful' constituted either by the other.[2] Persons in
their private capacity are plainly indebted totally to the collective past of doctrine and definition through which alone the
faith came to them and still avails. Yet it is only theirs by actual
participation and the personal equation. It was, indeed, that
personal equation, through the long centuries, which enabled
the faith to endure. How then does the personal commitment
belong with the historic sequence? Individuals have no right
to be cavalier with what they inherit. But nor have they the
option to see it as a deposit in a bank, its security – or, so
to say, its meaning – guaranteed without them. It is persons,
through the exchanges of the daily world, who most encounter
the implications of pluralism for religious authority and doctrine. Systems and collectives as such come much more slowly
and ponderously to meeting and relation.

There are, therefore, endless points of tension implicit in individuals relating across religious frontiers and in the implications of their ventures for the long legacies that make the frontiers. John Henry Newman's consuming desire to come to the end of all 'private judgement' and be wholly submissive to and ruled by 'authoritarian faith' can hardly obtain where faiths are required to meet.[3] For his stance of holding only what 'mother Church' had infallibly authenticated for him (though that stance itself was a deep occasion of a 'private judgement') is just the posture which, duly reciprocated by all, would foreclose everything. To adopt it would simply be to refuse all cognizance of pluralism and so to opt out of this world. It would be to enthrone one authority unilaterally or to imprison one and all incommunicado.

Requiring, or allowing, religious authority to be, in those terms, arbitrary and self-sufficing would be effectively the end of ecumenical impulses from personal believers. Yet how should such believers square their ventures with their loyalties? How, through them and because of them, will those loyalties be handled, read or re-read, by the collectives – time-sanctioned, culture-housed, prejudice-prone, power-ridden – which define and hold them?

Faiths, traditionally and temperamentally, differ in their attitude and capacities in this regard. Each has to react and speak for itself alone, affected as response must surely be by the quality that others bring. Our duty here is with the broad relation of the Christian concept of itself, as 'Christianity', to the searching issues the foregoing chapters have raised. There is much to which that self-image and definition must address itself in respect, for example, of the 'unity' of the Bible, the limitations of the finality of the New Testament Canon, the recognition of Christian incorporation of meanings wider than the Hebraic heritage and their liturgical expression. Hence the term *fiducia*, used here to denote the whole corpus of Christian doctrine and tradition which the *fides* of Chapter 1 possesses and fulfils. We are asking: What does the faith enjoin on faithfulness? How does faithfulness hold the faith? The two questions are really one.

This faith/faithfulness situation has sometimes been thought to admit of some ambiguity, or even discrepancy, between what is institutionalized and regulated in dogma and what is personally sustained by intellectually active adherents. The three

Semitic faiths, for example, for all their instinctive definiteness, give persistent evidence of personal or private deviance within a formal recognition of what orthodoxy or orthopraxy categorically require. Hinduism, in its capacity to be amorphous and indefinable, may need this tact less frequently. But it is no surprise to find, among others, Roman Catholic Christians, or Sunnī Muslims, or Mahāyāna Buddhists, readily conceding, indeed upholding, doctrines seen proper to corporate identity and the continuity of church or *Ummah* or *Sangha/Dharma*, while retaining a private freedom to see them, or think them, differently for purposes of their own integrity. Some find it permissible to see their adherence to a public orthodoxy privately doubted, as a deliberate oblation of individual intelligence to institutional authority. Liberty of thought is then, as it were, privatized, on behalf of the necessary working of the dogma-system which limits or denies it.

This paradox has certainly to be reckoned with in studying how loyalty reacts with tradition and how tradition commands loyalty. Faith-systems differ in their concepts and practice about the range, temper and quality of dogma and the room they give or deny to mind and spirit within them. The issues, also, are sharply affected by passions political and national whence springs so much currently, in Islam and Judaism and some forms of Christianity in the Middle East, to make tradition vociferous and loyalty unbridled. In that setting the theme we are discussing is darkly overridden by zealous obscurantism and blind assertion. The question then passes to a dimension beyond either dogma or loyalty in themselves, to the ability of a religion truly to be religious, that is, to know itself obligated to truth and love against, if need be, its own self. Such an ability is more likely to characterize private minds than public masses.

In this whole context, it will not do to say, for example, 'Islam is what Muslims say it is',[4] unless one allows 'Islam' at the same time to determine who are the Muslims with the 'say'. There is, necessarily, what Lesslie Newbigin has recently called a 'fiduciary framework'[5] in which every faith subsists and by which its relationships are governed. A theology cannot keep faith with contemporary challenge and play false with its past. To be *bona fide* in the one means *bona fiducia* in the other. The ultimates by which religions live are not, as it were, negotiable under popular pressures or in the pursuit of mutual relations.

To think them so would deny to them that quality of givenness and finality by which alone they proceed. It is only a few brave souls who can, so to speak, sustain absolutes for which their own will to believe them is the only warrant. All the great faiths, in their diversity, have availed, and do avail, by virtue of an authority inherent in themselves. Hence, of course, the psychology of 'fundamentalism' when it is feared that this authority is coming into question. Hence, too, the drift of scepticism into irreligion and secularity; or its taking refuge in another 'fundamentalism'. It is not in the nature of religion to consent to be indifferent about its own claims. Indifferent to the evils within it and around it, it may well be, and the claims made on it by time, society, memory and duty, but not indifferent to its claim for the transcendent or its version of what is final.

When such versions meet, when they effectively discover that they are not alone in interpreting mystery and the world, but must converse and articulate their finality where it can no longer be assumed, it is then that they face, or it may well be evade, the double obligation to waive their finality and relearn how to commend it.

Both go very much against the grain, not merely of inertia, or fear, but of emotional allegiance and cultural sanction. The will to be authentic wrestles with the yearning to be secure. Thought may point forward to where the psyche is unwilling to go. Theology in the context of inter-faith somewhat resembles a caravan impatient with itself both about movement and delay. Both its direction and its pace are in dispute. The global vision struggles with the parochial scene. How should ventures of spirit relate to deposits of faith? The latter have the creeds, the liturgies, the symbols, the practices by which the former should be weighed but may well also be inhibited. Then there are the tender souls to whom tradition is so dear, puzzled at the seeming threat to their familiar world, or daunted by the forbidding face of the other worlds of believing presented to their minds. A theology of cross-reference will have pastoral tasks at home in broaching its intellectual and spiritual tasks over the frontiers. Both aspects of this vocation belong together and neither should thwart the other.

III

That there are radical questions to be asked and decisions taken, if Christian theology is to respond truly to world religions, is

evident from all the foregoing chapters and their review of
things at issue with the major living four. To take up those
questions under the rubric of *fiducia Christiana* – what the trust
is and being entrusted with it – requires five related honesties.
Seeing the duty they impose as both pastoral and intellectual,
a spirituality both to nourish and to communicate, it will be
useful to borrow the accents of the first of the Pastoral Epistles
of the New Testament.[6] The First Epistle to Timothy is imbued
with the sense of the gospel in trust and in that context it has
intriguing turns of phrase and points of vocabulary which can
well carry the thrust of the present argument. These will fall
shortly into place. But let us first list the five honesties in broad
outline before setting a commendation of them within the *fiducia*
that lives and speaks in 1 Timothy. The first is a present realism,
free of proud illusions. The second is a resolute sense of 'the
gospel of the blessed God' (1 Tim. 1.11). The third is its hospitality to *and from* all cultures. The fourth is how that openness
has to relate to Scriptures canonized once and for all. The fifth
is the nature of the theological will and warrant by which faith
is confessed.

The alert reader of the New Testament can be under no illusions about what Paul called 'the magnitude of the struggle
in which I am engaged . . .' as to how mankind might be 'led
to a complete comprehension of God's secret which is nothing
less than Christ' (Col. 2.1–2). The Pastoral Epistles, too, in their
more prosaic style, breathe a deep spirit of concern and make
sober reckoning with the world around. 'Take heed to yourself
and to the doctrine', Timothy is told, significantly, in that order
(1 Tim. 4.16). His church, or churches, lived as a despised
minority with no pretension to power, or status. But they were
keenly aware of society around noting their conduct and testing
their nerve. Hence the meticulous directives about due order,
godly discipline and well-knit community, and a patient vigilance against aberrations both of thought and character.

It all reads very simply and precisely when we try to translate
it into the idiom of our contemporary complexity, our legacies
and accumulations of twenty centuries. Christain faith, at least
in Europe, its main historical area of strength, far from a scorned
minority, has been the theme of culture and the mentor of
power, the legatee of long tradition. That situation is now ended
and the experience of secularity, indifferentism and vehemently
hostile philosophies like Nazism, has yet to be fully digested

in theological response or reckoning. Mentalities are always slow to adjust to vital but protracted reversals of their familiar and cherished assumptions, the more so when these still enjoy physical tokens of what they once were, in architecture or the calendar or cultural remnants of their dominance.

The main point here about this western secularity and its implications for Christian fidelities is its significance, real or alleged, for other faiths. Their readings and reactions are various, sometimes boasting a proud immunity from the contagion, at others apprehensive of the same corrosives and proposing inter-religious concert to arrest them. But in and beyond these is the frequent impression other faiths have, especially Islam, that Christianity has somehow failed to discipline and retain its allegiance even in its own civilization. Jews may assess the situation, by perspectives of Judaism, as a Christian form of their long tussle with minority status and host-culture, a Christian education in the vocation to persist and survive against the odds. But Muslims are more liable to a contrast of triumphalism, a proof of the sounder religious sinews of Islam as a faith more durable if less idealist, tougher because wiser about power and theological 'simplicity'. Buddhists, of course, read western malaise and, within it, Christian effeteness, as merely demonstrating the mistaken reading of human existence which theism entails.

It is evident that there can be no relating of Christian faith to others in cross-reference which does not take lively account of this 'domestic' crisis obtaining for Christianity itself. There are some cynics who note that Christians are in the van of 'dialogue' – often with little reciprocal enthusiasm elsewhere – and who, therefore, read dialogue-seeking from the Christian side as a way of forgetting, or disguising, the crisis within. Is it all somehow a loss of nerve, a paradox of confidence being sought in 'encounter' because it has been forfeited in 'mission'? Certainly the Christian mind is chastened by the evident relinquishment, by and large, of missionary expectation *vis-à-vis* the four major faiths we have been studying. That expectation was buoyed in the nineteenth century, and earlier in this twentieth, by the conditions of imperial government across much of Asia, and by the apparent weakness or inertia of Asian religions under disadvantage or disillusionment.[7] It looks differently now in the age of new nationalisms, the recovery and reform of faiths in their neo-forms or in new vibrancy of the old. Cross-reference theology has to be a theology of mission in retrospect taking due cognizance of historical exper- ience.

This duty of present realism is underlined by the presence of numerous minorities within European society, possessing and defending their faiths from comparable cultural disadvan- tage or privation to that of Christian minorities in Asia and elsewhere. Those religious minorities have immediate aware- ness of the crisis for Christianity because of secularity and the recession of faith and practice alike within the increasing vulgar- ity, scepticism and hedonism of western society. They must estimate Christianity by different criteria from those, of their allegiance formerly and elsewhere, who encountered an evan- gelizing Christianity whose missionary presence could be read, however erroneously, as suggesting that all was thoroughly and securely Christian in the lands from which it came. This means that Christian commendation of the gospel is compelled to a more discerning, more lowly, more contrite relation to other faiths in *their* postures and resources. It need not mean any less urgent or less proven warrant for such commendation. It does mean an honest humility in its ventures, an honesty which is ready to face and feel the onus for patient interpre- tation and genuine realism. 'Judgement', it was written in a New Testament Epistle, 'must begin at the house of God' (1 Peter 4.17). There is no true theology with external relations today which is not first introspective. The areas of inward inquest cannot be isolated from the hopes of outward mission or meeting.

IV

The great positives of the faith certainly invite to such realism, where that we called the second honesty belongs: 'the gospel of the glory of the blessed God' (1 Tim. 1.11). This resounding sentence holds the vital clue. It is a *theo*logy which we have in trust, a vision of the transcendent, a divine Lordship self- disclosed and faith-identified in self-expending, world-embrac- ing love of which Christhood according to Jesus is the point and symbol. 'Self-disclosed and faith-identified': that is the mutuality, within history, of event and experience, of being-in- meaning and meaning-in-being, God's and ours. The gospel through and through is about God. But it is about God in dimensions and *via* indices which are nowhere else reached or read as they are in Jesus as the Christ and the Christ as crucified for love of man.

The clear distinctiveness of this faith has concerned us throughout this book. 'Unique' is not a word to use here. For it has an exclusiveness, even a hostility, about it, as that which is totally 'other'. The gospel, however, has many 'overlaps' but with them, and indeed because of them, possesses a quality, holds a content, in terms affirmed and cherished nowhere else. Buddhism would never allow history to contain redemption as the cross is understood to do, nor read in such concreteness the glory of transcendence. Yet its prescripts about the self have implicit relevance to the 'why' though not to the 'whence' of such redemption, its bearing on the human predicament though not its issue from the heart of God. Judaism, from Hosea to Heschel, deeply partners – indeed must be said to originate – Christianity's vision of divine pathos, of painful divine yearning over earth. But Judaism finally focuses that yearning around its own humanity rather than the human whole, and would never find it once for all enshrined in a cross as messianic fact. There is what is gratefully common in what is deeply distinctive.

Consistent also with Islamic monotheism is the affirmation of divine sovereignty from which 'the gospel of the blessed God' proceeds. Divine greatness is nowhere in question between Muslim and Christian, only our comprehension of its measure and criterion. The Christology which Christian *fiducia* treasures has an evident continuity with the mission of prophethood so central to Islam. As we have seen, truth-bearing from God, *via* prophethood, to the human realm reveals a logic in which message and messenger become indistinguishable, word passes into life and life becomes the word. When it does so, given human passion and prophetic steadfastness, the word that becomes life is likely to be the life that becomes suffering. There is nothing alien to the implicit sequence here in the rationale of pre-Hijrah Islam. What is distinctively Christian and repugnant to Islam is the conviction that it happened so in Jesus and happened so, conformably to the very nature and glory of God. The crux of Christianity is anathema for Islam. But they are one in pleading, so disparately, 'the glory of the blessed God'.

Honesty, then, with distinctiveness is, in every direction, the nature of the Christian *fiducia*. It is just this which compels attentiveness on our part to the *whole* reaction of others, in their capacity to share as well as in their mind to reject. This posture, at once hopeful and forthright, is consistent with the very nature of the gospel. It is determined to find allies wherever it can precisely because it has so much at issue. Since it is about God over all, it could not well do otherwise. A thing in trust exacts right dealing not only with its content but with its destination. It must be passed unimpaired but it must not miscarry in the passing.

There are many, surveying the contemporary scene, who suggest that somehow the great symbol of Christianity has lost its power and its appeal. The man on the cross seems so far in the past. Easter, we are told, is a premature celebration. Faith in Jesus is a sort of auto-persuasion of good and of goodness which hardly tallies with the enigma, the violence, the tedium, of the real world. Jewry cries out that all thinking must now be post-Holocaust, that evils now have a range, a horror, a depth, a persistence, which no single event in the past, however cherished, however sacred, can possibly enshrine, still less retrieve or save. The nettle of power, say the Muslims, must be firmly grasped so that we may 'pluck this flower – safety'.[8] A gospel about God and grace, which thinks somehow to proceed, political power and its guilt apart, on the resources of love and long-suffering, has no credible purchase on things as they are and must be allowed to be. Hinduism, in measure, pays tribute to saviours and devotion, but only by fantasizing them into myth and saga, with no sacrament in history. Perhaps the Christian, though, is only fantasizing when he sees Calvary, however actual in time and place, as admitting of the claim: 'Be of good cheer; I have overcome the world' (John 16.33).

All these voices of disavowal may perhaps be gathered into the irony with which Dickens in *Bleak House* introduces Jo, the crossing sweeper, crouching on the doorstep of the Society for the Propagation of the Gospel. In a later scene, we find him gnawing some scraps of charity within sight of St Paul's, before police arrive to move him on.

There he sits, looking up at the great Cross on the summit of St. Paul's Cathedral ... From the boy's face one might suppose that sacred emblem to be, in his eyes, the crowning confusion of the great confused city – so golden, so high up, so far out of his reach.[9]

Deepen that irony, banish the sentiment by which Dickens charmed his readers, let the enigmas that beset faith and the wrongs that flout it be what they are and, paradoxically, it will appear that it is only a theology of the cross, not a theology of bland omnipotence or divine immunity, which can undertake the burden of the mystery. In architecture it may be said about the arch that its ability for loads comes oddly from the loads themselves. It is a piece of engineering designed to make the thrust of weight upon it the very strength by which to bear it. Being held together by its keystone and springing from secure foundations, its arms turn their burden into strength. Its solidity and the pressure strangely combine. In this way the arch creates and secures the space beneath where things can happen because of it. It is thus a true paradigm of love and of redemption. At the heart of 'the gospel of the blessed God' is a proven divine capacity to love and the cross is where we can know it so. There too is a bearing of evil which is a bearing away of it. It is the way of love, like the arch, to turn its obligations into its achievements. What the gospel holds in trust is an event 'in the world of all of us' worthy to be acknowledged as the point and pledge of a divine love responding redemptively to human wrong. It is an acknowledgement which Christian thought and experience find the more authentic as awareness of other faiths makes its distinctiveness the more compelling. The ground of such a conclusion will concern us again in our fifth 'honesty'. It has, meanwhile, much to preoccupy in the areas earlier set down.

V

The third in the sequence had to do with the hospitality of this *fiducia* to and from every culture. Both prepositions are important. We can state the point usefully by reference to the familiar words in 1 Timothy 1.15 as to the 'faithful saying' which deserves complete *apodochē*, i.e. acceptance or reception. The writer repeats the phrase in 1 Tim. 4.11 and it reads like an emerging formula for things credal. *Apodochēs axios* means 'worthy of welcome', and with *pasēs* 'universal welcome'.[10] The immediate sense is that the faith merits an acceptance which is entire and unreserved. But this can hardly be unless it is a welcome springing genuinely from within a free responsiveness and motivated there. Acceptance can never result from sheer dictation or assertion from without, or not, at least, in respect of gospel. That which results from coercion or duress is not acceptance.[11] It is, in this respect, with grace as it is with humour: the prosperity of either is in the hearer's recognition.

What merits entire welcome merits entire circulation. *Omni acceptione dignus* says the Vulgate, in the 1947 English translation: 'What a welcome it deserves!' The universal range must be argued from the all-commendable content. This means that our theology must always be alert for the impulses of welcome which must therefore be latent everywhere and with all faiths. Not so to believe, and anticipate accordingly, would be to call in question the merit of the gospel as something which cannot rightly be privatized or read as belonging restrictedly to bits of humanity, however privileged or circumscribed, and not to the whole. The Christian faith is not to be delimited to these, and not those, to some and not to others, without violation of its very nature.

It is often assumed that the gospel makes its way only by a total otherness, by contradiction of what it finds. Its authority is then one of judgement. It must disavow what it meets before it can enter. The sequence to its impact, paradoxically, is discontinuity. This can hardly be so, if it is truly to 'merit welcome'. That it has, in its 'blessedness of God' a wholly distinctive ground of welcome, we have already seen. But sheer otherness could neither show merit nor kindle welcome. Nor is total discontinuity a feasible thing in human perception of truth. That moral transformation must be radical is not in doubt. 'Old things are passed away . . .' But things conceptual must interact. The reception of what is new always turns upon categories already present.

Hence the duty honestly to perceive the gospel as open to a hospitality from within other faiths and therefore ready for a hospitality to them. Previous chapters have sought to indicate where this might happen, where the Christian can readily welcome meanings read elsewhere. Such meanings are then the points on which the gospel's meriting acceptance will turn. These may well be disconcerting as the discovery of unrealized love, the unlocking of mystery, or the realization of hope, are liable to be. None of these, however, occur without a positive readiness in the way of them. Exciting such readiness is the very communicability of truth.

It is easy to see how such a stance in respect of 'God in Christ' tallies with the doctrine of God in creation and, in creation, of the legitimate diversity of peoples, cultures and mentalities, as these are shaped and sustained by factors of the created order, territory, climate, race and memory. The exchange of hospitality on Christian part, consistent with *fiducia*, is no more than acknowledgment of the bond between the order of nature and the order of grace. In no way does it mean that we become sanguine about man in nature or oblivious of the perversities in all religion. But these, heinous as they are and present in all systems, have no final veto on the initiatives grace can arouse in its own direction through ministries that kindle expectations by being themselves expectant in their relationships.

This theme of 1 Tim. 1.15 about 'meriting acceptance' helps to clarify the temper of 'dialogue', that much over-used word in current theology. Too often dialogue can appear to be an exercise on which one does not enter without a prior assurance of winning. Or it is not genuine because either party is already sure of the issue and merely wants to demonstrate it. Or it is a mere exchange of statements, elucidatory perhaps but nontransactional. The analogy of hospitality helps escape from these assumptions of 'debate' so liable to artificiality. 'I will sup with him and he with me' (Revelation 3.20) in a different context was how the Lord described his venture with the soul. Dietary laws, in some quarters, have long been a symbol of estrangement and separation. Whatever rationale they may have in hygiene, they are humanly divisive. For long, even in faiths which do not enforce them, they have had their theological counterparts. 'Come eat of my bread' was the invitation from wisdom and her seven-pillared house (Proverbs 9.1–6). Between faiths, Christians must make themselves guests and learn thus to be hosts.

If we need neutral areas for these arts of hospitality we can readily find them outside theological or other doctrine – Scripture, Torah, *Dharma*, or whatever. We can find them in themes of common urgency: the family and its preservation, the mutual issues in parenthood and the new generation, communal relationships, the control of technology, ecology and ethics, the obligations and limitations of political power, religion itself as a structure of pride. We need a shared hospitality to, and because of, all these themes of our time. We recall that Peter in Acts 10 and 11 went furthest in both discovery and effectiveness, when he was not on his own ground, securely set in his tradition. Yet he was on Cornelius' ground, within a Roman's walls, only by invitation. This his repute and certain heavenly intimations had earned him. But his own response, however guarded and tentative at first, was vital to the outcome. And it all happened then because men, whether young or old, were 'seeing visions . . . dreaming dreams'. The intriguing narrative of Peter and Cornelius would seem to illustrate perfectly the two sides of 'meriting acceptance', a *fiducia* in risk.

VI

But, if this sort of openness, offered and evoked, is what *fiducia* in the gospel must bring in order to 'deserve welcome', there is much to be done with its own traditions. The third of our suggested duties merges into the fourth. If the Christian will to the *apodochē* of 1 Tim. 1.15 takes in the wideness of the world, it is served by its Scripture in terms of a very limited part of it. The issues here are spiritually very searching: psychologically they may be, for many, quite beyond their ability to face. The question remitted to us from all the foregoing, and especially from the chapters on India, is what we are to do, in the will to universality, with the severe geographical limitation of the New Testament and the closed-ness of the Canon. 'Jerusalem, round about unto Illyricum', – all of it 'westward ho!' (Romans 15.19) – is hardly a recipe for a documentation 'meriting acceptation' in further Asia, India, China, and the lands of the Buddha. Yet the formulation of the faith, and thus the terms of the *fiducia* with it, 'in letters of Hebrew and Greek and Latin' – for all their wealth and range still very partial – are the only ones scripturized, canonized and authorized as 'sufficient'. Clearly culturally they are painfully insufficient. A gospel that intends the world draws its articulation only from the Mediterranean.

The problem needs to be stated starkly before we can reassure ourselves about a solution. For the solution we can discern has difficult implications for our *fiducia*. Our theological task with 'the Christ and the Faiths' has to include our most treasured assumptions: the finality of the New Testament, the unity of the Bible, the range of lectionary in liturgy, and the extra-biblical antecedents of the incarnate Word. We are not asking whether Marcion, after all, was right.[12] We are asking whether Christian thought – and, no less important, devotion – have failed, in their biblical loyalties, to 'belong with mankind'.

It happens that 1 Timothy has a word in its vocabulary which may serve us to develop this fourth 'honesty'. It is *hedraiōma* in 3.15, where the Church is described as 'the pillar and ground of the truth'. *Hedraiōma*, the second term here, is linked closely with the first, *stulos*. It is uncannily close to that blessed word 'establishment', *via* the cognate verb. The Church is to the truth what pillars and their bases are to an edifice. *Stulos*, for a 'pillar' is also applied to an apostle or teacher (cf. Gal. 2.9 and Rev. 3.12). The role of persons in structures is always significant, not least in the things of faith. *Hedraiōma* is then the 'stay' on which the building stands, the solidity which 'establishes' the whole.[13]

The problem, however, with foundation metaphors and building imagery is how to provide for life and change. None can doubt that definition, doctrinal identity, spiritual security, are vital dimensions of faith. There can be no *fiducia* if there is no explicitness, no certitude, no dependable meaning institutionalized in creed and symbol. Conserving is inseparable from belonging, as guarding is from cherishing. There has to be 'contention for what is once for all delivered' (Jude 3). *Hedraiōma tēs alētheiās* is not in question. Church and Scriptures, in their interdependence, are its dual agency.

That Church, however, by its very nature, is not uni-national. It is not national at all, in its nature. Nor is it tribal, uni-cultural, or monolingual. Its Scriptures, nevertheless, were finalized within a highly partial phase of its universal destiny and at an early juncture in its history. There is no doubt that the Canon, through prolonged debate, was understood as a vital factor in any *fiducia* rightly discharged. It was a means of defence against vagary and heresy, a necessary element in conscious and vigilant identity. Indeed, to a degree, Canon-shaping and theology belonged together. We have, therefore, to align the closure of the Canon and theology ongoing, and ask what the consequences have been.

Many minds here will register immediate alarm, insist that the question of the Canon will not be reopened, and suggest that the point is too drastic to be allowed to arise. They may well be right that no reopening is practicable and that emotions about the sanctity, the inviolability, of Scripture must not be aroused. If so, the implications still have to be faced. Was the New Testament Canon premature? Was its instinctive association with the Hebraic Canon imperceptive, its unilateral loyalty to *one* heritage unimaginative or over-cautious? Having courageously affirmed a supra-racial, Jew *cum* gentile, quality, did it compromise it by a scriptural perpetuation of a partiality which left other cultures no canonical share or partnership? If we protest that New Testament and Patristic Christianity had no occasions to let Asia in, the point is dubious historically. But if we accept the point, we cannot plead it now without disowning a destiny said to be as wide as the world. For our geography is not that of the Fathers. Yet the Canon's remains so, and the Canon is the referent for faith, and loyal Bible translators are still painstakingly rendering Leviticus or Esther for the tongues of the far Pacific.

There were, of course, strong instincts behind the unity of the Bible idea. When Christian writings, letters and *logia* began to circulate in the churches and to be read in public worship and moral nurture, it was natural to associate the practice with synagogue lectionary habits and so, in turn, to develop the idea of a Christian Canon, complementing but not displacing the Hebraic one. There was obvious wisdom in that assumption in respect of past retrospect. But should it have been allowed to ride uncritically with future calling? To be historically formative is one thing: to be truly future-oriented is another.

Before turning to how we might respond to a situation we cannot now change and keep a critical loyalty to biblical unity, it may be useful to exemplify how an uncritical, undiscerning loyalty to it has actually or potentially compromised Christian integrity in *fiducia*. Painful and emotive as the theme must be, the honesty we are after cannot ignore it.

VII

If we agree that peoplehood under God, in the New Testament, is genuinely open to all on the sole ground of faith and indifferently as to birth, Jewish or otherwise, then we cannot ignore how continual liturgical use of Hebraic Scriptures which did not proceed upon such openness, has inculcated in the Church

the very proneness to national, ethnic, particularist consciousness which does not belong there. For all their deep and splendid quality of devotion and adoration, the Psalms breathe a
very powerful and insistent identity-vigilance which has passed
over into the ethos of the users. Its terms in the Psalms have
bolstered people-consciousness at the expense of the meaning
of the Church, or, worse still, identified the two. The bent of
all of us towards ethnic, political, even tribal, pride has no
doubt connived. But there is a 'them-and-us' divide about so
much in Old Testament history and psalmody which collides
with the ecclesial accessibility to all and stimulates what is all
too ready to be stimulated, namely the English, Russian, German, etc., or just human, tendency to recruit God for their
own exceptionality and ally his providence to their designs.

Even the loveliest of psalms have this sad ambivalence. There
is scarcely one rich *vade mecum* of the heart before God which
may not link its piety with enmity and its praise with its animad-
versions about others as foes. The exquisite Psalm 84 is pre-
ceded by Psalm 83. 'Thine enemies (i.e. God's) . . . have taken
crafty counsel against thy people . . . Let them be put to shame
and perish' – a sentiment negating the parallel plea: 'that they
may seek thy Name, O Lord'. 'Truly my soul waits upon God',
cries the psalmist in Psalm 62, but his mind moves at once to
his enemies and his maledictions on them: 'You shall be slain
all of you . . .' Examples are everywhere. The danger is that
this spirit of confrontation makes identity between a people's
foes and God's, and all subsequent users liable to the same
assumption, thus nourishing the very particularism of nations
or sects or causes which the will to be Church must renounce.

It may be argued that all this, like the Book of Joshua, can
be spiritualized into allegory. This hardly suits, for example,
Psalms 58 or 137, and in any event it must be doubtful whether
a right repudiation of inward evils marries well with sharply
nationalist or political animosity. Or it may be pleaded that
much psalmody relieves pent-up anger just in giving voice to
it and yielding its occasions up to God. Tensions may be mastered in being allowed to explode verbally. Whether this plea
is valid for Scripture and liturgy must surely be denied. Or
again, it may be said that psalmody is authentic and necessary
protest against the reality of evil, against what flouts the very
majesty whose worship all psalmody intends. Indeed, both
authentic and necessary: but only if in reading and repudiating

real evil we do not identify it wholly in others or in malice against ourselves. There *is* an innocence which suffers but it is not always our own and everything turns on the quality of the suffering. This the gospel of the cross knows only too well. It is not conspicuously in the mind of psalmists voicing national wrongs.

It seems sadly right to conclude that within the Bible the earlier Scriptures proceed in general from a quite different understanding of peoplehood than the later Scriptures. Whereas the Church achieved, albeit precariously, a definition of peoplehood quite contrasted in its non-ethnic, non-territorial character, it still continued loyally to nourish its piety and frame its worship in the language inherited from Moses, Samuel and David. Was the loyalty, loving and earnest as it was, insufficiently alert to the logic of gentile inclusiveness, and to the ease with which subsequent generations, lacking its own pristine virtues, would interpret some psalms and psalmists as meant to sanction identity of interest between God and themselves? The theme of 'the heathen come into thine inheritance' could augur dark counsels from Cromwell, leading 'God's own Englishmen'. The Psalms have worthily celebrated nature, bared the soul and fortified mortality. But they have also been invoked to celebrate battle, to bare the arm of power, and to fortify collective pride.

There are similar issues in the unthinking iteration of Israeli history from the Judges to Zedekiah faithfully rehearsed in Christian fidelity to biblical story and hero. The episode of Samuel and Agag is horrific; the wanderings of the Ark, and sundries in royal chronicles, are trivial or inconsequential. They have their fascination for historians but should they monopolize the ground of Scripture to the degree they do, when they thus exclude so much from liturgy and life richer and worthier, albeit non-canonical? It is true that godly ingenuity has extracted homilies and meditations of warm spirituality from these sources.[14] But this is often done at the expense of realism or in neglect of original meanings and implications left to silence.

But the heart of the matter of the Canon is not, finally, these tensions or worries with which we have lived for so long and from which there is no obvious escape. It is rather that if we are serious about a theology of other faiths we cannot be content to find ourselves under the constraints of a Canon and a concept of Scripture so unilateral in their character. We are called to a theology serving its *fiducia* in Christ from a wider range of idiom and vocabulary, and responsive to other verdicts of experience. The search for 'Christ in all the Scriptures' – the biblical Scriptures – has long been a faithful task of Christian study through typology and the will for interpretation. It would be false and foolish to envisage a 'Christ in all the Scriptures' meaning 'all'. What is right and wise is to bring to the expression of Christ whatever the world's Scriptures afford to illuminate what we have found in him. Should we look for outlines of what Christhood means only in Hebraic sources? Joseph and Jonah, for example, have served well as partial types. Are there none in the literature of Asia? Or, if paradigms of the Christ are tenuous and remote, there are surely analogies of the wistfulness and lostness of soul which Christian salvation claims to meet. May these find no place in the spiritual stock-in-trade of a Church meant for universal mankind and no echo in its liturgy? If a once-for-all Canon serves a regulative purpose need it be also a restrictive one? For what, then, would it regulate? Surely the antecedents of *all* discipleship should find their way into its ecumenical confession. Otherwise we would have to conclude that the Canon of Christian Scripture had been both premature in time and parochial in content and on both counts a problematic servant of a *fiducia* in Christ for all mankind.

Before turning to how the *hedraiōma* of 1 Tim. 3.15 might 'establish' faith rightly in this regard, it is important to take note of one contemporary area of tension within this biblical Canon-authentic Church issue, one that is insufficiently appreciated outside the Middle East. It might be likened in some respects to the grievance Jewish readers feel about the New Testament portrayal of the Pharisees.

In the parable, for example, of the two men in the Temple one cannot well have the lesson of the penitent humility of the tax-gatherer without the pride of the Pharisee. He provides the contrast inseparable from the lesson. Scholarly concern for a right estimate of Pharisaism resists its being cast as a foil to sincerity in this way. Something of the same situation occurs, this time in ethnic, not ethical, terms, in the Jew/Gentile distinction on which the Hebraic tradition proceeds. The Philistine is always the *bête noire*, the other, whose enmity throws into contrast the exploits, the legitimacy, the specialness, of Israel. The Gentile is the butt of all those items of contrast by which, as morally in the parable, the point at stake has always to be made.

This familiar situation, implicit in chosen peoplehood in Hebraic terms, and present throughout Hebrew history, ritual and literature, casts the Gentile in that role of contrast by which Hebraic consciousness is sustained. It was precisely this binding factor that the new Christian faith and community emerged to undo, liberating Jew and Gentile alike into a single equality. To see how some aspects of Christian adherence to the unity of the Bible impede that liberation or habituate us to go on with differentiations unknown to grace, is to become aware of the peculiar incidence of that factor in the Middle East.

There, the campaign for, and culmination of, political Zionism in the creation and defence of the State of Israel has recruited some expressions of Christian biblical loyalty for support and vindication. These cast present-day Palestinians in the same obstructionist role as the old Philistines, namely resistance to the divinely legitimated possession of disputed territory. Modern Israel has enjoyed massive approval and commendation from western Christian sources who saw in its emergence what the Bible required all Christians to celebrate and assist. For those sources, the moral and spiritual issues in the tortured sequence of events had little or no part in the assessments. Whatever events might be in impartial reckoning, they were legitimated, as for Joshua, so for Ben Gurion. Human considerations of justice or compassion or of undifferentiated humanity under God were not to be set against divinely mandated Zion. There have been occasions, almost bizarre in their paradoxical character, of 'Bible-Christians' enthusiastically upholding all things Israeli, in line, as they saw it, with the Bible's unity, despite the secular realism of the State, and despite the witness of the New Testament to the equal status of all peoples, under grace.

It is, of course, a harsh and painful experience to be, on this reckoning, the 'Philistines' of the drama, the people arbitrarily cast as the villains of the piece, when they are on all counts the sufferers. There is, for Arab Christians, an almost unbearable ambiguity in singing: 'Blessed be the Lord God of Israel . . .' Israelis themselves are not agreed about him and if his 'visiting and redeeming his people' has to be read in terms of contemporary Palestinian history, how is he to be called 'blessed'?

This sharp anguish is only pondered here as a stark, telling example of how the uncritical assertion of the unity of the Bible can stray from the integrity of the New Testament, and the equal community of all, in undifferentiating grace, within the gospel. That there are deep *positive* meanings in the fact of Israel is not in doubt. We have tried to think them through in the chapters on Messiah and Jewry. But those meanings do not alter, and should not be allowed to obscure, the urgent compromise of Christ into which some forms of Bible invocation are led, in current context in the Middle East. It is perhaps ironical that those who, in their security, are farthest away can so readily, even aggressively, waive the truths of grace and peace, in favour of the mandate heaven had with Joshua. Egyptians, Amorites, Amalekites, Canaanites, Philistines, are always cast in adverse roles in the Hebraic scripture drama. In the New Testament they are not the foil of 'the people of God'. They are equal candidates for participation.

There is a very different drama in the New Testament story – not of a people and a territory and the history pertaining, but of a ministry coming to messianic climax and so to Christ-community. In that climax there were what long centuries counted as adverse roles – the part of Jews and Romans. It is fair to say that the New Testament struggled not to have it so. The roles are there. But the same preaching in the Acts which rehearses the story invites the participants into its welcome.[15] 'The promise', it says, 'is to you'. The story is not about the making of a nationhood in territory, of politics and confrontation. It is a story of redemption, of evil overcome by good. It is true that when the preaching and the welcome it offered were caught in the tensions of new and old, of allegiances at issue, then enmities developed. Hence the word 'struggled' four sentences back.[16] Those enmities measured the intensity of things at stake: they did not touch the deep diversity of the stories that make the Testaments nor diminish the inherent will to inclusion of the theme that centres in the cross. Our task is how to surmount the enmities which particularize and thus serve the theme of open grace.

This brings us back where the Canon of Scripture both takes and leaves us – a Mediteranean source book (might we say?) for a world theology.

VIII

The *hedraiōma* of 1 Timothy 3.15, refers in context to behaviour in office of bishops, deacons and members and their moral character. It has to do with what 'establishes' or undergirds the authenticity in discipleship, of faith and life within the Church, 'the ground of truth'. Such truth of character stands in truth of mind. Due order in community means due ordering of community faith. Scripture, in liturgy and devotion nourishes the one; in teaching and theology it informs the other. The Canon and its formation had much to do with both, but within the cultural limits of its time and place. These have every right to be definitive. For they, and their Hebraic dimension, were the matrix of all things messianic – the long hope, the Jesus-form and the open Christ-people. It would be crass thinking and a hopeless proceeding to suggest that the Canon might now be reopened. But for that very reason any sound theology, caring for the world and not merely for the past, must do two things. It must actively make good in its sympathies the severe unilateralism of the first Testament in the Bible, and it must handle the second with appropriate initiatives from and beyond it.

Plainly there are more proverbs than those of Solomon, be he king or pseudonym. All Asia is rich in them and they deserve recruiting for Christ. There are more providences in tribal migrations and people histories than those of Exodus from Egypt. Amos 9.7, with rare boldness, tells us so. As Psalm 87 bravely confesses Jerusalem has more citizens than those of natural progeny. Ethiopia, even Philistia, may claim a holy lineage. 'From farthest east to farthest west', according to Malachi 1.11, there is worship in 'the great Name'. Any Christian doctrine of the pre-incarnate Word must believe it so. It is urgent that a theology of the Word should loyally and ardently seek out and treasure the *consummatio evangelii* latent in the Scriptures and cultures of mankind. Is it not also urgent that such treasures should find their place in lections and liturgies which confess a world's Messiah? The heritage abiding from Genesis to Malachi will not be threatened by such usage. In being de-monopolized it will abide more suitably within a Christian loyalty.[17]

The vital duty of cross-reference theology in the trust of the New Testament is one consistent with this custody of the Old. The Canon, from Matthew to John the Theologian, is sealed.

If the *fiducia* for which it exists is faithful, it must be interpreted
world-widely. This means that the self-monitoring commended
to Timothy in *hedraiōma* must characterize the Church in its
intellectual and spiritual context of cultures never encountered
by New Testament writers. The concern, which was pastoral
in the Epistle and had to do with pagan society as the arena
of Christian purity of life, has still the same dimension today.
That is why it must also undertake the self-monitoring which
responds to all human situations and the religious doctrines
reading them.

Are not the Epistles rightly received when they are read as
yielding precedents rather than strictures? They care pastorally
rather than command arbitrarily. If taken in the same temper
they have an open-ended quality and must be received in the
liberty Paul, for example, so often extols. What he enjoins about
vain partisanship, or what is truly legitimate but spiritually
inexpedient, or the primacy of love, may be translated into
every situation. The closed Canon need not mean a static theology. The finality it symbolizes – the completeness of the faith
– has perennial quality.

In this way the trust of the New Testament can know and
prove itself open to the demands of a world-conscious theology.
Logic in Corinth can obtain in India. Idolatry in either can be
countered in the solicitude which also feels with the apprehen-
sions it entails. 'The weaker brother' within the Church edu-
cates us about the stranger outside it. For all are 'brothers for
whom Christ died'. The faith which can transcend both circumcision and uncircumcision will be alert in comprehending its
own baptism lest it become merely a badge or a boast. If the
preacher-teacher, humorously, can be likened to 'the ox that
treads out the corn' (1 Tim. 5.18),[18] the metaphor of grist and
mill must be right for his theology. It is an ill mason who refuses
any stone. The fact that the New Testament is culturally circumscribed need not mean that it is theologically inhibiting,
given custodians and interpreters alive to its nature as a document. What is confined by its geography instructs and releases
its wise interpreters for duties as wide as humanity.

It is well to understand how this sense of things about the
New Testament is borne out by the very shape of its own genesis. It did not happen as literature by divine *ipse dixit* – as we
have seen in Chapter 3. In a real sense the Church was left
to document its own faith. Its own mind, memory and muse

gave literary form, in Gospel and Epistle, to the meaning that gave it being. We cannot, then, rightly inherit that documentation, in its canonical form, in a temper of passivity or slavishness altogether incompatible with its own progress into being as text and authority. Further, the Canon's dependence on the Church, reciprocal to the Church's dependence on the Canon, must make for a lively relation between the text then and the context now. It must be the task of exegesis to let the demands of inter-faith relationships come strongly into its study. The truth of New Testament universality is seen to depend on the patient trust of its particularity. Or, in words of 1 Timothy, *apodochēs* turns on *hedraiōma*, meanings found welcome from meanings made authentic. Meanwhile, is it not right for the Church generously to open out the reach of its liturgical readings to include worthy expression outside the Canon, whether from sources Christian or extra-Christian?[19]

IX

The fifth honesty to which experience of cross-reference calls us concerns the very will to theology, the warrant for believing and belonging on which all else rests. 'By what authority?' is the perennial question underlying all religion and, as we saw throughout, the keener the awareness of how plural religions are the sharper the issue. Bunyan's 'a think so too', with which we began in this chapter, will amuse, tantalize, engross, or haunt us, according to temperament or mood. But it will not go away unless we choose to banish it by drowning its insistent whisper with loud assertiveness or make peace with it – the peace of indifference.   When we truly concede what pluralism implies for all faiths – the discovery, as it were, of their optionality – we become aware also that there is no feasible or agreed arbiter to adjudicate their claims. For vast numbers of differing adherents this may have no conscious consequence, for they are secure in their religious identities. But for those who, through whatever factors, are alerted out of such security, there comes a disconcerting sense that authority is, so to speak, competitive, that absolutes are alternates. The thought arises that these, as it were, neutralize each other, there being no agreed frame of reference in which their differing *confessiones fidei* can be resolved.

Reason cannot well serve as any final umpire, whatever contributory relevance it may claim. For there is no agreement about its competence, its range, or its application. Appeal to powerful minds or saintly characters as vindicating faiths they have held or adorned is inconclusive, for all faiths possess them. Likewise the plea of wide dispersion and long persistence. Islam, for example, cannot but be true having spread so far, endured so long and held sway over so many. Every major faith can plead the same and there is no calculus by which to judge such grounds. Intuition, feeling, emotion, capacity for idealism, capacity for realism, coherence of belief, psychic serviceability: all these might be proposed as decisive evidence. But all of them are themselves on trial.

Nor does 'revelation' settle the puzzle of diversity. For it is itself diverse. There attends it an old paradox, namely that the revelation can only be identified as such if we know the criteria which warrant its recognition. However, if we know enough to identify revelation we are hardly in need of it. Revelation has somehow to be self-authenticating. But the several authentications of its diversely alleged incidence concede *some* things to each other but none the total ground to any. They only sanction further the competitions they do not resolve.

It is natural for each to maintain its explicitness as foreclosing the questions. We can aver: 'God chose the Jews'; or: 'Muhammad is his apostle': or 'God so loved the world that he gave his only begotten Son': or *Sruti* Scripture (as distinct from *Smrti*) 'heard the sound of eternal truth and reproduced it like an echo'. The faithful within will agree: their consensus will be confined to themselves. If we could think what meets us in 'revelation' by the analogy of knowing ourselves loved, the teasing intellectual problem would depart. For, in the experience of being loved, the credentials we need are in the experience itself. Such a sense of love, divinely real and embracing all, would point to Christianity as truth. But other faiths have the instinct to reject it, either for something more particular to themselves, or as too 'human' to be divine, simply our wishfulness. So pluralism seems to leave truth an ever open question.

The same would seem to be concluded from all claims to institutional finality. Many in Christianity have wearied themselves to identify 'the one true Church of God, founded by Jesus Christ', so that by submission to it they could live within

absolute assurance guaranteed by an authority they consent
fully to accept, relieving themselves of acts of private judgement
thus reliably concluded in the infallible mentor. Yet they have
not thereby escaped a personal decision. They have made a
vital one in opting for no more. They must surely allow for
at least the surmise that the faith-truth relation should not have
been thus summarily, perhaps lazily, foreclosed. Should not
the logic in such submission be always under review?

X

How should our theme of 'the Christ and the faiths' respond
to this situation? We seem to be left squarely with the fact
that all of us, in whatever tradition, must take personal responsibility for our beliefs. There is no authority, no 'truth' in fact
or claim or dogma, in what we call 'religion', exempt from
dependence on the credence brought to it, freely or otherwise,
from human wills and minds. That the credence believes itself
indisputably required by what it finds 'objectively real' does
not make the credence less germane to the objectivity. This
situation, captured in the very term *fiducia*, clearly makes religious pluralism a *de facto* pluralizing of 'truth', in the sense
that credences are multiple. We are not responding in Christ
unless we take fully upon ourselves the onus of this situation.

This is the more urgent because, while personal responsibility
for faith, in the light of the foregoing, is religiously implicit
in the nature of things, vast numbers of mankind are unable
to bring it. Though, when truly aware of themselves, faiths
– however adamant their authority – stand in the credence of
their faithful for reasons and motives on which the faithful
stand, they are tenaciously held in fact by multitudes quite
*un*aware in those terms. Birth, tradition, communalism, illiteracy, inertia, fear, pride all combine to locate and perpetuate
believers in their believing. Belonging is a decisive dimension
of faith and belonging is, for the very many, an unexamined
fact of their existence. Compassion, in Christ, is surely bound
to weigh this fact and care for its human consequences sensitively. Otherwise any challenge to it is liable to entrench it
further, provoking enmity and negation.

It is often found that faith-advocacy across frontiers proceeds
only from within a dogmatism which is unaware of this basic
issue of authority and simply aims to substitute one claimant

for another in complete inattention to the truth-question in the mandate of the one and the psyche of the other. Faith-commendation can even be a form of communal pride or an exercise in self-corroboration.

Those temptations apart, it is clear that the alert Christian, committed to good faith with *fiducia*, cannot ignore the givenness of other faiths, the permanence of their psychic tenure in the societies and cultures of the world, and the near inability of masses of their people – as of his own – to take a conscious critical personal responsibility for the truth by which they live. That inability will mean that they are, in a certain sense, inaddressable by what proposes their displacement. Where fanaticism, obscurantism, and bigotry obtain, that inaddressability will be intensified. For these emotions and attitudes are precisely the form which unexamined allegiance can take in order to remain so.

Where commitment to a faith *is* cogent, self-aware, and personally liable for its credentials, it is likely to fall back squarely upon its own system of authority and rely upon it to counter whatever is addressing it from within the prescripts of another faith-currency. Thus 'the Bible says' will be met by 'the Qur'ān says'. Wesley Ariarajah in his Postscript to Bishop Lesslie Newbigin's *The Other Side of 1984*, recognizes the rightness of being 'based unashamedly on the revelation of God made in Jesus Christ', and continues:

> The only standpoint from which a theologian can raise questions is that of faith. The theologian does not ask questions in order to arrive at faith. He or she can only start by asking: What can I say to this from the perspective of my faith?

Whether this can be wholly true even internally to any faith he leaves aside. But, between faiths, he makes the obvious point that they possess their own fiduciary framework and would be minded to make it similarly definitive in all their responses. In his response to Newbigin's plea for a resolute return to dogma in confronting the spiritual bankruptcy of the scientific, secular world-view, Ariarajah says: 'Yes, indeed. But other cultures, other dogmas.'[20] If we have to take pluralism in this unaccommodating temper, faiths even in alertness and responsiveness to the contemporary scene will be forgoing in self-sufficiency the duty most crucial to them. A faith that

intends to be responsible must be responsible to all mankind
if its framework of dogma and cult is not to be either a fortress
or a communal preserve. We are not religiously authentic in
a plural world if our singularity only dogmatizes on its own
terms and has no burden, no compassion, no mind, for the
puzzles and conflicts it excites. What we do with diversity will
test what we mean by dogma. *Fiducia* has no meaning if taken
out of this world. Pluralism is where faith must prove itself
both in temper and in trust.

XI

What, then, finally, is required of Christian theology in trust
with the Christ among the faiths? An answer can be formulated
in three interrelated tasks. The first is to be the custodial house
and home of the gospel so that its meaning and its invitation
are hospitably accessible to all, an evangelism which appre-
ciates its vocation within pluralism. The second is to seek and
find the utmost possible relation to the themes and tensions
of other faiths in positive hope. The third is to set the other
two squarely in the denominators common to us all both of
human wistfulness and present history. All three can be well
comprehended within a word much used in the New Testament
Letters and found alongside the others noted here from
1 Timothy. It is the word *parrhēsia* (1 Tim. 3.13). It is a well minted
word from *rhēsis* or 'speaking' and *para* (intensive) or, perhaps
pan, 'all'. It has to do with the freedom of the citizen in civic
assembly to speak his mind without fear or favour – a freedom
about the substance as well as the right to voice it. Translations
like 'frankness', 'assurance', 'openness', 'readiness' have to be
rolled into one. The Epistles characteristically employ it to describe the ministry of the Word and the liveliness of its ministers. It is the antithesis of secretiveness, whether of content
or manner, and marries well with Paul's ringing assurance:
'I am not ashamed of the gospel of Christ' (Romans 1.16). *Parrhēsia* responds to *apodochē*; it is the corollary in the theologian
of the worthy-of-welcome quality of the Christian faith.

The Church, then, is the trustee community of the gospel
which interprets the nature of God as responsible love, for ever
grounds that interpretation in the person and the wounds of
Jesus as the Christ, and presents him as, for all mankind, the

where and how of grace, of forgiveness, and peace. There is no doubt of the distinctiveness of that gospel and, equally, there is no doubt of its bearing upon the perceptions and anxieties of every other religion. These we have tried to trace in preceding chapters. Within, through and, at times, even against, their corporate tradition, Christians must take personal responsibility for the faith that is them. It is presented to them, and through them, as reading in the cross of Jesus the sacrament between God and men of all that so variously, so anxiously, engages and diversifies the religions of the world. Neither the Church, nor the personal Christian, may pontificate or guarantee, still less coerce or overbear. We walk by faith. The other options exist and multitudes exist who can exercise none. Compassion must determine all. But the Christ-faith has shaped for its credential to all others a custodial community, a house and home from which to pursue the hospitality of God in the homelessness of the world.

In such care with Christ and in the *parrhēsia* of his credentials, a Christian wisdom will seek out all the insights and explore all the preoccupations of other faiths as a duty vital to its own outspokenness. The citizen with *parrhēsia* in the debate is not in monologue ignoring other speakers. His freedom moves with them. He is articulate in response to them. It is precisely in their context that his confidence belongs.

Some Christian theology, to be sure, has proceeded on the opposite idea of its task, and some mission likewise. It was outspoken not because it listened but because it did not need to. Its plainness was that of bare assertion. It expected to prevail by sheer unlikeness. But that posture would seem disloyal to the Incarnation of the Word, where that *to* which the Word reaches is that *in* which it comes. *Verbum caro factum est.*

The task of a theology with the Word similarly to fulfil its trust within the idiom and the compass of humanity, in all the forms of its engagement with its own mystery, would seem to be clear: 'As my Father has sent me even so do I send you' (John 20.21). We need not fear that such referencing of the gospel within the mental universe of other faiths is some kind of compromise or that so doing we jeopardize our own faith-security. This is not ensured by ignorance of others or seclusion from them. Rather we disserve evangelism and impede the free course of the Word, if we isolate vocabulary in a kind of private currency, as some have sought to do.[21] For then we forgo all occasions of communication through words and metaphors stretched and new-weighted after the manner, for example, of Paul.[22]

Some who question and distrust this will to lively cross-reference, do so with a strange lack of Christian *parrhēsia*. Thus, for example, Wesley Ariarajah, earlier quoted, writes:

> In a Muslim, Buddhist or Hindu nation there can be no question of replacing their Scriptures with the Bible. There are some who advocate that we identify the biblical perspectives within these faiths and name them. This is a strange solution. I have never been able to understand why a Hindu perception should suddenly become 'Christian' simply because a Christian is able to respond to it and accept it as biblically valid. Not only people, even principles can become victims of the proselytizing zeal![23]

Such a verdict is to assume that things Hindu, or things Christian, are commodities with a trade-mark only marketed by the sole proprietors. The Buddhist sense of human transitoriness is not an awareness exclusive to Buddhism, only its interpretation is. The Islamic sense of divine transcendence cannot carry a label: 'Muslims only'. The Christian is not proselytizing a principle in staking out a share in these. Nor, conversely, would the Buddhist be doing so in discerning the Christian dimension of his own emphasis in the sign of baptism. Nor again is the Muslim on unIslamic ground in facing, as Christianity does in Jesus, the relation of the divine will and human wrong which we all call prophethood. 'A Hindu perception' does not 'suddenly become "Christian"' by a Christian ability to recognize it. It was so already, unless we mean to define 'Christian' by the trade-mark mentality which allows only brand names and no open truths in common. This would be a shopkeeper's mentality indeed. To think we were 'proselytizing' when acknowledging truth wherever we find it would imply that the Bible, the gospel, the Christian faith, either have everything true under their own jealous copyright or have commandeered what does not rightly belong to them. Both positions would be quite inconsistent with the unity of mankind and the universal ambition belonging to Christ. Relevance and total otherness cancel out each other.

So it emerges from all the foregoing that theology in cross-reference is the only theology there is. There is no good faith that is not attentive, no *fiducia* not set to *merit* its welcome. It is precisely by a steady attention to the questionings from which other faiths reach for their answers that the gospel makes its way, taking up those very questionings into the answer it holds for them through 'God in Christ reconciling the world'.

More than in any previous time or culture the world is deciding, even dictating, the themes within which the Christian theologian must serve the faith of Christ. How are we to read the flux of history, its cumulative meaning and the bearing of its content on our interpretation of ourselves? How are science and its technology to be duly subservient to the health, sanity, community and well-being of mankind? How, indeed, are these to be understood in the light of the secular tide? How is secularity to be redeemed from its misreading of experience? How are the religions to be saved from their pride, or panic, or sloth? A sense of the good earth, of the sacrament of things, of the limits of nationality and the reach of community, of the guilt of selfish structures and idolatries of vested interest, is mandatory for all religions and, in search of it, the self-criticism of all faiths in their varying contributions to the circumstances which confront them all. The faiths have never had more urgent tasks with themselves than those which the world now sets each of them alike. Theology, therefore, never had more reason to be ecumenical.[24]

XII

So we return to the Christian theme underlying all the complexities of a pluralism intelligently faced – the theme of the faith as having in trust 'the Gospel of the blessed God' and the people of that faith being the custodial community by whose loyalty that trust 'shall not perish from the earth' but will always avail for mankind as long as they avail to serve it.

NOTES

1   John Bunyan, *Grace Abounding*, Paragraphs 97 and 98.

2   This point is the central theme of Wilfred C. Smith's *Towards a World Theology* (New York 1981), although he lays the emphasis on the 'faithful', seeing the 'faith' which identifies them as such in terms only of a residual tradition. This emphasis belongs with his entire concept of religion as 'a humane science', essentially constituted by religious experience. As a

protest against undue formalization of dogma and system without attention to the personal equation it is salutary. But we are not wholly convinced when he affirms, for example, that 'Muslims . . . religiously [are] not carriers of a pattern but participants in a process' (p. 29). The process, surely, is somewhat patterned and 'orthodoxy' has powerful sanctions.

3   See John Henry Newman, *Apologia pro Vita Sua*, London 1864. Hence, of course, the sad echoes of his phrase about 'the parting of friends'.

4   In an aphorism, Wilfred Smith's position. See note 2 and, even more confidently, his: 'The True Meaning of Scripture: An Empirical Historian's Non-Reductionist Interpretation of the Qur²an', in *International Journal of Middle East Studies* (1980), vol. 11, pp. 487–505.

5   Lesslie Newbigin, *The Other Side of 1984* (Geneva 1984), pp. 27, 31, 58.

6   On the relation of the Pastoral Epistles to Paul and the linking of their authorship with his authority, see Robert Falconer, *The Pastoral Epistles* (Oxford 1937); and P. N. Harrison, *The Problem of the Pastoral Epistles*, Oxford 1921.

7   Henry Martyn, for example, with his keen sense of the embarrassment to evangelism of the East India Company auspices under which he worked, wrote: 'How marvellously is India put into the hands of a Christian nation for a short time. May we lay a lasting foundation for the Gospel in it' (S. Wilberforce, *Journals and Letters of Henry Martyn* [London 1837], vol. ii, p. 56; written, 3 May, 1807). After the First World War, Samuel M. Zwemer's *The Disintegration of Islam* summed up what appearances then seemed to argue following the defeat of Turkey and the collapse of the Caliphate.

8   William Shakespeare, *King Henry IV*, Part 1, Act 2, Sc. 3, line 10.

9   Charles Dickens, *Bleak House* (London), Chap. xvi and the last paragraph of Chap. xix.

10 There are several translations of 1 Tim. 1.15: NEB, 'merit full acceptance'; Jer. Bible, 'nobody should doubt', 1947 trans. from the Vulgate, 'what a welcome it deserves'. On 'Faithful is the saying', see Excursus 3 in C. F. D. Moule, *The Birth of the New Testament* (New York 1962), p. 222.

11 The point is, of course, implicit also in the concept of 'good news'. That quality is identified by the hearer. Humour, likewise, does not pass unless it generates recognition at once.

12 Marcion, the second century heresiarch, of Pontus and Rome, in his gnostic fashion, derived the mission of Jesus from the supreme God whom he radically distinguished from the God of the Hebrew tradition. His vagaries, and the resistance they urgently merited from such writers as Tertullian, have tended to obscure the quite different and equally urgent issue as to the due role of the Old Testament within a world-extensive Church.

13 'Stay' is a useful word here for it incorporates the twin ideas of 'abidingness' and the material that ensures it.

14 'Potters . . . who dwelt with the king for his work' (1 Chron.4.13) affords a very sweet homily on lowliness and ordinariness dignified by divine presence. I remember a devotional discourse from 1 Chron. 29.22 on 'mak-

ing Solomon ... king a second time' in the form of a recall of the hearers from 'backsliding'. All this is devotionally to the good. But why does it need to be derived from one single source, and to resort to such ingenious – and ingenuous – devices?

15 All the early apostolic 'sermons' in Acts are not only altogether free from 'anti-Semitic' feeling but positively belong within Judaic norms and meanings.

16 See, further, this writer's *Jesus and the Muslim* (London 1985), Chap. 9.

17 Reference may be had to a Research Seminar on Non-Biblical Scriptures whose findings were published under that title and edited by D. S. Amalorpavadass, Bangalore 1974. It explored the varying philosophies of Scriptures and the use of sources outside the biblical tradition in Christian worship and theology. The Roman Church in India, and the Jesuit Order within it, have taken some significant initiatives in this field. See also a related study: *The Word in the Experience of Revelation in Qur'an and Hindu Scriptures*, by Ary A. Roest Crollius, Universita Gregoriana Documenta Missionalia, no. 8, Rome 1974.

18 This verse is surely a warm pleasantry. Treading out corn is a wearisome, repetitive business and the ox (with apologies to Thomas Aquinas) is a sturdy but ponderous creature. Yet he must not be muzzled, and the preacher/teacher must be duly permitted to labour for his reward.

19 See, for example, the careful discussion and wise selecting of a 'liberated' Lectionary by T. R. Henn, *Passages for Divine Reading*, London 1963. Henn's Selections had a mind for oral readability as well as content. Plato and Plotinus and Rabelais are the only authors included from outside Christian – and largely Anglican – tradition. The two decades since his venture have seen no development along the lines he suggested. Numbers, Joshua, Nehemiah, etc. are still preferred to Andrewes, Baxter, Donne and Bunyan on whom Henn drew and for whom he pleaded.

20 Newbigin, op. cit., pp. 27 and 64.

21 There is a deep instinct among Arab Christians to hold off Quranic vocabulary from Christian meanings. Similarly some strong Islamic sentiment proscribes any Christian usage of terms, however legitimate, which Islam thus claims to monopolize. See relevant legislation and decree in Malaysia in recent years.

22 Examples in Paul would be *musterion*, sometimes of gnostic provenance for 'the secret of Christ', and what he does with his quotation from Psalm 68.18 in Eph. 4.8.

23 Newbigin, op. cit., p. 74.

24 Using the word 'ecumenical' in its ultimate sense, not of what is inclusive of all Christians, but of humanity in the *oikumene*. Terms like 'the wider ecumenism', however precariously, intend this wide inclusion. For 'Christian' substitute the word 'religious'.

Index of Names and Subjects

Index of Documentary Sources